FASHION MERCHANDISE INFORMATION

Textiles and Nontextiles

Dorothy D. Prisco, Ed.D.
Centenary College

Harold W. Moore, Ed.D.
University of Arkansas

John Wiley & Sons
New York • Chichester • Brisbane • Toronto • Singapore

The Wiley Retail Fashion Merchandising and Management Series

The manuscript for this book was developed under the guidance of Joseph C. Hecht, consulting editor for the Retail Fashion Merchandising and Management Series.
Dr. Hecht is a professor at Montclair State College, Upper Montclair, New Jersey.

RETAIL FASHION MERCHANDISING AND MANAGEMENT SERIES

Linda Cahan and Joseph Robinson
A PRACTICAL GUIDE TO VISUAL MERCHANDISING

Cynthia Easterling, Ellen Flottman, and Marian Jernigan
MERCHANDISING MATHEMATICS FOR RETAILING

Melvin Morgenstein and Harriet Strongin
MODERN RETAILING: PRINCIPLES AND PRACTICES

Pamela Phillips, Ellye Bloom, and John Mattingly
FASHION SALES PROMOTION: THE SELLING BEHIND THE SELLING

Dorothy D. Prisco and Harold W. Moore
FASHION MERCHANDISE INFORMATION: TEXTILES AND NONTEXTILES

Front and back cover fashion illustrations by Anterny Riley.

Copyright © 1986, by John Wiley & Sons, Inc.

Library of Congress Cataloging-in-Publication Data:

Prisco, Dorothy D.
    Fashion merchandise information.

    (Wiley retail fashion merchandising and management
series)
    Bibliography: p.
    Includes index.
    1. Textile fabrics.   2. House furnishings.
3. Clothing and dress.   I. Moore, Harold W.
II. Title.   III. Series.
TS1445.P89   1986   677   86-13337
ISBN 0-471-89577-6

Printed in the United States of America
10   9   8   7   6   5   4   3   2   1

Preface

Fashion Merchandise Information: Textiles and Nontextiles is a new addition to the John Wiley fashion merchandising series. It is directed to students preparing for buying careers, but it can also be used effectively in other courses that include information related to textile and nontextile merchandise.

The text is divided into two parts: textiles and nontextiles. The textiles portion covers the manufacturing process from fiber to finishing of fabrics. A practical chapter on care is included (see Chapter 8). The chapter on home textiles (Chapter 9) provides the future buyer with valuable information about soft floor coverings, upholstery fabrics, curtains and draperies, and household linens—important merchandise in today's market because of the increased interest in home and environment. The textiles section also includes two chapters not often found in textbooks of this kind. Chapter 1 focuses on textiles in the marketplace and covers textile legislation, generic and trademark names, and the importance of textile information to retail personnel. Chapter 2 presents a concise history of textiles, relating its importance to retail personnel.

The nontextiles portion of the book, also emphasizing merchandise information for the prospective buyer, covers major product categories. Pertinent information is covered completely yet concisely for rubber, glassware, wood and furniture, paper, plastics, furs, jewelry, flatware and hollowware, dinnerware, housewares, leather and footwear, and accessories including gloves, handbags, belts, luggage, and umbrellas.

The book contains special features that the instructor and student will find very useful and practical. Each chapter begins with clearly stated behavioral objectives that should be achieved with the careful reading of the chapter. At the conclusion of each chapter, there is a list of key terms as well as study questions and study activities. Thus each chapter is designed to provide well-coordinated, in-depth coverage of each topic. Throughout, the text is well-illustrated, a feature that serves to clarify the information and to add enjoyment to the use of the text.

The textbook will provide the prospective buyer and retailer with the necessary textiles and nontextiles information that today's market demands.

D.D.P.
H.W.M.

Acknowledgments

We would like to thank the following instructors for reviewing the proposal for our manuscript:

Sue Ellis, Polk Vocational-Technical Center, Eaton Park, Florida
Eleanor Kennedy, Fashion Institute of Design and Merchandising,
   Los Angeles, California
Joanne Maggio, Gateway Technical Institute, Kenosha, Wisconsin
Mary Alice Matthews, Florida State University, Tallahassee, Florida

We especially thank the following reviewers, who not only reviewed the proposal, but also offered their helpful advice during the development of the manuscript:

Helene Eiker, Patricia Stevens Career College, Milwaukee,
   Wisconsin
Judy Evenson, 916 Area Vocational School, White Bear Lake,
   Minnesota
Robert M. Fishco, Middlesex County College, Edison, New Jersey
Camile Garrett, Tarrant County Junior College, Fort Worth,
   Texas
Carol Bayer Styles, Southern Institute, Birmingham, Alabama

Special thanks are extended to Terri Lynch, assistant professor of fashion merchandising at Centenary College, who became part of this project in the last months of development. Professor Lynch worked on the nontextiles portion of the text and worked diligently to pull together that section in order to meet production deadlines.

   The authors also extend their thanks and appreciation to the following companies and other organizations that were generous and cooperative in providing various kinds of information, including many illustrations, requested by the authors.

Aero Draperies, Inc., a Division of Minnesota Fabrics
B. Altman & Company

American Apparel Manufacturers Association
American Cyanamid Company, FIBERS Division
American Enka Company
The American Fur Industry, Inc.
American Hoechst Corporation
The American Museum of Natural History
American Textile Manufacturers Institute
Armstrong World Industries, Inc.
Arnold Print Works, Inc.
Atlas Electric Devices Company
Bath House
The Bobbs-Merrill Company, Inc.
Bootonware Dinnerware
Celanese Fibers Marketing Company
The Columbus (Ohio) Zoo
Corning Glass Works
Cookware Manufacturers Association
Cotton Incorporated
Cranston Print Works Company
Crantex Fabrics, Division of Cranston Print Works Company
Deering Milliken
Diamond Information Center
E.I. du Pont de Nemours & Company, Inc.
Durand International
Engelhard Corporation
Ethan Allen, Inc.
Steve Fabrikant & Co., Inc.
Farberware, a subsidiary of Kidde, Inc.
Firestone Tire and Rubber Company
Footwear Industries of America, Inc.
The Gorham Company
Hoover Universal, Inc.
Jewelers of America
Karastan Rug Mills, a division of Fieldcrest Mills, Inc.
Lenox, Inc.
Liberty of London Fabrics
Library of Congress
Macmillan Publishing Company
Man-Made Fiber Producers Association, Inc.
The Maytag Company
The Metropolitan Museum of Art
Monarch Marketing Systems, Inc.
Monsanto Textiles Company
National Board of Fur Farm Organizations, Inc.
National Cotton Council
National Housewares Manufacturers Assocation
National Knitwear and Sportswear Association

New York Public Library Picture Collection
Oneida Silversmiths
Oster, Division of Sunbeam Corporation, Allegheny International Corp.
The Paper Trade Journal
Philadelphia College of Textiles & Science
Porcelain Enamel Institute
Proctor Silex
Regal Ware, Inc.
Russell Harrington Cutlery, Inc.
Scientific American, Inc.
Sportowne®, a division of The Metzger Group, Inc.
Springs Industries, Inc.
Spunize
Sunbeam Appliance Company, a member company of Allegheny
    International Corp.
Travelware Magazine
U.S. Dept. of Agriculture, Forest Service
U.S. Dept. of Agriculture, Southern Regional Research Center
Viscosuisse
The West Bend Company
Woods Glass, Inc.

Contents

CHAPTER 1

Textiles in the Marketplace

OBJECTIVES

After completing this chapter, you should be able to:

1. Explain consumer expectations of textiles.

2. List and explain textile labeling legislation.

3. Identify the existing generic fiber names and selected trademarks.

4. List reasons why knowledge of textiles is important to the consumer.

5. List reasons why knowledge of textiles is important to the retailer.

This chapter presents a number of topics related to textiles in the marketplace. Since the buyer must make selections that will be accepted by the customer, consumer expectations of textiles are discussed. Textiles labeling and generic/trademark information are covered. Many products in the market today are actually made, entirely or in part, of textile fibers; these are included. Knowledge of textiles is as essential to retail personnel as it is to the consumer, and attention is given to reasons for this.

1

CONSUMER EXPECTATIONS OF TEXTILES

Consumer motives and expectations are closely linked. If a customer is motivated to purchase a garment because of its practicality, he will have expectations of durability, ease of care, and perhaps versatility, if it is a basic wardrobe component. Expectations, like motives, can range from simple (a desired color that is flattering) to complex (a garment that will be versatile, comfortable, attractive, and easy to care for). The following are expectations the customer may possess in the textiles/apparel decision-making process.

Beauty (Aesthetics)

A consumer's first reaction to any product is often emotional; this is as true for a consumer's reaction to fashion apparel as it is to furniture or a new automobile. In reference to textile products, beauty usually incorporates one or all of the following: color, appealing design, interesting texture, pleasing hand. (*Pleasing hand* is an industry term meaning pleasant to touch.) Standards of beauty change with various fashion influences, but the consumer trend today is for beauty of a classical, enduring quality, not faddish whims that will be outmoded in a season.

Performance and Care

The concepts of performance and care are closely interrelated. If a fabric performs well and fulfills its intended purpose, its care will probably be minimal. If the fabric is wrinkle-resistant, retains its shape and size, and is colorfast, care will not be a problem for the consumer. Today, fabrics that are machine washable and dryable are highly desirable to the busy consumer. If a fabric needs to be dry-cleaned, the consumer will have to decide if the added expense and time are worth the investment.

Comfort

Consumers today will not sacrifice comfort for fashion. Fashion dictates are no longer shaping consumer choice; therefore, comfort, often a stepchild to fashion in years past, is more important to consumers than ever before. Consumers will not tolerate textiles that scratch, tickle, restrict, or pinch. More than ever, consumers want to enjoy the textiles they select.

Quality and Durability

Quality and durability are closely related in the buying patterns of the modern consumer. With the high cost of textile products and the added expense of frequent replacement, the consumer trend today is to shop for quality with the understanding that durability and long life are also being purchased. Consumers cannot afford to replace textile products each season. More and more, consumers are opting for quality merchandise that will be durable and long-lasting.

Value

Although consumers want quality, they also seek value. A high price tag must be justified by high quality; many consumer expectations will have to be met. Whether on a budget or blessed with limitless funds, today's consumer shops for value. Consumers along all points of the economic spectrum will accept higher prices if they are convinced they are receiving good value for money invested.

Status and Prestige

The designer influence upon all textile products has made the elements of status and prestige integral parts of consumer choice. These elements enable people to feel good about themselves and their selections and to feel more confident in their relationships with others.

End-Use of the Garment

Consumer expectations may vary in relationship to the end-use of the garment. Consider the purchase of a blouse for two different types of end-uses. Table 1.1 lists the expectations previously discussed and the rating of each for the purchase of a blouse for either career dressing or social dressing. The possible ratings may range from 1 to 5 as follows:

1 = least important
2 = fairly important
3 = moderately important
4 = very important
5 = most important

The individual surveyed in Table 1.1 ranks value equally important for both types of garments but ratings vary greatly for Performance and Care, and Quality and Durability. While these expectations are most important for Career Dressing, they are only fairly important to this individual when considering the blouse for Social Dressing. See Figure 1.1 for an ad with an appeal to career dressing.

TABLE 1.1   RATINGS OF EXPECTATIONS FOR A BLOUSE PURCHASE BASED ON TWO DIFFERENT END-USES

EXPECTATIONS	END-USES CAREER DRESSING	SOCIAL DRESSING
BEAUTY (AESTHETICS)	4	5
PERFORMANCE AND CARE	5	2
COMFORT	5	3
QUALITY AND DURABILITY	5	2
VALUE	5	5
STATUS AND PRESTIGE	3	4

Your hard-working suit deserves something sweet: A whipped cream treat with plenty of pleats.

Delicious. **Rich**. And (unlike a hot fudge sundae) good for your ego and your image. This trio, designed by **Lloyd Williams**, comes in cream and other tempting tones of fine polyester georgette. Not only flattering. Today, pleats tell the world you've got a high **fashion I.Q.** See these and more modeled Monday in Better Blouses, third floor of the store that always treats you like a **guest**.

See these and more new Lloyd Williams blouses in our Fifth Avenue windows and at informal modeling tomorrow, 12:30 to 1:30.

A. Pleated double collar, pleated sleeves. Pearl gray or cream. 6 to 14. **72.00**
B. Pleated and lace-trimmed jabot, lace-edged cuffs. Wild rose or sweet cream. 6 to 14. **54.00**
C. Pleated Pierrot collar, sleeves and cuffs. Cream or rose. 6 to 14. **72.00**

B. Altman & Co

It's always a pleasure

Fifth Avenue, White Plains, Manhasset, N.Y., Short Hills, Ridgewood/Paramus, N.J., St. Davids, Pa.

Figure 1.1
Career dressing emphasized in an ad.
Courtesy of B. Altman & Co.,
Fifth Avenue and branches.

TEXTILE LABELING ACTS

With the availability of more and more textile products on the market and the increased variety of man-made fibers and blends, a need for legislation developed. Legislation provides the consumer with information and protection. Competent retail personnel, too, must be aware of legislation. This information will enable buyers to make wise choices in the marketplace and to serve their customers better. The following is a brief, chronological summary of mandatory standards enacted by the government.

1938–Federal Trade Commission Ruling on Weighted Silk

If silk products contain more than 10 percent weighting (the addition of metallic salts to improve hand and drape), they cannot be labeled *silk* or *pure dye silk*. The only exception is black silk, which may contain 15 percent weighting. A *weighted silk* label is given to products not complying with these standards. (Refer to the discussion of silk in Chapter 3.)

1939–Wool Products Labeling Act

This legislation was enacted in 1939, became law in 1940, and was amended in 1980. Any apparel, wool fabrics, and other products made of 5 percent or more wool (excluding ornamentation, upholstery, and floor coverings) must be labeled. The kind of wool and the amount must be stated in the label. In the case of a blended product, the amount of wool as well as the other fibers must be indicated. The various kinds of wool are defined as follows.

Wool, new wool, or *virgin wool* refers to a wool fiber that has been manufactured but not used. Wool fiber is the fleece from sheep or lamb, goat hair (Cashmere or Angora), or other similar animal fibers that have never been processed into a textile fabric.

Reprocessed wool refers to a wool fiber that has not been used by any consumer but that has been manufactured from another wool yarn or a knitted, woven, or felted wool (usually in scrap form).

Reused wool refers to a wool fiber reclaimed from products used by a consumer. These may have been woven, knitted, or felted fabrics in the form of rags or clothing.

The 1980 amendment deleted the terms *reprocessed wool* and *reused wool,* stating that any reclaimed fiber can be labeled *recycled wool.*

1951–Fur Products Labeling Act

This legislation was enacted in 1951 and became law in 1952. Fur products must carry the true English name of the animal and state the country of origin. If the fur is used, damaged, or scrap, and if it has been dyed or bleached, this information must also be included on the product labeling as well as in advertising.

1953–Flammable Fabrics Act

This act was passed in 1953 and amended in 1967. When standardized testing reveals a high flammability, wearing apparel (excluding hats, gloves, or footwear) and fabric cannot be sold. This act was amended and broadened in 1967 to cover a wider range of clothing and household fabrics, including carpeting and mattresses.

1960–Textile Fabric Products Identification Act

This act became law in 1960. Every textile fabric (except upholstery fabric attached to the frame) must have an attached, durable label with specific information, including (1) the generic name and registered trademark or trademark of each fiber (generic names and trademarks are discussed on p. 6); (2) the percentage of each fiber, listing the dominant fiber first; (3) designation of fibers of less than 5% as "other fiber"; (4) unidentified fibers listed as "undetermined fiber"; (5) full information on all imported items; and (6) identification of the manufacturer. See Figure 1.2 for an example of a hangtag found on a garment selling at retail.

1972–Care Labeling Act

This law became effective in 1972. The Federal Trade Commission ruled that all clothing as well as fabric sold by the yard requires labels stating care instructions. These labels may be permanently affixed to apparel (see examples in Figure 1.3); in the case of yard goods, the label must be available if requested by the customer (see examples in Figure 1.4).

Figure 1.2
A hangtag will often include the retailer's name as well as complete fiber information.

AB 1234	Machine Wash Warm	Machine Wash
72% Acrylic	Wash Darks Separately	Medium
28% Polyester	Tumble Dry Low	Gentle cycle; no bleach
Machine wash warm.	Hang Immediately	Made in U.S.A.
No bleach. Tumble	Use Cool Iron If	82% Nylon
dry low.	Desired.	18% Lycra Spandex
SMALL		Style 150

Figure 1.3

Permanent care labels provide complete care instructions and may include additional information.

The care instructions include procedures for regular garment maintenance including specifics for washing, drying, ironing, or professional dry cleaning. This has been a controversial piece of legislation with different and often competing points of interest debated by manufacturers, retailers, and consumers. There have been confusing labels affixed to garments, apparently for the sole purpose of having a label in place, although in some cases no testing had been conducted to determine proper labeling. Some manufacturers have simply labeled a garment "Dry Clean Only" even when it might have been handwashed; this is often done as a safeguard against those consumers who would throw the garment in the washing machine rather than take the time and care to handwash. Dishonesty and carelessness in maintaining the standards of this act can only hurt all concerned—manufacturer, retailer, and consumer.

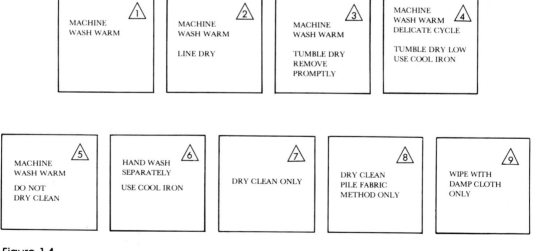

Figure 1.4

Care labels are available when requested with the purchase of yard goods.

Voluntary Labeling

Some manufacturers and retailers provide consumers with supplementary information. On a voluntary basis, the following may be included:

1. Country of origin of cloth garments
2. Union label
3. Specific fabric quality, characteristic, or design/printing information
4. Indication of affiliation with the Bureau of Consumer Protection of the Federal Trade Commission
5. Designer and/or company profile
6. Maintenance of performance standards and quality other than those mentioned

Figure 1.5 illustrates voluntary labeling that may appear in garments sold at retail.

This garment has been carefully inspected.

Due to the nature of silk, and our unique dye application, slight irregularities may be noticeable. We do not consider fabric nubs, and/or inconsistency of color application as constituting a flaw.

Your understanding of the uniqueness and total individuality of this garment will be appreciated.

Figure 1.5
Voluntary labeling referring to fabric quality and characteristics.

GENERIC AND TRADEMARK NAMES FOR MAN-MADE FIBERS

Generic names for man-made fibers are the result of a system established by the Federal Trade Commission that permitted the grouping of similar fibers produced by various manufacturers. Such a system was required when the number of man-made fibers became so large that confusion developed about their similarities and/or differences. A specific generic name was assigned to those fibers that were similar in chemical structure. Currently, there are twenty-one generic names to classify man-made fibers. New generic names will be added only when fibers are manufacturered that are different from those currently classified.

There are two basic types of man-made fibers: cellulosic and noncellulosic. Cellulosic fibers—acetate, triacetate, rayon—are manufactured from cellulose found in soft-wood trees. The eighteen noncellulosic fibers are manufactured from molecules composed of various combinations of carbon, hydrogen, nitrogen, and oxygen which are obtained from air, water, petroleum, and natural gas. Five of the eighteen noncellulosic fibers are not currently manufactured in the United States. They are anidex, azlon, lastrile, novoloid, and nytril.

Manufacturers give their own fibers trademark names to distinguish them from other fibers classified within the generic name category. While generic names are not capitalized, the trademark names always are capitalized. Table 1.2 lists the generic fibers that are currently encountered in the marketplace and gives selected trademark names, characteristics, and major domestic and industrial uses.

TEXTILE FIBERS: DIVERSITY OF END-USES

Textiles for apparel are only one part of the wide range of fiber/textile end-uses; some of these were referred to in Table 1.2. Consumers will make decisions about textiles for many uses. Buyers must be prepared to meet these needs. All of the following products use textile fibers in a variety of forms.

Apparel	Medical supplies/equipment	Umbrellas
Carpeting	Toys	Wigs
Draperies	Basketball nets	Tents
Linens	Rope and cable	Hammocks
Upholstery	Adhesive tape	Tires
Dental floss	Typewriter ribbon	Luggage
Aircrafts	Fishing line	Cookware
Insulation	Artificial grass	Space suits

IMPORTANCE OF TEXTILES FOR CONSUMERS AND RETAIL PERSONNEL

Consumers and retail personnel often face each other in the textiles decision-making process. Consumers often rely heavily on retail personnel's knowledge of textiles; unfortunately, that knowledge is often minimal. Retail personnel, on the other hand, often go about their jobs hoping they will never be put on the spot

TABLE 1.2 A GUIDE TO MAN-MADE FIBERS

GENERIC FIBERS AND MAJOR TRADENAMES*		CHARACTERISTICS	MAJOR DOMESTIC AND INDUSTRIAL USES
ACETATE		Luxurious feel and appearance; wide range of colors and lusters; excellent drapability and softness; relatively fast-drying; economical; shrink-, moth-, and mildew-resistant.	*Apparel:* Blouses; dresses; foundation garments, lingerie; linings; shirts, slacks, sportswear. *Fabrics:* Brocade, crepe, double knits, faille, knitted jerseys, lace, satin, taffeta, tricot. *Home Furnishings:* Draperies, upholstery. *Other:* Cigarette filters, fiberfill for pillows, quilted products.
Acetate by	Estron[12]		
Avron[6]	Lanese[8]		
Avtex[6]	Loftura[12]		
Celanese[8]			
Chromspun[12]			
Ariloft[12]			
ACRYLIC		Soft and warm, wool-like, lightweight; retains shape; resilient; quick-drying; resistant to moths, sunlight, oil, and chemicals.	*Apparel:* Dresses, infant wear, knitted garments, skirts; ski wear; socks; sportswear, sweaters, work clothes. *Fabrics:* Fleece and pile fabrics; face fabrics in bonded fabrics; simulated furs; jerseys. *Home Furnishings:* Blankets, carpets, draperies, upholstery. *Other:* Hand-knitting and craft yarns.
Acrilan[14]	So-Lara[14]		
Bi-Loft[14]	Zefran[7]		
Creslan[2]			
Fi-lana[14]			
Fina[14]			
Orlon[11]			
Pa-Qel[14]			
Remember[14]			
ARAMID		No melting point; highly flame-resistant; high strength; high resistance to stretch; maintains its shape and form at high temperatures.	Hot-gas filtration fabrics; protective clothing; military helmets, protective vests; structural composites for aircraft and boats; sailcloth; tires, ropes, and cables; mechanical rubber goods; marine and sporting goods.
Kevlar[11]			
Nomex[11]			
GLASS		Resistant to chemicals, soil and wrinkles; strong; quick-drying; low abrasion resistance; nonflammable	*Home Furnishings:* Curtains and draperies. *Other:* Insulation in buildings and in vehicles such as trains, boats, airplanes; reinforcement for molded plastic parts in boats, airplanes.
Beta[17]	Vitron[19]		
Fiberglas[17]			
401[17]			
PPG[18]			
METALLIC		High sheen and glitter; very decorative; helps to eliminate static; heat-resistant; colorfast; resistant to moths, mildew, shrinkage.	*Apparel:* Dresses, blouses; lingerie; shirts, slacks, sweaters, sportswear. *Fabrics:* Used as a decorative element in brocade, crepe, crepe de chine, satin, taffeta, tricot. *Home Furnishings:* Draperies, upholstery, table linens. *Other:* Braids, ribbons.
Lurex[20]			
Mylar[11]			
MODACRYLIC		Soft, resilient, easy to dye; abrasion- and flame-resistant; quick-drying; resists acids and alkalies; retains shape.	*Apparel:* Deep pile coats, trims, linings; simulated fur; wigs and hairpieces. *Fabrics:* Fleece fabrics; industrial fabrics; knit-pile fabric backings; nonwoven fabrics. *Home Furnishings:* Awnings; blankets; carpets, flame-resistant draperies and curtains; scatter rugs. *Other:* Filters; paint rollers; stuffed toys.
SEF[14]			
Verel[12]			

NYLON

A.C.E.[1]
Anso[1]
Antron[11]
Blue "C"[14]
Cadon[14]
Cantrece[11]
Caprolan[1]
Captiva[1]
Celanese[8]
Cordura[11]
Courtaulds Nylon[10]
Crepeset[3]
Cumuloft[14]
Eloquent Luster[1]
Eloquent Touch[1]
Enkalure[3]
Enkasheer[3]
Golden Touch[3]
Lurelon[3]
Matte Touch[3]
Natural Touch[3]
Multisheer[3]
Natural Touch[3]
Natura Luster[1]
Shareen[10]
Shimmereen[3]
Softalon[3]
T.E.N.[3]
Ultron[14]
Zefran[7]
Zeftron[7]

Exceptionally strong, supple, abrasion-resistant; lustrous; easy to wash. Resists damage from oil and many chemicals; can be dyed in wide range of colors. Resilient; low in moisture absorbency.

Apparel: Blouses, dresses, foundation garments; hosiery, lingerie and underwear; raincoats; ski and snow apparel; suits, windbreakers. *Home Furnishings:* Bedspreads, carpets, draperies, curtains, upholstery. *Other:* Air hoses; conveyor and seat belts; parachutes; racket strings, ropes and nets; sleeping bags, tarpaulins, tents; thread, tire cord; geotextiles.

OLEFIN

Herculon[13]
Marquesa[5]
Marvess[16]
Patlon[5]
Polyloom[9]
Vectra[9]

Unique wicking properties that make it very comfortable. Abrasion-resistant; quick-drying; resistant to deterioration from chemicals, mildew, perspiration, rot and weather; sensitive to heat; soil resistant; strong; very lightweight.

Apparel: Pantyhose, underwear, knitted sports shirts; men's hose; men's knitted sportswear; sweaters. *Home Furnishings:* Indoor and outdoor carpets; carpet backing; slipcovers, upholstery. *Other:* Dye nets, filter fabrics; laundry and sandbags; geotextiles.

POLYESTER

A.C.E.[1]
Avlin[6]
Blue "C"[14]
Caprolan[1]
Crepesoft[3]
Dacron[11]
Encron[3]
Fortrel[8]
Golden Glow[3]
Golden Touch[3]
Hollofil[11]
Kodel[12]
KodOfill[12]
KodOlite[12]
KodOsoff[12]
Matte Touch[3]
Natural Touch[3]
Plyloc[3]
Polyextra[3]
Shanton[3]
Silky Touch[3]
Spectran[14]
Strialine[3]
Trevira[4]
Twisloc[14]

Strong; resistant to stretching and shrinking; easy to dye; resistant to most chemicals; quick-drying; crisp and resilient when wet or dry; wrinkle- and abrasion-resistant; retains heat-set pleats and creases; easy to wash.

Apparel: Blouses, shirts, career apparel, children's wear; dresses; hose; insulated garments; ties; lingerie and underwear; permanent press garments; slacks, suits. *Home Furnishings:* Carpets, curtains, draperies, sheets and pillow cases. *Other:* Fiberfill for various products; fire hose; power belting; ropes and nets; thread, tire cord, sails, V-belts.

RAYON

Absorbit[3]
Avril[6]
Avsorb[6]
Beau-Grip[15]
Coloray[10]
Durvil[6]
Enkaire[3]
Enkrome[3]
Fibro[10]
Rayon by Avtex[6]
Zantrel[3]

Highly absorbent; soft and comfortable; easy to dye; versatile and economical; good drapability.

Apparel: Blouses, coats, dresses, jackets, lingerie; linings, millinery, rainwear; slacks, sports shirts, sportswear, suits, ties; work clothes. *Home Furnishings:* Bedspreads, blankets; carpets, curtains, draperies; sheets, slipcovers, tablecloths; upholstery. *Other:* Industrial products; medical/surgical products; nonwoven products; tire cord.

TABLE 1.2 *continued*

GENERIC FIBERS AND MAJOR TRADENAMES*	CHARACTERISTICS	MAJOR DOMESTIC AND INDUSTRIAL USES
SPANDEX Lycra[11]	Can be stretched 500 percent without breaking; can be stretched repeatedly and recover original length; lightweight; stronger; more durable than rubber; resistant to body oils.	*Articles (where stretch is desired)*: Athletic apparel; bathing suits; delicate laces; foundation garments; golf jackets; ski pants, slacks, support and surgical hose.
TRIACETATE Arnel[8]	Shrink- and wrinkle-resistant; resistant to fading; easily washed; good pleat retention and crisp finish.	*Apparel (where pleat retention is important)*: Dresses. *Fabrics*: Faille, flannel, jersey, sharkskin, taffeta, textured knits, and tricot.
VINYON Vinyon by Avtex[6]	Softens at low temperatures; high resistance to chemicals; nontoxic.	Used in industrial applications as a bonding agent for nonwoven fabrics and products such as tea bags.

*Number or letter after the fiber tradename indicates the manufacturer. [1] = Allied Fibers and Plastics Company (e.g., Caprolan polyester). [2] = American Cyanamid Company (Creslan acrylic). [3] = American Enka Company (Crepeset nylon). [4] = American Hoechst Company (Trevira polyester). [5] = Amoco Fabrics Company (Marquesa olefin). [6] = Avtex Fibers Incorporated (Avril rayon). [7] = Badische Corporation (Zefran acrylic). [8] = Celanese Corporation (Celanese acetate). [9] = Chevron Fibers, Incorporated (Polyloom olefin). [10] = Courtaulds North America, Incorporated (Fibro rayon). [11] = E.I. duPont de NeMours & Company, Incorporated (Orlon acrylic). [12] = Eastman Chemical Products, Incorporated (Verel modacrylic). [13] = Hercules Incorpoated (Herculon olefin). [14] = Monsanto Textiles Company (Cumuloft nylon). [15] = North American Rayon Corporation (Beau-Grip rayon). [16] = Phillips Fibers Corporation (Marvess olefin). [17] = Owens-Corning Fiberglas Corporation (Fiberglas glass). [18] = PPG Industries Incorporated (PPG glass). [19] = Johns-Manville Fiberglass Incorporated (Vitron glass). [20] = Dow Badische Company (Lurex metallic).

Note: From *Man-Made Fibers: A New Guide*, copyright © 1982 by the Man-Made Fiber Producers Association, Inc., Washington, D.C., pp. 6-7. Reprinted by permission. [Information on glass and metallic fibers added by author.]

about textiles. Often, salespeople do not know even the very basic kinds of textile information, such as the difference between a woven and a knit! Consider the importance of textiles for both consumers and retail personnel.

Why Should Consumers Know about Textiles?

1. To make wiser purchases and ensure value
2. For maximum durability of textile products
3. For wardrobe coordination; home decor
4. To judge suitability of the product for the individual or the home
5. To understand advertising, labeling, legislation
6. To identify quality
7. To develop manufacturer awareness and preferences
8. To have power in the marketplace

Why Should Retail Personnel Know about Textiles?

1. To perform job requirements satisfactorily (whether salesperson, buyer, merchandise manager, advertising artist, copywriter, etc.)
2. To assist and please customers; to develop customer rapport
3. To develop store credibility; prestige
4. To educate coworkers
5. To minimize returns based on poor textiles knowledge or misinterpretation of labels/hangtags
6. To enhance opportunities for advancement through expertise

KEY TERMS

1. Cellulosic fibers
2. Generic names
3. Noncellulosic fibers
4. Recycled wool
5. Textile legislation
6. Trademark names
7. Virgin wool
8. Voluntary labeling
9. Weighting

STUDY QUESTIONS

1. List six consumer expectations of textiles and explain each.
2. Why is end-use important when considering a garment for purchase?
3. Explain the textile labeling legislation that applies to silk, wool, and care factors.
4. How many generic fibers are currently being produced in the United States? List them according to cellulosic and noncellulosic categories.
5. What is meant by voluntary labeling?

6. Why has the Care Labeling Act been controversial?
7. Why is it important for consumers to know about textiles?
8. Why is a thorough knowledge of textiles necessary to the retailer?
9. Why are quality and durability important to the retailer and the consumer?
10. Study the ad in Figure 1.1. How would you evaluate the specific elements of beauty, care, quality, and prestige inherent in the blouses? Did the buyer who selected these blouses make choices that will sell? Why?

STUDY ACTIVITIES

1. Consider a recent textile/apparel purchase; which consumer expectations discussed affected your purchase?
2. Randomly select from this season's wardrobe five to ten items that you enjoy wearing. List the man-made fibers contained in the fabrics. Which predominate in your clothing? Are you surprised by your findings?
3. Visit a local department store. Select three types of garments that will reflect various aspects of textiles legislation in their labeling. Copy this information to bring to class for discussion.

CHAPTER 2

Textiles in Perspective

OBJECTIVES

After completing this chapter, you should be able to:

1. Explain the importance of textile history to retail personnel.

2. List several resources for researching textile information.

3. Identify major cultures and their textile/fiber usage and advances.

4. Identify major inventors whose inventions had impact on the textiles field and its advancement.

5. Discuss some major textile advances of the twentieth century.

The purpose of this chapter is to place textiles in historic perspective so that you can appreciate their long, colorful history and the unique way in which textiles have reflected the customs and advances of humankind. A brief history of textiles is presented highlighting major textile advances, fashion preferences of each period, and the sometimes humorous aspects of textiles that make their study even more enjoyable.

IMPORTANCE OF TEXTILE HISTORY TO RETAIL PERSONNEL

The current fashion scene is the product of the history that preceded it, and in many ways that history is vividly alive. Designers of clothes and textiles often turn to the past for inspiration, as do fashion publicists, coordinators, copywriters, and visual merchandisers. Buyers with a knowledge of textile history can understand more in depth the current trends in fashion, can better appreciate the cyclical nature of fashion and the inspiration for today's fabrics and garments, and thus can perform their job requirements more intelligently. It is therefore vital for today's retail personnel to develop an appreciation of the rich history that influences contemporary textiles and fashion.

DERIVATION OF TEXTILE INFORMATION

Reaching back into history to research textiles often requires some detective work for the material is often scattered about in a variety of places. Being aware of all the sources for textile information underlines the richness and diversity of this area of study.

Valuable textile information may be gathered from the following sources:

1. Tomb relics and paintings
2. Art forms—sculpture, paintings, pottery, monuments, frescoes, tapestry
3. Old manuscripts, diaries, fashion magazines, newspapers
4. Old garments and textile fragments
5. Accessories, including jewelry and medals, hats, gloves, parasols, shoes, shawls, undergarments.

Figure 2.1 illustrates sources from which textile information may be derived.

HISTORICAL PERSPECTIVE ON TEXTILES

Prehistoric Period

Textiles were part of human life before history was recorded. Archaeology has brought to the modern world spinning and loom equipment thousands of years old. In the Egyptian tombs were fabric fragments woven over 4,000 years ago. These fabulous finds give us great insight into the people and customs of their day.

In the earliest days of man, plant and animal fibers were used to construct a simple weave, or were knotted or braided. It is possible that first attempts at weaving, the interlacing of two sets of yarn at right angles, were in the construction of baskets or fishing nets. The first common tribal covering was a loincloth made of woven grass. The earliest Polynesians made body coverings from grasses and palm leaves. Hawaiians constructed tapa, or bark cloth, by soaking the fibrous inner bark of the mulberry or fig tree and beating together several

Figure 2.1

Sources of textile information.

Photo of ancient sculpture courtesy of New York Public Library Picture Collection. Egyptian XII Dynasty necklace courtesy of The Metropolitan Museum of Art. Contribution from Henry Walters and the Rogers Fund, 1916. Eighteenth century painting (by Joshua Reynolds) courtesy of Bath House. Nineteenth century American magazine (*Godey's Fashions,* May, 1867) from the collection of the Library of Congress.

layers. Similarly, human and animal hair could be soaked, placed in layers, and beaten to make a feltlike fabric, a compact sheet of matted fibers.

Ancient cave dwellers wore animal hides as capelike coverings and skirts. Figure 2.2 depicts this mode of early dress. Since sewing techniques were not perfected, the original animal shape was maintained. In cold climates, the fur side was worn against the body; this could easily be reversed in warmer climates. Goat, sheep, and leopard hides were worn in such a manner. Before tanning techniques were developed, however, the hides became brittle and uncomfortable.

Neolithic Age

People of the Neolithic Age had sheep that provided food as well as wool for clothing; llamas and alpacas also provided wool. Before the spread of weaving techniques, developed in ancient China, the animal wool was made into feltlife material as described earlier. Weaving, however, was done in the Neolithic period, especially in the Middle East, before being transmitted to Europe.

The Egyptians

The Egyptians used cotton, ramie, linen (flax), and wool. The tombs of ancient Egypt reveal the popularity of some of the earliest examples of textiles. Although a variety of colored fabric was worn during the Old Kingdom and excellent mineral and vegetable dyeing was possible, by 1400 B.C. the national Egyptian cos-

Figure 2.2
Cave dweller in animal hide skirt.
Painting by Charles R. Knight. Nega. #39441-A, Courtesy Department Library Services, American Museum of Natural History.

tume emerged, characterized by beautifully draped garments of diaphanous woven linen in white. Although Egyptian linen was woven with hundreds of threads to the inch, it was characterized by a fine transparency that, even in light of modern technology, is a marvel. The Egyptians also used fabric, such as wool and palm-leaf fiber, to fashion artificial wigs and beards. Ancient tomb drawings picture the Egyptians weaving cloth on an upright loom.

The Greeks, Romans, and Byzantines

The Greeks wore garments of wool, linen, and silk. They often combined linen and silk in one of the earliest blends (a fabric composed of two or more fibers) known to man; it is believed this was initially done because silk from China was very costly. To give a pleated effect to fabric, the Greeks dipped garments in thin starch, twisted each piece, and placed them in the sun to dry. It is interesting that this twist and dry procedure is a home method today for maintaining the pleated look in gauze fashions.

The Romans wore fabrics of wool, linen, cotton, and silk. It was a practice for a typical Roman garment, such as the palla, which could be a practical or decorative wrap, to be made from any one of several fibers, depending on its purpose. Thus, the wool palla provided warmth and practicality, while the silk palla was luxurious and decorative. Embroidery was a source of great pride to Roman women, who often embellished garments with lively embroidery. The Roman toga, as well as other garments, was symbolic of a highly stratified society. Ordinary people wore plain white togas while stripes signified rank of a higher order. The senator, for example, wore a tunic with a wide purple stripe or band.

During the Byzantine period, in the fourth century, the shuttle, probably developed by the Syrians, made it possible to weave fabric with more elaborate patterns than had been previously possible; this would often replace embroidery. Silk, light and very sheer, became the predominany fiber, with genuine gold threads often worked into the weave for a sumptuous cloth. The Byzantines produced their own silk from silk worm eggs from China that had been smuggled into Constantinople in 551 by two Persian monks.

Medieval Period

Probably the first written "how-to" booklet on the care of clothing was written during the Medieval period; it included information about the proper attire and procedure for dressing, and how to fold garments when they were not being worn. Medieval garments were primarily of wool, cotton, silk, and linen, woven into a great variety of fabrics such as canvas, brocade, velvet, flannel, satin, lawn, batiste, chiffon, and crepe. An interesting textile blend of the time was a fabric woven of camel's hair with a silk warp. This period also gives us insight into the relationship between the law and textiles throughout history. In 1464, an English decree prohibited the use of gold cloth, purple silk, and sable by anyone with a title below that of baron. In 1490, women were prohibited from weaving certain types of cloth. It was during the Middle Ages, in France, that the weaving of tapestries reached the heights of excellence.

Renaissance Period

By the sixteenth century, at the height of the Renaissance, the fashion silhouette became quite broad, and sumptuous garments of heavy fabrics were the mode. Primary textile centers, such as Milan, Florence, and Venice, produced exquisite silks, satins, velvets, and brocades. At this time, it was a popular practice to use furnishings fabric for clothing because of its opulence. Italy was the home of expert weavers; as some of them migrated, excellent weaving centers were developed elsewhere. The extraordinary Renaissance fabrics had a tremendous impact on fashion and style. Body movements became difficult in the often cumbersome silhouettes and a formal, dignified fashion look resulted. One royal gown of the day was decorated with 32,000 pearls and 3,000 diamonds; imagine its weight and the difficulty of wearing it! The male costumes were as elaborate as those worn by women, as can be seen in Figure 2.3. An important male accessory—hose—improved during the Renaissance. The industry grew, especially after better fitting, less costly hose were available after 1590; this was due to the

Figure 2.3
Renaissance man and woman wearing typical dress of that time.
Courtesy of New York Public Library Picture Collection.

invention of the stocking frame (later a knitting loom) by William Lee. Up to this time, hose had been cut on the bias for better fit, but knitted hose were far superior.

Seventeenth Century

The use of lace had grown in popularity during the Renaissance, but it was used judiciously since it was in short supply. By the seventeenth century, however, lace was an important trim on apparel. Venetian lacemakers were brought to France so that beautiful laces could be readily available. The popularity of lace and embroidery and the use of a wide range of fabrics characterized dress of the seventeenth century. Heavy, elaborate fabrics were worn, as well as lighter calico, dimity, and lawn. A unique use of textiles, seen during previous periods, but more popular than ever during this time, was as a beauty/status symbol applied to the face! Patches of black taffeta were a necessity to men and women of style. Patches were available in a variety of motifs, such as stars, crescents, circles, ships, and animals. They were sometimes symbolic, having romantic or political connotations. Patch boxes—holding a mirror, patches, and adhesive—were probably history's first makeup kits. The church objected to this fad that it considered excessive, but it continued for many years.

Eighteenth Century

The use of heavy textiles and elaborate designs continued and reached an extreme during the eighteenth century. At this time, gowns were so large and cumbersome that doorways, carriages, and even stairways had to be modified for fashion's sake—or a lady had to learn to walk sideways. Figure 2.4 depicts the dress of this period.

In the rebellion against the aristocracy that led to the French Revolution, lavish dress was discarded by the wealthy to eliminate identification; luxury fabrics and silk were abandoned. Depression hit towns that manufactured beautiful French fabrics. The lace industry was crippled, lace factories like that at Chantilly closed, and some lace makers were sentenced to death. Many aristocrats fled to England and their influence there led to a flowering of English fashion. The English manufactured high quality cottons (such as Liberty) and established a tailoring reputation known worldwide to this day.

Important developments during this period were the mass production of spools of thread and the invention of the cotton gin by Eli Whitney in 1794, a major breakthrough which facilitated the separation of the cotton from its seed. Spinning machines and automatic looms were other inventions that marked the beginnings of the industrialization of the textile field.

Following the American Revolution and the French Revolution, there was a dramatic change in dress. Politics and fashion were influenced by classical Greek culture. Men's garments changed more than women's, emphasizing practicality in design. From this time on (except for the 1960s), changes in men's clothing have been negligible compared to those for women. A narrow silhouette

Figure 2.4
Large, cumbersome dress of the eighteenth century.
Courtesy of New York Public Library Picture Collection.

Liberty
Regd. Trade Mark

Figure 2.5
Liberty cotton label.
Courtesy of Liberty of London Fabrics.

was in mode for women. Fabrics such as lawn, dimity, and muslin were chosen for the popular empire-waisted chemise, as seen in Figure 2.6. Women soaked their garment-clad bodies to achieve a clingy Grecian line; unfortunately, they often became ill afterward. Hoping to put an end to this odd fashion practice, French officials declared it illegal.

Figure 2.6
The empire-waisted chemise, graceful and narrow in silhouette, was a dramatic change in women's fashions.
Courtesy of New York Public Library Picture Collection.

Napoleon, to prohibit this spare dressing, ordered fireplaces bricked up in the palaces to necessitate warmer garments. Napoleon, nevertheless, was very interested in fashion. Fashion designer Leroy was commissioned to establish sumptuous court fashions using velvet, heavy silk, brocade, and lace. Platinum was the favored metal for embroidery since it did not tarnish. Napoleon required all fabric to be manufactured in France to revive this depressed industry. In the last decade of the eighteenth century, ready-to-wear shops became popular, each specializing in specific items such as hose, hats, or gloves.

The year 1793 was a momentous one for the American textile industry. This marked the opening of The Slater Mill in Pawtucket, Rhode Island, the first successful textile mill in the United States.

Nineteenth Century

In the nineteenth century, many important advances were made. In 1801, the Jacquard loom was invented by Joseph Marie Jacquard in Lyon, France (refer to Chapter 5). In 1805, the first fabric store opened in France. In 1808, Camus patented the invention of hooks and eyes. Charles Macintosh, in 1819, made a notable advancement in the development of waterproof fabric; he joined two layers of cloth with a rubber core, resulting in the famous covering named after him. In 1827, fabric-covered buttons were produced by Samuel Williston on a machine he invented. An embroidery machine was invented by Heilman in 1834. Jacquard, in 1837, modified his loom to mass produce laces in Calais (thus the name "Calais lace," which referred to a flowered netting). The sewing machine, invented in France by Thimmonier, was further developed by Elias Howe (1846) and Isaac Singer (1851) in America. By this time, full mechanization of the textile industry had been accomplished.

The Industrial Revolution was a time of dramatic change for fabric manufacture. Technical advancements and factories enabled the industry to grow and flourish and to move out of the home where there were major restrictions on its development. Furthermore, the need for diversified, practical fabrics could be met. Inexpensive, gingham day dresses could be easily manufactured for those with modest incomes. A demand for a variety of fashions and accessories grew, and the first department stores appeared where assortments of merchandise could be collected in one place. Fashion trends paralleled the rapid social, cultural, and economic changes of the period. It was common to see seasonal fashion change as we have today, rather than the prolonged fashion trends that previously existed. Fashion was becoming a vibrant, exciting field of merchandising. Feminism, a popular movement among the middle and upper classes, was responsible for placing women in a more dominant position during this period. Perhaps as a reflection of this, the first women's pantsuits were introduced around 1840.

Twentieth Century

The twentieth century marked the development of man-made fibers. In 1910, the first manufactured fiber, rayon, was available to the general consumer.

Rayon was called *artificial silk* but was not the first attempt to produce a fiber characteristic of silk; this had first been suggested in 1664 by the English scientist Robert Hooke, and in France in 1889 Count Hilaire de Chardonnet presented his artificial silk fabrics at the Paris Exhibition. Chardonnet later merited the title Father of the Rayon Industry. The first commercial rayon plant was built by him in Besancon, France, in 1891.

In 1924, acetate was first introduced. Since then, scientists have produced many new fibers and have developed a great variety of fabrics and finishes. In 1939, nylon was produced by DuPont; it was soon known as the miracle fiber and used in items from hose to tires. It was such a desirable fiber for hosiery that women waited in line to purchase the new product. During World War II, nylon was taken off the market because it was required for military uses. When it was available after the war, women were anxious to wear hosiery once again. One very enthusiastic consumer could hardly wait to try on her new hose; see Figure 2.7.

In 1950, acrylic, the wool-like fiber, was introduced. *Wash and wear* fabrics appeared in 1952, first in an acrylic/cotton blend and later in a polyester/cotton blend after the first production of polyester in 1953. These fabrics could be machine washed and were easy to care for. This marked the beginning of modern blends which combined the best qualities of two or more fibers. Among other things, fibers were engineered for comfort, flame resistance, whiteness, and soil release. The sophistication of the textile industry grew through the 1960s and 1970s; textiles played a significant role in the most exciting adventure of the times—space exploration. Nylon and aramid fibers are used in the astronauts' spacesuits. Graphite fibers, made from rayon or acrylic, reinforce the nozzles of booster rockets. The consumer has been the primary benefactor of the scientific research that has improved textile performance, appearance, versatility, and care requirements. Despite all that has been accomplished in the twentieth century, the future is an exciting one for textiles.

KEY TERMS

1. Blend
2. Felt
3. Tapa/bark cloth
4. Wash and wear
5. Weaving

STUDY QUESTIONS

1. What sources may be utilized for the study of textile history?
2. What were two of the earliest fibers known to people? How were they used to construct "cloth"?
3. What did each of the following cultures contribute to the advancement of textiles: Egyptian; Greek; Roman; Byzantine?
4. Discuss three examples of the relationship of textiles to status and/or social position through history.
5. List three inventions of the eighteenth century that marked the beginning of the industrialization of the textile field.

Figure 2.7
A woman eagerly trying on hose after World War II.
Courtesy of E.I. duPont de Nemours & Co., Inc.

6. What major effect did the Industrial Revolution have on the production of fabric?
7. List five advances of the nineteenth century that are related to textiles.
8. Give an example in history when clothing reflected the position of women.
9. Why should buyers and other retail personnel have a knowledge of textile history?
10. What is artificial silk?

STUDY ACTIVITIES

1. Select one of the cultures discussed, such as Egyptian, Greek, Roman, or Byzantine. In the library, locate illustrations pertaining to the culture that illustrate their preferences for fabric, garment design, and color.
2. Look through recent newspapers and magazines for fashion advertisements. Find several examples of garments that reflect women's place in society today. Does the ad copy refer to women and their status today?
3. Department stores first developed during the Industrial Age. Research the early types of department stores. How did they differ from today's department stores? Are there similarities?

CHAPTER 3

Textile Fibers

After completing this chapter, you should be able to:

1. Define what a fiber is and what characteristics make a fiber suitable for production.

2. Differentiate between natural and man-made fibers.

3. Identify the three types of natural fibers and their sources.

4. List the fibers included in each type of the natural fibers, and identify characteristics, including advantages and disadvantages.

5. Identify the two general types of man-made fibers.

6. List the fibers included in each type of man-made fiber, and identify characteristics, including advantages and disadvantages.

7. Develop a profile of man-made fibers including U.S. mill consumption, per capita availability, and fiber consumption in end-use products.

This chapter provides information about the major fibers—natural and man-made—that the retailer will encounter. A general introduction to fibers is presented and a discussion of each of the major fibers follows. For each of the fibers, a general overview and historic perspective is included as well as production procedures. The advantages and disadvantages of each fiber are included to provide you with specific, concise information about individual fibers; this establishes a basis for selling and merchandising information related to the finished products. The entire production and merchandising process, from fiber to customer, is illustrated in Figure 3.1 and will be discussed in subsequent chapters.

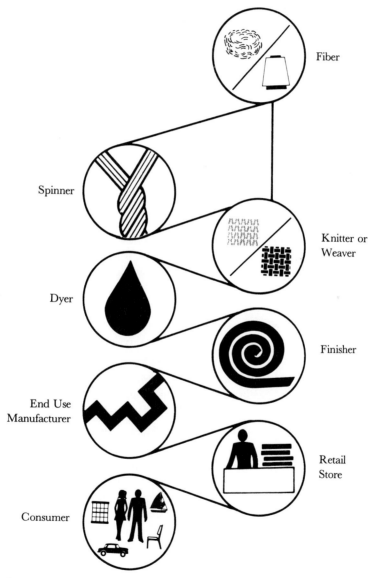

Figure 3.1
From fiber to customer: The entire production and merchandising process.

This chapter concludes with general information about man-made fibers, including the U.S. mill consumption of fibers, per capita availability, and fiber consumption in end-use products.

WHAT ARE FIBERS?

Fibers vary in their physical appearance. They may be straight or crimped. Their chemical properties vary as well. Both the physical and chemical properties are very important since they determine the end characteristics of the fabric.

Fibers may be of two basic lengths: *staple* and *filament*. A staple fiber has a length of less than one yard. A filament fiber is longer than one yard; in fact, it may be hundreds of yards in length.

Fibers, in order to be suitable for production into textiles, must be evaluated according to specific characteristics. The following characteristics are important because they relate to the end-use of the fiber and the ultimate success and satisfaction with the fabric constructed from the fiber:[1]

1. Adequate length—fibers that possess a substantially longer length than width (at least 100 times longer than wide) are more easily made into fabric than fibers not possessing this characteristic.

2. Strength—the tenacity, or strength, of the fiber must be adequate enough to undergo the production process for making cloth. Withstanding chemical treatment is important. Once the fabric is made and various textile articles produced, the fiber must be strong enough to survive the stresses of use and care. Tensile strength is the fiber strength measured in pounds per square inch.

3. Spinning quality—the ability of the fiber to adhere to other fibers is necessary in the yarn construction process.

4. Flexibility—fibers with this quality can be made into cloth that is drapable and creaseable, comfortable to wear, and durable.

5. Elasticity—the ability of the fiber to recover after stretching will result in a cloth and in products that retain their shape and resist wrinkling.

6. Resiliency—this is the ability of the fiber to retain its shape after bending or being deformed. This is related to crease recovery in the finished fabric.

7. Moisture absorption—fibers with high levels of moisture absorption accept dyes and finishes more successfully than those fibers with low levels. Hydrophilic fibers have a high degree of moisture absorption, while hydrophobic fibers have a low degree.

8. Density—this is the weight of the fiber compared to water; fibers of low density provide more yarn per pound and are produced into lighter

---

1. Adapted from Marjory L. Joseph, *Introductory Textile Science,* 2d edition. (New York: Holt, Rinehart & Winston, 1972), pp. 11–19.

cloth compared to high density fibers; the latter certainly affect an individual's comfort.

In constructing yarns or cloth, fibers may be used alone or in combination with other fibers. Blends—the combination of fibers—can result in unique fabrics that combine the best qualities of the incorporated fibers. The use of fibers in blend combinations can compensate for undesired characteristics that one fiber may possess. For instance, a 100 percent cotton shirt may wrinkle easily and require constant ironing, but a shirt of 65 percent cotton and 35 percent polyester will be easier to care for. Some consumers may prefer the pure cotton shirt, specifically because of appearance and comfort; other customers will make a choice based only on ease-of-care considerations. There are many blended fabrics in today's marketplace (see Figure 3.2).

Two main classes of textile fibers will be discussed in the following sections:

1. Natural
2. Man-made or manufactured (sometimes referred to as synthetic fibers)

NATURAL FIBERS

Natural fibers have been part of man's existence since civilization began. Cotton, linen, wool, and silk were the four major fibers until the end of the nineteenth century when rayon, a man-made fiber, was produced. This marked a dramatic shift from the exclusive use of natural fibers to the availability of manufactured fibers. The three types of natural fibers are *protein, cellulosic,* and *mineral.*

Protein Fibers

The protein fibers are either animal hair (wool and specialty fibers) or animal secretions (silk).

Figure 3.2
Blended fabrics are made up of a variety of fiber combinations.

Animal Hair Fibers

The major fiber of this group is wool, the covering of sheep. A variety of other animals supply the specialty fibers, which are given individual names:

- cashmere from the Kashmir goat
- mohair from the Angora goat
- camel hair from the camel
- vicuna from the vicuna
- alpaca from the alpaca

Wool, once a major textile fiber, is less used today than it once was. This is due to its high cost and to the variety of man-made fibers which are less expensive and easier to care for. Wool is still, however, a highly desirable fiber utilized to make beautiful and fashionable garments, accessories, and home furnishing fabrics.

Since there are about 200 different kinds of sheep that produce wool, its variety and quality can vary greatly. The finest wool is that of Merino sheep and their descendants, the French Rambouillet sheep, which are in the United States.

The fleece is sheared from the sheep in the spring. This fleece is called lamb's wool, provided the sheep is no older than eight months old; it is soft and fine wool. Wool from animals who have either died or been slaughtered is called pulled wool.

The grading and sorting of wool is based on the fiber's length and fineness. The fleece is then scoured to clean it of natural oils, perspiration, and dirt. After drying, the wool is carded to separate and straighten the wool fibers. If the fibers are long, a combing process is utilized to further straighten them; these are the strong, smooth, long fibers used in worsted wools. (See Figure 3.3 for a picture of a wool fiber.)

The advantages of wool are as follows:

1. Wool fibers have a natural crimp or wave which increases their elasticity and resiliency; this also provides excellent spinning quality.

2. Elasticity and resiliency enable wool to recover from or resist wrinkling (if wrinkled wool garments are hung, the wrinkles will fall out).

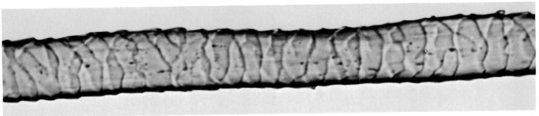

Figure 3.3
Wool fiber.
Courtesy of U.S. Dept. of Agriculture, Southern Regional Research Center.

3. Low density of wool makes it feel light in relationship to its bulk.

4. Although wool is highly absorbent, spilled liquids will generally run off the surface because of its scalelike structure that inhibits wicking (moisture passing through the fabric).

5. Wool is especially comfortable in cold weather because the crimp and the loose structure of the wool fibers enable air to be trapped between them, thus providing insulation.

6. It has excellent dyeing qualities.

The disadvantages of wool are as follows:

1. The clothes moth will feed on wool.

2. Poor dimensional stability—wool will shrink if not cared for properly (laundering, dry cleaning).

The speciality fibers, previously mentioned, have many of the same characteristics as wool, but they are considered to be more luxurious and are more expensive. The major use of the specialty fibers is in the manufacture of luxury garments.

Silk Fibers

Silk has been a valued and prestigious fiber for thousands of years. Both wild and cultivated silkworms produce silk. Today, cultivated silkworms are housed by the thousands in factorylike conditions where they live out their life cycles. They feed on enormous amounts of mulberry leaves for six to seven weeks, often consuming 30,000 times their weight. After the feeding period, they attach themselves to special straw frames, extrude the silk secretions from two tiny holes in the head, and form cocoons around themselves. A fine silk fiber is obtained by unreeling the cocoon. Some silkworms die in the process and others are used for breeding. Thousands of cocoons are required for one yard of silk. The wild silkworm feeds on oak leaves, rather than mulberry, and produces a silk that is coarse and duller in appearance than the cultivated silks; one type of wild silkworm produces tussah silk. Figure 3.4 presents a longitudinal and cross-section view of silk fiber; the smooth, rodlike filaments give silk its lustrous, shiny appearance and smooth feel.

The reeled silk filaments are combined to make yarns called *thrown silk,* which is wound on spools and is then ready for fabric construction. The gum (sericin) that is still in the fiber is removed by boiling the fiber is soap and water; the result is soft, fine fiber with a luster. If the gum is not removed, the silk remains coarse and dull; it is called *raw silk.* When the sericin is removed from the silk yarn, the weight of the silk is reduced by 20–30 percent. Silk in this cleansed condition and reduced weight is considered *pure silk.* If the weight is replaced by the absorption of metallic salts, for which the silk has a great attraction, it is known as *weighted silk.* Weighting may give silk more body and drapability, but overweighting may cause the silk to deteriorate more quickly.

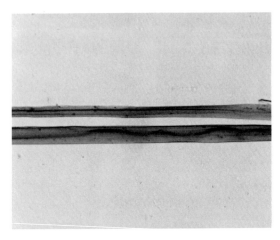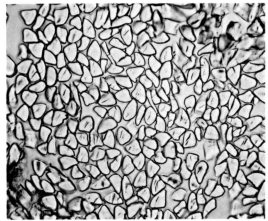

Figure 3.4
Longitudinal view and cross-section of silk fiber.
Photomicrographs courtesy of E.I. duPont de Nemours & Co., Inc.

The advantages of silk are as follows:

1. It is a luxurious and prestigious fiber; sometimes called the queen of fibers.
2. Strong, yet fine, silk is the strongest natural fiber.
3. It has good resiliency—wrinkles tend to fall out when fabric is hung.
4. It has good shape retention.
5. It is absorbent and accepts dye easily, resulting in rich, vibrant colors, if desired.
6. Lightweight, it is a comfortable fabric year-round; good for travel.

The disadvantages of silk are as follows:

1. Long production process and its complexity makes the fiber expensive.
2. It scorches easily when ironed with temperatures above 149 degrees Celsius (300 degrees Fahrenheit).
3. Care usually suggests dry-cleaning process, which adds to the maintenance costs.
4. Aluminum chloride, an ingredient in many deodorants and antiperspirants, can damage silk; dress shields may be required to maintain the original beauty of the fiber.

Cellulosic (Vegetable) Fibers

Cellulosic fibers are derived from various plants, including seeds, stems, and leaves. Cotton and flax are two common examples.

Cotton

It is believed that cotton was first available in India about 3000 B.C. Cotton is a seed-hair fiber that, in the United States, dates back to the early seventeenth century, when it was first planted for its fiber. The growth of cotton in the United States, which has been most successful in warm climates, reached its peak production in the late 1930s when almost 20 million bales were produced. Production has declined since then; the popularity of man-made fibers, and the fluctuation of interest in cotton as a fashionable fiber, have been in part responsible.

About six months after the cotton is planted, the fleecy cotton fibers emerge from the boll (see Figure 3.5) and are ready to be picked; today, this is done primarily by machine. After picking, the fiber is processed through a gin which separates fiber from seed and cleanses it of foreign matter.

The grading process that follows is based on consideration of the following: color, presence of foreign substances, fiber length and strength, uniformity, spinning quality, elasticity, flexibility. Of all the fibers utilized worldwide, cotton is the most popular, accounting for about 50 percent of the world usage. Figure 3.6 depicts the cotton fiber.

Figure 3.5
Cotton boll.
Courtesy of the National Cotton Council.

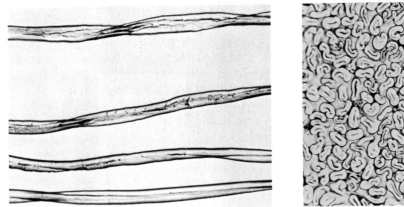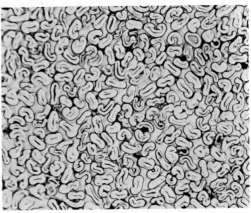

Figure 3.6
Longitudinal view and cross-section of cotton fiber.
Courtesy of U.S. Dept. of Agriculture, Southern Regional Research Center.

Flax

Flax (or linen) was probably the first fiber used in the Western world and dates back to the Egyptians. It was during the early American settlement that flax was introduced in this country. Flax is a stem, or stalk, fiber. When the plant has grown for several months, it is mechanically or manually pulled with roots attached so that the root fibers will not be damaged. Once dried, the flax is processed according to the following steps:

1. Rippling—the seed pods and bolls are removed by threshing machines.

2. Retting—the outer stalk is removed (usually by soaking) so that the fiber is accessible.

3. Braking—the outer, woody covering of the flax is further broken down to free the fiber.

4. Scutching—the outer covering is separated from the part of the fiber that can be utilized.

5. Hackling—the fiber is drawn through pins which separate the long fibers (line) from the short fibers (tow).

6. Spinning—fibers are combined to form a yarn.

A cross-section view of flax is seen in Figure 3.7.

Cellulosic Fibers: Advantages and Disadvantages

The advantages of the cellulosic fibers are as follows:

1. They absorb moisture and conduct heat well; comfortable in hot weather.

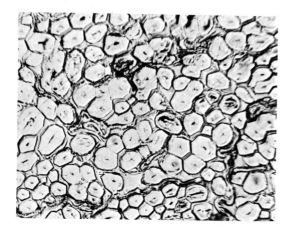

Figure 3.7
Cross-section of flax fiber.
Courtesy of U.S. Dept. of Agriculture, Southern Regional Research Center.

2. They are good conductors; do not build up static electricity.

3. Good dimensional stability; they neither shrink nor stretch.

The disadvantages of the cellulosic fibers are as follows:

1. Resilience and elastic recovery are low; therefore, they tend to wrinkle unless special finishes are used.

2. High density will often result in heavy fabrics.

3. Prolonged exposure to sunlight can weaken fibers, especially cotton.

4. They will ignite and burn quickly.

There are many other cellulosic fibers, other than those discussed. They are included here according to type.

Bast Fibers: jute, ramie, hemp, nettle, kenaf

Leaf Fibers: sisal, pina, abaca, henequen

Seed Fibers: coir, kapok

Mineral Fibers

The important fiber in this category of natural fibers is asbestos. The major characteristic of asbestos is its ability to withstand fire, a fact that has perplexed and intrigued people since the Greeks. Because it is difficult to obtain asbestos fiber and to produce yarn due to its smooth, rodlike structure, it was not commercially important until the late nineteenth century. The Industrial Revolution brought new demands for products made of a fire-retardant fiber.

The asbestos fiber is found in mineral deposits. The rock is mined and the fiber extracted from the crushed rock. The fiber is graded by length. The longer lengths, suitable for spinning but weak and difficult to handle, are often combined with cotton or rayon; the blended yarns, however are not fireproof. Asbestos is primarily used in industry.

The advantages of the asbestos fiber are as follows:

1.   Excellent fire resistance; it will not burn.

2.   It has good abrasion resistance.

The disadvantage of the asbestos fiber is:

1.   It is cancer causing or carcinogenic; it is prohibited in consumer clothing and many other products.

MAN-MADE FIBERS

It was the magic of the silkworm and its ability to extrude a liquid which turned to solid fiber in the surrounding air that inspired scientists to develop fibers through chemistry. Patterned after the silkworm phenomenon, scientists developed liquids that could be forced through a spinneret (see Figure 3.8). Through

Figure 3.8
A spinneret is used in the manufacture of man-made fibers.
Courtesy of Viscosuisse.

various means, the liquid was hardened into filaments. Because these fibers are manufactured, they can be produced in a variety of lengths and widths and with different characteristics that will affect the finished textile and its use. Man-made fibers tend to look similar in the longitudinal view and are characterized by a smooth, rodlike appearance. The cross-sections, however, are more distinctive and some of these are included in the discussion. The following modifications may be made to man-made fibers when they are produced:

1. Optical brighteners may be added, resulting in clear, bright fibers.
2. Delustrants can be added to diminish the brightness of the fiber.
3. The strength of the fiber may be controlled for various end-uses (whether the fiber is intended for industrial applications where superior strength is required, or for home textiles or apparel with less strength required for product satisfaction).
4. Cross-section diameter and shapes can be controlled—this may affect appearance, hand, and level of brightness.
5. Crimp can be set in the fiber—more crimp results in bulkier fiber.
6. Filaments may be stretched to improve strength and elasticity of the fiber.

There are general advantages and disadvantages common to all man-made fibers, although each fiber has specific characteristics and, as previously explained, can be engineered with a range of modifications.

General advantages of the man-made fibers are as follows:

1. Dimensional stability—shape retention; will not stretch or shrink
2. Resilience—will resist wrinkling
3. Strength—toughness and durability
4. Abrasion resistance—resist damage from rubbing
5. Ease of care—machine washing and drying
6. Resistance to damage from the sun—resist fading

General disadvantages of the manufactured fibers are as follows:

1. Thermoplasticity (sensitive to heat)—makes extra care necessary in laundering and ironing
2. Nonabsorbent (hydrophobic) qualities may affect comfort
3. Static electricity which tends to build in the fiber as a result of low absorbency

Since they were first introduced, manufactured fibers have increased in number and have been improved to meet the demands of the sophisticated consumer. Today, the most creative, innovative designers utilize manufactured fibers for their contemporary, exciting fashion designs (see Figure 3.9). Manufactured fibers are divided into two categories—*cellulosic* and *noncellulosic*.

giraffe neck

dropped shoulders

hip belt

full sleeve

pleats

wrap closure

winter polo

full sleeve

dropped shoulder

suspenders

high waist

straight leg

Figure 3.9
Designs for man-made fibers are creative and innovative.
Courtesy of Celanese Fibers Marketing Company.

Cellulosic Fibers

The cellulosic fibers are rayon, acetate, and triacetate. All three are derived from cellulose.

Rayon

Known as *artificial silk* when it was first produced in 1891, the first manufactured fiber was renamed *rayon* in the 1920s. The common types are:

1. Viscose rayon—discovered in 1892 by three English chemists, the name is derived from the thick, syrupy viscous solution forced through the spinneret.

2. Cuprammonium rayon—discovered in 1890 by a Frenchman, the name is derived from the copper oxide and ammonia used to dissolve the cellulose.

3. Modified rayon—these are the rayons that have been introduced as a result of technical advancements. Their special qualities include increased strength, added texture and warmth, dimensional stability, and aesthetic qualities.

See Figure 3.10 for a cross-section view of rayon.

The advantages of rayon are as follows:

1. Absorbent and comfortable to wear
2. Accepts dyes readily
3. Versatility—can be made to resemble wool, silk, linen, cotton
4. Inexpensive production

The disadvantages of rayon are as follows:

1. Low strength compared to noncellulosics
2. Low resiliency—tends to wrinkle
3. Low dimensional stability—tends to stretch and sag
4. Low wet strength

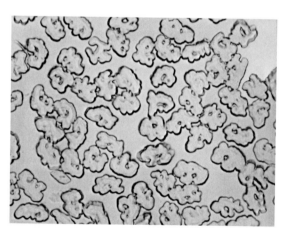

Figure 3.10
Cross-section of rayon fiber.
Photomicrographs courtesy of E.I. duPont de Nemours & Co., Inc.

Acetate and Triacetate

Discovered in 1869, the cellulose acetate solution was not commercially used until after World War I. Acetate fibers were produced in the United States by the

Celanese Corporation in 1924. Today, there are many other producers of acetate fibers. (See Figure 3.11 for a cross-section view of acetate.)

In 1954, Celanese produced triacetate, which differed from acetate because of its higher ratio of acetate to cellulose. One of the advantages of triacetate, compared to acetate, was its lower level of sensitivity to heat, which made ironing triacetate much easier. The Celanese triacetate is called Arnel and is the only one manufactured in the United States.

Acetate and triacetate have been popular both in apparel and in home furnishings.

The advantages of acetate are as follows:

1. Attractive appearance and hand (appealing to the touch)
2. Excellent drapability
3. Fairly absorbent, but less so than cotton

The disadvantages of acetate are as follows:

1. Low abrasion resistance
2. Low tensile strength
3. Extremely sensitive to heat — can melt or shrink
4. Poor resistance to sunlight damage — sun weakens fiber
5. Poor elasticity and low resiliency — tends to wrinkle and deform

The advantages of triacetate are as follows:

1. Good resiliency — resists wrinkling
2. Good colorfastness to light and laundering

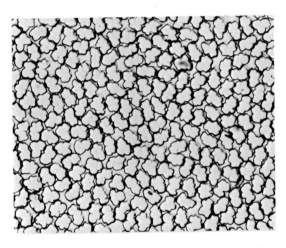

Figure 3.11
Cross-section of acetate fiber.
Courtesy of U.S. Dept. of Agriculture, Southern Regional Research Center.

3. Its ability to be heat set—a popular fiber for pleated fashions

4. Excellent for traveling—packs compactly and without wrinkling

The disadvantages of triacetate are as follows:

1. Low abrasion resistance

2. Low tensile strength

3. Sensitivity to heat

4. Low absorption level which can be uncomfortable for the wearer

Manufactured Noncellulosic Fibers

The fibers in this classification are not formed from natural bases, but from complex chemical compounds.

Nylon

Years of research at the DuPont Company were necessary to develop nylon, the first truly manufactured fiber. (See Figure 3.12 for a cross-section of nylon fiber.) Launching nylon stockings to introduce the new fiber, and backed by an exciting advertising campaign, the marketing of nylon began on a grand scale in 1940. Immediate success followed and continued with a temporary absence of nylon on the market because of its military use during World War II.

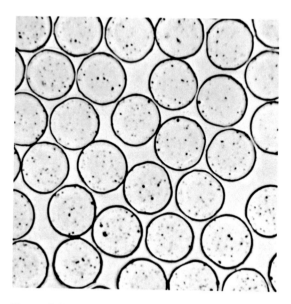

Figure 3.12
Cross-section of nylon fiber.
Photomicrographs courtesy of E.I. duPont de Nemours & Co., Inc.

Why was nylon so popular, especially as hosiery? Nylon resembled silk, but was more durable and not as expensive. Considering the other fibers available in hosiery in 1940—cotton, wool, and rayon—it is easy to understand why women quickly placed silklike nylon as their first choice.

DuPont introduced Qiana in the 1960s. It has been a very fashionable fiber because of its lovely hand, draping qualities, and silklike characteristics, while being completely machine washable and dryable.

Nylon, one of the most popular and widely used fibers today, is suitable for lingerie, a wide variety of apparel, home textiles, and industrial use. (See Figure 3.13.)

The advantages of nylon are as follows:

1. High strength
2. Easy care—resists staining, washes easily, dries very quickly, does not require ironing
3. Excellent resilience—resists wrinkling
4. Excellent abrasion resistance (however, pilling may be a problem as a result)
5. High elasticity and good recovery—maintains shape
6. Does not support combustion

Figure 3.13
Nylon lingerie of "Antron" III nylon is pretty and comfortable.
Courtesy of E.I. duPont de Nemours & Co., Inc.

The disadvantages of nylon are as follows:

1. Low absorption can make nylon feel uncomfortable and clammy (in swimwear, this can be an advantage because the suit will not absorb water well and will dry quickly).

2. Sunlight weakens fiber.

3. Low moisture absorbency causes the fiber to be a conductor of static electricity (special finishes have been developed to alleviate this problem).

Polyester

Research with polyester fibers had been conducted a number of years in the United States by DuPont and then in England before two British scientists finally introduced a workable polyester fiber in 1941. Further development of the fiber was interrupted by World War II so that it was not introduced to the public until 1946. DuPont manufactured polyester in the United States, and it was first available to consumers in 1951. Since that time, many manufacturers have developed polyester fibers, resulting in a proliferation of varieties and trademarks on the U.S. market. (See Figure 3.14 for longitudinal view and cross-section of the polyester fiber.)

Polyester was well accepted by consumers, particularly because of its superb crease resistance and carefree maintenance. Polyester fibers are used in all kinds of clothing for the entire family and in many kinds of home textiles. Polyester also has many industrial applications, such as use in conveyor belts, fire hoses,

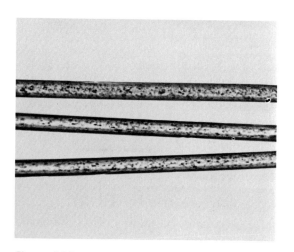
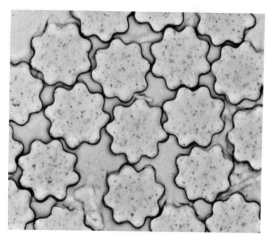

Figure 3.14
Longitudinal view and cross-section of polyester fiber.
Longitudinal view, courtesy of U.S. Dept. of Agriculture, Southern Regional Research Center. Cross-section photomicrographs courtesy of E.I. duPont de Nemours & Co., Inc.

rope, and sailcloth. Polyester fibers have been phenomenally successful world-wide, and their use surpasses that of any other fiber.

The use of polyester fibers in blends has been very popular, especially because of the incorporation of polyester fibers makes blends easy to care for and attractive to wear because of their wrinkle resistance. Popular polyester blends and their usage include the following:

Polyester/Cotton Blends. This blend was first incorporated in one yarn by Du-Pont. A 65/35 blend of polyester/cotton offers the comfort of cotton and the wrinkle resistance of polyester. The major disadvantage is that stain removal can be a problem because the cotton attracts water-borne stains and the polyester attracts oil-borne stains; thus, cleaning these stains from the blend is more difficult than cleaning stains from the pure cotton or pure polyester.

Polyester/cotton blends may also have ratios of 50/50, 35/65, 80/20, or 20/80. These blends have been popular in the marketplace, appealing to many different customers with varying preferences for blends of different ratios.

Polyester/Wool Blends. These blends have been widely used in both men's and women's clothing. While the wool offers warmth, absorption, aesthetic qualities (drape and texture), and resiliency, the polyester increases abrasion resistance, crease retention, and wrinkle resistance. It is lighter in weight than pure wool, tailors well, packs easily, is less expensive than pure wool, and is often washable. Blends include polyester/wool ratios of 50/50, 55/45, and 65/35. Figure 3.15 illustrates a fashion in a polyester/wool blend.

Polyester has also been blended in unique combinations such as polyester/rayon/flax which results in fabrics that are nicely textured, comfortable to wear, and easy to care for (see Figure 3.16 for an example).

The advantages of polyester are as follows:

1. Excellent resilience—resists wrinkles
2. Excellent dimensional stability—resists shrinkage and retains shape
3. Easy-care; quick drying and needs no ironing
4. High strength and abrasion resistance (this can be a disadvantage, as explained later)

The disadvantages of polyester are as follows:

1. Low absorption—can feel clammy and tends to build static
2. Weakening of fibers when exposed to direct sunlight (there is much less damage behind glass, so the fiber is suitable for window hangings)
3. Tends to absorb oily stains (polyester is oleophilic); also tends to pick up soil from other clothes in the wash
4. High strength and abrasion resistance which encourages pilling (these tiny fiber balls stay on the surface of the fabric rather than falling off, due to the high strength of the polyester fiber)

Figure 3.15
Polyester/wool fashion.
Courtesy of Hoechst Fibers Industries (Division of American Hoechst Corporation).

Figure 3.16
Polyester/rayon/flax fashion.
Courtesy of Hoechst Fibers Industries (Division of American Hoechst Corporation).

Acrylic

DuPont developed the first acrylic fiber, Orlon, during the early part of World War II; full scale commercial production began in 1950. Two years later, Monsanto introduced Acrilan. American Cyanamid manufactured Creslan, which appeared in 1958. The tradename Zefran is applied to all the synthetic manufactured by Dow Badische. Different generic classes are labeled Zefran orlon, Zefran acrylic, Zefran nylon, etc. A careful reading of labels and hangtags will supply necessary information to the customer. (See Figure 3.17 for a cross-section view of acrylic fiber.)

Bicomponent acrylic fibers were introduced by DuPont in 1959. The fiber is formed by simultaneously extruding from the spinneret two types of acrylic fiber. Because one variety shrinks more than the other, the resulting *bicomponent* (a combining of two types of the same fiber or polymer) fiber has a permanent spiral crimp (see Figure 3.18) and possesses resiliency, elasticity, high bulk, and

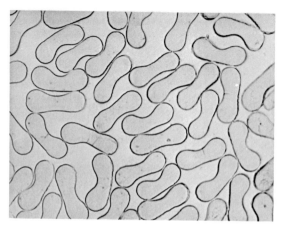

Figure 3.17
Cross-section of acrylic fiber.
Photomicrographs courtesy of E.I. duPont de Nemours & Co., Inc.

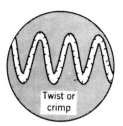

Figure 3.18
The spiral crimp in acrylic fiber adds to its high bulk, wool-like appearance.
From MODERN TEXTILES, 2nd Ed., by Dorothy Lyle. New York: John Wiley & Sons, 1982, p. 225.

Figure 3.19

Left: Casual fashions in So-Lara and Bi-Lofe acrylic.
Courtesy of Monsanto Textiles Company.
Right: Garments bearing the American Fleecewear® label and made with Creslan® acrylic fibers.
Courtesy American Cyanamid Company, FIBERS Division.

wool-like appearance. It is especially aesthetic when used for sweaters, outer-wear, craft/knitting/crochet yarns, and carpets.

Acrylic fibers are widely available in the marketplace and are especially suited for use in soft, bulky treatments (see Figure 3.19). Acrylics are used in both apparel and home textiles.

The advantages of acrylic are as follows:

1. Good resiliency—resists wrinkles
2. Good abrasion resistance
3. Good dimensional stability—retains shape
4. Aesthetic, with a wool-like appearance
5. Easy care; most can be machine washed and dried

6. Moderately strong
7. Resistant to sunlight damage

The disadvantages of acrylic are as follows:

1. Tendency to hold oil-borne stains
2. Shrinkage due to heat exposure

Modacrylic

Modacrylics are modified acrylic fibers that were included in the acrylic classification until 1960 when the Federal Trade Commission required a separate category. Whereas acrylics must be composed of at least 85 percent acrylonitrile units, only 35–84 percent of these units are necessary in producing modacrylics.

Modacrylic fibers, called Dynel, were initially produced by Union Carbide in 1949. They have been especially popular in pile and fleece fabrics for apparel, home textiles, and accessories such as wigs and hair pieces. Various texturizing techniques result in modacrylics that resemble fur or hair, thus their popularity in "fake" fur outerwear and hair pieces. Both acrylic and modacrylic have been successfully engineered to simulate luxury fur (see Figure 3.20).

The advantages of modacrylic are as follows:

1. Lightweight but warm, making attractive outerwear
2. Good resilience and abrasion resistance, making suitability for pile fabrics excellent
3. Good dimensional stability
4. Inherently fire resistant—are self-extinguishing when removed from flame
5. Pleasing, luxurious hand

The disadvantages of modacrylic are as follows:

1. Lower melting point than that of acrylic makes the fibers more sensitive to heat.
2. Its sensitivitiy to heat may result in some shrinkage if dried at a high temperature in a dryer.

Olefin

Polypropylene and polyethylene are the two major categories of olefin fibers. The latter was developed in the 1930s but polypropylene, the more widely used olefin today, was not developed until 1951 by the Montecatini Company in Italy. Since then, foreign production of olefin has increased and many American companies are today producing olefin fibers.

While polyethylene is of minor importance today and is used primarily for plastic films, polypropylene is extensively used for various apparel (blends are common) and home furnishings, especially carpeting including the indoor-outdoor variety. Polypropylene is also used for craft yarns, for artificial ski slopes, and in industrial applications.

Figure 3.20
An acrylic/modacrylic fur coat looks like the real thing!
Courtesy of Sportowne®, a division of The Metzger Group, Inc.

The advantages of the polypropylene olefin fiber are as follows:

1. Very strong
2. Good abrasion resistance
3. Easy to maintain—washes well, dries rapidly, and requires little or no ironing
4. Good resiliency—wrinkle resistant
5. Resists acids, alkalies, microorganisms, insects
6. Lightweight—provides good insulation
7. Excellent resistance to water-borne stains

The disadvantages of the polypropylene olefin fiber are as follows:

1. Almost totally nonabsorbent and difficult to dye
2. Oleophilic (oil-staining); stains may be difficult to clean
3. Slowly degrades in sunlight

Elastomeric Fibers

In this category are included fibers with characteristics similar to those of natural rubber. They can be stretched several times their length, but will recover almost to their original length. Rubber and spandex are currently being manufactured. (See Chapter 10.)

Rubber is available in both natural and synthetic forms. Natural rubber is obtained from the rubber plant; rubber fibers were developed by the U.S. Rubber Company in the 1920s. The rubber filament formed the core of fiber-covered yarns. These yarns are used in hosiery, elasticized bands, and foundation garments. The advantages of rubber include the elastic, flexible, high-strength qualities; the major disadvantage is the damage caused by sun and age. Synthetic rubber has replaced natural rubber to a great extent; its qualities are similar to those of natural rubber and the synthetics also resist deterioration.

Spandex fibers were first made in the United States in 1959. They have replaced natural rubber in many items and have been widely accepted for use in stretch fabrics for sportswear, foundation garments, hosiery, swimwear, and stretch laces and trims. Like rubber, spandex is used in combination with other fibers (see Figure 3.21 for fashions of spandex).

The advantages of the spandex fiber are as follows:

1. It is stronger than rubber.
2. It has excellent stretch qualities.
3. Low absorbency and moisture regain make the fiber excellent for swimwear/beachwear.

The disadvantages of spandex are as follows:

1. Excessive heat will cause melting.
2. Chlorine bleach damages, degrades.

Figure 3.21
Spandex activewear made of "Lycra" spandex.
Courtesy of E.I. duPont de Nemours & Co., Inc.

Glass

Glass fiber production was first undertaken by Owens-Corning Fiberglas Corporation in the 1930s; other companies manufactured glass fibers after World War II. Glass is made from sand, limestone, and other minerals. Glass fibers have been used in draperies and bedspreads; however, glass fibers have not been accepted by consumers in clothing or upholstery since they irritate the skin. Glass has been combined with plastic to form fiberglass used in construction, draperies, lampshades, sportscars, and boats.

Advantages of the glass fiber are as follows:

1. Very strong
2. Excellent elastic recovery, but low elongation
3. Excellent dimensional stability
4. Excellent resiliency — resists wrinkles

5. Nonflammable
6. Stain resistant
7. Good insulation

The disadvantages of glass fibers are as follows:

1. Low abrasion resistance—the fibers may be damaged by rubbing and friction.
2. Alkalies damage the fibers.
3. Allergic reactions in some people—skin irritations result.
4. Residue from fiber after washing can be transferred to other wash loads, causing skin irritation when garments are worn.

Metallic

Metallic fibers were used before recorded history and were the first man-made fibers. The ductility of the metal—its ability to be beaten and drawn into a fine filament—determines its suitability for fiber. Gold and silver have excellent ductile qualities, but are costly and weaken; in addition, silver tarnishes. To reduce costs, other metals (such as aluminum) are coated with gold or silver and made into fiber; metallic fibers may also be coated with plastic or polyester. Today, the available technology makes a variety of metals appropriate for fiber.

Metallic fibers are used for decorative accents in clothing and household textiles. In carpeting the metallic fibers are used to diminish static charge, and in other household textiles the fibers are utilized for heating purposes.

The advantages of the metallic fibers are as follows:

1. Fashion accents enhance many fabrics, but these are not always in fashion.
2. These fibers can diminish static charge and can be used for heating purposes in household textiles.

The disadvantages of the metallic fibers are as follows:

1. They have low strength.
2. Special care is often required—read labels carefully.

Saran

Dow Chemical introduced saran fibers in 1940; later, other manufacturers developed saran fibers. Saran is used for home textiles, automobiles, upholstery, and patio furniture.

The advantages of saran fibers are as follows:

1. Excellent elastic recovery
2. Very good resiliency
3. Nonflammable

The disadvantages of saran fibers are as follows:

1. Low strength
2. Could melt when ironed
3. Susceptible to static electricity

Vinyon

This fiber was produced commercially in the United States in 1937. It is generally used in industrial applications, theaters, and vehicles, especially because of its nonflammable qualities.

The advantages of the vinyon fiber are as follows:

1. Nonflammable
2. Moderate to good stain resistance

The disadvantages of the vinyon fiber are as follows:

1. Strength varies considerably—low to high
2. Softened by dry-cleaning solvents
3. Very heat sensitive
4. Low to moderate resiliency
5. Fair elastic recovery

Aramid

These fibers are somewhat similar to nylon, but differ sufficiently to warrant a separate category by the Federal Trade Commission. Nomex and Kevlar, both manufactured by DuPont, are the two aramid fibers on the American market today. Aramid fibers are used in protective clothing, upholstery, drapery and carpeting, ironing board covers, sporting goods, and space exploration.

The advantages of aramid are as follows:

1. High strength
2. Good abrasion resistance
3. Good dimensional stability
4. Excellent flame resistance—does not melt
5. Excellent resiliency

The disadvantages of aramid are as follows:

1. Can be damaged by sun
2. Relatively low absorbency

Novoloid

Kynol is the only novoloid fiber manufactured today. It is used in aircraft, protective clothing, car racing outfits, and for draperies.

The advantages of the kynol fiber are as follows:

1. Good resiliency
2. Excellent dimensional stability
3. Resistant to sun damage
4. Excellent flame resistance—will not burn or melt

The disadvantages of the kynol fiber are as follows:

1. Poor abrasion resistance
2. Damaged by chlorine bleach

The following three fibers are not currently being produced in the United States.

Azlon

Azlon is a manufactured protein fiber, the protein extracted from original sources such as milk, corn, soybean, peanuts. Azlon fibers have a nice hand, are warm and soft, resist sunlight damage, and have good draping qualities. They are weak, however, and have a tendency to develop an unpleasant odor when wet.

Anidex

Anidex is an elastomeric fiber. It was first introduced in 1970 by Rohm & Haas. Among its qualities are the following: excellent elasticity and recovery; easily dyed, printed, finished, or bleached; blends well with other fibers whether natural or manufactured.

Nytril

In 1955, the first commercial nytril fiber was introduced by B.F. Goodrich Company. Purchasing the rights to manufacture the fiber in 1960, Celanese then made an agreement with Hoechst in 1961 to manufacture the fiber in Europe. The fiber is not currently manufactured anywhere. Nytril was characterized by ease of care, a soft hand, resiliency, and nonpilling qualities.

FIBER FACTS

Table 3.1 and Figure 3.22 present information about U.S. mill consumption of fibers for designated years between 1940 and 1980. Table 3.2 and Figure 3.23 present information related to per capita availability of cotton, wool, and man-made fibers. Table 3.3 presents information related to fiber consumption in end-use products.

TABLE 3.1 U.S. MILL CONSUMPTION OF FIBERS

	(MILLION POUNDS)		
	1970	1975	1979
Polyester	1,600	3,100	3,800
Nylon/Aramid	1,300	2,000	2,700
Glass	400	500	900
Olefin	200	500	700
Acrylic/Modacrylic	500	500	600
Rayon	900	500	500
Acetate/Triacetate	490	285	280
Other	10	15	20
Total Man-Made Fiber	5,400	7,400	9,500
Cotton	3,800	3,100	3,100
Wool	300	100	100
Silk	+	+	+
Total	9,500	10,600	12,700

In 1940, the man-made fiber industry supplied only 10% of the fibers used by American textile mills. By 1960, their share had increased to 29% and then to 58% by 1970. Today, man-made fibers account for 75% of the approximately 12.7 billion pounds of fiber used by domestic mills annually. Polyester alone represents more poundage than does cotton and is the most widely used fiber today. To the right is a breakdown of U.S. Mill consumption by fiber.

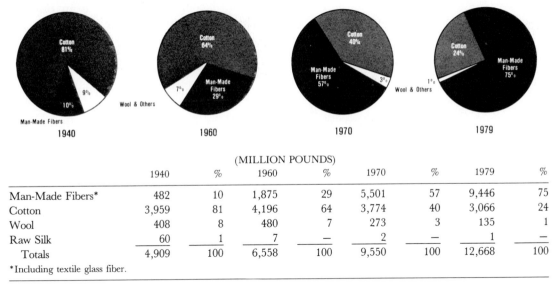

	1940	%	1960	%	1970	%	1979	%
				(MILLION POUNDS)				
Man-Made Fibers*	482	10	1,875	29	5,501	57	9,446	75
Cotton	3,959	81	4,196	64	3,774	40	3,066	24
Wool	408	8	480	7	273	3	135	1
Raw Silk	60	1	7	—	2	—	1	—
Totals	4,909	100	6,558	100	9,550	100	12,668	100

*Including textile glass fiber.

Courtesy of Man-Made Fiber Producers Association, Inc.

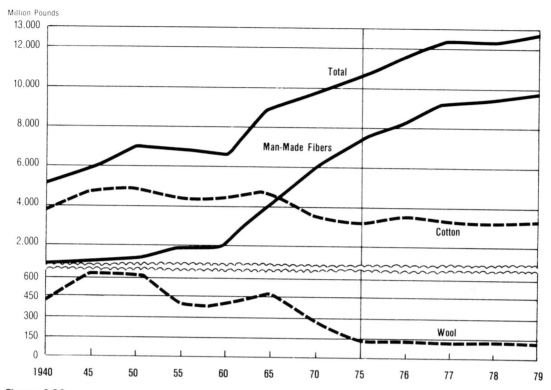

Figure 3.22

U.S. textile mill consumption of cotton, wool, and man-made fibers.
Courtesy of the Man-Made Fiber Producers Association, Inc.

TABLE 3.2   PER CAPITA AVAILABILITY OF COTTON, WOOL, AND MAN-MADE FIBERS

Each year the U.S. population increases and each year more fiber is made available for individual use. The 1979 U.S. availability of man-made fiber, cotton, and wool in all forms, including imported products, aggregated 58.7 pounds per capita. The chart below shows how availability and population have increased since 1940.

(POUNDS)

	1940	1960	1970	1975	1979	Percentage Increase 1960–1979
Man-Made Fibers*	4	10	28	35	43	+ 330
Cotton	30	23	20	15	15	− 35
Wool	3	3	2	1	1	− 71
Totals	37	37	49	51	59	+ 59
Population (millions)	132	181	205	213	220	+ 22

*Including textile glass fiber.
Courtesy of Man-Made Fiber Producers Association, Inc.

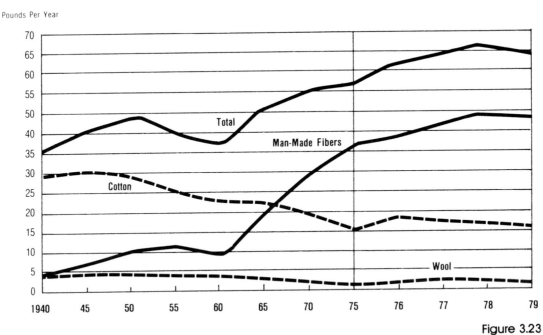

Figure 3.23

U.S. per capita availability of cotton, wool, and man-made fibers.
Courtesy of the Man-Made Fiber Producers Association, Inc.

TABLE 3.3   FIBER CONSUMPTION IN END-USE PRODUCTS

Man-made fibers are found in all types of textile products manufactured in the United States for apparel, home furnishings, industrial and other consumer uses as well as exported fabrics and yarns. The following table shows the millions of pounds of major fibers used during 1970, 1974, and 1978 for selected articles. The figures do not include imports of these articles.

	Year	Man-Made Fiber	Cotton	Wool	Total
		(MILLION POUNDS)			
Apparel	1970	2,355	1,805	240	4,400
	1974	3,054	1,692	90	4,836
	1978	3,289	1,614	144	5,047
Home Furnishings	1970	1,683	1,257	90	3,030
	1974	2,464	962	33	3,459
	1978	3,092	908	35	4,035
Industrial and Other Consumer Uses	1970	1,391	711	9	2,111
	1974	2,124	600	10	2,734
	1978	2,406	506	9	2,921
Exports of Yarns and Fabrics	1970	105	132	1	238
	1974	249	255	15	519
	1978	289	220	4	513

KEY TERMS

1. Absorption
2. Bicomponent fiber
3. Delustrant
4. Density
5. Elasticity
6. Elastomeric fiber
7. Filament
8. Raw silk
9. Resiliency
10. Spinneret
11. Spinning quality
12. Staple
13. Thrown silk
14. Wild silk

STUDY QUESTIONS

1. What is the difference between natural and manufactured fibers?
2. List and explain five characteristics required of fibers that will be used in textile production.
3. Why have blends been so popular in the marketplace?
4. Identify the three types of natural fibers and their sources.
5. Identify the two general types of manufactured fibers and give three examples of each.
6. Explain the difference between pure silk and weighted silk.
7. What inspired researchers to develop a method for producing manufactured fibers?

8. Explain five modifications that can be made to manufactured fibers and the purpose of each.
9. List and explain three advantages and disadvantages that apply to manufactured fibers in general.
10. What has been the trend in U.S. mill consumption of natural and manufactured fibers in the last forty years?

STUDY ACTIVITIES

1. A loyal customer is planning a business/pleasure trip to New York in July. She has asked you, her favorite salesperson, to help her make wardrobe selections. She has $350 to spend. List each piece you select for her, giving the fiber content and price. Justify selections.
2. Visit the sportswear department of a local store. List at least ten items sold, the fiber content of each item, a description, and the price. What relationships can you draw about fiber/design/price? Explain your reaction to your findings.
3. Read a selected newspaper every day for a week. Record the information found in fashion advertising that relates to fiber information. What fibers were found, in what kinds of garments, and for what prices? Can you draw any conclusions from your findings?

CHAPTER 4

Textile Yarns

OBJECTIVES

After completing this chapter, you should be able to:

1. Define what a yarn is.

2. Outline the procedures for making spun and filament yarns.

3. List and explain the methods for texturizing filament yarns.

4. Define and explain the importance of twist.

5. Explain yarn size as it relates to natural and man-made fibers.

6. Differentiate single, ply, and cord yarns.

7. Explain the difference between simple and novelty/complex yarns.

This chapter provides detailed information about textile yarns. Spun yarns and filament yards are discussed. Their characteristics are outlined, and comparisons are drawn. Steps for producing spun yarns and filament yarns are delineated. Texturizing procedures that have been developed to improve the aesthetics and performance of filament yarns are discussed. Single, ply, and cord yarns are discussed as well as simple and novelty yarns.

The information in this chapter will enable you to understand how yarn factors relate to and influence the specific end-uses and performance characteristics of the finished fabrics.

Textile fibers must be made into yarns before textile fabric can be constructed. Based on the definition of the American Society for Testing Materials (ASTM), the generic term *yarn* is a continuous strand of textile fibers, filaments, or other material in a form that is appropriate for knitting, weaving, or other type of construction to form a textile fabric.

Yarns are made from either short, staple fibers or from long, continuous filament fibers. The staple fibers may be natural fibers that are available only in short lengths (except for silk, which is the only natural fiber in filament form), or they may be man-made fibers that have been cut or broken into short staple lengths. Filament fibers may be made into yarn from a single strand (monofilament) or several strands (multifilament). The processing required for converting staple fiber into yarn is more complex than that required for converting filament fiber into yarn.

MAKING NATURAL STAPLE FIBERS INTO YARN

Originally, staple fibers were twisted together by hand to make yarns suitable for spinning. You may wish to try the following to simulate this process. Take a small cotton ball and gently pull out a mass of fibers. From this, isolate one fiber and observe its length, diameter, and shape. Return this fiber to the mass of cotton fibers and begin to pull the fibers out into an elongated formation. Gently pull and twist the fibers in one direction to form a yarn (moistening the thumb and index finger will facilitate the yarn making). This is the most primitive type of yarn construction.

Before fibers can be twisted into yarns, they have to be straightened by a process called *carding*. This was originally performed by hand with several techniques possible. Fingers could be run through the bundle of fibers; this method straightened the fibers only minimally and was not terribly efficient. Nature provided a more efficient tool—the thistle head or teasel—which was often utilized to straighten the fibers. Another ancient device, the carder, was a pair of wooden paddle-type instruments studded with wire hooks; these were pulled in opposite directions in order to straighten the fibers. A teasel and a carder are illustrated in Figure 4.1.

After carding, another step called *combing* resulted in more completely parallel fibers to be used in smooth, fine, high-quality yarns. A comb-like device was utilized and the process was especially effective in separating short fibers from longer-length fibers.

Today, the manufacture of yarns from staple fiber involves a number of steps. The industry processes staple fiber according to two basic methods known as the cotton and wool systems. These differ in the machinery utilized, which is designed to handle the two fiber types: (1) the relatively strong and smooth cotton fibers or (2) the long, weak, crimped woolen fibers. The steps in each process are similar:

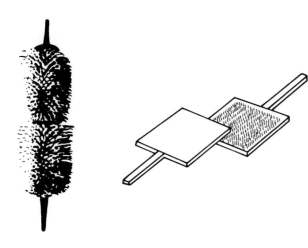

Figure 4.1
The teasel and carder were used to straighten fibers.

1. Opening and blending
2. Carding and combing
3. Drawing and roving
4. Spinning

These processes are illustrated in Figure 4.2.

Opening and Blending

The purpose of this step is to sort the fibers according to grade, and to clean, separate, and blend the fibers. Fibers from different bales or lots are fed through the chute of the opener/blender, which has a spiked, rotating cylinder.

Carding and Combing

During the carding procedure, the fibers are processed through moving brushes and wire needles, resulting in a thin web of fibers. During this step, the fibers are partially straightened, which will enable them to be more readily made into yarn. Short fibers are generally eliminated, which will later result in stronger yarns made primarily of the longer fibers. The short fibers may be used in the manufacture of lower-grade fabrics.

The combing procedure is similar to carding, but utilizes finer and more compactly spaced brushes and needles. The combing process is employed only when long staple fibers are to be spun into fine, silklike yarns to be used in fabric like percale. Figure 4.3 provides a comparison between carded and combed yarns. The carded and combed sheet of fibers is drawn through a funnel into an untwisted strand called a *sliver* (see Figure 4.2).

Fibers being pulled from the bale on new carousel opening equipment

Carding machine

Sliver being formed on carding machine

Sliver being fed into drawing machine

Roving frame

Spinning frame

Figure 4.2
Fiber processing.
Photos courtesy of Springs Industries, Inc.

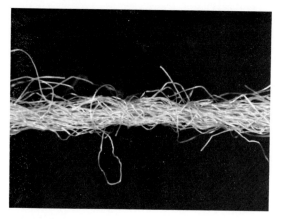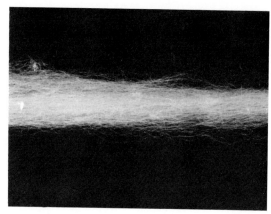

Figure 4.3
Carded and combed yarn.
Courtesy of E.I. duPont de Nemours & Co., Inc.

Drawing and Roving

The drawing frame, which has several pair of smooth revolving rollers, accepts five or six fiber slivers and combines these into one long drawn sliver. In the process, the original slivers are flattened, pulled out, and recombined, resulting in greater yarn uniformity. During the drawing process, different fiber blends can be produced, such as a polyester/cotton blend in which both polyester and cotton slivers are fed into the drawing frame in the desired amounts; half polyester and half cotton would result in a 50/50 blend.

The sliver then passes through the roving frame containing drafting rolls, which produces *roving* (a length of yarn about one-eighth the diameter and eight times the length of the sliver; see Figure 4.2). As the yarn is wound on a spindle, some twist is added.

Spinning

This is the final step in yarn manufacture, and a number of spinning methods may be utilized. The end result is that the yarn is stretched to its final diameter and twist is imparted into the yarn to the desired degree. Ring spinning and open-end spinning are the two most commonly used methods. In ring spinning, the roving is further processed to its final diameter and the desired amount of additional twist is imparted. Open-end spinning, the newer and more advanced process, is advantageous in that it converts a sliver of fibers into yarn without the necessity of forming the roving. This method increases productivity, requires less space, is more cost-efficient, and results in yarns that are uniform and smooth. The disadvantages of open-end spun yarns are that they are not as strong nor can they be made as fine as those produced through the ring-spinning method. Other methods of spinning include direct spinning, self-twist spinning, and twistless spinning.

Direct Spinning

In this process, tow fibers (filament fibers cut to staple length) are stretched until they break. They are drawn into sliver and twist is imparted. Because the fibers were not permitted to recover after stretching, the yarns have the capacity to shrink considerably. Consequently, these yarns are often used in novelty fabrics where this shrinking characteristic may result in a unique surface texture.

Self-Twist Spinning

Self-twist spinning is suitable only for two-ply yarns. Two rovings are passed between two rollers and are drawn out and given S-twist in some sections and Z-twist in other sections. When combined, they twist around each other to form the ply yarn, as seen in Figure 4.4. (Refer to pages 74 and 79 for a discussion of yarn twist and ply.) This process is advantageous because of its cost effectiveness; less space, time, energy, and labor costs are required.

Twistless Spinning

This process eliminates the twisting step. A drawn roving is coated with a starch-like sizing substance and wound. Bonding of the fibers is achieved through a steaming process which liquifies the sizing. After the sizing is removed, the yarns are soft and ribbonlike and, because they have no twist, are quite lustrous.

CHARACTERISTICS OF SPUN YARN

Spun yarns are made of staple fibers that have been twisted together; they have protruding fiber ends which affect their appearance and comfort. Since these ends hold the yarns a distance from the skin, they are more comfortable in warm weather than are filament yarns. These protruding ends also give a somewhat textured, fuzzy appearance and are subject to pilling and soiling. The spun yarns are absorbent, bulky, and warm. Their absorbency makes these yarns comfortable to wear and curtails static buildup.

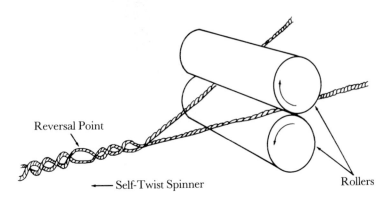

Reversal Point

Figure 4.4
Self-twist spinning.

◄── Self-Twist Spinner

Rollers

MAKING MAN-MADE STAPLE FIBERS INTO YARN

Man-made fibers produced in filament form can be cut or broken to staple lengths and converted into yarns in a manner similar to that previously outlined for natural fibers. Since man-made filament fibers that are converted to staple form are called *tow,* the spinning process is known as the tow-to-top system (top refers to the sliver). The length of the cut staple fiber will depend on the type of equipment available to the yarn manufacturer; the opening, blending, and carding steps are omitted.

At the drawing stage, blends of man-made fibers or natural/man-made fiber blends can be developed. The diameter and twist of the yarns may be regulated for various end-uses; yarns may be fine for sheer, lightweight fabrics or thick for heavier constructions. The yarns must possess sufficient twist to secure the fibers in place.

FILAMENT YARNS

The processing of natural and man-made filament fibers into yarn is much simpler than the processing of staple fibers. The only natural filament fiber is silk and production of the silk yarns was discussed in Chapter 3. Since silk makes up only about 1 percent of fibers and yarns, you can readily see that filament yarns are predominantly man-made.

Man-made filament yarns are produced by the continuous or the discontinuous methods. In the continuous method, the filaments are collected in multiple numbers (lengths) as they are extruded from the spinnerette. The number of filaments simultaneously grouped depends on the number required in the finished yarn. Twist is added to the collected filament group, and the result is a yarn ready for fabric construction. In the discontinuous process, single filaments are wrapped on cones. The yarn manufacturer may combine the filaments and impart twist as desired for a particular fabric construction.

Characteristics of Filament Yarn

Filament yarns are smooth, lustrous, silklike, and have little bulk. They can be produced with irregular surfaces for special fabric construction, and can be made in many weights and diameters, resulting in fabrics with sheer or heavy characteristics suitable for many items from hosiery to carpeting. Filament yarns may be delustered. Twist may be regulated as well, depending on end-uses; crepe yarns, for instance, require highly twisted yarns. Since filament yarns have no protruding ends, they resist pilling and tend to shed soil. Since the thermoplastic filaments (those that become pliable with heat application) are low in absorbency, they are not comfortable in warm weather and tend to build up static.

Other Spinning Systems for Filament Yarns

In addition to the traditional spinning procedure previously discussed, filament yarns may also be utilized in the following spinning systems.

Bobtex System

The Bobtex Spinning Machine forms yarns that combine a man-made monofilament core fiber and any other staple fibers. The core fiber is coated with a molten polymer resin which is in turn coated with staple fibers while twist is incorporated. As the center core hardens, the staple fibers are permanently secured to it. This type of yarn is strong because of the monofilament core, and the staple fibers add interest, texture, and additional strength.

Fasciated Yarns

Developed by DuPont, fasciated yarns consist of a bundle of parallel filaments wrapped, or bound, by other filament fibers. Their unique structure provides these yarns with a strength that surpasses that of conventionally spun yarns. See Figure 4.5 for an illustration of a fasciated yarn.

TEXTURIZING FILAMENT YARNS

The highly desirable characteristic of staple fibers—their bulk, texture, warmth, and comfort—are lacking in the filament yarns, which are smooth and strong. To compensate, the textile industry has developed methods for texturizing filament yarns so that they approximate the best features of spun yarns.

Textured yarns refer to yarns with stretch or bulk qualities; therefore, texturizing methods incorporate stretchability and bulkiness. The disadvantages are that the texturized filaments, compared to the plain filaments, can pill, pull, soil, or snag more easily.

Texturizing through the Addition of Stretch Properties

The following procedures are utilized primarily to add stretch properties to filament yarns. The three popular methods for incorporating stretch include *twisting, edge-crimp,* and the *knit-de-knit* processes.

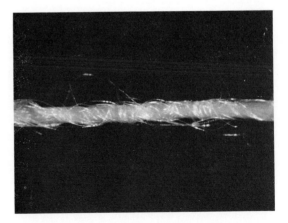

Figure 4.5
Fasciated yarn.
Courtesy of E.I. duPont de Nemours & Co., Inc.

Twisting

Twisting was the first texturizing process and included three steps: (1) twisting the yarn, (2) heat-setting, and (3) untwisting the yarn. The result was a kinked and coiled yarn. Because the original procedure was a slow one, it has been replaced with the false-twist process, based on the same principles, but more quickly and efficiently accomplished by the false-twist texturizing machine. Superloft and Helenca texturized yarns are made through this process. See Figure 4.6 for an illustration of a false-twist yarn.

Edge-crimp

In the edge-crimp process, heated thermoplastic filaments are drawn over a sharp hot knife edge causing the filaments to curl (a similar effect is achieved by pulling a scissor edge over narrow curling ribbon). Edge-crimp yarns have good stretch and are primarily used for hosiery. An example is Agilon nylon by Deering-Milliken. An edge-crimp yarn is illustrated in Figure 4.7.

Knit-de-knit

In this texturizing process, the yarn is first knitted into tubes resembling seamless, one-size-fits-all hosiery. The knitted tubes are heat-set and unravelled (de-knit), creating a permanently looped yarn with a crepelike texture that can be used in many types of clothing, swimwear, and home textiles. Crinkle is the trade name of a fabric produced through this process. Figure 4.8 illustrates a knit-de-knit yarn.

Texturizing through the Addition of Bulk Properties

The following procedures are employed primarily to add bulk properties to filament yarns. The bulk properties are desirable because warmth and textural appeal is inherent in the finished products. The three commonly used methods for incorporating bulk include the *air-jet, gear crimp,* and *stuffer box* processes.

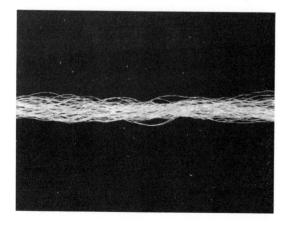

Figure 4.6
False-twist yarn.
Courtesy of E.I. duPont de Nemours & Co., Inc.

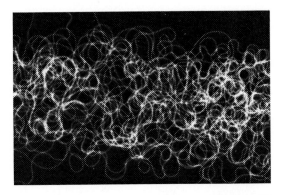

Figure 4.7
Edge-crimp yarn.
Reprinted with permission of Macmillan Publishing Company from *Modern Textiles* by Dorothy S. Lyle, originally published by John Wiley and Sons, Inc. (New York: Macmillan, 1982.)

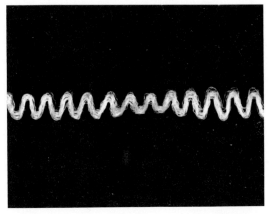

Figure 4.8
Knit-de-knit yarn.
Courtesy of E.I. duPont de Nemours & Co., Inc.

Air-jet

Thermoplastic and nonthermoplastic yarns may be texturized by air or steam which blow about the filaments so that they loop and curl. The volume of the yarn is increased up to 150 percent, but the stretch properties are not altered. This method was developed by DuPont for yarns marketed under the Taslan trade name. End-uses include wearing apparel, shoelaces, and home textiles. Air-jet yarns are illustrated in Figure 4.9.

Gear Crimp

In this process, heated filaments are passed through the teeth of two heated gears which imparts a sawtooth shape into the filaments. Spunized is a trade name for

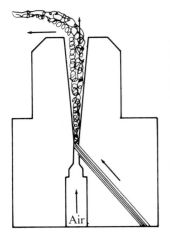

Figure 4.9
Left: Texturing of yarn by the air-jet method.
Right: Air-jet yarn itself.
Left: From "Yarn," by Stanley Backer. Copyright © 1972 by Scientific American, Inc. All rights reserved.
Right: Courtesy of E.I. duPont de Nemours & Co., Inc.

a gear-crimp yarn. These yarns are commonly used in women's apparel and lingerie. A gear-crimp yarn is illustrated in Figure 4.10.

Stuffer Box

In this process, filament yarns are fed into a small, heated box where they are pressed into crimped shapes and removed. The volume increase may be as high as 200–300 percent. Ban-Lon is a trade name for fabrics made from yarns processed in this manner. These yarns are used in carpeting and upholstery, as well as in many knits, including sweaters, skirts, and dresses (see Figure 4.11).

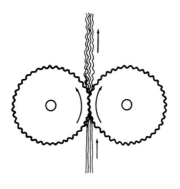

Figure 4.10
Left: Processing of yarn by the gear-crimp method.
Right: Gear-crimp yarn itself.

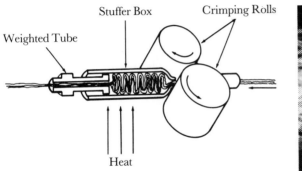

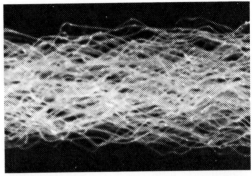

Figure 4.11

Left: Production of yarn with a stuffer box.
Right: Stuffer box yarn itself.

Right: Reprinted with permission of Macmillan Publishing Company from *Modern Textiles* by Dorothy S. Lyle, originally published by John Wiley and Sons, Inc. (New York: Macmillan, 1982.)

CHARACTERISTICS OF YARN

The characteristics of a particular yarn influence its appearance as well as its use in particular fabric constructions and the care required to maintain the fabric. As discussed previously, yarn characteristics also have a substantial effect on the comfort of a fabric. Understanding these factors is essential to the professional who works with fashion on a daily basis. The buyer, for instance, who can fully evaluate a garment (through knowledge of fibers, yarn characteristics, construction, etc.) will be better able to fulfill the requirements of the position.

Twist

Twist is the number of turns per inch in the yarn. Because this technical information is not always available, terms such as *low, medium, high,* or *hard, twist* are often substituted to describe the amount of twist in the yarn. Actually, a low twist filament yarn would have about 2–3 tpi (turns per inch); a medium twist yarn, such as a spun yarn used in nylon hosiery, has about 25–30 tpi; a high, or hard, twist crepe yarn may have 40–80 tpi. See Figure 4.12 for an illustration of the various levels of twist.

There are two possible directions for yarn twist. Yarns are either S-twist (twisting clockwise) or Z-twist (twisting counterclockwise) as illustrated in Figure 4.13. The student may wish to try a simple test to determine yarn twist direction.

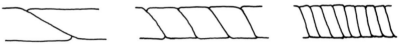

Figure 4.12

Low, medium, and high twist yarns.

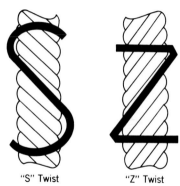

"S" Twist   "Z" Twist

Figure 4.13
S-twist and Z-twist are the two basic types of yarn twist.
From MODERN TEXTILES, 2nd Ed., by
Dorothy Lyle. New York: John Wiley & Sons,
1982, p. 220. Courtesy Cotton Incorporated.

Attach a paper clip to the end of a single yarn about 12 inches long, and allow to
hang free. If the yarn rotates clockwise, it is an S-twist yarn; if it rotates counterclockwise, it is a Z-twist yarn.

Cotton and linen yarns are usually produced with a Z-twist while woolens
and worsted yarns usually have an S-twist. Centuries ago, this was especially important so that the customer could verify a purchase of wool by examining the direction of the yarn twist.

In reference to twist, yarns may be balanced or unbalanced (see Figure
4.14). As yarns are twisted, internal forces, known as torque, are built up in the
yarn. A balanced yarn is one in which the twist has been uniformily distributed,
resulting in a straight hanging yarn. In an unbalanced yarn, the amount and
direction of twist has been varied throughout the yarn so that it untwists and re-
twists in opposite directions (a torque effect), resulting in a coiled and looped
yarn suitable for creped or highly textured fabrics.

You may perform a simple exercise to demonstrate torque. Cut an 18-inch
length of worsted weight yarn. Holding the ends in the left and right hands, and
keeping the yarn fairly taut, twist the yarn ends in opposite directions a few
times. Now bring the yarn ends together and you will observe a torque effect (as
illustrated in Figure 4.14).

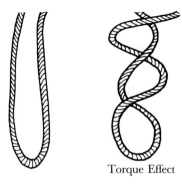

Torque Effect

Figure 4.14
A balanced and an unbalanced yarn.

Yarn Size

The size of a yarn refers to its weight and fineness and is designated by numbers. First devised during the Middle Ages, the yarn numbering system provided a standard by which yarns could be bought and sold. For spun yarns, yarn number may be defined as the number of standard hanks for each pound of yarn. The following terms are used to designate the size of spun yarns:

- *number* or count—the size of cotton, wool, and spunsilk yarns
- *lea*—the size of linen yarn

To illustrate how yarn size is designated, consider cotton. For cotton, the correct term is number or count. The standard used is 840 yards of cotton yarn to the pound which is equal to one hank and is therefore a #1 cotton. Table 4.1 supplies information related to four sizes of cotton; note that as the count or number becomes higher, the yarn is finer.

TABLE 4.1   YARN SIZE FOR COTTON YARNS

YARDS OF COTTON YARN	WEIGHT	HANKS	NUMBER/COUNT	CHARACTER
840	1 lb.	1	1	Coarser to
4200	1 lb.	5	5	finer
8400	1 lb.	10	10	
42000	1 lb.	50	50	↓

Wool numbering is based on whether or not it is worsted. Worsted yarn size is based on the number of hanks of 560 yards weighing one pound. A count of #1 indicates one 56-yard hank of one pound, while a count of #10 is 5600 yards of worsted yarn weighing one pound. Higher numbers indicate finer yarns. For nonworsted wool yarn, a 1600-yard hank weighing one pound has a count of #1; this low number corresponds to a coarse yarn.

Lea is the term designated for the size of linen yarns; there are 300 yards per lea. One 300-yard hank weighs one pound and is a lea of #1. The higher the number, the finer the yarn.

For reeled silk and man-made filament yarns, the term *denier* is used to indicate yarn size. Denier is equal to the weight in grams of 9000 meters of yarn which equals 9842.4 yards. If 9000 meters of yarn weigh 5 grams, the denier is 5; if 9000 meters weigh 50 grams, the denier is 50. The higher the denier number, the coarser the yarn. The number of filaments may also be included with the denier. For instance, 50/50 indicates a 50 denier yarn containing 50 filaments. You can then calculate the size of each filament in the yarn. In the 50/50 example, each of the filaments is a denier of 1 ($50 \div 50 = 1$). The amount and direction of twist may also be indicated. Thus, 50/50/5S designates a yarn with 50 denier, 50 filaments, and 5 twists per inch in the S direction.

Tex System

In 1873, in Vienna, a universal yarn numbering system was proposed. Many years later, in 1956, ten nations attending an international textiles conference voted unanimously to adopt such a system, known as Tex. The Tex system expresses the weight in grams of 1000 meters of yarn and can be applied to all fibers. For example, if 1000 meters of yarn weighs 1 gram, it is a #1 Tex yarn.

You can immediately see the advantages of one universal system replacing the variety of existing yarn numbering systems, and it is expected that the Tex system will gradually replace the others.

Yarn Strength

Twist adds strength to fibers and to yarns. Without twist, yarns have no strength because the fibers have not been intertwined, or interlocked, through the twisting process. Generally, more highly twisted yarns tend to be stronger, but too much twist will render the yarn too brittle, leading to weakness and breakage. Filament yarns are very strong and do not have protruding fiber ends; therefore they do not pill unless the filaments are broken. When this occurs, the loose fiber ends that collect on the surface of the fabric remain attached because of the strength and length of the filament yarns.

Yarn Elasticity

Highly twisted yarns tend to be more stretchy and elastic. Within these yarns is developed a high degree of interfiber friction which maintains elasticity and stretchability. With lower twist yarns, the ability to stretch may be excellent, but recovery is diminished and the yarn's elasticity decreased because these yarns have a much lower degree of interfiber friction.

Yarn's Tendency to Soil

High twist, tight yarns tend to have less space between fibers where soil can collect while low twist yarns are easily penetrated by soil. On the other hand, high twist yarns may not show the soil as readily as low twist yarns. You can see that a variety of factors must be considered when evaluating yarns and fabrics.

Yarn Comfort/Insulation

The insulating properties of finished cloth are related to the cloth's ability to keep the wearer warm or cool. The fiber type is, of course, important, but the yarns themselves — specifically their construction and bulk — are also very important in determining the insulating capacity of the finished fabric. Yarns will be considered first, and then the construction of the finished fabric will be considered.

A yarn with low twist and high bulk (such as a wool yarn) will have the ability to trap air among the fibers; as this air warms, it becomes an insulating layer on the body. Conversely, a yarn of higher twist and low bulk (such as a silk crepe) will not trap the air as well and will not provide as much warmth to the wearer.

The construction of the fabric must also be considered. If it is a loose, open fabric, such as a lacy wool evening sweater, the insulating properties of the yarns will not compensate for the open construction and the garment will be cool to the wearer. A tight, compact construction utilizing the silk crepe previously mentioned might actually provide more warmth, in comparison, because the warmth between the body and the garment will not escape as easily. The comfort and insulating capabilities of the finished fabric depend, therefore, on the construction of the yarn and the finished fabric. You cannot truly evaluate the garment without considering both.

Closely related to the insulating factor is the moisture permeability of the yarns and fabric. The skin has a top layer of moisture that evaporates and this affects body temperature. Fabrics made of predominantly filament yarns tend to lay close to the body. It is more difficult for moisture to penetrate the long, smooth yarns, and uncomfortable clamminess may result. Fabrics of spun yarns have a tendency to improve moisture permeability since the shorter fibers keep the cloth further from the skin and at the same time, the short fiber ends attract the moisture; the garment feels more comfortable.

Yarn Aesthetics

Fibers and yarns affect the appearance of the finished fabric. A smooth fiber, such as silk, reflects more light than a crimped fiber such as wool; therefore, it has more shine. Low to moderate twist yarns tend to reflect more light than highly twisted yarns and exhibit more luster because of the light reflected on the surface of the fabric. Aesthetics cannot be evaluated without the consideration of the fabric end-use as well as the wearer's preferences.

CONSTRUCTION OF YARN

Yarns are commonly categorized according to their inherent structure. The major categories are as follows:

1. Yarns classified by basic structure
   A. spun
   B. filament
2. Yarns classified by number of parts
   A. single
   B. ply
   C. cord
3. Yarns classified by similarity of parts
   A. Simple
   B. Novelty or complex
4. Other types of yarns

Since spun and filament yarns have been discussed, attention will now be given to the other means of classifying yarns.

YARNS CLASSIFIED BY NUMBER OF PARTS

Single Yarns

A single yarn is made up of a basic structure of fibers, staple or filament. It is a one-strand yarn that may be of any fiber. Single yarns are fairly smooth and even.

Ply Yarns

Two or more single yarns twisted together are called ply yarns. A 2-ply yarn is composed of two yarns; a 3-ply yarn is composed of three yarns, and so on. Ply yarns may be of all staple or all filament fibers or a combination of staple and filament fibers.

If you examine a worsted-weight yarn, and untwist the yarn so that the plies are separated, a typical 4-ply construction will be observed.

Thread

Thread is a plied construction. Thread is reeled into hanks, as is yarn, and can be bleached, dyed, or mercerized (these processes are discussed in Chapters 5 and 6). A satisfactory thread must have the following characteristics:

1. Strength—the thread should adequately secure seams, buttons, trims, and withstand various care procedures such as laundering and dry cleaning.
2. Elasticity—the thread should have some elasticity so that the stitches do not break or pucker.
3. Even diameter and smooth surface—the thread should easily pass through various surfaces in the sewing process and must resist damage through friction.
4. Dimensional stability—the thread should retain its original dimensions without shrinking and stretching.

Sewing threads on the market include those made of cotton, polyester, nylon, and silk. Cotton-covered polyester is a popular sewing thread that combines two fibers for strength, durability, easy care, and smooth sewing.

Cord or Cable

A cord or cable yarn consists of two or more ply yarns twisted together. A cord made of three ply yarns with each ply yarn contining six strands would be a ³⁄₆ ply cord.

Figure 4.15 illustrates single, ply, and cord yarns.

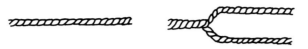

Figure 4.15
Single, ply, and cord yarns.

YARNS CLASSIFIED BY SIMILARITY OF PARTS

Simple Yarns

Simple yarns have the following structural characteristics:

1. Even in size
2. Equal number of turns per inch throughout the length
3. Relatively smooth and uniform

Simple yarns may be of one or mixed fibers and may be single, ply, or cord yarns. Fabrics made of simple yarns tend to be relatively smooth and flat, but a combination of yarns may result in fabrics of varying texture and surface interest. The smooth fabrics resulting from simple yarns will generally wear better than those made of novelty yarns because there are not the protrusions and extensions that can result in the easily snagged, pulled, and soiled novelty yarns.

Novelty Yarns

Novelty, or complex, yarns are characterized by the following:

1. Irregularity in size and in surface characteristics
2. Usually plied
3. A structure often consisting of three parts: a single core yarn; another single yarn with a special novelty characteristic, often called a *fancy;* a third single yarn that functions as a binder (see Figure 4.16)
4. Varying degrees of twist
5. Are unique and are used primarily for aesthetics and design variety

Popular novelty yarns include boucle, chenille, core-spun, flock, nub, slub, thick-and-thin, and spiral (or corkscrew).

Boucle Yarns

Characteristics. These yarns are complex ply yarns and are characterized by loops that project from the core at fairly regular intervals. Ratine yarns are similar to boucle yarns, but the loops are continuous. Boucle yarn is illustrated in Figure 4.17.

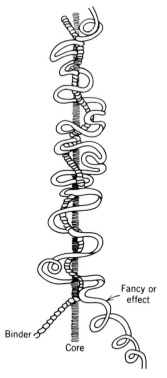

Fancy or
effect

Binder

Core

Figure 4.16
A typical structure of a novelty yarn.
From MODERN TEXTILES, 2nd Ed., by Dorothy
Lyle. New York: John Wiley & Sons, 1982, p. 221.

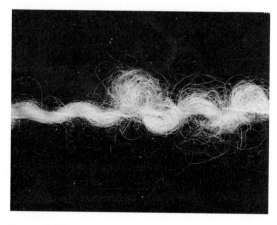

Figure 4.17
Boucle yarn is characterized by a loop structure.
Courtesy of E.I. duPont de Nemours & Co., Inc.

Uses.   Boucle and ratine yarns are used in knitted and woven constructions, in
separates, dresses, and in textiles for the home.

Chenille Yarns

Characteristics.   A leno-weave fabric is woven and then cut into strips that are used as yarns. (See Chapter 5 for a discussion of leno-weave construction.) These pile yarns inspired the name *chenille,* which is the French word for caterpillar. The tight pile surface of the chenille yarn is similar to the appearance of a pipe cleaner (see Figure 4.18).

Uses.   Chenille yarns are especially popular for robes and for household textiles, including draperies and carpeting.

Core-Spun Yarns

Characteristics.   A core yarn of one fiber is wrapped by a second yarn of a different fiber. For example, a core yarn of elastic may be covered with cotton for a stretchy yarn.

Uses.   Core-spun yarns with elastic core are very popular in sportswear and swimwear. Sewing threads are often core-spun with a core of polyester and a cover of cotton fiber. A core-spun yarn is illustrated in Figure 4.19.

Figure 4.18
Chenille yarn is similar in appearance to a pipe cleaner.
Courtesy of E.I. duPont de Nemours & Co., Inc.

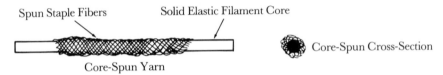

Spun Staple Fibers   Solid Elastic Filament Core

Core-Spun Yarn   Core-Spun Cross-Section

Figure 4.19
Core-spun yarns contain a core yarn and an outer yarn.

Flock Yarns

Characteristics. These are also referred to as flake, or slub, yarns. Small fiber tufts are applied to a core yarn and are secured by the twist in the yarn (see Figure 4.20).

Uses. Flock yarns are used in all kinds of clothing, including dresses, suits, and lingerie. Tweed fabrics are commonly made with flock yarns.

Nub Yarns

Characteristics. A nub, or knot, yarn (also referred to as a spot or knop yarn) is made of a core yarn around which a novelty yarn has been wrapped. At intervals, the wrapping is tight and close to form an enlarged raised segment (see Figure 4.21).

Uses. Nub yarns are used in all kinds of apparel for the entire family, as well as in textiles for the home.

Figure 4.20
A flock yarn is made of fiber tufts applied to a core yarn.

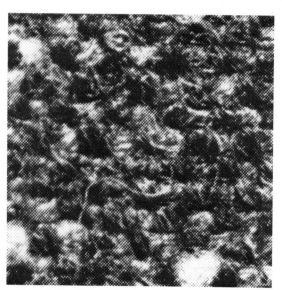

Figure 4.21
A nub yarn is made of a core yarn around which a novelty yarn has been wrapped.
Reprinted with permission of Macmillan Publishing Company from *Modern Textiles* by Dorothy S. Lyle, originally published by John Wiley and Sons, Inc. (New York: Macmillan, 1982.)

Slub Yarns/Thick-and-Thin Yarns

Characteristics. The slub yarn is made of single or 2-ply yarns. When single, this yarn is left with little or no twist at irregular intervals, producing a thick bulky section; sometimes, tufts of fiber are incorporated at intervals. When a 2-ply yarn is used, the bulkier section is stabilized by a more highly twisted yarn (see Figure 4.22).

Thick-and-thin yarns are made of filament yarns. The filament has been extruded from the spinnerette with varying degrees of pressure, resulting in a thick-and-thin effect (see Figure 4.22).

Uses. These yarns are especially popular in knitted constructions, but are also found in wovens. They are used in many kinds of apparel, including outerwear, and are also used in textiles for the home.

Spiral, or Corkscrew, Yarns

Characteristics. Spiral yarns combine two yarns of different diameter, fiber content, twist, or color, resulting in one yarn spiraling around the other. A common construction is to wrap the heavier novelty yarn around the finer, more highly twisted core yarn. A spiral yarn is illustrated in Figure 4.23.

Uses. Spiral yarns are popular in knitted items such as sweaters, caps, and scarves.

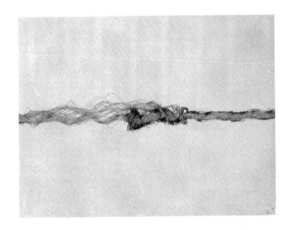
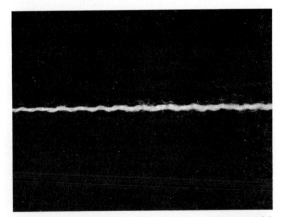

Figure 4.22
Slub (left) and thick-thin (right) yarns can be made of single or 2-ply yarns.
Courtesy of E.I. duPont de Nemours & Co., Inc.

Figure 4.23
A spiral yarn combines two different yarns for a novelty effect.

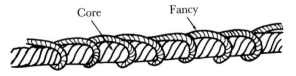

Core   Fancy

Color plus pattern adds interest to textiles used in clothing. Three coordinated prints provide a focal point for this two-piece dress and shawl. Courtesy of Crantex Fabrics Division of Cranston Print Works. Cotton takes intense dyes and intricate designs. Courtesy of Cotton Incorporated.

Black and white and red all over makes a sophisticated color scheme for a contemporary baby. Crib linens in a delightful panda design include a warm, lightweight quilt and snuggly pillows. The shelves are stocked with colorful stuffed toys. Wall-coverings have a border design. Bright carpeting adds a final touch. Courtesy of E.I. duPont de Nemours & Co., Inc.

The beauty of a traditional wood table is enhanced by gleaming china, crystal stemware, and elegant silverware. An Oriental rug and silver hollowware accessories complete this semiformal dining setting. Courtesy of Lenox China and Crystal.

A spare but comfortable contemporary look is created with overstuffed furniture, a blend of neutral colors, and a textured carpet, placed in a room with clean lines and large windows. Courtesy of Philadelphia Carpets.

A more traditional living room uses a plain, dense carpet in a striking color as a luxurious foil to patterned fabrics in the upholstery and draperies. The fabrics and carpet were chosen to bring out the pink in the marble fireplace facing. Courtesy of Philadelphia Carpets.

Carpeting today comes in a vast array of colors not dreamed of a generation ago. Courtesy of Philadelphia Carpet.

This bedroom combines delicate furniture, thick carpeting, softly draped window treatments, and ruffled linens for a coordinated look. The full-length draperies and the coverlet, dust ruffle, and pillow shams add softness to the traditional furnishings. Oriental-style accents and fresh flowers and plants add warmth. Courtesy of Ethan Allen.

Other Types of Yarns

Recent advancements in technology permit the development of yarns directly from synthetic polymers without the necessity of fibers. The following are common.

Split Films

To make split film yarns, a sheet of polymer is drawn lengthwise and broken down into a mass of interconnected fibrils, a process called *fibrillation*. The yarn is developed from the drawn out fibrils to which twist is added. The yarns are fairly coarse, rough, plasticlike and have an appearance similar to that of burlap; their use is limited by these characteristics. Olefins are commonly made into split film yarns, but any thermoplastic fiber would be suitable. End products include bags, upholstery webbing, and industrial applications.

Slit Films

These yarns are made by cutting film into narrow, ribbonlike strips. In the drawing process, some fibrillation may occur as discussed in split films. The resulting tapes or yarns are used in similar ways.

Network Yarns

These yarns are made from a foam polymer in which air has been injected. As the foam polymer is drawn, it is broken into interconnected fibers from which the yarn is developed. These yarns have bulk and resemble staple yarns, but are not as hairy. Currently, network yarns are in the experimental stages. Although they are coarse and have low resiliency (they crease easily), there seems to be a future for network yarns.

Laminated Yarns

Laminated yarns are a variation of slit film yarns. They are made from a sandwich construction, placing aluminum foil between two layers of plastic film, bonded by adhesive or heat, and cut into yarns (see Figure 4.24). Since the metal is apparent in the yarns, they are unique and eye-catching and are used in a variety of fabrics for apparel and for the home. A very practical use is their inclusion in carpeting where, because of their metal core, they conduct electricity and eliminate the static buildup often found in widely used nylon carpeting. Laminated yarns require careful maintenance since they have a low melting point and may be broken down by dry-cleaning solvents.

Plastic Film — Aluminum Foil

Figure 4.24
Laminated yarns are made of a sandwich construction.

KEY TERMS

1. Carding
2. Denier
3. Novelty yarn
4. Number
5. Roving
6. Simple yarn
7. Sliver
8. Spinning
9. Texturizing
10. Torque
11. Tow
12. Twist

STUDY QUESTIONS

1. What is a yarn?
2. Is it easier to construct yarn from staple or filament fibers? Explain your answer.
3. List and explain briefly three kinds of spinning suitable for staple fibers.
4. What is the difference between spun and filament yarns? How are these differences related to the appearance and wearer comfort?
5. Define twist; twist direction. Discuss three ways in which yarn twist affects the appearance, performance, or care of the finished fabrics.
6. Define texturized yarn. What are the two types of texturization? Give two examples of each.
7. What is yarn size? Why is this important? How is yarn size designated for the major natural and man-made fiber yarns?
8. Define single, ply, and cord yarns.
9. Distinguish between simple and novelty yarns, referring specifically to their construction, aesthetics, and performance characteristics.
10. Discuss three ways in which yarns may be constructed without fibers.

STUDY ACTIVITIES

1. You are a salesperson in a trendy sportswear shop in a department store. A group of cardigan jackets, made of chenille yarns, has recently arrived and you are about to sell the first one. What selling points can you make to the customer? (Students may want to role-play this activity.)
2. Go to a local department store and visit an apparel department and a furnishings department. Observe the types of yarns used in clothing as well as in carpeting or upholstery fabrics. List at least ten items and the type of yarn utilized (spun, filament, novelty, simple, etc.).
3. Collect scraps of fabric made from a variety of yarns. Isolate yarns from the fabric and study them under a magnifying glass. Consider degree of twist, direction of twist, ply, fiber length, elasticity, appearance, etc. Record your observations on individual index cards with a sample of the yarn attached; these can be shared for general class discussion and observation.

CHAPTER 5

Fabric Construction

OBJECTIVES

After completing this chapter, you should be able to:

1. Define what a fabric is.

2. Define the structural characteristics of fabric, such as warp, filling, courses, wales, yarn count, gauge, selvage, etc.

3. Differentiate the broad types of fabric constructions–woven, knit, nonwoven, films, foam, specialty constructions.

4. List examples of end-uses of the various constructions.

5. Explain how fabric construction affects end-use and performance of fabrics.

The focus in this chapter is on the various kinds of fabric construction found in the marketplace today. Each type of fabric construction is described, examples of the particular type of fabric are listed where appropriate, and end-uses and performance characteristics are discussed. The following construction methods are discussed: woven, knitted, knotted, felted, lace, bonded, laminated, and specialty construction methods. The chapter information will enable you to appreciate the wide range of fabrics available today, the means of identifying them through their representative characteristics, the end-uses of the fabrics, and standards for evaluation.

WHAT IS FABRIC?

Due to advancements in technology, the definition of fabric has changed over the years. Originally, the definition encompassed only woven, knitted, or felted constructions. Today, this definition is not adequate since fabrics can refer to many types: woven gingham, knitted qiana, vinyl for tablecloths, felt for crafts, and the foam that backs carpeting. A more appropriate definition for fabric, therefore, is as follows: A material made from fibers, yarns, film, foam, or a combination of these.

WOVEN FABRICS

Weaving is the interlacing of two or more sets of yarns which are usually at right angles to each other. Weaving, the oldest method of fabric construction, is done on a loom (see Figure 5.1). The ancient Egyptians wove lovely linen fabric on looms, which have changed through history, although the basic principles remain the same.

First, the loom must hold the warp yarns (see Figure 5.2) which run parallel to the selvage in the length-wise direction; the individual warp yarns are known as ends. Next, the loom must separate these yarns to form an opening, or shed, for the weaving of the crosswise yarns, known as filling, weft, or woof; the individual filling yarns are known as picks. The shuttle carries the filling yarns through the shedding; this process is called *picking*. Although the textile industry commonly uses the terms *ends* and *picks,* the consumer refers to the lengthwise and crosswise yarns as *warp* and *filling*.

Finally, the loom must pack or beat together each of the crosswise yarns in order to set them in place; this is known as *beating up*. The terms *taking up* and *letting off* refer to the release of the cloth and the warp yarns from the warp beam.

Until the early nineteenth century, weaving was done primarily by hand. Today, handweaving continues to be a practiced and treasured craft, but for the industry, automation and computer technology have been the essential developments to meet the demands of the marketplace. The three basic weaves are plain, twill, and satin.

Structure of Woven Fabric

To prevent unraveling of the fabric, a narrow, closely woven edge, called the *selvage,* is constructed on each side of the crosswise width.

The closeness of the weave may be regulated, depending on the required end-use of the fabric. The yarn count indicates the closeness of the weave, and is the number of warp and filling yarns per square inch. Yarn count is notated by stating the number of warp yarns, then the number of filling yarns. For example, a sheer, soft cotton batiste fabric may have a count of 88 × 80, while a muslin may have a count of 100 × 60. The batiste is the higher count fabric because it has, in total, more warp and filling yarns than does the muslin. If the thread count is 60 square, it indicates that there are 60 yarns per inch in the warp and 60 yarns per inch in the filling.

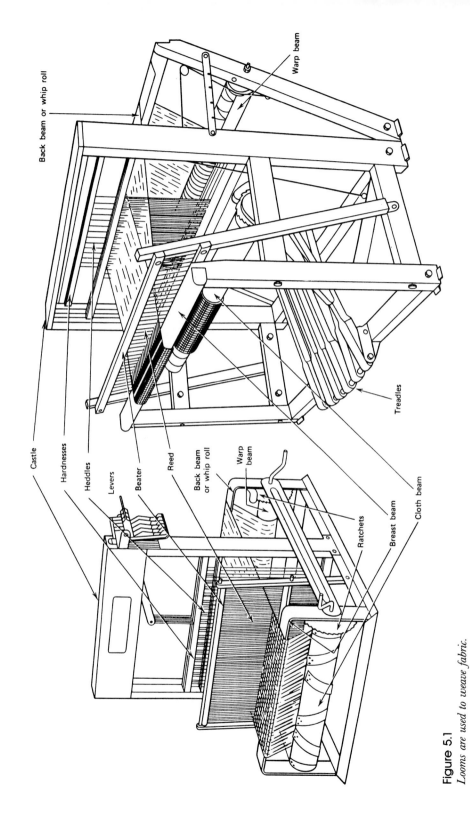

Figure 5.1
Looms are used to weave fabric.
Left: Table loom. Right: Floor loom.
From MODERN TEXTILES, 2nd Ed., by Dorothy Lyle. New York: John Wiley & Sons, 1982, p. 248.

89

Figure 5.2
Structure of woven fabric.
Reprinted with permission of Macmillan
Publishing Company from *Modern Textiles*
by Dorothy S. Lyle, originally published
by John Wiley and Sons, Inc.
(New York: Macmillan, 1982.)

The proportion of warp yarns to filling yarns is the balance of the fabric. The batiste previously mentioned, with the 88 × 80 count, is a well-balanced fabric because the warp and filling yarns are within a close range (there is not more than 10 yarns difference between them). The muslin (100 × 60) is poorly balanced, and this could affect performance. The fewer filling yarns could shift, causing weak spots in the weave. A well-balanced fabric tends to be more durable because the fabric will wear evenly. However, a high count fabric (even if poorly balanced) will generally give better wear than a low count fabric with good balance.

Fabric grain refers to the positions of warp and filling yarns in the woven fabric. The warp and filling yarns should be straight and perpendicular to each other. If they are not, the fabric is off-grain. Garments made of off-grain fabric will not hang and drape properly and printed designs will often look crooked.

Plain Weave

This is the simplest form of weaving and is sometimes referred to as a tabby weave or a 1 × 1 weave. The plain weave is formed by each filling yarn passing over and under each warp yarn; each warp yarn, in the same manner, passes over and under each filling yarn (see Figure 5.3).

The basic plain weave may be modified to produce variations, such as the rib weave and basket weave.

Rib Weave

Rib, or cord, fabrics have a noticeable line of emphasis on the surface design and texture; this may be in the warp or filling direction (see Figure 5.4). The rib, or cord, weave may be constructed in several ways:

1. Using more yarns grouped together in the warp or filling direction before they are interlaced with yarns in the opposite direction

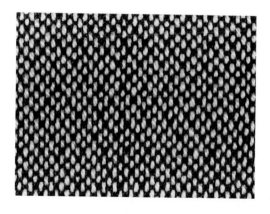

Figure 5.3
Plain weave fabric.
Courtesy of Philadelphia College of Textiles & Science.

Figure 5.4
Rib weave variation.
Courtesy of Philadelphia College of Textiles & Science.

2.   Utilizing heavy yarns in the warp or filling
3.   Utilizing more warp yarns and fewer filling yarns

Examples of rib weave fabrics are broadcloth, dimity, faille, grosgrain, otto-man, pique, poplin, and rep.

End-Use and Performance.   The rib weave is a widely used construction in apparel and home textiles, but it is not as popular as the plain weave. Rib fabrics are subject to abrasion because of the raised surface area or due to the smaller yarns that cover the larger yarns, thus exposing more surface area to year. The latter problem can be alleviated by using closely woven, strong yarns to cross the larger yarns.

Basket Weave

This fairly loose weave is constructed by using two or more warp yarns and one or more filling yarns (see Figure 5.5). A basket weave with two warp yarns and one filling yarn is designated 2/1; other types of basket weave are 3/2, 2/2, 4/3, 4/4. Basket weave fabrics include monk's cloth, hopsacking, and oxford cloth.

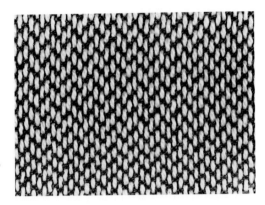

Figure 5.5
Photo of a 2/1 basket weave.
Courtesy of Philadelphia College of Textiles & Science.

End-Use and Performance. Basket weaves are attractive, interesting fabrics because of the various surface effects that can be achieved. Basket weave fabrics are found in coats, suits, separates, and in textiles for the home. The basket weave is not as durable as the plain or rib weaves. Because of its characteristic loose construction, a difficulty of the basket weave is yarn slippage; openings in the weave, snagging, or stretching may result. Basket weave fabrics can fray easily.

Other Varieties of the Plain Weave

The following variations of the plain weave can be achieved without major alteration of the structure of plain weaves. The result is often beautiful and very interesting fabrics. Variations of the plain weave may be constructed by the following methods:

1. Using complex yarns or a combination of simple and complex yarns to achieve textural interest
2. Altering the amount or direction of twist in the yarns
3. Varying the tension of the yarns while on the loom
4. Combining yarns of different fiber content
5. Combining yarns of different colors in unique ways
6. Varying yarn spacing—a loose structure or a dense, more compact, structure is possible

These techniques for creating interesting fabric variations may be adapted to all the constructions where yarns are the foundation of the structure.

Twill Weave

The second basic weave is the twill, characterized by a diagonal line that appears on the face, or face and back, of the fabric. The angle of the twill may range from low (a 14-degree reclining twill) to steep (75-degree angle). The most common is the 45-degree regular twill (see Figure 5.6).

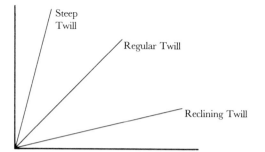

Figure 5.6
Twill weave angles.

Twill weaves can be simple to complex in structure. A simple twill is constructed by the filling yarn crossing over two warp yarns, then under one warp yarn, with this 2/1 sequence consistent throughout, but beginning one yarn over in each row to form the diagonal (see Figure 5.7). The area in which one yarn crosses over other yarns is called the *float*. The lines created by the twill pattern are called *wales*. Twills may run in a right- or left-hand direction, or may run both ways in the fabric to form the herringbone pattern as illustrated in Figure 5.8.

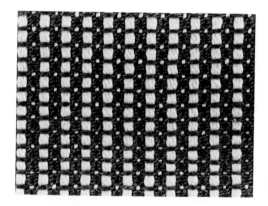

Figure 5.7
A 2 × 2 hand twill.
Courtesy of Philadelphia College of Textiles & Science.

Figure 5.8
Herringbone twill weave.
Courtesy of Philadelphia College of Textiles & Science.

The majority of twill fabrics are right-hand twills. A variety of twill weaves are constructed from combinations of warp and filling crossings or floats, such as 2/2, 3/1; the first number indicates the number of times the warp yarns cross the filling yarns (the second number).

In the twill weaving process, the yarns can be packed or beaten closely together because the yarn interlacings do not occur as frequently as in the plain weave. This can increase the strength and durability of the twill weave. Examples of twill weave fabrics are chino cloth, covert cloth, denim, drill, foulard, gabardine, serge, surah, and whipcord.

End-Use and Performance. Twill weaves are always in demand, especially in tailored suits, coats, and separates because they are handsome fabrics and are durable. The twills are stronger than plain weaves and are usually heavier; they have interesting texture and surface design. Twill weaves generally cost more to produce than plain weaves. Twills do not show dirt as readily as plain weaves, but may be more difficult to clean because of their texture. Depending on the type of twill, the fiber used, and the end-use, snagging could be a problem.

Satin and Sateen Weaves

These are the last of the basic weaves and are based on the principle of the twill weave. The satin or sateen weave is characterized by a high surface sheen because of the reflection of light on the fabric surface, which is constructed of low twist floats that pass over a few filling yarns or as many as ten to twelve filling yarns. The difference between satin and sateen is as follows:

Satin—there are more warp yarns than filling yarns on the right side of the fabric; these weaves are made of filament yarns and have a bright shine (see Figure 5.9).

Sateen or satine—there are more filling yarns than warp yarns on the right side of the fabric; these weaves are made of spun yarns and have a lustrous shine duller than in satin (see Figure 5.10).

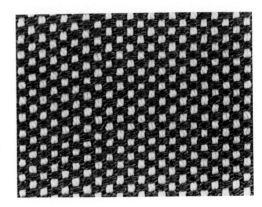

Figure 5.9
Satin weave.
Courtesy of Philadelphia College of Textiles & Science.

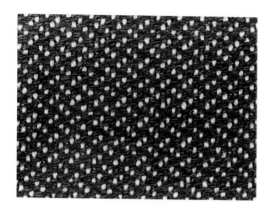

Figure 5.10
Sateen weave.
Courtesy of Philadelphia College of Textiles & Science.

A popular variation of the satin weave is crepe-back satin, a fabric which has been widely used in women's fashions. Low-twist, lustrous warp yarns float on the right side of the fabric, while high-twist, duller yarns (crepe) appear on the back.

Satin weave fabrics include antique satin, bridal satin, charmeuse, crepe-back satin, and cretonne. The sateen weave is known as sateen and is usually a cotton or cotton-blend fabric.

End-Use and Performance.   These lustrous fabrics are decorative and suitable for fashions for apparel and in the home; they have long been a popular choice in the marketplace. Satins often line coats and suits because they are smooth and slide easily over garments. They tend to shed dirt readily because of the smooth surface. The floats, however, are subject to snags and abrasion, and the longer the float, the more the likelihood of surface damage. Durability depends, too, on the choice of fiber and the density of the weave.

Fancy Weaves and Constructions

These include weaves and constructions which are decorative and structurally unique. The following are discussed: Jacquard, dobby, and leno weaves and lace, net, and braid.

Jacquard Weave

Both Jacquard and dobby weaves are characterized by all-over raised designs woven into the fabric. The most elaborate and costly designs are possible on the Jacquard loom, invented in 1801 in France by Joseph-Marie Jacquard. Up until that time, regular harness looms could construct only plain, twill, and satin weaves where the series of warp yarns did not require individual regulation to make the final product. The Jacquard machine provided control of each warp yarn, allowing much greater creativity to the fabric designer. Figure 5.11 illustrates a Jacquard loom and Figure 5.12 illustrates a representative fabric design constructed on the Jacquard loom.

Figure 5.11
Jacquard loom.
Courtesy of the American Textiles Manufacturers Institute.

Figure 5.12
A Jacquard fabric.
Courtesy of the American Textiles Manufacturers Institute.

The Jacquard loom is expensive and occupies a great deal of space. At one time, it took months to prepare the loom for a design which was worked out on perforated cards much like punched computer cards. In recent years, however, the computer has greatly facilitated the operation of the loom. The Jacquard weave combines two or more of the basic weaves.

Jacquard weave fabrics include brocade, brocatelle, damask, matelasse, and tapestry.

End-Use and Performance.   Fabrics constructed by the Jacquard method are used in apparel and home textiles, where they have been especially in demand for table linens, draperies, and upholstery. Jacquard weaves are expensive because the construction process is relatively slow and complicated. Since the Jacquard weave often incorporates the satin construction, the same performance factors must be considered. The Jacquard designs are beautiful but are subject to snagging, abrasion, and soiling. The end-use must determine the suitability of a Jacquard weave fabric.

Dobby Weave

The dobby weave can be achieved by the dobby attachment, invented in England, which is fit into the harness loom. The resulting patterns are characterized by their small size, repetition on the fabric, and geometric shapes. Figure 5.13 illustrates a dobby design. The dobby weave is similar to the Jacquard weave, but is less complicated.

Examples of dobby weave fabrics include bird's-eye or diaper cloth, huck toweling, Madras shirting, pique, waffle cloth.

End-Use and Performance.   Dobby weaves are used on their own or in combination with other weaves; they are used in apparel and in textiles for the home.

Dobby weaves are similar to the Jacquard weaves because they incorporate two or more of the basic weaves and the design is raised. Performance of the dobby weave, therefore, is similar to that of the Jacquard weave.

Leno Weave

The leno attachment makes it possible to construct fabrics that are open and have geometriclike spaces. This is achieved by crossing over adjacent warp yarns with the filling yarn passing through, as illustrated in Figure 5.14. The leno weave may be combined with one or more of the basic weaves.

Leno weaves fabrics include marquisette and mosquito net. Leno weaves are also used in laundry and hosiery bags, and in needlepoint canvas.

End-Use and Performances.　Leno weaves are widely used in dresses, shirts, and blouses, and in curtains. Despite their open construction, leno weaves are generally durable. The combining of the pair-warps provides strength and also holds the filling yarns securely.

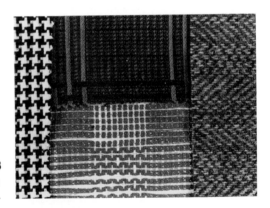

Figure 5.13
Dobby weave.
Courtesy of Philadelphia College of Textiles & Science.

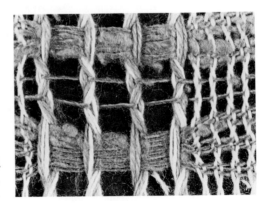

Figure 5.14
Leno weave.
Courtesy of Philadelphia College of Textiles & Science.

Lace

Lace is considered by many to be the loveliest and most romantic of fabrics. Characterized by its open and intricate designs formed by a network of yarns, lace combines the twisting, interlooping, interlacing, and knotting processes. The lace-making Leavers machine, invented in 1837, is an extraordinary device that can produce an almost infinite array of patterns. Genuine lace is quite expensive and is less common in the marketplace than are the lacelike constructions achieved through the raschel knitting process and Schiffli embroidery procedures (these are discussed later in the chapter).

Genuine lace fabrics are products of the places in which they were originally handmade. These include Alencon, Belgian, Breton, Brussels, Chantilly, and Cluny laces.

End-Use and Performance.   Lace has traditionally been associated with wedding gowns, but has in practice been used for all kinds of apparel, accessories, and home textiles. Because of the open design, lace requires careful handling and care. The man-made fibers, such as polyester and nylon, have made it possible to manufacture lace that is strong and durable. A genuine lace fabric is one to treasure.

Net

A net is a fabric characterized by an open-mesh construction in which the yarns are knotted (see Figure 5.15). Netlike fabrics may also be made by the tricot and raschel knitting methods, which will be discussed later in this chapter. These knitted netlike constructions, in which the yarns are looped, are not as durable as the traditional knotted net. Net, like the leno weave, has geometriclike spaces in the design.

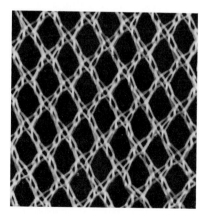

Figure 5.15
Net construction.
Reprinted with permission of Macmillan Publishing Company from *Modern Textiles* by Dorothy S. Lyle, originally published by John Wiley and Sons, Inc. (New York: Macmillan, 1982.)

Macrame is related to net construction in that looping and knotting are the structural foundation of macrame, which is a far more decorative, artistic construction. Macrame is mentioned here for general information; it is primarily a handcraft.

The terms *net* and *mesh* are usually used synonymously. Tulle is a net construction used in evening fashions and for veiling. Net is usually called *net* or *netting*.

End-Use and Performance.   Nets are used in veiling, apparel, window screens, curtains, laundry bags, fishing nets, and sports equipment. Like lace, nets require sensible handling and care.

Braid

These fabrics are constructed by plaiting or interlacing three or more yarns together; a diagonal surface pattern is achieved. Braids may be flat or tubular. This construction is usually called *braid, braiding,* or *plaiting.*

End-Use and Performance.   Braided constructions are found in many decorative trims or bindings, shoelaces, rugs, cords, and hoses. Braids may be loosely or tightly woven. Since braids are often made to be used as trim or binding, they are loosely woven and have stretch. These characteristics, however, may require special handling and care so that the original shape is maintained. Depending on the article, this may mean hand-washing and hang-dry care, or dry-clean only.

KNIT FABRICS

The increased popularity of knits since the early 1960s has been largely due to their suitability for a variety of end-uses for apparel and the home, and to their comfort and ease of care. Knits readily conform to body shape and movement. They are easy to pack and easily adapt to today's fast-paced lifestyles. Knits are wrinkle-resistant, durable, and usually require only machine wash-and-dry care. Knits have become a fashion item for both women and men (see Figure 5.16). In addition, knitted fabrics can be produced efficiently and inexpensively (see the last section of this chapter).

For general information, it should be noted that crochet is in reality a handcraft and not a machine construction as is knitting. In the marketplace, what is referred to as crochet is a knitted construction made on the raschel knitting machine.

Structure of Knitted Fabric

Knitted fabric is constructed by interlocking one or more yarns through a series of loops. The lengthwise stitches are called *wales* and the crosswise stitches are called *courses* (see Figure 5.17). Knits may be constructed in a flat or tubular form.

Figure 5.16
Both men and women enjoy knit fashions.
Left: Courtesy of E.I. duPont de Nemours & Co., Inc.
Right: Design by Steve Fabrikant, Steve Fabrikant & Co., Inc.

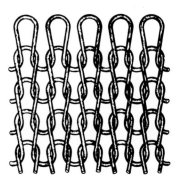

Figure 5.17
Knit construction.
Reproduced by permission of National
Knitwear & Sportswear Association,
New York, N.Y.

The term *gauge* is equivalent to the term *yarn count* in woven cloth. In knits, gauge refers to the number of needles or yarns per inch. The higher the gauge number, the finer the knit; a 45-gauge knit is not as fine in texture as a 60-gauge knit.

Full-fashioned is a term often used in describing a particular type of knit garment. A full-fashioned garment or other item is completely made and shaped on the knitting machine rather than being cut to shape and stitched, which is another method of sizing and shaping both knitted and woven products. In constructing full-fashioned items, such as cashmere and other fine sweaters, stitches are added or dropped to shape the garment, resulting in evenly spaced "fashion marks" that are perforationlike marks in the knit, as illustrated in Figure 5.18. These marks indicate better quality because the item will retain its shape, which is structured into the garment in the manufacturing process.

Mock fashion marks are sometimes manufactured into a garment to simulate the appearance of the higher quality merchandise; if examined carefully, it will be evident that these mock fashion marks do not correspond to an alteration in the number and/or direction of stitches as is the case in genuine full-fashioned items. Figure 5.18 illustrates mock fashion marks as well as the genuine full-fashioned marks. Note that, in the mock drawing, the marks do not correspond to a change in the number and/or direction of the stitches.

Weft Knits

Weft knits are also known as filling knits. This construction is characterized by crosswise loops linking one row to another. Handknitting is done in this manner as well. Weft knits include jersey or plain knit, rib and purl stitch knits, and interlock and double knits.

Jersey Knit

Jersey knit is also known as plain knit and is constructed on machines with one set of needles. Therefore, these are also single knits. They are characterized by a knit face (wales) and a purl back (courses) as illustrated in Figure 5.19. Jersey machines may also construct pile fabrics (discussed later in the chapter), knitted terry and velour, and full-fashioned knits which are often encountered in the retail store and which customers may specifically request.

End-Use and Performance.   Jersey knits are widely used in all kinds of garments and accessories. Jersey drapes beautifully and is a highly desirable construction

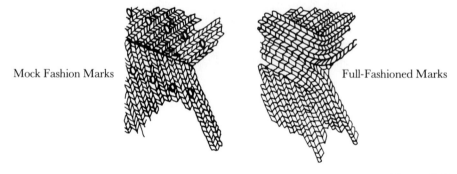

Mock Fashion Marks   Full-Fashioned Marks

Figure 5.18
Genuine full-fashioned marks indicate shaping of the garment in the construction process.

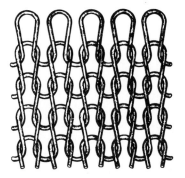 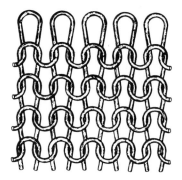

Figure 5.19
Knit and purl stitches.
Reproduced by permission of National Knitwear & Sportswear Association, New York, N.Y.

Figure 5.20
A jersey evening dress is soft and graceful.
Courtesy of Celanese Fibers.

for lovely dress creations such as the one illustrated in Figure 5.20. Jersey has good stretch both in the length and cross direction. Jersey is easy and fairly economical to produce and is therefore readily available and affordable. Possible difficulties are that jersey tends to run, may shrink, and may curl at the edges, which could lead to distortion of particular designs.

Rib Stitch Knits

These are constructed by knit and purl wales that alternate, forming raised and depressed columns as illustrated in Figure 5.21. A simple rib is a 1 × 1 construction, alternating one knit row and one purl row; variations are common, such as 2 × 1, 2 × 2, etc.

End-Use and Performance.   Rib stitch knits are very popular in sweaters for the entire family and in separates for women. They are often combined with other knits and are particularly suitable for wristband, neckband, and waistband sections of sweaters which require extra stretchability. Rib knits have more stretch in the width than in the length. They retain their shape well.

Purl Stitch Knits

These stitches are constructed by utilizing the purl stitch throughout the fabric; thus, the fabric is the same on the front and back and is considered reversible. Production is more slow and costly than for other types of knits.

End-Use and Performance.   This is a knit that will stretch and recover fairly well in the length, but can be stretched out of shape in the crosswise direction. Because they have only fair shape retention qualities, the purl stitch knits are not highly desirable for most garments. They are often used, however, in scarfs, stoles, and afghans.

Interlock Knits

These are a variation of the rib stitch, constructed on a knitting machine with two sets of needles, as are the double knits. Interlocks are produced by alternating knit and purl stitches in both the length and cross directions.

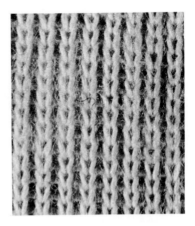

Figure 5.21
Rib knit fabric.
Reprinted with permission of Macmillan Publishing Company from *Modern Textiles* by Dorothy S. Lyle, originally published by John Wiley and Sons, Inc. (New York: Macmillan, 1982.)

End-Use and Performance.   Interlocks are soft and drapable, yet they are stable and have a good hand. They are closely knit and will not ravel. They resemble jersey, but are more durable, stronger, and more suited to a wider variety of garment constructions.

Double Knits

Like interlock knits, these are produced by a two-needle construction resulting in fabrics that are similar on both sides.

End-Use and Performance.   The double knits are thicker and less drapable than the single knits; they also have better dimensional stability, are less prone to runs, and are suitable for a much broader variety of clothing. Double knits have been used for women's fashions, children's clothing, and men's suits. Because twice as much yarn is required for double knits as is required for single knits, they tend to be more expensive.

Warp Knits

Warp knits can be constructed only by machine. They are characterized by vertical loops. Warp knits tend to be tighter than the weft knits and have less stretch, especially in the vertical direction. Warp knits are usually stronger than weft knits. Warp knits include tricot and raschel knits and the less popular simplex and milanese knits.

Tricot

Tricot knits, originating in England in the late 1700s, were not made in the United States until the latter part of the next century. The tricot machine was originally used to knit silk for hosiery. The same machine can knit plain or patterned tricot and can be controlled to produce a variety of sheer, lacelike constructions or fabrics with a brushed surface.

End-Use and Performance.   Tricot knits are popular for lingerie, as illustrated in Figure 5.22. Tricot knits have a pleasant hand, are soft, wrinkle- and run-resistant, and retain their shape. In recent years, tricot knits have been utilized for men's and women's shirts. They are also commonly used as linings and in bonded fabrics, which are discussed later in this chapter. They are very easy to care for and retain their shape and good looks through many washings and dryings.

Raschel Knits

The versatility of the raschel knitting machine permits the manufacture of a wide range of fabrics of varying weights, sheerness, and patterns, as well as fabrics that simulate wovens, crochets, nets, and laces.

End-Use and Performance.   The versatility of the raschel knits may be seen in their end-uses: foundation garments, thermal fabrics, carpeting, apparel for the fami-

Figure 5.22
Tricot lingerie of DuPont fibers.
Courtesy of E.I. duPont de Nemours &
Co., Inc.

ly. In lacelike constructions, the raschel knits have provided durable and afford-able fabrics. In general, raschel knits are durable and easy to care for and have been enthusiastically accepted in the marketplace.

Simplex Knits

These are similar to tricot knits, but are heavier. They are actually double knit tricot fabrics. Simplex knits are used in items that require more fabric strength.

End-Use and Performance.   Simplex knits are used in handbags and gloves. They are strong and durable.

Milanese Knits

These, too, are similar to the tricot knits, but are more expensive and time-con-suming to produce; pattern possibilities are very limited. Milanese knits are characterized by an argyle-type diagonal pattern.

End-Use and Performance.   Milanese knits are highly run-resistant and have good elasticity. They have been used in gloves and lingerie. Because the production process is relatively slow and the pattern range very limited, they are not widely available in the American marketplace.

OTHER FABRIC CONSTRUCTIONS

Included in this section are special constructions which have not been covered previously. They are pile fabrics, nonwoven fabrics, layered or multicomponent fabrics, decorative embroidery fabrics, and fabrics made from solutions.

Pile Fabrics

Pile fabrics have been very popular over the years, offering comfort, warmth, aesthetic appeal, luxury, and beauty. Figure 5.23 illustrates a contemporary outerwear fashion in which a pile fabric is used for accent. The majority of pile fabrics are relatively economical to make and are easy to care for.

Pile fabrics have cut or uncut loops which project on the surface of the fabric; the back of the fabric is smooth. Pile fabrics may be constructed by weaving, knitting, tufting, and flocking. Chenille yarns may also be used to construct pile fabrics.

Woven Pile Fabrics

If a pile fabric is woven, the ground fabric may be a plain or twill weave. The pile is made of an extra set of yarns; all woven pile fabrics are constructed of three yarns or more. A typical woven pile construction is seen in Figure 5.24. Woven pile fabrics include velvet, velveteen, corduroy, terry cloth, and velour.

Figure 5.23
Pile fabric trim adds a fur-like accent to a simple coat.
Courtesy of Sportowne®, a division of The Metzger Group, Inc.

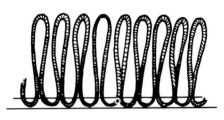

Figure 5.24
Woven pile construction.

End-Use and Performance.   Woven pile fabrics are widely utilized in apparel for the family, in luxury fabrics for the home, in accessories, and in automobile interiors. The durability of the pile construction will depend on the fibers selected and the construction quality. Woven pile fabrics can be poorly constructed and have a short life or can be high quality and strong-wearing. Care varies from easy to special care requirements; for instance, silk and rayon velvets are dry-cleaned while cotton corduroy and velveteen are generally machine washable.

Knit Pile Fabrics

Knit pile fabrics are also constructed with an extra yarn which is pulled from the ground cloth to form surface loops. The ground fabric is usually a plain filling or weft knit. Knit pile fabrics include fake furs, corduroy knits, terry, and velour.

End-Use and Performance.   Knit pile constructions have been very popular in the fake fur coats that have increased steadily in the marketplace. All kinds of clothing, accessories, and textiles for the home may be made from knit pile fabrics. The performance characteristics are similar to those for woven pile fabrics.

Tufted Pile Fabrics

In the tufting process, yarns are stitched into the finished fabric to form the pile. The pile may be left uncut or may be cut. Surface patterns may be achieved by varying the height of the pile yarns and by cutting some loops and leaving others uncut.

Tufted pile fabrics are simply called tufted fabrics and do not have more specific names as are associated with other constructions.

End-Use and Performance.   The most common use for tufted fabrics, because of the speed and efficiency at which they can be produced, is in carpeting. Tufted pile fabrics are also used for stuffed toys, robes, outerwear, upholstery, draperies, bedspreads, and blankets. The performance of tufted fabrics will especially depend on the density of the tuft and the manufacturing process. In items such as carpeting, where heavy wear is likely, the pile yarns must be bonded to the ground cloth with an adhesive.

Flocked Pile Fabrics

This type of pile fabric is made by attaching very short fibers to the surface of a finished fabric that has been coated with adhesive. This basic flocking technique has been around for centuries and has been utilized for a great variety of end-uses. Flock fabrics have been especially popular in recent years because of the improved adhesives available. The flock fibers may be sifted onto the fabric or may pass through an electric field which orients the fibers, allowing them to penetrate the adhesive in arrowlike fashion. The sifting method is less expensive and is the most common one used in the United States. Flocking may cover the entire fabric surface or selected areas to form interesting surface designs.

Flock pile fabrics are referred to as flocked fabrics. Flock can be made of a variety of fibers, including cotton, rayon, nylon, acrylic, polyester, and olefin. The important characteristic is that the fibers have no crimp.

End-Use and Performance.   Flocked fabrics are used widely for apparel and home textiles, wall coverings, automotive fabrics, accessories, and in industrial applications. Like other pile fabric types, if they are manufactured carefully, they will be durable, long-lasting, and will maintain the original pile.

Although not a major category, it should be noted that chenille yarns may also be utilized to create a particular type of pile fabric, often referred to as chenille. Chenille yarns were discussed in Chapter 4. Chenille fabrics are used for robes, bedspreads, and in various home textiles.

Nonwoven Fabrics

These fabrics do not require yarn for construction and are made directly from the fiber. The fibers are held together by chemical, heat, or mechanical means. This is the oldest method of fabric construction. The nonwovens that are popular today include felt and the web fabrics. Tapa cloth is discussed since it is the oldest of the nonwovens and is still seen today.

Tapa Cloth

This is the oldest of the nonwoven fabrics and is also known as bark cloth since it is made from the inner bark of trees, such as the fig or mulberry. The bark is softened in water and beaters pound the bark in order to interconnect the fibers; textural effects may be produced. The finished product appears and feels much like paper.

End-Use and Performance.   Even in the South Pacific, the use of tapa cloth is very limited, primarily because it is not suitable for a variety of apparel and cannot be easily stitched. Tapa cloth is still used in native handcrafts, the tapa being colorfully painted and often used as pictures.

Felt

Although included in this section of nonwovens, felt is not technically considered to be a nonwoven since felt is traditionally of all or part wool fibers and nonwovens are usually of man-made fibers. Wool is, in fact, ideal for the felting process since the fibers are pressed into a flat sheet and the scaly structure of wool facilitates the interlocking of the fibers.

End-Use and Performance.   Felt is widely used in industrial applications (sound-proofing, insulation, filters), but has not been accepted for clothing because it lacks the required flexibility and elasticity. Felt has been popular as a craft fabric and is used for accessories such as hats and slippers.

Web Fabrics

In this construction process, fibers are made into a weblike structure and bonding permanently sets the fibers into a fabric. Bonding may be achieved by applying an adhesive, using heat and pressure, or entangling the fibers through a stitch-through or a needle-punch process, as follows:

- Stitch-through process — the fabric is constructed by stitching through the assembled fibers and yarns.
- Needle-punch process — the fabric is constructed by punching needles through a bat of fibers, thus entangling them into a uniform mass.

End-Use and Performance.   The web fabrics have been used in medical and surgical supplies; disposable diapers, towels, and clean-up cloths; bedding; interfacings; and filters. They are generally durable and are more and more evident in the marketplace.

Layered or Multicomponent Fabrics

These fabrics include bonded, laminated, and quilted fabrics. Each type is discussed below.

Bonded Fabrics

In this construction, two layers of fabric are joined together by an adhesive, bonding agent, or heat. A popular bonded fabric has been a woven or a knit bonded to a tricot. The resulting layered fabric is intended to offer better end-use properties. For instance, the tricot back on a woven provides a self-lining stability and helps retain the shape.

End-Use and Performance.   Bonded fabrics have been used in a great variety of products, including clothing for the family, draperies, tablecloths, and other household items, and in accessories. If the bond is secure, the fabrics will be durable and very serviceable. Most bonded fabrics require only wash-and-dry care.

Laminated Fabrics

These fabrics are constructed by joining fabric to polyurethane foam or film as in the bonding process where two layers are joined.

Fabric Joined to Foam.   This may be a two-layer structure or a three-layer one which consists of two outer fabric layers and a center foam layer. These fabrics have been used in apparel and home textiles where they have been especially successful, particularly in carpeting where the foam backing provides insulation, extra thickness, and noise reduction.

Fabric Joined to Film.   In this construction, the film is laminated to a woven or knitted fabric. But in this case, the film is the face fabric and the woven or knit is the backing which provides the stability.

End-Use and Performance.   Laminated fabrics are commonly used in upholstery and, depending on fashion trends, have been popular for apparel and outerwear, especially rain or all-weather coats. A problem with early laminates was the separation of the layers or peeling of the top film layer. Laminates have been greatly improved, and performance depends on the manufacturing quality and on the customer following the manufacturer's care label.

Quilted Fabrics

Quilted construction is usually of three layers, two outer fabrics and an inner filler selected for its softness, thickness, or insulation properties. The layers are then stitched together or secured through ultrasonic welding which bonds all the layers in a manner that simulates stitching.

End-Use and Performance.   Quilted fabrics have been very popular in the marketplace. They are used for robes, comforters, apparel for the family, and textiles for the home where they have provided both warmth and aesthetic appeal (see Figure 5.25). Performance depends primarily on the quality of the fabrics used and the stitching or bonding quality. If threads break or bonds loosen, the quilt effect will be damaged; the inner layer will loosen and shift, forming lumps in the fabric. Well-made quilted fabrics provide lightweight, warm fabrics available in a broad range of colors and patterns.

Decorative Specialty Weaves and Embroidery

Lovely and varied decorative fabrics may be constructed by the use of extra warp or filling yarns to weave raised designs on the fabric. Genuine embroidery is decorative stitching on an already finished fabric. Although the clipped-spot, swivel, and lappet designs are not applied after the fabric is finished, but are woven into the fabric itself, the end effect is an embroiderylike design. Schiffli embroidery, worked on the finished cloth, is a classic embroidery process.

Clipped-Spot Weave

An extra filling yarn or warp yarn is utilized to achieve a small pattern in the ground fabric, which is usually a cotton or a cotton-blend. The extra yarn is usually of a different size and color to emphasize the design (see Figure 5.26). The spots are clipped.

Swivel Weave

In the swivel weave, extra filling yarns are wound around a group of warp yarns producing a tied effect; the extra filling yarns are carried by small shuttles called swivels. Dotted swiss, made in Switzerland, may be constructed in this way. The swivel weave is not generally used in the United States since other techniques

Figure 5.25

Quilted bedroom fashions add warmth and beauty to a room.
Courtesy Liberty of London fashions.

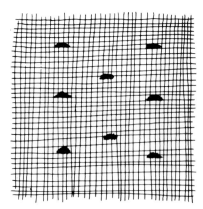

Figure 5.26
Clipped spot weave.

have been more successful; these include the clipped-spot weaves, flock designs, and fabrics made on the Jacquard loom.

Lappet Weave

A lappet design, characterized by a zigzag design, as in Figure 5.27, is achieved by the use of extra warp yarns in the construction process. The design is usually

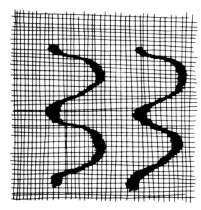

Figure 5.27
Lappet weave.

left unclipped. Like the swivel weave, the lappet design is not popular in the United States since other designs and methods of construction can produce similar fabrics more cost efficiently.

Schiffli Embroidery

The Schiffli embroidery machine permits the creation of beautiful embroidered designs, including eyelet, on many kinds of fabric. It is also possible to make Schiffli lace by embroidering on a ground cloth which is later dissolved.

End-Use and Performance.   These specialty fabrics are used in apparel as well as in decorative fabrics for the home that may be used for curtains, table linens, bedspreads, etc. Modern manufacturing techniques have provided durable embroidery fabrics which are easy to care for.

Fabrics Made From Solutions

These fabrics include film and foam fabrics. Each category is discussed below.

Film Fabrics

Films are made in sheets from solutions similar to fiber solutions. These films vary from very thin, such as plastic wrap, to heavy gauge vinyl. Many films are laminated, as previously discussed, to provide support while maintaining the desired characteristics of the film itself.

End-Use and Performance.   Films have frequently been used in rainwear where they are serviceable and practical; this use is usually predicated on current fashion trends. Films are also widely used for shower curtains, upholstery, and table coverings. Nonsupported, thin films are not durable and long-lasting; the laminated films are far superior. Films can be easily kept clean by wiping with a damp cloth or hand- or machine-washing with cold water. Films cannot usually withstand the heat of the automatic dryer; melting occurs.

Foam Fabrics

Foams are produced in sheets by incorporating air in elastic substances such as rubber and polyurethane.

End-Use and Performance.   Foams are widely used in furniture and carpet padding, pillow forms, and stuffings. They are also laminated for use in apparel and textiles for the home and industry. Sun discolors foam and will damage rubber. Generally, however, they are practical, serviceable, and widely used.

FABRIC CONSTRUCTION IN TRANSITION

In order to meet the challenges of the future, the textile industry is in a period of transition and modernization. Revolutionary technological changes will affect the entire industry and how fabric is constructed. Two important advancements that affect fabric and knitting constructions are mentioned here.

The shuttleless loom is one advancement affecting the weaving process. Until recently, a wooden shuttle carried filling yarns through the shed. Today, it is possible to propel the yarns by water or air jets. This shuttleless system produces fabric much more quickly and efficiently. The shuttleless loom is also quieter and safer to use.

In the knitting area, the advent of electronic knitting machines is changing the industry; this is looked upon by many to be the most exciting innovation in knitting in many years. The electronic machine allows the sweater design to be programmed on computer tapes which automatically operate the knitting machine. When a new design tape is inserted, the machine will knit the new design with no additional operation necessary. Again, speed and efficiency of production result. The computer also allows the knit designer to work out line and color on the computer screen and to make desired changes quickly, accurately, and in full color!

These innovations in fabric construction are extraordinary advancements for the industry. They hint at the many exciting possibilities for the future of fabric construction and for the textile industry in general.

KEY TERMS

1.	Balance	9.	Knit
2.	Bonded	10.	Laminated
3.	Courses	11.	Wales
4.	Filling	12.	Warp
5.	Float	13.	Weave
6.	Full-fashioned	14.	Web
7.	Gauge	15.	Yarn count
8.	Grain		

STUDY QUESTIONS

1. What is a fabric? How has the definition changed over the years?
2. Name the three kinds of woven fabrics and describe each.
3. What is the difference between yarn count and gauge?
4. What is a float? How do floats affect fabric performance?
5. Which of the three basic weaves would be most appropriate for a business suit? Support your answer.
6. Which of the knits is most versatile and why? Support your answer.
7. Considering wovens and knits, discuss three ways in which construction may affect performance.
8. Describe three ways in which web fabrics may be constructed.
9. Name two types of fabrics made from solutions. Describe each and its end-uses.
10. Explain two recent innovations affecting fabric construction.

STUDY ACTIVITIES

1. Visit a local department store. Focusing on two of the clothing areas below, list ten items from each area, the basic construction of each, and what you predict the performance of each item will be.
   Department store areas:
   women's sportswear
   men's sportswear
   household linens
   children's wear
   lingerie
   activewear
2. Complete an inventory of ten items you have in your wardrobe and have worn. What is the construction of each? How would you evaluate the performance of each? Relate the fabric construction to the performance, based on the information included in Chapter 5.

CHAPTER **6**

Fabric Finishes

OBJECTIVES

After completing this chapter, you should be able to:

1. Define what a finish is.
2. List and define six ways in which fabric is prepared for finishing.
3. List and define the two broadest classifications of finishes, giving examples of each.
4. Explain why it is often the finish that determines the ultimate marketability and success of the fabric.

Fabric, once it is constructed, may appear to be ready for the marketplace. But, in reality, it is not. The application of one or more finishes is in order. In many ways, this step is vital because it is often the finish that will determine the ultimate success and acceptance of the fabric.

WHAT IS A FINISH?

Fabric, after it is constructed, is known as grey, or griege, goods. This does not refer to the color of the fabric, but the fact that it is essentially uncolored, undyed, and unfinished. Muslin, with its off-white color and coarse appearance, is similar to the look of most grey goods.

The term *finish* refers to a treatment applied to a fabric that will improve it. For purpose of this discussion, a finish is a processing of fabric to improve the aesthetic qualities (specifically the appearance and/or hand) or the performance characteristics. Finishes may alter only the aesthetic qualities or only the performance of the fabric. Or finishes may also alter both the aesthetic and performance qualities of a piece of fabric.

Finishes may be classified as mechanical or chemical, permanent or nonpermanent. Chemical finishes may also be called *wet finishes* while mechanical finishes are *dry finishes*. Permanent finishes are those that are not altered through wear and care as are the nonpermanent finishes. Durable press may be applied as a permanent finish. Finishes applied to man-made fibers tend to be permanent. *Durable* is the term used to describe finishes that are long-lasting but not permanent; durable finishes probably will be diminished before the garment is discarded. Semidurable finishes last through several washing and dry-cleaning processes. Beetling may be durable or semidurable, depending on the finish and home care. Temporary finishes are usually removed substantially or entirely in the first laundering or dry-cleaning process; some antistatic finishes are temporary finishes. A renewable finish may be applied during the dry-cleaning process or during home care; a soil-repellent finish is an example.

In the textile industry, it is generally the converter who is responsible for applying finishes to fabrics. Some companies, however, produce fabrics and apply finishing techniques as well; these are known as vertical organizations.

PREPARATION OF FABRIC FOR FINISHING

Prior to the application of the various finishes, the grey goods must be properly prepared to accept the finishes. This preparation involves cleaning the grey goods or, in the singeing process, smoothing the fabric surface. The following steps should be followed before applying finishes to fabrics.

Bleaching

The purpose of bleaching is to whiten the cloth to prepare it for dyeing or printing. For instance, if silk is to be a pale pink in the final garment, it would be bleached so that the pale pink dyeing will be accurate and sufficiently pale in the finished product. Bleaching may occur at the yarn or fabric stage. Bleaching is more common among the natural fibers, which are naturally off-white in color. Man-made fibers are inherently white and do not require bleaching. Bleaching tends to weaken the fiber and fabric.

Removing Sizing

Sizing is often applied to the warp yarns before weaving so that they have a protective coating to withstand the strain of the weaving process. Sizing is similar to starching which adds temporary body to the fabric. The sizing is cleansed from the yarns prior to finishing.

Scouring

Many types of scouring procedures are employed, depending on the fibers and the particular construction. Scouring is meant to remove such impurities as dirt, sizing, and oils. It is done in large vats called kiers in which the piece goods are scoured in large batches.

Degumming

This is a special scouring process for silk. Degumming may take place at the yarn or fabric stage and is utilized to remove the natural gum, seracin, which held the cocoon together. When scoured, the fabric is boiled in a mild soap solution and then it is rinsed and dried, resulting in a silk fabric with a high sheen and soft, pleasant hand.

Carbonizing

This process removes vegetable matter from the wool cloth that was not completely removed in the carding process. In the carbonizing process, wool is placed in sulfuric acid which destroys the burrs and vegetable matter without harming the protein fiber. Finally, the wool is scoured and ready for finishing.

Singeing

This process removes the surface fiber ends or fuzz from cotton to ensure a smooth surface for successful printing of the fabric. Singeing may be necessary if the type of fabric being produced, such as percale, requires a smooth surface. The fiber ends are brought to the surface by a brushing process, and then they are burned off. Following singeing, the fabric is passed through water or steam to completely halt the singeing process.

AESTHETIC FINISHES

The following finishes affect the visual or the textural appeal (hand) of the fabric, or both.

Brighteners

Special chemical compounds may be used to affect fabric whiteness and brightness. These have been referred to by various terms, including *optical brighteners, optical whiteners, optical bleaches,* and *flourescent brighteners.* The most correct term, based on their function, is *flourescent* since they transform invisible ultraviolet light into visible "light" off the fabric. Brighteners may be added at various stages in the finishing process, including the point at which the fabric is dyed. Although the flourescent brightener loses its effectiveness through wear, it is included in many commercial soaps and detergents used in the home so that the brightening agents may be replenished.

Deluster

Delustering is commonly utilized with the man-made fibers which are naturally bright and need to be toned down for aesthetic purposes. Delustering, through the utilization of pigments, may take place at the fiber solution stage. Delustering is also possible at the fabric stage.

Calendering

The calendering procedure involves the pressing of fabric through two or more rollers, as illustrated in Figure 6.1. This procedure smooths the fabric, thus giving the appearance of surface luster. Calendering is a finish applied to almost all fabrics whether they are man-made or natural. As the damp fabric passes through the rollers, the heated rollers flatten and set the yarns.

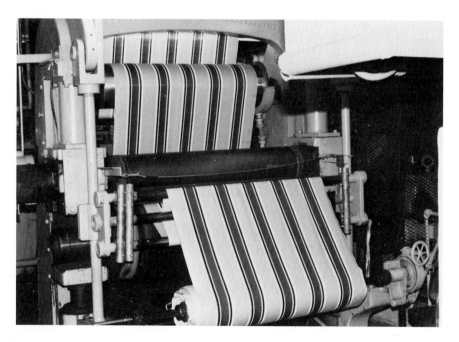

Figure 6.1
The rolling calender smooths the fabric and gives the appearance of a surface luster.
Courtesy of Cranston Print Works Company.

Variations of the calendering process produce special permanent or temporary effects on the fabric which may be achieved mechanically, chemically, or through the combination of treatments. A number of the variations are discussed below.

Glazing

A highly glazed or polished surface may be produced by the friction calender. The fabric is first coated with starch or resin and passed through the heated rollers which, through friction, polish the fabric surface. While resins produce a permanent finish, the starches produce only a temporary one. Chintz and polished cottons are finished in this manner.

Cire

This is a finish as well as the name of a fabric. Cire is characterized by a highly polished or so-called "wet look" which, at various times, has been a popular fashion look. The fabric is coated with wax or thermoplastic resin and processed through the friction calender.

Embossing

Through the embossing process, a raised surface design is achieved by passing fabric through hot rollers which imprint the desired motif (see Figure 6.2). At

Figure 6.2
Embossing rollers are used to apply raised surface designs.
Courtesy of Cranston Print Works Company.

one time, this embossed process was considered temporary and deteriorated in the laundering process. The use of resins, however, has resulted in durable embossing. Thermoplastic fibers, which can be heat set, are good choices for embossing finishes.

Moire

A moire design is characterized by a wavy or watermark surface pattern (see Figure 6.3). It is used in ribbed fabric such as taffeta and faille. The moire pattern may be produced in two ways:

1. The rollers, through heat, moisture, and pressure, press one layer of fabric against another layer (face to face), causing the flattening of the rib in various areas and the varied reflection of light in a watermark or woodgrain fashion.

2. A roller with a moire pattern etched into it presses the watermark pattern onto the fabric.

Schreinering

A special calender is required that is engraved with almost nondetectable, fine diagonal lines (about 250 per inch). Schreinering results in fabrics that are softly lustered, smooth, and have a pleasant, soft hand. This finish is often used on cotton, linen, and nylon tricot fabrics.

Tentering

Tentering is a mechanical process utilized to stretch fabric to the proper width and length and to straighten the warp and filling yarns so that they are at right angles to each other and are "on grain." The tenter frame has adjustable pins or clips to accommodate various fabric widths along the selvage edges (see Figure 6.4). The tiny holes or perforations evident along the selvage edges of some

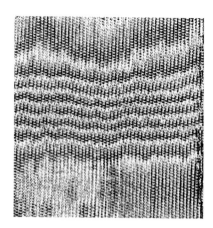

Figure 6.3
A moire finish is applied by rollers.
Reprinted with permission of Macmillan Publishing Company from *Modern Textiles* by Dorothy S. Lyle, originally published by John Wiley and Sons, Inc. (New York: Macmillan, 1982.)

Figure 6.4
A tenter frame stretches fabric to the proper width and length.
Courtesy of Cranston Print Works Company.

fabrics are from the tenter frame. The fabric is placed on the frame while wet, is stretched and straightened, and is dried. Tentering is one of the processes that may occur at different finishing stages and is a very important one. If done improperly, the fabric will dry off-grain and will be an inferior product.

Napping

To form napped fabrics, the loose fiber ends on the fabric surface are brushed up. This is achieved by passing the fabric over rolls that are covered with small wire hooks. Unlike pile fabrics, napped fabrics do not require additional yarns to form surface texture. Napping may be done on one or both sides of the fabric, and may be done on wovens or knits. Napping is particularly suitable to fabrics made of yarns with low twist and staple fibers because the yarns are easily brushed up. Napped fabrics are soft and comfortable to wear. Examples are flannel and simulated suede cloth. *Gigging, raising,* or *sanding* are other terms that refer to napping techniques.

Shearing

Once fabrics are napped, shearing may be done. Shearing is a process that may be used in several ways. The nap may be uniformly cut across the surface to produce a fabric with a smooth, even surface thickness. Or, sculpted effects may be achieved by shearing the nap to different levels of heights. Shearing may also be utilized to eliminate surface yarn ends or defects. The shearing machine, with its revolving blades, has often been compared to a lawn mower. Shearing may be performed on most fabrics.

Brushing

Brushing often follows napping and/or shearing. Napped fabrics may be brushed to run the nap in one direction. Brushing may follow shearing in order to remove the short loose fibers from within the nap.

Beetling

The general purpose of beetling is to impart a linenlike look to cotton and to finish linen so that it is smoother and has more sheen. Wooden hammers strike the cloth in order to flatten the yarns, to increase light reflection, and to make the surface more lustrous. Although beetling is a temporary finish, it becomes permanent with the addition of resins.

Fulling

Fulling is a process in which wool fabrics are exposed to moisture, heat, and friction, thereby shrinking the yarns and drawing them closer together. The resulting fabric is dense and feltlike. Melton, a popular coat wool, is an example of a fulled fabric.

Crabbing

This process, used to finish worsted wool, flattens and smooths the fabric. In the crabbing procedure, the fabric is run over rollers while steam or hot water is applied. A cold-water application follows to complete the process.

Decating

This is a mechanical process utilized to give the fabric luster, smoothness, a soft pleasant hand, and dimensional stability. Decating also prepares the fabric for the dyeing procedure and aids in producing an even, uniform color. Rollers and steam are utilized in this process. Fabrics such as wool, cotton, rayon, silk, and blends may be subjected to the decating process.

Sizing

The purpose of sizing is to impart body, strength, stiffness, and weight to yarns or fabrics. Starch is the most common sizing, but gelatin and resin are often used. Wax, glycerine, or oil is used with the sizing to act as a softener. Starch and gelatin sizings are temporary. Laundering and dry cleaning will easily remove them. Resins, also used as sizing, result in a durable finish.

Weighting

In the degumming process, when seracin is removed from silk, as much as 30 percent of the weight is lost from the silk fiber. The weighting procedure restores some of the lost fiber weight and adds body. This chemical procedure, in which the silk is treated with metallic salts, must be carefully monitored since surplus weighting results in silks with a stiff unpleasant hand, low luster, poor abrasion resistance, and the tendency to break because of the excess weighting and brittleness.

Flocking

Some authorities consider flocking a finish. For a complete discussion of flocking, see page 108.

Acid Finishes

The use of acid or caustic liquids results in several interesting, decorative-type finishes. Several acid finishes are discussed below.

Parchmentizing

In this process, sulfuric acid is applied to cotton to produce a parchmentlike (transparent) fabric with a stiff quality, such as organdy. Because of the destructive potential of the acid, the timing of this process must be exact. One of the oldest finishes of this type is the Heberlein process which originated in Switzerland. The parchmentizing process may also be used to produce fabrics with opaque designs on the surface by printing the design with an acid-resistant substance before the fabric is immersed in acid.

Burnt-Out

This process requires fabric made of two types of fibers, one that is destroyed by acid (such as rayon or acetate) and one that is not (such as silk or wool). When treated with acid, the acid-sensitive fiber will dissolve, and the acid-resistant fiber will be unaffected, resulting in a fabric with a sheer and opaque surface design.

Plisse

This is a finish and the name of the fabric that has undergone this finish. Sodium hydroxide is painted on selected areas of fabric, such as cotton, and these areas pull and shrink, causing puckering in the untreated sections. This finish is durable, but excessive ironing will damage and flatten the surface texture. Therefore, no ironing or light pressing with a cool iron is recommended.

FINISHES AFFECTING PERFORMANCE

The finishes discussed in this section affect the wear and care characteristics of fabrics. These finishes also increase the marketability of fabrics by improving their overall appeal and practicality for consumers.

Stabilizing Fabrics to Control Shrinkage

Stabilization of fabrics involves control of stretching or shrinking. Shrinking is an undesirable reduction in the size of a fabric or the finished garment. The three kinds of shrinkage are as follows:

1. Relaxation shrinkage—this occurs in the first washing of a fabric. This type of shrinkage may also occur in dry-cleaning if wet processing is utilized. Shrinkage occurs because the fibers and yarns, which were constructed under tension in a wet process, were stretched while wet and dried in the enlarged state. When the fabric is wet again, without tension, it returns to the original size before construction. In other words, relaxation occurs. Cotton, linen, and rayon are particularly susceptible to relaxation shrinkage.

2. Progressive shrinkage—this occurs each time a fabric is laundered and may not abate until the item is cleaned or laundered several times. As with relaxation shrinkage, this is often a problem with cellulosic fibers, especially rayon.

3. Felting shrinkage—this occurs particularly with wool and involves the entanglement of the scaly surface during washing. This entanglement is intensified by the pressures of agitation and spinning, heat, water, and the cleansing product used. The fibers become more compact, causing shrinkage.

Several finishing processes have been developed to control shrinkage. These processes are the result of a Federal Trade Commission ruling in 1938 which stipulated that manufactured cloth, if sold as preshrunk, had to meet rigid standards for shrinkage control. If fabrics were not labeled preshrunk, or shrunk, they were exempt from the ruling. The following finishes are meant to control shrinkage.

Compressive Shrinkage

This mechanical finishing method requires several exacting steps. The principle may be applied to wovens or knits. The sample fabric is measured, laundered to produce maximum shrinkage, and measured again. From these measurements the percentage of shrinkage is calculated. At this point, the processor knows exactly how much to compress (or preshrink) the fabric to ensure satisfactory performance.

The Sanforized Company, a division of Cluett, Peabody, & Co., Inc., includes a number of familiar trademarks that label fabrics that have undergone compressive shrinkage and will not shrink more than 1 percent. These trademarks include the following.

- Sanforized R — this label is found on many types of fabrics, where some ironing is required to retain satisfactory appearance.
- Sanforized plus & Sanforized plus 2 — these indicate easy care, durable press fabrics.
- Sanfor Set R — this label is used on all-cotton garments such as denim jeans.
- Sanfor Knit R — utilized on knit clothing, these labels identify garments that are comfortable, fit properly, and require only easy machine wash-and-dry care.

Other trademark names for preshrunk knit fabrics are Pak-nit, Shrink-No-Mor, Perma-Size, and Redmanizing.

Chemical Shrinkage Control

Rayon and wool fabrics are often treated with resins to stabilize them. For rayons, the resin treatment often follows compressive shrinkage; this is a combination of mechanical and chemical shrinkage control. In the manufacturing of washable woolens, a resin coating is applied to bind the scaly fibers and prohibit felting shrinkage. Trademarks of these resin-finished washable woolens include Superwash, Sanforlan, and Bancora. The use of resins must be carefully monitored since the amount of resin often required for shrinkage control may make the fabric stiff, producing an unpleasant hand. In addition, the resin coating may last through only several washings.

Wool may also undergo chlorine treatment to modify the scale structure to alleviate the felting shrinkage. Since chlorine is a harsh chemical and often imparts a harsh texture, this process must be used judiciously.

Sponging

This is a damp relaxation shrinkage control method used for high quality worsted woolens. The fabric is wet or steamed and then dried in a tensionless state. London Shrinking is another term used, although it is more common in England than the United States.

Heat Setting

The synthetics so prevalent in today's marketplace are stabilized by heat setting. The heat temperature is near the melting point, but must not exceed this point. Permanent dimensions are thus established if heat setting is properly employed.

Wrinkle Resistance

A fabric that is resistant to wrinkles will recover from folding or creasing and regain a generally smooth, attractive appearance. Although the discussion here focuses on finishes that inhibit wrinkling, the fiber and fabric structure may be selected so that wrinkling is unlikely or undetectable. For instance, wool is resistant to wrinkling and a boucle structure, because of its surface texture, would disguise wrinkle lines. The correct heat setting of synthetic fibers can control wrinkling very successfully.

Cellulosic fibers tend to wrinkle badly and, since the 1920s, attention has been given to remedying this problem. Years of research and experimentation led to the emergence of the durable-press and permanent-press finishes in the early 1960s. Up until this point, the only finish that had provided some relief was the wash-and-wear finish, which required some ironing. The wash-and-wear finish was replaced by the newer finishes in the 1960s. The wash-and-wear fabrics were precured at the mill before the garment was actually constructed. A discussion of the precure procedure is found below.

Durable Press or Permanent Press Finishes

The terms *durable* and *permanent* press are used interchangeably to describe these finishes, although some of the finishes are not permanent. Most fabrics with such finishes are treated with resin and may be precured, postcured, or recured.

Precure.   The fabric is treated with resin, which is then set by heat in a curing oven. The fabric is sold as yard goods. Because these fabrics were set when flat, clothing manufacturers and home sewers found them to be difficult to sew into garments which required various types of shaping. Therefore, the following two procedures became prevalent.

Postcure.   After the fabric is treated with resin, it is not cured, but only dried. After the finished garment is constructed, it is cured with the entire item permanently set as manufactured.

Recure.   This process is a combination of the precure procedure and the application of heat after garment construction. The resin initially applied is recured and, in addition, heat sets the thermoplastic fibers usually incorporated into the durable press blend. Therefore, the durable press is achieved in a two-step procedure that should be effective. This is the newest of the procedures. Durable press trademarks include Dan-Press, Never-Press, Koratron, Super-Crease, and Coneprest.

Problems of Durable Press

Following is a list of some of the problems resulting from the durable press finish. Despite the problems, durable press fabrics have been accepted by the general buying public. Many of the problems have been alleviated.

1. Durable press fabrics may be difficult to handle in some phases of garment construction. For instance, stitching may cause puckering and adjustments in thread, tension, and needle may be required.

2. The durable press finish will deplete cotton of up to half its strength and must be blended with a thermoplastic fiber (such as polyester) to compensate for this loss of strength.

3. Durable press finishes adversely affect the abrasion resistance of cotton. Frosting, which is a discoloring on a garment area that is subject to pilling, may result. In these areas, the weak cotton fibers wear away, but the stronger polyester fibers do not, leaving pills.

4. On durable press garments, it is difficult to make alterations, especially when the hem is let down and a previous crease must be removed for aesthetic reasons. Because alterations of this type are most often made by the customer, dissatisfaction with the garment and/or the durable press finish will result.

5. Durable press finishes result in poor moisture absorption and the fabric will not be comfortable on warm days.

6. Resins may cause stiffness in the fabrics, and they will not be suitable for designs requiring a soft drape.

7. Fishy odors may be associated with durable press finishes, although they can usually be removed with washing.

8. During home care, durable press fabrics should not be permitted to sit in a dryer after completion of the dry cycle because wrinkling will result.

9. The synthetic fibers and resins used in durable press fabrics attract and hold oil-borne stains. Because the durable press fabrics will also resist water, the stains will be difficult to remove.

Soil-Release Finishes

Since the durable press fabrics tended to attract and hold oily stains, particularly because of the polyester and resins used, soil-release finishes were developed. The soil-release finish permits the "release" of these oily stains and also discourages soil redeposition by which the fabric picks up the soil that has been transferred into the wash water. As the soil release finishes increase water/moisture absorbency, they also inhibit static electricity. Unfortunately, these finishes are not permanent and are gradually worn away through washing. Soil-release finishes include Visa and Zip-clean.

Soil-Repellent Finishes

A soil-repellent finish is achieved by using chemicals that are also used for water repellency. Some of the finishes resist water-borne as well as oil-borne stains. Soils such as coffee, tea, fruit juice, catsup, fats, and ink are all easily removed. These finishes are usually applied during the manufacturing process, but spray-on soil-repellent finishes may also be applied by the consumer. Soil-repellent finishes include Scotchgard, Visa, and Zepel. Many of these finishes are durable, lasting the life of the garment.

Water-Repellent and Waterproof Finishes

Although water-repellent fabrics resist water penetration, they are not water-proof. Most early water-repellent fabrics were renewable; that is, the finish was removed during laundering and dry-cleaning and had to be reapplied. The durable water-repellent finishes are more permanent and are achieved by coating the fibers with fatty or oily-based chemical compounds or by using fluorochemical compounds.

Waterproof fabrics prohibit the penetration of water through the fabric. These fabrics are generally coated with rubber or plastic. Since they are not porous and do not allow air permeability, waterproof fabrics are generally uncomfortable to wear.

Abrasion-Resistant Finishes

Abrasion is the damage of the surface of the fabric from rubbing or friction which is usually done by another fabric. Although this finish is not a common type, there are basically two methods for preventing abrasion damage. The highly resistant fibers, usually in the man-made category, may be blended with the fibers that have low abrasion resistance. When polyester and cotton are blended, the abrasion resistance of the cotton is improved. Technically, however, this is not a finish. Another method to improve resistance to abrasion is to apply synthetic resins to the fabrics.

Absorbency Finishes

The cellulosic fibers—cotton, linen, rayon—have good absorbency, but with specific end-uses, such as towels, undergarments, and diapers, the absorbency level should be increased. This is achieved by adding ammonium compounds to the fabric. With regard to the man-made fibers, there are several finishes to improve absorbency. These include Nylonizing and Nylonex (for nylon fibers), Fantessa (for polyester), and Hysorb.

Antislip Finishes

Slippage is the undesirable shifting of yarns which leaves flaws in the fabric. This is especially a problem with the filament yarns which are smooth and slip easily. It is also a problem with loosely woven fabrics. The common method to alleviate slippage is to treat the fabrics with resin which will hold the yarns in place.

Antistatic Finishes

Static electricity in fabrics is one of the common annoyances frequently mentioned by customers. Synthetic fibers are the biggest problem because they are poor conductors of electricity. Reducing static electricity involves coating the fiber or adding moisture to the fiber to improve its conductive properties. For home use, there are antistatic sprays and fabric softeners which impart antistatic finishes. The permanency of the finishes varies.

Moth-Repellent Finishes

Moths feed on wool and other animal hair fibers, sometimes causing extensive damage and ruining the garment. This problem may be prevented in the home by keeping the garments clean, exposing them to sunlight when possible, and storing the items with moth-repellent products. Finishes to inhibit moth damage may include insecticides such as Moth Snub. Another type of finish is to altar the chemical structure of the fiber so that it is indigestable to the moth.

Mildew and Rot-Repellent Finishes

Cellulosic and protein fibers may be damaged by molds and mildew. The consumer can prevent such damage at home by keeping the fabrics clean and dry; a boric acid rinse will prohibit mildew. Rotting, like mildew, is caused by exposure to wet, damp environments. Rotting and mildew may be inhibited by a variety of chemicals that prohibit the growth of microorganisms. Resin finishes will also retard mildew and rotting; Mil-tron and Arigal are two trade names.

Antibacterial Finishes

Antibacterial or antiseptic finishes are chemical treatments that inhibit bacterial growth, such as that caused by perspiration. This type of bacterial growth often causes irritation and/or odor in fabric. These finishes are semipermanent, lasting up to forty to fifty washings. Sanitized and Pacificate are trademarked finishes that protect fabrics from deteriorization and odor.

Heat-Reflectant Finishes

In clothing or home textiles, heat-reflectant fabrics function in two ways: (1) to reflect heat to the wearer or interior or (2) to draw heat away from the body or interior. Heat-reflectant finishes usually consist of a spray-on coating of a resinated metal, such as aluminum, which is a superior reflectant metal. A trademark of this process is Milium. To provide heat-reflectant properties, a thin layer or film of aluminum may be applied to the fabric; Scotch-Shield is a trade name for such a process.

Flame-Retardant Finishes

The flammability of fabrics has long been a consumer and market concern. Therefore, in 1953, Congress enacted the Flammable Fabrics Act so that fabrics that were readily ignitable could be removed from the marketplace. With increased concern with this problem, the act was amended in 1967 to include a wider range of wearing apparel and home textiles. In 1972, the act was expanded to include children's sleepwear in sizes 0–6X; the 1975 modification of the act included sizes 7–14. In 1972, the Consumer Product Safety Act was passed and the U.S. Consumer Product Safety Commission established; the CPSC regulates the Flammable Fabrics Act.

A number of flame-retardant chemical finishes have been used, such as those sold under the trade names THPC, Pyroset, and Pyrovatex. There are problems associated with using these finishes, including:

1. Stiff, unpleasant hand often results.

2. Loss of finish qualities due to improper washing with chlorine bleach, soap, and nonphosphate detergents may occur.

3. Washing in phosphate detergents restores flame-retardant finish, but phosphates pollute the water and are banned in some states.

4. Dry-cleaning may destroy the finish.

5. Unpleasant odors are associated with some of the finishes.

6. Finishes that work with one type of fiber may not be effective on another type; therefore, blends may not be truly flame-retardant.

Fibers may be made flame-retardant by incorporating special chemicals into the spinning solution; this obviously will add to the cost of the fiber. Other difficulties include a harsh, unpleasant hand, requiring modifications in the dyeing and finishing processes of these fibers. Examples of flame-retardant fibers are Acrilan Plus, Trevira 271, and Trevira 692.

Some of the man-made fibers, such as modacrylic and vinyon, are inherently flame-resistant. Nomex, an aramid fiber from DuPont, is used chiefly in industry. Kynol, a novoloid fiber, is used widely in industry. Glass fibers will not burn; they are used in home textiles but not in apparel.

Mercerization

Cotton or linen may be mercerized, but cotton benefits most from mercerization, since linen inherently possesses some of the qualities mercerization imparts (such as luster and strength). Mercerization may be done on yarns or fabrics. The fabric is immersed in a tension state into sodium hydroxide and then rinsed.

Slack mercerization, in which fabrics are mercerized without tension, produces stretch fabrics (woven or knitted) and yarn. The yarns shrink during the process and elasticity results. Compared to regular mercerization, yarns that have undergone slack mercerization are not as lustrous, but are stronger.

The general advantages of mercerization are as follows:

1. The process adds luster and strength to the fabric.

2. Fabric becomes more absorbent and is more easily dyed.

3. It improves receptivity of the fibers to the finishes.
4. The process is cheap and permanent.

KEY TERMS

1. Beetling
2. Bleaching
3. Brushing
4. Calendering
5. Carbonizing
6. Decating
7. Degumming
8. Embossing
9. Finishes
10. Fulling
11. Gigging
12. Glazing
13. Mercerization
14. Moire design
15. Napping
16. Preshrunk
17. Shearing
18. Singeing
19. Sizing
20. Soil release
21. Tentering
22. Weighting

STUDY QUESTIONS

1. What is a finish? Why are finishes necessary?
2. Explain why fabrics must be prepared for finishing; explain six ways in which this preparation is accomplished.
3. Explain the two broad classifications of finishes.
4. Define calendering; define five variations of this basic finishing procedure.
5. Discuss three finishes that affect the size, shape, or dimensional stability of fabrics.
6. List and explain four ways in which shrinkage is controlled through special finishing procedures.
7. Wrinkling of fabrics was a major problem until an appropriate finish was developed. Describe this finish, and discuss five associated problems.
8. Discuss mercerization and slack mercerization.
9. What is the difference between water-repellent and waterproof finishes?
10. Indicate the kind of fabric that would benefit most from each of the following finishes:
    a. moth-repellent finish
    b. absorbency finish
    c. soil-release finish
    d. antistatic finish
    e. antislip finish
    f. mildew finish

STUDY ACTIVITIES

1. Visit a large fabric store that stocks fabrics suitable for apparel as well as fabrics for decorating. Study the bolt labeling on the various types of fabrics. List ten different fabrics, their names, fiber content, care instruc-

tions, and any information related to finishes included in the chapter. What is an appropriate end-use for each of the fabrics, and is the finish appropriate for the end-use? If this activity cannot be completed in a fabric store, or if a supplement activity is desired, you should visit a department store and check finished garments or home textile products for the information stated above.

2. To experiment with the effects of finishes, do the following exercise. Cut two pieces of muslin, each about sixteen to twenty inches square. Leave one piece as is, but spray the second with a soil-resistant finish available over the counter in a spray can; follow manufacturer's directions carefully. On both swatches of fabrics, apply stains of tea, coffee, fruit juice, catsup, vegetable oil, and ink. Observe what happens to the staining on both pieces of cloth. Try to remove the stains with paper towels. What do you observe? Machine wash and dry the two pieces of fabric; press. What conclusions can you draw about the finish you applied?

CHAPTER 7

Color and Design

OBJECTIVES

After completing this chapter, you should be able to:

1. Define dyeing and printing.

2. List and define major factors affecting colorfastness.

3. Define the difference between natural and synthetic dyes.

4. List twelve categories of synthetic dyes, their characteristics, and end-uses.

5. List and explain the five stages of fabric manufacture in which the dyeing process may be implemented.

6. List and define three basic methods for printing fabrics and provide specific examples of each.

7. List and define eight additional examples of printing methods.

The color and design of fabrics are their aesthetics and excitement in the marketplace. Color and design—or dyeing and printing—are the beauty and prestige of fabrics, the qualities by which customers immediately make a judgment and register their interest or disinterest. Even the most perfectly constructed fabrics or garments will likely be dismal failures in the marketplace if they do not reflect current fashion trends in color and design, or if they do not instantly stimulate interest and enthusiasm. The correct selection and merchandising of color is a significant ingredient for success.

Consequently, although the dyeing and printing procedures are indeed technical, many trained fashion specialists—designers, stylists, fashion directors—are involved in decisions about dyeing and printing so that the finished products do have broad fashion appeal. This chapter details the background information and processes that ultimately bring to the marketplace fashion products that are not only eye-appealing in their color and design, but that are serviceable, durable, and easy to care for.

DYEING AND PRINTING

Adding color and design involves the final dyeing and printing of the fabric. Each of these is a separate, distinct process. Dyeing involves the impregnation of dyestuff at the prefiber, fiber, yarn, fabric piece, or garment stage. The printing process involves the application of color to the fabric surface in a broad range of patterns and designs.

SELECTION OF DYE FOR BEAUTY AND PERFORMANCE

In the selection of dyes for fabrics that will be attractive as well as practical, two factors are of major importance:

1. Fiber identification and characteristics—dyes may have an affinity for vegetable, animal, or man-made fibers. Therefore, a dye perfectly acceptable in coloring a wool fabric may be inappropriate for a rayon fabric.

2. End-use of the fabric—since the most important requirement of the dye is to maintain its original color—remain colorfast—the end-use of the fabric must be considered in dye selection. For instance, in draperies, fastness to light is essential, but in clothing, fastness to washing and perspiration are more important.

Since colorfastness is essential for a satisfactory textile product, it is important to consider those factors that may affect color: care methods, light, fumes, perspiration, and crocking. These factors usually result in fading, but they may also darken some dyes or distort the quality of the color.

Care Methods

Washing and bleaching procedures, dry-cleaning, spot removal, and ironing may all affect dyes. Occasionally, many garments may be affected, for example, a whole washload may turn pale blue due to the color loss from a navy shirt! Such a color loss from one fabric to others in the wash is called *bleeding*. A too-hot iron may also affect color quality and permanence.

Light

The absorption of light can cause the chemical order of dyes to change, usually resulting in fading. Light can damage curtains and draperies. It can also cause fading in other items in a room, such as carpeting and slipcovers.

Fumes

Atmospheric gases, especially serious in industrial areas, can cause fading of dyes. Auto exhaust may also be a problem. *Gas fading* or *fume fading* are terms used to describe this kind of color fading or distortion.

Perspiration

Dyes may fade or change color when exposed to perspiration. Use of protective deodorants or antiperspirants may inhibit perspiration fading, but these products in themselves can also cause color changes in garments.

Crocking

Dyes can rub off through friction of one fabric upon another. Such crocking can remove the red coloring from a poorly dyed red jacket, and transfer it to a pair of white pants in the course of daily wear.

TESTING COLORFASTNESS

Scientifically controlled, laboratory procedures are often utilized by the industry to test colorfastness to ensure the best textile product possible. Some of these tests may be simulated at home (see Study Activities at the end of this chapter). Several commercial test procedures, their purposes, and equipment utilized are discussed here. The American Association of Textile Chemists and Colorists (AATCC) has outlined specific test procedures.

Fastness to Light

The Fade-Ometer is used for testing colorfastness to sunlight. After textile samples have been exposed to rays of light for a prescribed period, they are compared to unexposed, protected samples, and rated. (A Fade-Ometer is illustrated in Figure 7.1.)

Fastness to Laundering

The Launder-Ometer is used for washing fabric samples under carefully controlled conditions. The specimens are than rated for performance and change in color.

Figure 7.1
Fade-Ometer.®
Courtesy of Atlas Electric Devices Company.

Fastness to Crocking

The Crockmeter is utilized to test color rub-off from a dyed sample piece to a white fabric test sample. Both dry and wet tests are conducted. The dyed fabric is evaluated for resistance to crocking. A Crockmeter is illustrated in Figure 7.2.

TYPES OF DYES

Dyes may be broadly classified as natural or synthetic. Each classification is discussed below.

Natural Dyes

As the name indicates, natural dyes were found in nature and were derived from mineral, animal, or vegetable sources. Use of such dyes dates back to the beginnings of civilization. Natural dyes are still used today, mostly in home dyeing, not commercially. Mineral colors were the least utilized. Animal dyes included the brilliant red obtained from the cochineal insect of South America and the Tyrean purple derived from small shellfish. The broad spectrum of vegetable dyes could be made from flowers, berries, nuts, roots, and grasses, among others.

Figure 7.2
Crockmeter.
Courtesy of Atlas Electric Devices Company.

Synthetic Dyes

The use of synthetic dyes, derived from coal tar, may be traced back to the research of English chemist William Perkin, who created the first synthetic dye in the color mauve in 1856. The development of the American dye industry, however, did not take hold until World War I when imports were curtailed. Through the years, the primary goals of the industry have been based on commitment to satisfactory end-use performance. These industry goals involve the improvement of dyes in the following ways:

1. Colorfastness—the primary requirement of satisfactory dyes
2. Color aesthetics—quality, intensity, and beauty of color for general fashion appeal
3. Color variety—an ever-increasing range of colors to appeal to broad customer tastes and changing fashion trends

The synthetic dyes have been categorized in a number of ways. Included here are the twelve major categories, their characteristics and end-uses: (1) basic dyes, (2) acid dyes, (3) mordant dyes, (4) oxidation dyes, (5) direct dyes, (6) developed dyes, (7) azoic dyes, (8) disperse dyes, (9) vat dyes, (10) sulfur dyes, (11) reactive dyes, and (12) pigment dyes.

Basic or Cationic Dyes

Characteristics. These were the first of the synthetic dyestuffs, derived from coal tar. They may be used directly on silk and wool, but on other fibers they must be used with a mordant, which binds the dye to the fiber. When used on natural fibers, however, basic dyes are not fast to light, washing, perspiration, or fading from atmospheric gases. Colors are possible in a broad range, including bright flourescents.

End-Uses.   Basic dyes are used largely on acrylics where their performance is best. These dyes are also used on modified polyester and nylon. They are suitable for direct prints on acetate. Basic dyes may also be used as "topping" colors —that is, they are layered on top of previous dyes to increase brilliance and brightness. Discharge prints may also be produced with basic dyes (see page 146 for a discussion of discharge prints).

Acid or Anionic Dyes

Characteristics.   Available in a complete range of color, acid dyes are inexpensive, but do not have a high level of performance. Their fastness to light and drycleaning may vary considerably, and they have poor fastness to washing and to perspiration. They are highly resistant to crocking.

End-Uses.   Acid dyes have been most widely used on silk and wool, but are also used on acetate, nylon, acrylics, spandex, and on some olefin fibers.

Mordant or Chrome Dyes

Characteristics.   Mordant dyes are available in a range of colors not quite as broad as the selection of acid dyes. They are duller than the acid hues. Their performance level is fair to good in all care procedures, and they are not seriously affected by gas fading and perspiration. Bleeding may be a problem, however.

End-Uses.   These dyes are most widely used on wool. They may also be used on cellulosic fibers, silk, and nylon.

Oxidation Dyes

Characteristics.   These are among the oldest of the synthetic dyes. Among the colors within the group is aniline black, a true and fast black color that is one of the best black dyes available. An excellent brown dye also belongs to this group. Performance qualities in every category are good to excellent.

End-Uses.   Used most often for cotton, oxidation dyes may also be used in wool, silk, and acetate.

Direct or Substantive Dyes

Characteristics.   Available in a broad range of colors, direct dyes are duller in intensity than either the basic or acid dyes. The direct dyes are sometimes topped with basic dyes to brighten the color. Their performance is good to excellent in all categories, except washing, where they can lose color.

End-Uses.   Commercially, direct dyes are the most important group today, particularly because they are inexpensive, easy to use, and offer a wide color range. They are most often used in cellulosic fabrics, but are also used for wool, silk, and nylon. They are used extensively in discharge printing.

Developed Dyes

Characteristics.   A group of direct dyes, the developed dyes are applied directly to a fabric and then chemically treated with developers to establish the final color, which may be quite different from the primary dye applied. They perform well in most ways, but washing may affect the color quality.

End-Uses.   The same as those for direct dyes.

Azoic or Naphthol Dyes

Characteristics.   A third category of direct dyes, these dyes are often called ice colors since ice is used in the application process. The range of colors is wide and includes darks, pastels, and brights. They can be produced at relatively low cost. Performance qualities are good, although bleeding may occur on white fabrics.

End-Uses.   Azoic dyes are used primarily on cottons, but they may be used on acetate, nylon, acrylic, and polyester. Since they launder well, they are often used for household linens. They are well-suited to printing procedures, since the colors are dischargeable and can be easily used with other types of dyes.

Disperse Dyes

Characteristics.   The disperse dyes are available in a good color range and were originally called acetate dyes because they were developed for acetate fibers. Today, they are called disperse dyes primarily because they do not dissolve in the dyebath, but disperse and attach to the fibers to be colored. Performance quality may vary from fair to good in most categories. The major weakness with disperse dyes is that, especially when the color blue is used to dye acetate, it fume fades badly, the blue often turning to pale pink in time.

End-Uses.   Today, disperse dyes can be used on most fibers, except for silk and wool. Because of their dispersing qualities, they have been successfully used in combination in one dyebath to add multicolors to knit goods which are then unraveled to produce craft yarns.

Vat Dyes

Characteristics.   The vat dyes are so called because of the large vats originally used for applying the dyes. The earliest vat dye was indigo, developed in the late nineteenth century. The color range is not as broad as that available from the acid or the direct dye groups, but is adequate enough to provide some variety. It is a good-to-excellent dye for colorfastness and, indeed, vat dyes are often considered the best dyes in this regard.

End-Uses.   Most often used for cotton, but also for wool and silk, vat dyes are widely used for all kinds of textiles, including those utilized for sportswear, work-clothes, and household textiles.

Sulfur Dyes

Characteristics.   The sulfur dyes were created about the same time as the vat dyes. Although color variety is broad, the colors tend to be dull, and red is not producible. Resistance to colorfastness varies in terms of light, washing, and bleeding. Sulfur dyes do resist color loss from dry-cleaning, gas fading, and perspiration.

End-Uses.   Sulfur dyes are used primarily for cotton, especially for heavy wovens suitable for work apparel. Black sulfur dye is a commonly used black dye.

Reactive Dyes

Characteristics.   The reactive dyes, developed in 1957, are so called because they combine chemically with the fibers to which they are applied; thus, they have very good color retention. Reactive dyes produce some of the brightest colors possible and exhibit very good fastness to light, washing, dry-cleaning, gas fading, crocking, and perspiration.

End-Uses.   Most widely used in cottons, reactive dyes are also used on wool, silk, rayon, nylon, and acrylic.

Pigment Dyes

Characteristics.   Technically, pigment colors, which have no affinity for fibers, are not dyes. They are applied to the fiber or fabric with resins, adhesive, or some other type of bonding agent. The quality of the bonding agent is directly related to the colorfastness; if the bonding is not excellent, it will wear away and take the color along with it. Pigment dyes have good-to-excellent performance qualities, although crocking is a problem with dark colors.

End-Uses.   Although cotton is often pigment dyed, almost all types of fibers are suitable for this process.

DYE PROCESSES

Color can be applied at various stages of fabric manufacture:

1. The solution or prefiber stage before the man-made fiber is extruded from the spinneret
2. Fiber stage
3. Yarn stage
4. Fabric or piece stage
5. Finished garment or product stage

Solution Dyeing

In this process, color is added to the spinning solution before the man-made fiber is extruded from the spinneret. There are several advantages to this process:

1. It is quick and economical.
2. Color, since it becomes part of the fiber itself, is highly colorfast and far superior in this regard to colors established through dyeing at other points.
3. This method has been successful even with fibers that tend to resist dyeing.

Fiber or Stock Dyeing

In this process, the staple fiber is dyed before spinning. This is accomplished in large vats through which the heated dye solution is continuously passed in order to permeate the fiber mass. This process is effective, but expensive. Except for solution dyeing, stock dyeing is the best of the remaining dye methods in penetrating the entire fiber.

Similar to the stock dye method is the top dyeing process. Top, the ropelike form into which wool is combed, is wound on spools and placed into a tank where the dye is pumped through it.

Yarn Dyeing

This process takes place after the yarn has been spun from the fiber. Yarns may be dyed in skeins, in spools or cones (package dyeing), or on warp beams; Figure 7.3 illustrates package dyeing. Deeply colored and aesthetically pleasing yarns result. They are utilized by textile designers in yarn-dyed fabrics in which various colored yarns may be combined to produce lovely patterns such as plaids,

Figure 7.3
Package dyeing.
Courtesy of the American Textile Manufacturers Institute.

checked ginghams, and stripes. Yarn dyeing is less expensive than fiber dyeing, but more expensive than piece or garment dyeing. A variation of this basic process is space dyeing, in which the length of yarn is dyed at intervals.

Fabric or Piece Dyeing

By far the most commonly employed method used today, piece dyeing affords the manufacturer flexibility in quickly meeting changing fashion trends while providing the marketplace with fabrics that are evenly dyed, colorfast, and fashionable. Piece-dyed fabrics may be of one fiber or of blends. When blended fabrics are piece dyed, variations of the basic technique may be utilized, such as cross dyeing or union dyeing.

Cross Dyeing

In this process, a fabric made of two or more fiber types (such as a protein fiber and a vegetable fiber) is dyed according to one or more methods that will result in a fabric in which each fiber type is a different color. This is achieved because each of the fiber types has an affinity for a specific dye type utilized. The methods employed may vary according to the end result desired, but may include the following:

1. A combination of stock or yarn dyeing, followed by piece dyeing
2. Using two or more separate dyebaths, each meant to color a different fiber in the fabric
3. Piece dyeing in one dyebath containing two or more dye types, each affecting the fiber types in different ways.

Utilizing the cross-dyeing process, a broad variety of patterns is possible.

Union Dyeing

In this process, a fabric made of two or more fiber types is dyed but, in contrast to cross dyeing, the finished fabric will be a solid color. Dyes appropriate for the fibers involved are combined in the dyebath into which the fabric is submerged. The final result will be a uniformly dyed, single-color piece.

Garment or Product Dyeing

Garment or product dyeing involves the dyeing of the entire garment (such as a sweater or dress) or product (such as a towel or sheet) in its finished state. This method is economical and quick, and can allow for rapidly changing fashion trends in color. However, shrinkage has been a problem. Consequently, this method is more practical where some size variation is acceptable, such as in non-tailored items or in household linens.

PRINTING

Printed fabrics are fabrics that have been decorated by the application of dyes to the surface of the fabric. The color is generally for surface decoration only, so that the wrong side of the fabric usually remains pale by comparison. If a yarn is pulled from a printed fabric, it will be uneven in color because the dye has not penetrated the whole yarn. In contrast, a yarn taken from a yarn-dyed cloth or a piece-dyed cloth will be evenly colored throughout. The art of printing is as ancient as fabric itself. Fragments of printed fabric have been discovered in the tombs of ancient Egypt. There are three basic methods for printing fabrics: direct printing, discharge printing, and resist printing.

Direct Printing

This has been the most popular method of printing fabrics, particularly the roller print technique.

Block Printing

This is probably the oldest printing technique and dates back to ancient civilizations. Each color in the design requires a separate block, usually made of wood or metal. The design portion of the block is raised as the rest of the block area is carved out. The block is coated with the required dye and pressed firmly onto the fabric (see Figure 7.4).

Since this is a slow, costly method that is best done by hand, it is not commercially significant today. Hand-blocked prints, however, continue to be prized fabrics in the handicraft field.

Roller Printing

This efficient, economical, and rapid method of printing designs on fabric is achieved by engraving the design onto rollers, usually made of copper (see Figure 7.5). This method requires that each color in the design be printed by a separate roller; some designs may require up to sixteen rollers. Each time the roller completes a revolution, a repeat of the design is printed. The smooth areas of the roller that are free of the etched design are kept clean in the process by blades that remove the dye.

Figure 7.4
Block printing.

Figure 7.5
Roller engraving.
Courtesy: Arnold Print Works, Inc.

Discharge Printing

Discharge prints are executed on fabrics that have been piece dyed a solid color. The design itself is achieved by removing or bleaching out this color in the desired areas through a chemical process. A popular type of discharge print is a solid ground fabric with a white design motif where the color has been removed (see Figure 7.6). An additional step, or series of steps, may add one or more colors to the discharged areas.

Figure 7.6
Discharge printing.

Resist Printing

Resist printing, a very early form, is achieved when portions of the fabric are protected (often with a wax layer) from the dye to be applied. The fabric maintains its color in the protected areas while the exposed areas undergo a color change (see Figure 7.7). Examples of resist printing include batik, tie dye, stencil printing, and screen printing.

Batik

A method originating in Java, batik prints are achieved by applying melted wax to areas to be protected from the dye. When the dye has dried, the wax is removed by submerging the fabric into boiling water. The wax may be reapplied to other areas on the fabric if subsequent dyes are to be applied for more varied, intricate fabric designs, such as that illustrated in Figure 7.8. Primarily a hand process, batik continues to be popular in the handicraft arena.

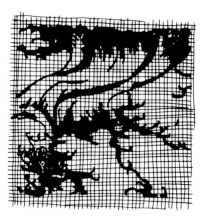

Figure 7.7
Resist printing.

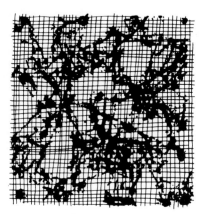

Figure 7.8
Batik print.

Tie Dye

Technically, this is not a printing method, but it is based on the resist principle. Fabric is wrapped, tied securely in places, and then piece dyed; the tied, protected portions do not accept the dye. The basic process may be repeated until the desired effect is achieved. In recent years, this has been a very popular method of decorating fabrics at home.

Stencil Printing

This resist method was first developed in Japan and is primarily a handicraft process. Today, it is a little-used procedure, not suited to commercial production because it is costly and time-consuming. A design stencil is cut from paper, plastic, or thin metal; a separate stencil is required for each color. The stencil is placed on the fabric and color applied with a brush or spray gun. Each color application requires complete drying before the next is applied. Stencil prints are illustrated in Figure 7.9.

Screen Printing

Screen printing is derived from the stencil process. A fine, mesh screen is used for each color; the screens were originally of silk and the process was called silk-screen printing. Today, however, screens may be of silk, metal, nylon, polyester, or other materials. The design area of the screen is left open while remaining areas are protected by a film or resist material. A squeegee forces the color through the open design areas. A series of screens is required to produce the finished print. This process was originally done by hand, a costly and time-consuming procedure. Today, most screen printing is automatic and done either by flat-bed screen printing machines or rotary screen printers.

Flat-bed Screen Printing. In this process, each flat screen, which is secured to a frame, is lowered onto the fabric, dye is applied, and the fabric is moved into ovens for drying.

Figure 7.9
Stencil printing.

Rotary Screen Printing.   A newer technique, this procedure involves quick and efficient rolls that print the design onto the fabric. Rotary screen designs cannot be as large as flat-bed screen designs since the roller size establishes the repeat of the print. The rotary method, however, can more easily produce designs of more color and complexity since it is easy to increase the number of rotary screens required to execute a print. Rotary screen printing is illustrated in Figure 7.10.

Today, screen printing produces some of the most beautiful fabrics in the marketplace and is widely used as a printing process.

Figure 7.10
Rotary screen printing. First the design is painted on a cylinder screen. Dye is forced through holes in the screen as the cylinder is rolled over the cloth. The final photo shows the printed cloth.
Courtesy of the American Textile Manufacturers Institute.

Other Printing Methods

Additional printing methods, utilized to varying degrees in the industry today, include the following: transfer printing, duplex printing, flock printing, electrostatic printing, jet spray printing, airbrush printing, warp printing, and photographic printing.

Transfer Printing

This procedure involves the transfer of design from paper to fabric through applying dry heat or wet heat, and pressure. In this process, the dye on the paper evaporates and transfers to the fabric surface. This process is related to the home decorating of T-shirts with iron-on transfers. This is a growing printing technique, especially since it is efficient and less expensive than roller and screen printing, requiring only special paper rather than copper rollers or silk screens. Advancements in technology now permit highly successful transfer printing of many natural and man-made fibers and all types of fabric including wovens, knits, and piles. Indications are that the transfer printing technique will continue to grow in the industry.

Duplex Printing

When a fabric is intended to be reversible, both sides may be exactly and simultaneously printed on the duplex printing machine. The result is a fabric in which the design or pattern appears to be woven in rather than applied to both surfaces. Another method for duplex printing involves printing of each side separately, a two-step rather than a one-step process.

Flock Printing

The application of short fibers in a pattern onto a ground fabric is flock printing. This may be accomplished through the use of adhesives or passing the fibers through an eletrostatic field onto the fabric (refer to Chapter 5 for a related discussion).

Electrostatic Printing

Similar to electrostatic flocking, in this process a screen with the design on it is covered with a dye-resin mixture. When placed in an electrostatic field with the fabric just below it, the print is pulled or transferred to the fabric and heat-set to complete the process.

Jet Spray Printing

In this process, designs are applied to fabrics through the use of jets which spray on the color as the width of fabric passes beside the jets. The polychromatic process permits the application of several dyes in one process. The fabric then moves between heavy rollers which allows the penetration of dye to the back of the fabric and sets it. The microjet process is another jet spray printing procedure which is totally computerized and produces Jacquardlike patterns, especially popular for carpeting and upholstery fabrics.

Airbrush Printing

Another type of spray-on method is the airbrush technique in which color is sprayed or blown onto the fabric. Interesting shaded patterns may be easily achieved.

Warp Printing

This technique, which results in interesting, subtle designs, is achieved by printing the warp yarns only before the fabric is constructed; these are often combined with white filling yarns. A variation of warp printing is Vigoureux printing or melange utilized with wool; in this process, the ropelike tops or slubbings are dyed, before spinning, in a striped pattern. When woven, the effect is a fabric with color flecks throughout.

Photographic Printing

Any photograph, black-and-white or color, may be roller printed. Photographic techniques are used to engrave the picture onto the roller and the fabric is printed.

KEY TERMS

1.	Acid dye	15.	Flock print
2.	Airbrush print	16.	Fume fading
3.	Azoic dye	17.	Jet spray print
4.	Basic dye	18.	Mordant
5.	Batik	19.	Oxidation dye
6.	Bleeding	20.	Pigment dye
7.	Crocking	21.	Reactive dye
8.	Developed dye	22.	Resist printing
9.	Direct dye	23.	Screen print
10.	Direct printing	24.	Stencil print
11.	Discharge printing	25.	Sulfur dye
12.	Disperse dye	26.	Transfer print
13.	Duplex printing	27.	Vat dye
14.	Electrostatic print	28.	Warp print

STUDY QUESTIONS

1. Define dyeing and printing. What is the basic difference between the two?
2. Explain the origin of synthetic dyes. What is the difference between natural and synthetic dyes?
3. What is the difference between cross dyeing and union dyeing?
4. List and explain the five categories that must be considered when evaluating textiles for colorfastness.
5. Why are pigments technically not dyes?

6. Explain the function of each of the following pieces of textile testing equipment: Crockmeter, Fade-Ometer, Launder-Ometer.
7. Define mordant and explain its function.
8. Why do reactive dyes have excellent colorfastness?
9. List and explain the five stages in which dyeing may take place.
10. List and define three basic methods for printing fabrics.

STUDY ACTIVITIES

These three study activities are simple tests for colorfastness. Several fabrics, suited to various end-uses (apparel, table linens, draperies, etc.), may be used for each of the tests. Evaluations should be written and presented to the class. It is suggested that fabric swatches at least four inches square be used, two swatches for each test.

1. *Colorfastness to Sunlight.* Expose the fabric test sample to sunlight by placing on a window ledge that receives sun for several hours between 9:00 A.M. and 5:00 P.M. daily. Leave for one week, checking daily and recording observations. Finally, compare the exposed sample with the unexposed sample at the end of the week. Evaluate the fabric's colorfastness to light.

2. *Colorfastness to Laundering.* In a large, clean screw-top jar, place one cup of warm water and one teaspoon of detergent. Place one test swatch at a time in the jar and shake frequently during a fifteen-minute period. Let sit for ten minutes. Has the water changed color? Write down your observations. Dispose of water, rinse jar, add one cup of clear warm water, and rinse sample thoroughly. What do you observe? Evaluate the performance of the test swatch against the control, or unwashed, swatch.

3. *Colorfastness to Crocking.* You will need a four-inch square of white plainweave fabric. Rub the white swatch against the test swatch (a solid color or a print) about twenty-five to thirty times. Record your observations and evaluate, comparing the test swatch with the second swatch of fabric. This test may be conducted with wet or dry fabrics, or both.

CHAPTER 8

Care of Textiles

OBJECTIVES

After completing this chapter, you should be able to:

1. List the factors to be considered in determining the proper care of textile products.

2. Correctly interpret the care labels used today.

3. List and give examples of the products utilized in home laundering.

4. List the procedures to be followed for proper hand washing, machine washing, and drying.

5. List the general procedures followed by professional laundries and dry cleaners.

6. List the factors related to successful spot and stain removal at home.

As the cost of textile products increases, proper care becomes more and more important to insure the consumer's investment. This chapter provides a broad overview of textile care. The following topics are covered: the meaning of care labels, home laundering, professional dry-cleaning, and stain removal. For store personnel, this information provides a broad basis for the buying and selling of products made from textiles.

TEXTILE CARE FACTORS

Textile care involves the removal of soil, drying of the textile after laundering, and if required, pressing. Removal of soil is achieved by two basic methods: laundering or dry-cleaning. For overall, proper textile care, many factors must be considered:

1. Fiber content—various fibers, such as silk and mohair, require special care and cannot be treated as ordinary laundry. Blends, too, may need special attention, depending on the combination of fibers used.

2. Yarn structure—complex yarns may require hand washing and air drying on a flat surface to maintain the yarns properly.

3. Fabric construction—simple constructions, such as a plain weave, generally require different care from more intricate constructions, such as lace or pile.

4. Dye type and dyeing process—colorfastness as well as the performance of the dye may be questionable if it is exposed to bleach, too-hot water, or the machine-drying process.

5. Printing—the printing process, or the dyes utilized, may affect care procedures.

6. Finishes—the type of finish used may affect care requirements; the finish may require dry-cleaning rather than laundering.

7. Design and construction—unusual designs may be supported by special interfacings or construction details that may not be apparent, but that require special handling. Garments of intricate construction (e.g., lots of pleating, tucks) require more careful attention than items of simple construction.

8. Decorative or functional trims—these may include buttons, zippers, braid, piping, etc. When laundered or dry-cleaned, these trims may be undesirably altered, resulting in discoloration, shrinkage, fraying, or separation from the garment or product.

9. Extent and type of soil—if possible, textiles should be cleaned before soil accumulates; knowledge of the type of soil is also very important in removing it satisfactorily.

10. Equipment and products used—these include the types of washing and drying machines used, the dry-cleaning process, the temperature or character of the water or dry-cleaning solvents, and the kinds of detergent, bleach, or softener.

It is evident that the care of textiles can be a complicated endeavor. Fortunately, care labeling must be attached to garments; the law governing care labeling was passed in 1972 (see Chapter 1). Generally, if the care labels are followed precisely, successful maintenance is assured. Also, most products are manufactured today with ease-of-care as a priority factor, since customers have demand-

Figure 8.1

Proper textile care should take into account a variety of factors, including fiber content and yarn structure. Pleating must always be considered, as must the dye content and fabric sheerness.
Left: Courtesy of E.I. duPont de Nemours & Co., Inc.
Right: Courtesy of American Enka Company.

ed this of the industry. Some customers insist upon textile items that can be completely cared for the home; they avoid purchases of items that need to be dry-cleaned. Whatever the method, care of textile products must be approached with some caution to insure serviceability and long-term satisfaction.

Table 8.1 provides a list of textile care labels and the meaning of each.

HOME LAUNDERING

Laundering involves wetting the fabric and adding detergent or soap to aid in soil removal. Today, home laundering usually means machine washing, especially since washing machines can be most satisfactory in washing everything from delicate hosiery to denim or corduroy workclothes. Yet, there are times when hand washing is best.

Hand washing may be preferred for economic reasons—for example, it would be energy-wasteful to run a washing machine for a few items. Also, hand washing may be required for items such as as a silk shirt or a knitted wool sweater on which the care label unequivocally states: HAND WASH ONLY. Hand washing is the safest method when the colorfastness of the product is in question.

Before the procedures for home laundering are discussed, available products to aid in laundering must be considered.

TABLE 8.1 CONSUMER CARE GUIDE FOR APPAREL

	WHEN LABEL READS:	IT MEANS:
MACHINE WASHABLE	Machine wash	Wash, bleach, dry and press by any customary method including commercial laundering and dry cleaning
	Home launder only	Same as above but do not use commercial laundering
	No chlorine bleach	Do not use chlorine bleach. Oxygen bleaches may be used.
	No bleach	Do not use any type of bleach.
	Cold wash; Cold rinse	Use cold water from tap or cold washing machine setting
	Warm wash; Warm rinse	Use warm water or warm washing machine setting
	Hot wash	Use hot water or hot washing machine setting
	No spin	Remove wash load before final machine spin cycle
	Delicate cycle; Gentle cycle	Use appropriate machine setting; otherwise wash by hand
	Durable press cycle; Permanent press cycle	Use appropriate machine setting; otherwise use warm wash, cold rinse, and short spin cycle
	Wash separately	Wash alone or with like colors.
NONMACHINE WASHING	Hand wash	Launder only by hand in luke warm (hand comfortable) water. May be bleached. May be dry cleaned.
	Hand wash only	Same as above, but do not dry clean.
	Hand wash separately	Hand wash alone or with like colors.
	No bleach	Do not use bleach.
	Damp wipe	Surface clean with damp cloth or sponge.
HOME DRYING	Tumble dry	Dry in tumble dryer at specified setting—high, medium, low or no heat.
	Tumble dry; Remove promptly	Same as above, but in absense of cool-down cycle remove at once when tumbling stops.
	Drip dry	Hang wet and allow to dry with hand shaping only
	Line dry	Hang damp and allow to dry
	No wring; No twist	Hang dry, drip dry, or dry flat only. Handle to prevent wrinkles and distortion.
	Dry flat	Lay garment on flat surface.
	Block to dry	Maintain original size and shape while drying.
IRONING OR PRESSING	Cool iron	Set iron at lowest setting.
	Warm iron	Set iron at medium setting.
	Hot iron	Set iron at hot setting.
	Do not iron	Do not iron or press with heat.
	Steam iron	Iron or press with steam.
	Iron damp	Dampen garment before ironing.
MISC.	Dry clean only	Garment should be dry cleaned only, including self-service
	Professionally dry clean only	Do not use self-service dry cleaning
	No dry clean	Use recommended care instructions. No dry cleaning materials to be used.

This care guide was produced by the Consumer Affairs Committee, American Apparel Manufacturers Association, and is based on the Voluntary Guide of the Textile Industry Advisory Committee for Consumer Interests. *The American Apparel Manufacturers Association, Inc.*

Laundry Products

Products that are probably in every home for the purpose of textile care include the following: pretreatments, soaps and detergents, bleaches, fabric softeners, starch, and finishing products. Just as it is very important to follow the care labels in textile items, it is just as important to follow product directions to assure success.

Pretreatments

Stained or very soiled items may need special treatments before they are actually washed with a soap or detergent. Soiled cuffs or collars or isolated stains may be treated with a pretreatment such as Spray 'n Wash or Clorox Pre-Wash. Heavily soiled workclothes or playclothes require a presoak. Enzyme presoak products such as Biz or Axion are especially effective in removing many kinds of stains and soils, in maintaining whites, and in keeping colors true.

Soaps and Detergents

Soap.   This is oldest cleaning agent known. It is a combination of soda and fat. Laundry soaps such as Ivory Snow are often recommended for delicate items. The problem with soap is that, when used in hard water, it reacts with the minerals present to create an insoluble, somewhat sticky film which adheres to textiles, often streaking them with a whitish film or making them dull and dingy. To avoid this problem, water may be conditioned or softened. Water-softening systems may be installed in homes in hard-water locations, or water softeners may be added directly to the water.

Detergents.   These are organic chemicals and are technically "synthetic" detergents. They were originally developed in the 1930s because of the previously described problem with the use of soap in hard water. Today a great variety of detergents is on the market, including light-duty detergents for hand washing and regular or heavy-duty ones for general laundry requirements.

Special formula detergents may also include bleach, softeners, and deodorizers to eliminate additional steps in the laundry process.

Bleaches

Two kinds of bleaches are used in home care of textiles:

1. Chlorine bleach—generally in liquid form, this product can be used to brighten whites and is safe for most fibers, except wool, mohair, silk, and spandex. These fibers can be damaged by the chlorine in the bleach, which oxidizes stains and color. Clorox and Purex are examples of chlorine bleaches.

2. Oxygen bleach—not as strong or effective as the chlorine type, this product works well for light bleaching requirements and is safe with all washables. Snowy and Clorox-2 are examples of oxygen bleaches.

Fabric Softeners

Fabric softeners that actually serve to lubricate fibers are used for several reasons. They add a soft, fluffy quality to fabrics. They also aid in preventing fabric wrinkling and static electricity. The use of softeners can actually decrease the necessity for ironing. They can, however, collect on fabrics and make them less absorbent in time; if absorbency is essential, as in towels, softeners should not be used in every wash. Many brands of softeners are available, usually in liquid form for the washer or sheet form for the dryer. Downy is a liquid form and Bounce is a sheet form.

Starch

Starch is used to add a fresh, crisp look. Since it smoooths the surface of fabrics and adds a coating, starch helps keep garments clean because the soil adheres to the starch and is easily removed with it in washing. Starch is usually sold in liquid or spray form. The aerosol spray types, such as Easy-On and Niagara, have been popular since they are quick, easy to use, and may be applied exactly where needed on the fabric.

Finishes

Spray-on fabric finishes are available that are not actually starch, but sizing. These finishes add body to the fabric and a professionally finished appearance. Such a product is Magic Sizing.

Another finishing type product is designed to protect and provide repellency for soil and water. An example is Scotchgard fabric protector.

Hand Washing

Hand washing may be completed as follows:

1. Check care labels for washability.
2. Hand washing is best on items that are not deeply soiled or have been worn just once.
3. Prior to washing, any mending of seams or buttons should be completed to avoid further damage in the wash process.
4. Remove ornamental attachments or pins securing bows, etc.
5. Select a soap meant for hand washing, such as Ivory Flakes or Woolite, and follow manufacturer's directions. Using too much soap may actually reduce cleansing action because a film is more likely to build up on the fabric.
6. Use warm water (100 – 110 degrees) into which soap has been dissolved before immersing items.
7. Do not rub, but squeeze the item to work the cleansing action.
8. Rinse in at least two waters; more if suds are still apparent or if water is not clear.

9. To absorb excess water, roll item in a thick towel; leave for just a minute.

10. Following care labeling, either hang to dry or shape to original dimensions on a flat surface that has been covered with a towel.

11. When dry, press as needed.

Machine Washing and Drying

The introduction into the marketplace of the automatic washing machine in the 1930s and the dryer in the 1950s has greatly eased the general care of textiles in the home. Selection of the proper washing machine for individual or family needs is absolutely essential for successful home care of textiles. Factors to consider in the selection of a washing machine are as follows:

1. Capacity—how large a load can be washed and can loads of varying sizes (small to large) be selected?

2. Cycles—are there different ones to handle delicate, permanent-press, or regular wash requirements?

3. Time of cycle—does it vary from several minutes for delicate items to ten minutes for regular, soiled washloads?

4. Temperature selection—this is energy saving as well as necessary for various types of wash. Can cold, warm, or hot water be selected for the wash and rinse cycles?

Selection of the automatic dryer, too, should be made with specific requirements in mind:

1. Capacity

2. Temperature selection

3. Cycle-length selection

For maximum performance levels and satisfaction, both the automatic washer and dryer should be kept clean, free of lint, and in top running condition.

Machine-Washing Procedures

The following are general procedures to follow when machine washing (see Figure 8.2):

1. Sort by color—whites and light colors should be separated from darks; if a garment is suspected of not being colorfast, it should be washed separately.

2. Sort by soil—very heavily soiled clothes should be washed separately from lightly or moderately soiled items.

3. Sort by size—it is best to wash delicates separately from heavy items which might snag or damage the delicates.

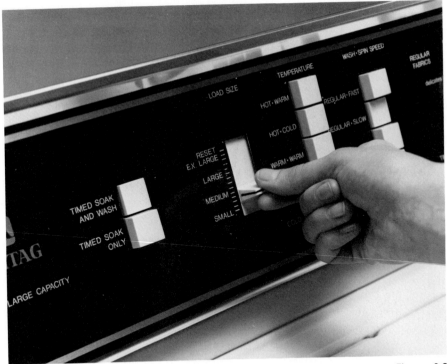

Figure 8.2

Proper machine washing involves several basic procedures.
Courtesy of The Maytag Company.

4. Sort by texture—highly napped or textured items (heavy corduroy or chenille) are best washed separately since they tend to collect or shed lint.

5. Prepare clothing—empty pockets, mend items, and sew on buttons, if necessary. Remove ornamental pins or buckles. Close zippers and fasteners to help prevent snagging.

6. Pretreat—remove stains, if any (see section on Spot and Stain Removal, page 163); presoak if necessary.

7. Wash in machine as directed by manufacturer; do not overload the machine.

8. After cycle completion, remove clothing immediately for best results; hang dry or flat dry items that cannot be automatically dried.

Automatic Drying Procedures

Although many individuals can still appreciate clothing dried in the fresh air outdoors, the popularity of automatic dryers has increased since they were first introduced into the marketplace. It is easy to understand why. In minutes, many clothes can be dried and ready for storage or to be worn once again. Yet the dryer, when not used correctly, can cause problems and damage to textile products.

To assure successful dryer use, the following guidelines should be implemented:

1. Follow care labeling—dry only those items that may be automatically dried according to their care labeling.

2. Do not overload the dryer—more even drying and less wrinkling is possible.

3. Do not overdry—leave items in the dryer just long enough to dry; remove them promptly. This discourages wrinkling and shrinkage and prevents buildup of static electricity.

4. Do not allow items to sit in the dryer after the cycle has ended—this will cause undesired wrinkling and setting of the wrinkles that have formed.

5. Be cautious with stained items—if items have been pretreated for stains and then washed, check that the stains have been removed before putting through the drying cycle. If stains are still apparent, drying will tend to set them further and they may never be removed from the fabric.

If these drying procedures are followed, most textile items will emerge from the dryer fresh-looking and wrinkle-free. In most cases ironing will not be necessary, or minimal touch-up ironing will be sufficient to achieve the best appearance possible.

Ironing

Although ironing is not the long, arduous task it once was when there were no easy-care fabrics on the market, it is necessary to iron some items. It is essential, of course, to invest in a good, dependable iron with features that will make the task easier. Among these, select irons with steam settings, self-cleaning systems, and Teflon-coated soleplates for easy gliding on fabrics. Most irons have easy-to-follow heat settings for the various fibers. Once the iron selection is made, the following guidelines should be followed:

1. Read thoroughly the instruction booklets packed with the iron—this is the best insurance for satisfaction with the iron.

2. If many items are to be ironed, begin with those requiring low heat, increasing heat as required for specific items.

3. For blends, choose the lowest heat setting. For instance, if a cotton/polyester blend is to be ironed, set the iron for polyester ironing.

4. Test the iron heat on a seam first; heat setting may be adjusted if necessary.

5. If fabric shows a shine when tested on the seam, iron on the wrong side or use a press cloth for protection. Caution should be exercised with wool, silk, linen, and rayon.

6. Care should be taken with textured, embossed, or raised fabric designs since ironing may permanently flatten the effect.

7. Do not iron soil or spots; ironing will set them.

Following the procedures just outlined for home washing, drying, and ironing, the self-service laundromat may be used for textile care. Another option is to send laundry to a commercial laundry establishment.

Commercial Laundering

The commercial laundry generally operates on the same principles used for home care. Although each establishment may operate differently, they will usually follow those broad guidelines:

1. Sorting and classification—this is based on color, fiber, and amount of soil.

2. Washing—soft water is used in commercial laundries. The other products used (soap, detergent, bleach, etc.) are based on the standards established by each company and analysis of the items to be washed.

3. Special care—items such as woolens and silks receive special handling for best results. Washable woolens and silks are processed in machines with lots of suds at a low speed and with a gently rolling movement.

4. Pressing and finishing—these services are performed, usually based on customer request. Various equipment is especially designed to press flat pieces, shirts, socks, etc.

5. Items are sorted, packaged, and ready for delivery back to customers.

PROFESSIONAL DRY-CLEANING

Although the dry-cleaning process is costly and time-consuming, it is certainly worth it to preserve the investment made in fine clothing. This is something retail personnel can emphasize to the customer. It is believed that the first dry-cleaning firm opened in Paris in the 1840s. The dry-cleaning process gets its name from the quickly drying solvents used in the cleaning process. However, these solvents will not remove water-soluble stains, which must be treated separately with water; this is called *wet cleaning*. Wet cleaning is the process of removing soil with water after the dry-cleaning process; therefore, wet cleaning is not the same as washing.

For thorough satisfaction, take the time to select a dry cleaner that is reputable and, preferably, one whose work has been recommended. A dry cleaner with high standards will be attentive to customer needs and requests, will be attentive to the items to be cleaned, and will likely perform the extras (mending, finishing, and pressing properly) that will result in garments that look almost better when they leave the establishment than when they were first purchased.

For satisfactory dry-cleaning, it is helpful to remember the following:

1. Dry-clean items regularly rather than waiting until they are very soiled and harder to clean.

2. Be able to identify spots and stains to aid the dry cleaner in removing them efficiently.

3. Do not store soiled garments during seasons they will not be worn. Insects or moths may be attracted to the stain or the stain may oxidize and discolor, thus becoming far more difficult to remove.

4. Before a trip to the dry cleaner, empty all pockets in a garment and remove decorative items, such as pins, leather belts, and ornate buckles, that cannot be dry-cleaned.

Self-Service Dry-Cleaning

Coin-operated dry-cleaning machines, first introduced in the 1960s, have been popular for self-service cleaning. These machines are best for items not requiring special pressing and finishing, such as sweaters, scarves, bedspreads, and draperies. It is advisable to leave fine tailored dresses, blazers, suits, and sportswear to the professional dry cleaners. For satisfactory results, the same principles outlined for home washing may be applied here.

SPOT AND STAIN REMOVAL

Fabric stains are caused by water-borne, oil-borne, or dry substances. Removing spots and stains successfully depends on a number of factors (see Figure 8.3).

1. Give immediate attention to the spot or stain.

2. Identify the spot or stain.

3. Identify the fiber on which the spot or stain appears.

4. Never use hot water as the first step in dealing with a stain. This will set the stain and make it difficult to remove.

5. On a nongreasy stain, a safe first step is to sponge with cold water.

6. On a greasy stain, a safe first step is to apply a solvent sparingly.

7. Do not press stains or soiled garments. The heat will set the stains and the pressure exerted on the fabric will drive the soil even deeper into the fibers.

8. Follow directions explicitly if any commercial products are used.

9. Work in a well-ventilated area since flammable products may be used in stain removal.

10. Work on protected surfaces. Absorbent toweling will protect surfaces and will often act as a blotter, drawing particles of the stain to it.

11. Work from the underside rather than the face of the stain since pushing the stain through the fabric may worsen it. Place the stain face down in the absorbent toweling.

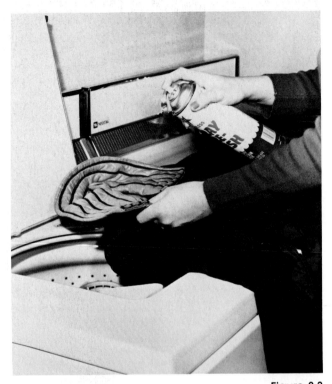

Figure 8.3
Stains can be successfully removed at home if the proper steps are taken.
Courtesy of The Maytag Company.

The following is a list of stains commonly encountered, including treatment for removal from washable fabrics. For fabrics that are labeled "Dry-Clean Only," it is best to refer a stain to the professional dry cleaner.

1. Alcoholic beverages — sponge in cold water or soak in cold water for at least thirty minutes. Wash in warm sudsy water. If stain remains, soak fifteen minutes in one quart of water mixed with one tablespoon chlorine bleach. Launder.

2. Blood — soak in cold water containing an enzyme presoak product. Launder.

3. Candle wax — rub with ice cube to harden wax. Carefully scrape wax away with a dull-blade knife. Place the fabric between layers of absorbent toweling and press with a warm iron to allow toweling to absorb stain. Sponge with cleaning fluid. Launder, using bleach appropriate for the fabric.

4. Carbon paper — dampen stain with cold water and rub in detergent. If stain persists, apply a few drops of ammonia and follow with additional detergent. Launder.

5. Catsup—scrape off excess with a dull-blade knife. Soak in cold water thirty minutes. Apply some detergent. Launder in hot water.

6. Chewing gum/adhesive tape—rub with ice cube to harden. Scrape off gum or tape with a dull-blade knife. If stain persists, sponge sparingly with cleaning fluid. Rinse and launder.

7. Chocolate and cocoa—soak in warm water with an enzyme presoak. Rinse and dry. If greasy stain remains, soak with cleaning fluid. Launder in hot water, using bleach if it is safe for the fabric.

8. Coffee and tea—follow directions for the removal of chocolate and cocoa stains.

9. Cosmetics such as eyeshadow, lipstick, liquid makeup—dampen stain and rub with bar soap or detergent. Rinse and launder.

10. Crayon—dampen stain and rub with soap such as Ivory Snow. Launder in hot water, using bleach if it is safe for the fabric.

11. Deodorants and antiperspirants—dampen stain and rub in detergent. Launder in hottest water safe for fabric. Some antiperspirants may alter the color of certain dyes; sponging with ammonia may restore color. Rinse thoroughly and launder.

12. Egg, meat juice, and gravy—if the stain is dry, scrape off as much as possible with a dull-blade knife. Soak in cold water. Rub detergent into wet area. Launder in hottest water safe for fabric.

13. Fruit and berry—soak in cold water with enzyme presoak. Launder in hot water.

14. Grass—soak with enzyme presoak. Launder. If stain remains, use chlorine bleach if safe for fabric. Launder.

15. Grease and oil (car grease or oil; butter, margarine, shortening, or cooking oil; salad dressing)—place stain face down on absorbent toweling. Sponge sparingly with dry-cleaning solvent using clean white cloth. Dampen stain with water and rub with detergent. Rinse and launder.

16. Ink and ballpoint—place absorbent toweling under stain. Apply dry-cleaning solvent. If stain persists, soak in warm water and detergent. Launder.

17. Milk, cream, and ice cream—soak in warm water with enzyme presoak product. Launder.

18. Nail polish—test nail polish remover on hidden piece of fabric, and use on stain if it is safe for the fabric. Do not use nail polish remover (acetone) on acetate, triacetate, or modacrylic since it will damage these fabrics; instead, use amyl acetate (banana oil).

19. Paint and varnish—treat immediately or stain may become permanent. Sponge with solvent recommended as thinner for product; if not available, use turpentine. While still wet, work detergent into stain and soak in hot water. Launder. Repeat process if necessary.

20. Perfume and cologne—launder immediately in detergent and warm water. Use safe bleach for fabric if stain persists. Do not allow stains to age as further discoloration may occur.

21. Perspiration—rub detergent into damp stain. Launder in hottest water safe for fabric.

22. Rust—use commercial rust remover. Launder. A rust stain may be impossible to remove.

23. Scorch—soak in warm water and enzyme presoak product. Launder in hot water, using bleach that is safe for the fabric. Severe scorching damages fabric permanently and cannot be removed.

24. Shoe polish (wax)—scrape off as much as possible with dull-blade knife. Sponge with warm water and detergent. Launder in hot water.

25. Tar and asphalt—treat immediately for best results. Sponge with trichloroethane (fireproof energine) without rubbing. Rinse and launder.

26. Urine—soak in cold water and enzyme presoak product. Launder, using chlorine or oxygen bleach.

27. Wine and soft drinks—soak in enzyme presoak. Launder, using the hottest water safe for the fabric.

KEY TERMS

1.	Bleach	6.	Pretreatment
2.	Detergent	7.	Soap
3.	Dry-cleaning	8.	Softeners
4.	Finishes	9.	Starch
5.	Laundering	10.	Wet cleaning

STUDY QUESTIONS

1. List three dos and three don'ts for spot and stain removal. Explain each response.
2. List six categories of laundry products. Describe the purpose of each and provide at least one example of each type.
3. Discuss three things you can do to assure successful dry-cleaning.
4. What method of sorting would you employ to prepare items for laundering? Why?
5. List eight factors related to proper textile care in general.
6. What is the difference between dry-cleaning and wet cleaning?
7. List three reasons for hand washing.
8. Explain how you would prepare a work area for stain and spot removal.
9. Before placing textile items in the automatic dryer, why is it important to check that any stains have been eliminated?
10. You are about to purchase a washer and a dryer. What factors would you consider before making your final choices? Why?

STUDY ACTIVITIES

1. Visit a department store. In various clothing areas throughout the store (children's, men's, women's, etc.), select ten items and write down the information found on the care labels. Explain why you think the care label is appropriate or inappropriate for the garment in which you find it.

2. Collect swatches from six different washable fabrics. Stain each with common substances, such as makeup, coffee, perfume, nail polish, ink, and catsup. Try to remove the stains, following the procedures for spot and stain removal.

3. Cut two large fabric swatches (twelve inches square) of a washable blend (such as cotton/polyester) and a nonwashable fabric (such as wool, silk, rayon, or novelty). Machine wash and dry, following procedures outlined in the chapter. Evaluate the performance of each fabric type. If these fabrics were to be selected for garments, write the care label that should probably be attached to each.

CHAPTER **9**

Home Textiles

OBJECTIVES

After completing this chapter, you should be able to:

1. List three ways in which home textiles are decorative, and three ways in which they are functional.

2. Differentiate between rugs, carpets, and broadloom; soft and hard floor coverings; curtains and draperies; upholstery and slipcovers; bedspreads, comforters, and quilts.

3. List and define the major methods for constructing rugs and carpeting.

4. Identify and discuss the factors considered when buying soft floor coverings, upholstery fabrics, curtains and draperies, and household linens.

5. Identify typical market selections for each of the categories of home textiles: soft floor coverings, upholstery fabrics, curtains and draperies, and household linens.

6. Discuss general care requirements for the products in each of the home textile categories: soft floor coverings, upholstery fabrics, curtains and draperies, and household linens.

Imagine a home without textiles—without the rich colors, intriguing textures, and infinite decorating choices that give a home a unique character, a special quality. Consider, too, a home without the functional, practical qualities offered by textiles—thick, absorbent bath towels, handy dish towels, cozy comforters and blankets, chill-chasing carpeting, and sun-screening curtains. Textiles transform an architectural shell into a warm, expressive environment.

This chapter provides information for salespeople and buyers about major textile products for the home, including soft floor coverings, upholstery, curtains and draperies, and household linens (including bedclothes). Emphasis is placed on the factors that influence the buying of these products, on the selection available in the marketplace, and on the care requirements.

SOFT FLOOR COVERINGS

Soft floor coverings is the term commonly associated with textile coverings that are soft and pliable and made of fibers and yarns. Rugs, carpeting, and broadloom are soft floor coverings. Hard floor coverings is the second major category, made of nontextile materials such as vinyl, rubber, cork, ceramic, and stone. The focus in this chapter will be on the soft textile floor coverings.

Rugs and carpeting represent major household investments. They not only add beauty, visual interest, and coziness to an area, but they are also heat and sound insulators. Although most soft floor coverings are bought for living rooms, dining rooms, and bedrooms, advances in technology and design have brought to the marketplace wonderful choices of rugs and carpeting for other areas of the home as well—kitchens, bathrooms, patios, and poolsides. Who would have thought just a few years ago that carpeting would move outdoors!

The terms *rug* and *carpet* are often used synonymously, but technically they are not names for exactly the same type of floor covering. Another term, *broadloom,* is also used today. These terms are clarified in this section.

Rugs

A rug is a soft floor covering that has finished edges; fringe is often added as a decorative touch. Rugs usually cover a portion of the floor rather than the entire floor space. Rugs are not attached to the floor. They are cut in standard sizes, small to very large. The largest size rugs (12 × 12 feet, 12 × 15 feet, 12 × 18 feet, or 12 × 21 feet) are often called room-size rugs. Smaller rugs are referred to as area rugs, scatter rugs, or accent rugs, in sizes such as 5½ × 8½ feet, 4 × 6 feet, or 27 × 45 inches. Smaller rugs are easily moved about and used as accent or protective pieces, or they can be layered on other floor coverings for special effects. Rugs are often selected to enhance, rather than cover up, lovely hardwood floors. Rugs may be square, rectangular, round, oval, or free-form to complement any decor and fit any space.

Carpets

A carpet is a soft floor covering that is sold by the square yard and is shipped in rolls. Widths may vary; twelve feet and fifteen feet are popular carpet widths. Carpeting is usually purchased wall-to-wall to cover an entire floor area, but it can be cut to any specifications. Carpeting, when installed wall-to-wall, is secured to the floor, usually with special stripping that hooks the carpet into place; this is the tackless method of installation. Because of their ease of care and beauty, carpets are purchased by many families for every room in the house, including the living room, as illustrated in Figure 9.1.

It is also possible to purchase carpet squares (usually twelve inches square) with adhesive backing. These have appealed to the do-it-yourself decorator.

Broadloom

Broadloom is seamless carpeting available in a variety of widths, generally up to eighteen feet wide. It is usually sold for wall-to-wall carpeting, but may also be cut into rugs. The term *broadloom* refers specifically to its wide width and its construction on a wide loom.

Figure 9.1

Formal living room featuring broadloom in a mix of cut and looped yarns.
Courtesy of Karastan Rug Mills, a division of Fieldcrest Mills, Inc.

Buying and Selling Factors

The variety of soft floor coverings is so vast that the customer often is confused and unsure about making the correct choice. The factors, affecting appearance and quality, to consider are as follows:

1. Face fiber
2. Yarn construction
3. Pile height
4. Pile density
5. Construction of the backing

Fibers

Wool was once the dominant, best-selling fiber for soft floor coverings, but the man-made fibers are the best sellers today, accounting for at least 98 percent of the face fibers used in soft floor coverings (see Figure 9.2). One reason for this is the expense of wool compared to the man-made fibers. Another reason is the improved performance and variety of the man-made fibers now available. Face fibers, however, must be judged on other criteria as well, which generally include the following:

1. Durability—is the fiber easy to maintain? Does it hold up to soiling and traffic?
2. Soil resistance—does the fiber resist common soils and how does soil affect the original appearance?
3. Abrasion resistance—does the fiber hold up to the pressures of foot traffic, to furniture, or to people sitting on the covering? Do the fibers remain whole rather than breaking under pressure?

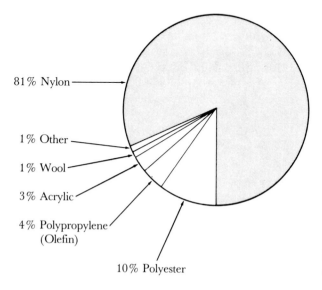

81% Nylon

1% Other

1% Wool

3% Acrylic

4% Polypropylene (Olefin)

10% Polyester

Figure 9.2
Face-yarn fibers used in soft floor coverings.

4. Resilience—does the fiber retain its original shape? After cleaning, does the fiber look fresh and restored to its original condition?

5. Care—how easy is it to keep the fiber clean and fresh-looking?

6. Aesthetic appeal—does the fiber dye and print well? Are the texture and hand desirable?

Each of the common floor-covering fibers on the market today will be discussed in the order of their popularity (see Figure 9.2).

Nylon. The nylon fiber dominates the marketplace, accounting for about 81 percent of face fibers used in soft floor coverings. Nylon is very durable, resilient, and abrasion resistent. It has good soil resistance and cleans easily. Nylon dyes well.

Polyester. Polyester is a good performer in most categories, but it may be just fair in soil resistance unless a special finish is applied. Oil-based stains may be difficult to remove. Polyester yarns dye well.

Olefin. The polypropylene fiber is highly stain- and abrasion-resistant. It resists moisture and mildew and cleans quite easily. Its resilience is often the weakest factor. It also has aesthetic limitations since the texture possibilities are limited, and it does not have a luxury hand. Olefin dominates the outdoor carpeting market.

Acrylic. Most closely resembling the wool fiber, acrylic has high aesthetic appeal. It is a good performer in all categories, and the yarns dye well. In recent years, the use of acrylic has declined because it is more expensive than nylon to produce.

Wool. Although wool accounts for only 1 percent of soft floor coverings, many people consider it the supreme carpet fiber. Wool has very good resilience, durability, and soil resistance. It cleans well and has good abrasion resistance. Wool dyes beautifully. It is, however, the most expensive carpet fiber, and the improved man-made fibers have gradually surpassed wool for soft floor coverings. Today, wool is more prevalent in the manufacture of rugs rather than carpeting.

Other Fibers. The dominant fibers in this small segment are cotton and rayon. Cotton dyes well and has been popular for small rugs that can be washed and dried at home. Cotton is not resilient and there is a tendency for the pile to flatten and mat. Rayon is an inexpensive fiber, and dyes and cleans well. Rayon is not resilient and has low abrasion resistance.

Construction of the Yarn

The yarn affects the aesthetics and durability of the carpet. The majority of carpet yarns are 2-ply and 3-ply, but carpets are manufactured with 1-ply and 4-ply yarns as well. Crimped, high twist, or bulky yarns (such as biocomponent acrylic) provide textural interest. Figure 9.3 illustrates three piles of varying twist, very low to high. Generally, high twist yarns are more durable. The weight and twist of the yarn determines the weight and density of the pile, which is directly related to the final quality. For aesthetic appeal, novelty colorations and tweeds may be constructed by combining various color yarns or space-dyed yarns.

Pile

Pile is the surface, or face, texture of the carpeting. In addition to pile weight, pile height and closeness affect quality. Pile height is the length of yarn from the backing up to the surface (see Figure 9.4). The closeness of the yarns is the density; density may be measured in terms of the number of tufts per square inch. Prized Oriental antique rugs can have close to 1,000 hand-knotted tufts per inch!

High density carpeting (see Figure 9.4) is more attractive and longer wearing, resists soil and stains better, and retains its original appearance much better than low density carpets, which crush and flatten with wear. High pile does not necessarily mean quality because, if the density is poor, the high pile will flatten and disfigure. Generally, the lower pile yarns that are densely packed are best for long wear and durability. In evaluating carpet density, the buyer should not be able to see or touch the carpet backing through the face yarns.

For a variety of effects, pile may be constructed in a number of ways (as illustrated in Figure 9.5). Level-loop is the most basic pile and provides a flat, even surface appearance. Cut pile is formed when all the tuft loops are cut evenly, giving an even surface texture. The multilevel loop pile is of varying heights and is the kind of pile construction used in sculptured carpeting. A variation of this is the cut and loop pile, in whch some loops are cut; this construction is also used for sculptured effects. Shag carpeting is created by constructing long yarn tufts.

These variations on the basic loop-pile construction result in a broad range of floor coverings that vary in surface texture and pattern, and can be coordinated with any decor. Figure 9.6 illustrates various types of carpeting.

Very Low Twist
Velvet Plush
Dense pile, level, smooth, rich surface

Medium Twist
Saxony Plush
Uneven surface with a textured look

High Twist
Frieze
Overall nubby effect; practical; very resilient

Figure 9.3
Yarn twist provides textural interest in carpets.

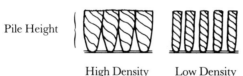

Pile Height

High Density   Low Density

Figure 9.4
Pile height and density affect the quality and durability of carpets.

Figure 9.5
Pile variations create carpeting suitable for any area of the house.
Courtesy of Karastan Rug Mills, a division of Fieldcrest Mills, Inc.

Backing

Although not as apparent as the yarn and pile characteristics, the backing warrants attention since it is the foundation of the carpeting and supports the pile. The primary backing is usually woven of jute or polypropylene (olefin). The yarns of the carpet are inserted into this base fabric. To secure the yarns, the backing is coated with some sort of adhesive, such as latex. For added support, stability, and body, a secondary backing may be laminated to the first (see Figure 9.7 for an illustration of this construction).

Figure 9.6
Carpet textures can be coordinated with various decors.
Courtesy of Karastan Rug Mills, a division of Fieldcrest Mills, Inc.

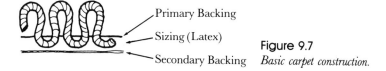

Primary Backing

Sizing (Latex)

Secondary Backing

Figure 9.7
Basic carpet construction.

Carpet and Rug Construction

Machine-made carpets and rugs may be categorized into four types:

1. Tufted
2. Woven
3. Nonwoven (needlepunched and flocked)
4. Knitted

Tufted

This method accounts for more than 95 percent of the carpet manufactured today. Yarn is inserted into a backing material, in loop form, by a machine with hundreds of needles working simultaneously. The tufted, looped pile is seen in Figure 9.7. Tufted carpeting can be made quickly, efficiently, and relatively inexpensively.

Woven

Woven carpets are made of the same principle as woven fabrics, with interlacing vertical and horizontal yarns. Four kinds of woven carpets are Wilton, Axminster, velvet, and chenille. These types of woven carpets differ in the technical manufacturing construction process and may vary in quality and asethetic appeal. Woven rugs and carpets are more expensive than tufted ones because they take longer to manufacture.

Nonwoven

This construction includes rugs and carpets that are needlepunched and flocked.

Needlepunched. This method is primarily used for indoor/outdoor carpeting made of olefin. This carpeting is nonwoven and has a flat surface. It is made by laying fibers on a base cloth and, through the use of barbed needles, entangling the fibers, and forcing them partially through the base where they remain secured.

Flocked. This construction requires a backing fabric coated with an adhesive to which electrostatically charged fibers are drawn in a prearranged pattern. The resulting floor covering looks similar to flocked wallpaper.

Knitted

In this process, three sets of needles knit together the backing, stitching, and pile yarns. Knitting machines can construct a pile yarn that is cut, uncut, or of varying heights. For additional body and support, latex is often utilized to coat the back of the construction. This is a simple and inexpensive construction.

Carpet and Rug Care

When a consumer purchases soft floor coverings, or when a retailer sells them, each should give special attention to the care requirements that should be followed throughout the life of the carpet. For general care procedures, most manufacturers recommend the following to insure the product's long life and satisfactory performance:

1. Vacuum frequently—doing this once or twice a week will not only remove fiber-damaging soil, but will restore and freshen the pile; vacuuming is actually good for the carpeting.
2. Use mats and runners in heavy-wear areas for protection and longer wear.

3. Rotate rugs to avoid wear in the same spots over a long period of time.

4. Remove stains and spills immediately.

5. Enlist professional-type cleaners on a regular basis.

UPHOLSTERY FABRICS

Upholstery and slipcovers are textile covers for stuffed or padded furniture, such as chairs and sofas. While upholstery is part of the piece itself, having been sewn or nailed to the frame, a slipcover is fitted over the original upholstered piece. A slipcover is easily removed for cleaning, redecorating, or seasonal changes. Fabric used for either upholstery or slipcovers is correctly called *upholstery fabric.*

Buying Factors

In buying or selling upholstery fabrics, particular qualities should be sought, including the following:

1. Abrasion resistance

2. Colorfastness to sunlight and cleaning

3. Resiliency

4. Soil resistance

5. Easy care

Some fibers and fabric constructions will meet these requirements far better than others.

Selection of Upholstery Fabrics

Fibers that have been most successful in upholstery have been cotton, linen, silk, wool, polyester, acetate, nylon, rayon and, in recent years, olefin. Fibers such as silk and wool are expensive and not as widely used today as are cotton, linen, or olefin.

Fabric that is best for upholstery should be tightly woven; a pile fabric, flat fabric, or knitted fabric may wear equally well if the construction is tight. Patterned fabrics do not show soil as readily as solid ones do but, patterned or plain, a soil-repellent finish is most desirable. Serviceable wovens for upholstery include brocade, chintz, corduroy, damask, denim, sateen, stain, rib weave, tapestry, velvet, and velveteen. A quilt-stitch outlining a floral pattern such as a chintz is a popular accent in upholstery fabric today, adding beauty, dimension, and strength to the covering. Such detailing is found on the upholstery pictured in Figure 9.8.

Upholstery Care

For successful care of upholstery, the care label provided with the furniture or fabric should be followed explicitly. If problems arise, the store in which the purchase was made should be consulted. For general upholstery care, the following are important:

Figure 9.8
This living room features fabric with quilt-stitch upholstery.
Courtesy of Ethan Allen Inc.

1. Guard against possible color fading—never expose upholstery fabric to direct sunlight.
2. Vacuum frequently to remove surface soil.
3. Treat stains immediately.
4. Professionally clean regularly.
5. If the fabric is wool and has not been mothproofed, mothproofing is recommended for maximum protection and long life.

CURTAINS AND DRAPERIES

Curtains and draperies are functional and decorative window treatments. Functionally, they provide privacy, insulation, light protection, and a sense of comfortable intimacy within the home. Decoratively, they help establish the interior mood of the room and add visual interest. Often, they are selected to match upholstery, as illustrated in Figures 9.8 and 9.9, thus creating a beautifully coordinated area.

Figure 9.9
This sitting room features matching draperies and upholstery.
Courtesy of Liberty of London Fabrics.

The terms *curtains* and *draperies* are often used interchangeably to describe window coverings; technically, they are not the same. They are defined as follows (refer to Figure 9.10):

- Curtains—usually sheer-type, or lightweight, textile window treatments that may be short (to sill or below apron) or long (to floor); curtains are informal in mood.

- Draperies—usually a heavier textile window treatment than is the curtain; draperies may be short (to the sill or below the apron) or long (floor length). Draperies are usually pinch-pleated at the top; they are formal in mood.

Curtains or draperies may be used separately or in combination, depending upon the functional and decorative requirements of the room. See Figure 9.9 where floor-length draperies and curtains are combined for a formal setting.

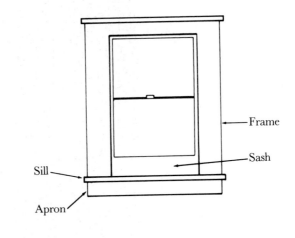

Figure 9.10
A basic window area.

Buying Factors

Although window treatments do not receive the same type of wear given to floor coverings and upholstery, the consumer should consider several factors when purchasing curtains or draperies. These factors are:

1. Colorfastness to sunlight.

2. Soil resistance.

3. Easy care.

Market Selection

A vast variety of curtains and draperies are available for immediate purchase or special order in many stores. The seasonal rotation of window treatments and the comparatively low cost of totally changing the mood of a room by replacing curtains or draperies have enhanced and broadened the market for these items.

Curtains.   Common curtain and drapery styles are illustrated in Figure 9.11. All of the styles illustrated may be adapted to the lighter weight fabrics from which curtains are traditionally made. Fabrics most popular for curtains include voile, gauze, organdy, lawn, batiste, dotted swiss, marquisette, muslin, ninon, and lightweight chintz. Fibers are often cotton, polyester, nylon, and rayon.

Draperies.   Usually establishing a more formal mood, draperies may be panel, tier, or cafe style (see Figure 9.11). The panel style is the most common. Priscilla styling is more appropriate for curtain treatments because this style is full, light, and airy in mood and is more appropriate for the lighter curtain fabrics. The val-

Figure 9.11
Common curtain and drapery styles.
Courtesy of Aero Draperies, Inc., a Division of
Minnesota Fabrics.

ence, a short fabric piece extending across the top, is appropriate for either draperies or curtains. A valence is used with the draperies pictured in Figure 9.9. The swag top is most often used with curtains, but may be adapted to drapery treatments. The more formal cornice is used with draperies; it is a sturdy, rigid frame covered with the drapery fabric or made of carved wood or another decorative material. Formal-type fabrics appropriate for draperies include antique satin, brocade, damask, velvet, velveteen, and flocked fabrics. Fibers include linen, cotton, acetate, rayon, polyester, and glass.

Size

In selecting curtains or draperies, several factors relating to size are important:

1. Window width—measure the width of the mounted fixture on which the fabric will be hung.

2. Window length—measure from the fixture to the desired length, whether to the sill, below the apron, or to the floor (see Figure 9.10).

3. Fullness—this is determined by the fabric weight, fullness, and effect desired. Width is usually between 1½ and 3 times the measured window width.

Care

As with the selection of the other types of textile products, ease of care is a top priority in buying curtains and draperies. To meet this demand, manufacturers have marketed many styles that can be machine washed and dried in the home. Generally, it is easier to care for curtains than for draperies, which are usually more elaborate, heavier fabrics that require special, professional attention. Also, draperies are often just too large or heavy to launder at home. The best care procedure is to save any instuctions accompanying purchases and to follow them precisely. If curtains or draperies are custom-made or special-ordered, questions about care and maintenance should be answered before the final decision is made.

HOUSEHOLD LINENS

The classification of what constitutes household linens may vary from store to store. Here, the category is used in a broad, general sense to include tablecloths, towels, and bedding (sheets, pillowcases, blankets, bedspreads, and comforters). The term *linens* is a carry-over from the past when linen was a primary fiber in the manufacture of many products in this classification.

This classification of household textiles has undergone a magnificent renaissance since the 1960s. At that time there was an explosion of color and design in household linens, and well-known national and international fashion designers turned their fashion flair to designing and merchandising household linens. In the past two decades, the importance of this area has continued to grow and flourish. Today the selections within this category are abundant.

Table Linens

Items within this category are tablecloths, napkins, and placemats.

Tablecloths and Napkins

Buying Factors.   In many homes, tablecloths have been replaced by placemats for informal, daily dining. Tablecloths, however, continue to be used for special occasions, holidays, and when guests come to dine. In selecting tablecloths, the following factors are important:

1.   Aesthetic appeal—they should set a beautiful table.
2.   Ease of care—the fabric used should be easy to wash and dry.
3.   Special finishes—permanent press and soil-release features are desired.

Market Selection.   Common fibers for tablecloths are cotton, polyester, nylon, rayon, and linen. Constructions such as damask, plain weaves, linen-looks, and lace are popular choices. Tablecloths are available in square, rectangular, oval, and round shapes in a variety of sizes. In selecting size, it is suggested that an allowance of six to twelve inches hang over the table edge, depending on the formality of the occasion and personal preference. Napkins are often purchased to match the tablecloth. Napkins are square-cut, available in sizes small (twelve inches) to very large (thirty inches).

Care.   Table linens are indeed easy care with their permanent press and soil-release finishes. Simple machine-washing and drying is usually all that is required. If stains do occur, they should be treated at once. Ironing is usually no more than a simple touch-up.

Placemats

Placemats are often chosen instead of tablecloths because:

1.   They are small and store easily.
2.   They are lovely accents on a beautiful wood tabletop.
3.   They are easy to care for.
4.   They are usually less expensive than tablecloths.

Placemats are available in a wide range of colors, patterns, and fabrications including straw or vinyl, which can easily be wiped clean after use. They are manufactured in many sizes and shapes. The general rule pertaining to size is that the mat should be large enough to provide a pleasing border to frame the place setting.

Towels

Included in the towel category are bath towels and kitchen towels. Bath towels include the very large bath sheet, bath towels, hand or face towels, guest or fingertip towels, and washcloths. Kitchen towels include dish towel for drying and dish cloths for washing. Table 9.1 provides a list of these items in typical dimensions that are available.

TABLE 9.1   TOWEL STYLES AND DIMENSIONS

	STYLE	DIMENSIONS (Inches)
BATH	Bath Sheet	36 × 68
	Bath Towel	22 × 42
	Hand Towel	16 × 26
	Fingertip Towel	11 × 18
	Washcloth	12 × 12
KITCHEN	Dish Towel	20 × 30
	Dish Cloth	12 × 12

Buying Factors

In selecting towels, the following factors are primary:

1. Absorbency—this feature is especially important for bath towels and dish towels.

2. Durability—in determining durability, it is necessary to consider the closeness of the weave, the tightness and uniformity of the selvages, stitching quality of the hems, and the fiber content.

3. Ease of care—although all towels are relatively easy to care for and can be machine washed and dried, it should be remembered that decorative edges or fancy trims may require special handling.

4. Aesthetics—customers look for a variety of colors and designs that will complement their home decor. Consumers also require that towels be colorfast and durable.

Market Selection

Traditionally, towels have been made of cotton. Recently, however, blends of cotton/polyester have been popular in the following blends: 86/14, 90/10, 84/16. These blends have been readily accepted since they are almost as absorbent and are as attractive as the all-cotton variety. The addition of the polyester fiber increases the strength and durability of the finished product and decreases shrinkage and drying time. The all-cotton and blend towels are available for both the bath and the kitchen.

Towel construction is generally a terry cloth, looped-pile construction or a flat-type weave. Velour or sheared velvety textures are achieved by cutting the loops on one side of towel. The flat-type weaves are usually for the kitchen and include plain and dobby weaves. Washcloths are made of terry to provide adequate friction when cleansing the skin.

Care
Towels are very easy, wash-and-dry care items. Precautions that may be used when washing towels include washing dark or bright colors separately and isolating for the laundering process those items that produce excess lint.

Bedclothes

The bedding classification includes sheets and pillowcases, blankets, bedspreads, and comforters. Each of these is discussed with reference to buying factors, market selection, and care.

Sheets and Pillowcases
Today's sheets and pillowcases are so varied, lovely, and visually appealing that they often form the focal point of the decor in the bedroom.

Buying Factors. In purchasing sheets and matching pillowcases, the most desired qualities are appeal of design and color, no-iron or permanent press finish for ease of care, colorfastness, price and brand considerations, and general durability. Durability can be judged by the following:

1. Closeness and uniformity of the weave, including the selvage
2. Small, even stitching (about twelve to fourteen per inch)
3. Nicely finished, even hems
4. Thread count (see discussion in Chapter 5) — a higher count usually indicates a better quality sheet; a 200-count sheet of percale is superior to a 130-count sheet of muslin.

Market Selection. Sheets and pillowcases are usually made of polyester/cotton blends (such as 50/50, 70/30), though all-cotton sheets and pillowcases are available. Pure linen bedclothes are rare and very expensive. Sheets and pillowcases are typically of muslin or percale; muslin has coarser yarns, a lower thread count, and is cheaper than percale. Various size sheets are available from crib to king size; see Table 9.2 for standard styles and dimensions. The fitted bottom sheet is used with a matching flat top sheet. Pillowcases are available in standard, queen, or king size to fit pillows appropriate for beds of varying sizes. Color and design choices are excellent, with many top designers represented in this particular market classification.

Care. Sheets and pillowcases are easy to care for, requiring only machine washing and drying and no ironing because of their special finishes. In order to get the longest wear possible from these items, do the following:

1. Have several sets of sheets and pillowcases to rotate use, rather than wearing out one set quickly.

TABLE 9.2   SHEET AND PILLOWCASE STYLES
              AND DIMENSIONS

	STYLE	DIMENSIONS (Inches)
SHEETS	Crib	42 × 72
	Twin Flat; Fitted	66 × 96; 39 × 75
	Full Flat; Fitted	81 × 96; 54 × 75
	Queen Flat; Fitted	90 × 102; 60 × 80
	King Flat; Fitted	108 × 102; 78 × 80
PILLOW-CASES	Standard	20 × 30
	Queen	20 × 24
	King	20 × 40

2. If possible, reverse the sheets and pillowcases so that the same areas are not subject to wear.

3. Mend sheets and pillowcases immediately, when necessary, to avoid further damage.

4. Use mattress covers and pads—they not only protect the mattress, but they help prevent early wear in the sheets and pillowcases.

Blankets

Compared to sheet sets, the purchase of blankets is a more long-term and costly investment.

Buying Factors.   When shopping for blankets, desired qualities include warmth without excess weight, color and design appeal, tactile appeal, and durability. The durability will depend on:

1. A balanced, even weave that is close and firm.

2. A nap that is uniformly dense and does not come loose when pulled.

3. Nicely finished edges and bindings that are securely and smoothly stitched in place with small, even stitches.

Market Selection.   Blankets are available in many fibers, including cotton, wool, acrylic, nylon, and polyester. Various blends are popular. Colors and patterns are rich and interesting and can harmonize with sheets, pillowcases, and bedspreads. Blankets are manufactured in many weights and thicknesses, from thin sheet-type blankets to the thick, heavy, all-wool variety. Most blankets are of a woven construction, but some are knitted, and others are nonwoven. Thermal-weave blankets provide lightweight coverings that can be used singly in the summer and with a second cover in winter for the best insulation. Electric blankets are an excellent choice for those who desire uniform heat and comfort that can be regulated—even while home thermostats are turned low for energy conservation.

Care.   Many blankets can be washed and dried at home, although the size and bulk of some are beyond the capacity of home equipment and must be professionally or commercially cleaned. The same care strategies outlined for sheets and pillowcases apply here. With proper care, a good blanket is indeed an investment and should provide years of warmth, service, and beauty.

Bedspreads, Comforters, and Quilts

Bedspreads, comforters, and quilts are the top, most visible layer of bedding. Comforters and quilts consist of a layer of batting or filling sandwiched and stitched between two outer layers in a standard, geometric-type quilting stitch. Quilts are usually thinner and lighter than comforters. Quilts and comforters may be used as informal throws on the bed, or they may be used as a type of bedspread in combination with a dust ruffle, as illustrated in Figure 9.12.

A bedspread is a covering that may be fitted or unfitted and, technically, extends to the floor around the bed. Bedspreads are referred to as throw-style when they are not fitted and seamed around the edges that fit the bed top. If they are

Figure 9.12
A bedroom featuring a comforter, dust ruffle, and pillow shams.
Photo courtesy of Ethan Allen, Inc.

seamed and fitted, they are called bedspreads. A bedspread and a throw-style bedspread are illustrated in Figure 9.13. Bedspreads may be quilted like comforters and quilts or they may also be flat-type single-layer spreads. Comforters and quilts are more informal in appearance and mood, while bedspreads give the room a more formal appearance.

Buying Factors.   In selecting bedspreads, comforters, and quilts, desired qualities include visual appeal, coordination with other bedding and decor, warmth, ease of care, and general durability. Durability will depend on:

1.   A close, even weave or construction.
2.   A batting, if used, that does not lump. Polyester fiberfill is better than cotton in this regard.
3.   Nicely finished edges and bindings, all evenly stitched.
4.   Quilting stitches that are close and even and are sturdy.
5.   Surface texture that will generally hold up better than flat surfaces.

Market Selection.   Bedspreads, comforters, and quilts are all available in a wide range of fibers such as cotton, rayon, polyester, acrylic, acetate, and nylon. Many types of fabrics are available such as broadcloth, chintz, chenille, taffeta, satin, brocade, and corduroy. However, very smooth fabrics, such as satin, should be avoided in comforters and quilts because they tend to slip from the bed and do not remain in place. The choices of colors and patterns are excellent and can certainly satisfy every decorating need. There are many weights and thicknesses to choose from, suitable for every season of the year and every climate.

Care.   Although some bedspreads, comforters, and quilts may be washed and dried in the home, their size and bulk often require professional or commercial maintenance. For long wear and serviceability, it is advisable to:

Figure 9.13
Bedspreads may be fitted or throw-style.
Photos courtesy of Ethan Allen, Inc.

1. Alternate spreads during the year so that one is not quickly worn out.
2. Reverse the spread on the bed, if possible, so that the same areas do not constantly receive stress.
3. Mend immediately, if required, so that further damage is inhibited.
4. Clean regularly so that soil does not wear the yarns and fibers.
5. Avoid the tendency to sit on the spread or to throw things on it.

KEY TERMS

1. Backing	9. Face fiber
2. Bedspread	10. Linens
3. Broadloom	11. Pile
4. Carpet	12. Quilt
5. Comforter	13. Rug
6. Curtains	14. Slipcover
7. Density	15. Upholstery
8. Draperies	

STUDY QUESTIONS

1. List five factors that are important in selecting upholstery fabrics; explain why each factor is significant.
2. List and explain three ways in which home textiles are functional and three ways in which they are decorative.
3. List and explain four methods used to construct soft floor coverings. Which is the most widely used today? Why?
4. List three differences between muslin and percale sheets.
5. List four reasons for the market acceptance of polyester/cotton blend towels to replace the all-cotton variety.
6. Explain the difference between the following home textile products: rugs and carpets; soft and hard floor coverings; curtains and draperies; upholstery and slipcovers; bedspreads and comforters.
7. List three reasons for the decline in the use of wool as a major fiber in soft floor coverings.
8. Explain why each of the following is important in judging the quality of a rug or carpet: fiber content; yarn twist; pile height and density; the backing construction.
9. List three styles appropriate for curtains and three styles appropriate for draperies; for each style, indicate the fiber/fabric selection you would recommend to a customer, based primarily on aesthetic appeal.
10. In selecting a comforter, list and explain six factors to be evaluated.

STUDY ACTIVITIES

1. Visit a store department or a specialty shop stocking floor coverings or upholstery fabric. In either classification, make ten to twelve selections that

vary in design and price. List all the information available with these items. How does your collected information relate to chapter information on buying factors and market selection?

2. Visit store departments or specialty shops selling household linens. Select those items, including table linens, towels, and bedding, you think a customer would like for her first apartment. The individual will be living alone for the first time. List all the items, including complete descriptions and prices. What factors were most important in making final selections?

3. Conduct an informal survey involving about ten individuals who have furnished their homes and have purchased carpeting within the last five years. Determine what factors were considered in buying the carpeting. Develop a prioritized list of the factors mentioned and discuss the implications of this list when chapter information is considered.

CHAPTER 10

Rubber

OBJECTIVES

After completing this chapter, you should be able to:

1. Describe the background and the process that latex goes through to become natural crude rubber for manufacturing into various products.

2. Explain the operations necessary in the manufacture of rubber from the raw to the finished products.

3. Explain why synthetic rubber has become the most used rubber in the United States.

4. Identify by their chemical names at least six kinds of important synthetic rubbers.

5. Describe the best methods of caring for rubber.

Rubber is one of a group of industrial materials, including fibers, glass, metals, plastics, and wood. The whole of modern technology depends on these industrial materials. About one-third of the rubber used is natural rubber, which comes from rubber trees in plantations located along the equator. The remaining two-thirds is man-made rubber derived from petroleum and other minerals from manufacturing plants located in industrialized countries. More than one-half of all the rubber produced—natural or synthetic—is used to make tires. The rest of the world's output goes toward the manufacture of a wide variety of industrial and consumer products. In many of its modern applications, rubber is used not alone but reinforced with textiles and plastics such as cotton, vinyl, acrylics, and other members of the thermoplastic and thermosetting families. By combining these materials with rubber, products can be produced that display many varied properties such as increased elasticity, flexibility, resistance to abrasion, increased chemical resistance, and increased resistance to weather.

HISTORY AND DEVELOPMENT

The South American Indians were the first to discover and make use of some of the unique characteristics of rubber. On his second voyage to the New World, in 1493 – 1496, Christopher Columbus saw Indians in Haiti play a game with elastic balls. He learned that the balls were made from a milky substance (natural latex) obtained from cutting the bark of a certain tree, and that this substance, when exposed to air, became dark and hardened into an elastic mass. In 1615 a Spaniard noted that the Indians brushed the milky substance on their cloaks and made crude footwear and bottles by coating earthen molds and letting them dry. These applications were of practical interest to Europeans because they lacked a continuous material that was airtight or waterproof until then.

The first serious descriptions of rubber production, the primitive native system of manufacture, and what could be done with the "elastic gum" were recorded in the eighteenth century. A member of a French geographical expedition sent to South America in 1735, C.M. de la Condamine, sent a sample from Quito to the Academie des Sciences in Paris, explaining that the Maina Indians called the condensed sap from the *Hevea* tree Caoutchouc (pronounced Koó chuck). Another Frenchman, C.F. Fresneau, searched for and eventually located rubber-bearing trees in French Guiana. He tapped them himself, used the sap to make a pair of shoes, and waterproofed an overcoat. His account was read by la Condamine to the Paris academy in 1751; in his report, Fresneau suggested how the material might be used to make such useful articles as tarpaulins, divers' suits, and waterbottles. The first accurate report of the botanical characteristics of the *Hevea* species was written in 1775.

The sap (natural latex) could not be sent to Europe in liquid form because it coagulated quickly after being tapped. The Indian methods of rubber production could not be used on the tough, dry gum. This problem caused the king of Portugal to send his boots to Brazil to be waterproofed.

In 1770 Joseph Priestley, the discoverer of oxygen, found that the solid gum material rubbed out pencil marks. He recommended it to English engineers and named it *rubber*. Two French chemists, P.J. Macquer and C. Herissant, discovered that the solvents ether and turpentine were both effective in making the coagulated gum liquid again after it reached Europe. Their experiments included using a rubber solution to waterproof cloth. By the end of the eighteenth century, the French professors Jacques Charles and F. Robert had utilized rubberized silk for their hydrogen balloons. This combination allowed for the increased containment of hydrogen inside the balloon due to the sealing effect of the rubber.

The first rubber factory was built in Paris in 1803 to produce elastic bands for use in garters and braces. All the early manufactured products were sensitive to temperature changes. In the cold they became brittle and in the heat, soft and sticky. In 1823 a Scotsman, Charles Macintosh, developed the double-textured raincoat that still bears his name. He sandwiched the sticky gum mixed with coal tar naphtha between two layers of close-woven cotton.

An English inventor, Thomas Hancock, became Macintosh's colleague and partner from 1820 to 1856. He invented some basic equipment for processing rubber, including a machine called a *masticator* that, instead of tearing the rubber to shreds, softened it and prepared it for compounding and mixing.

A complete solution to the problem of stabilizing rubber during hot and cold seasons came about in 1839 when an American inventor, Charles Goodyear, developed and patented a process of curing rubber called *vulcanization*. Vulcanization occurs when a mixture of rubber and sulphur goes through a heat treatment (or curing) process. The process of vulcanization made the modern rubber industry possible by permitting use of cured rubber in combination with machinery and in tires for bicycles, and later for automobiles. The vulcanization process remains basically the same today despite subsequent discoveries that have refined Goodyear's original techniques.

Others who helped to develop rubber as we know it today include Nathaniel Hayward, who showed Goodyear how to overcome the stickiness in rubber by dusting the surface with the chemical flowers of sulphur and placing it in the sun (solarization). Alexander Parkes invented the dipping process where rubber was vulcanized at room temperature using sulphur chloride. The first iron-roll, steam-heated mixer was invented by Edwin M. Chaffer. Nelson Goodyear, in 1851, patented the vulcanization process where large quantities of sulphur were used to form hard rubber (ebonite).

The pneumatic wheel was patented in 1845. The tire industry was founded by John B. Dunlop, a British veterinary surgeon. He patented and developed pneumatic tires for bicycles and tricycles in 1888. Several rubber companies began manufacturing solid rubber tires for horsedrawn carriages by 1900. As the demand for rubber increased, a worldwide shortage of rubber developed.

Until the end of the nineteenth century nearly all of the world's supplies of rubber came from the wild rubber trees tapped by Indian tribes along the Amazon River in Brazil. The British government in India conceived the idea of developing rubber plantations in Ceylon and the Malay Peninsula.

In 1866 the English adventurer, Sir Henry Wichham, visited Central America to survey the rubber scene. Later he was deputized to collect and deliver *Hevea brasilienses* (botanical name for the rubber tree) seeds to the director of the Kew Botanical Gardens, London. At least 70,000 seeds were smuggled out of Brazil in 1876. The first attempts at planting failed, but 2,600 seeds—less than 4 percent—sprouted. Thirty-eight cases of seedlings were sent to Ceylon before the year ended. These transplanted seedlings became the foundation of the plantations that were to thrive in Malaya and later in Indonesia.

It took two generations of growing mature trees to obtain enough seeds for planting on a commercial basis. From the planting of the seed until the trees were ready for tapping took seven years. By 1910 natural rubber was in such demand worldwide that the price had risen to $7.05 per kilogram. The thriving plantation system of producing rubber helped bring the price down to 4.5¢ per kilogram in 1928 and less than 7.7¢ per kilogram in 1932.

Modern production includes carefully selecting the seeds to avoid inbreeding; the selection of stronger young plants is desired. Plantations are scientifically laid out to follow natural contours of the land and to protect the trees from wind damage. The trees are inoculated against disease. The soil is fertilized by fixing atmospheric nitrogen. The young trees are grown in nurseries from handy rootstock. Standard horticultural techniques such as grafting, hand pollination, and vegetative propagation (cloning) are used to grow genetically uniform trees.

Rubber trees grow about ten degrees on either side of the equator in most soils. Annual rainfall must be about 100 inches, especially in the spring. Malaysia in Southeast Asia produces the majority of the natural rubber. Other countries that produce natural rubber include Brazil, Ecuador, India, Sri Lanka, Liberia, and Nigeria.

Rubber trees are ready for latex production when they are about six years old. At about ten years of age, they reach maximum output. The trees will continue to produce latex indefinitely, but the older trees (those about 30 years old) are usually replaced by younger ones. Due to effective management, research, and the use of chemical stimulants, the average yearly yield has increased from 300 pounds of rubber per acre in 1900 to 1,800 pounds per acre today. An average yield of somewhere between 3,000 to 5,000 pounds per acre annually is anticipated in the near future. About one ounce of latex is obtained per tree per tapping before the latex coagulates and stops flowing. New chemical stimulants, such as Ethrel, can be applied to the bark to help keep the latex flowing. The result has been to replace the small collection cup with a polyethylene plastic bag and to collect the latex every ten to fourteen days instead of daily.

The standard method of tapping a rubber tree for latex is to make diagonal incisions with a special knife to the depth of the bark (about one millimeter) up to halfway around the tree (see Figure 10.1). The incisions slant down from left to right at an angle of thirty degrees, starting at the highest point accessible to the tapper. Each subsequent cut is made immediately below the last one.

The milk-white fluid latex (Figure 10.2) is gathered from the trees, bulked in large containers, diluted with water, and sieved to remove foreign objects. The latex is run into troughs and treated with coagulants (acetic acid or formic acid) to allow the rubber to rise to the surface in white slabs. The slabs are cleaned by passing them through a succession of water baths and then horizontal rollers that remove most of the water and press the rubber into creped sheets. After further drying and processing, the sheets are baled for shipping. Natural latex can be shipped in liquid form by preserving it in ammonia, caustic soda, or formaldehyde to prevent bacterial action. In order to lower transportation expenses, latex is usually "creamed," or centrifuged, to raise the solids content from 30 percent to 60 percent.

Figure 10.1
A field worker tapping a rubber tree on a plantation in Liberia.
Courtesy of the Firestone Tire and Rubber Company.

Virgin Bark

Renewing Bark

Latex Channel

Tapping Cut

Spout

Cup Hanger

Latex Cup

Figure 10.2
Latex dripping from the spout into a cup.
Courtesy of the Firestone Tire and Rubber Company.

SYNTHETIC RUBBER

History and Development

As early as 1826, Michael Faraday determined that natural rubber was a hydro-carbon compound containing molecules of five atoms of carbon to every eight of hydrogen. Chemists tried to duplicate the natural product in the laboratory for over a hundred years. In 1860, an Englishman, Evanville Williams, distilled crude rubber from the right chemical formula and named it *isoprene*. In 1884, another Englishman, Sir William Tilden, prepared isoprene from turpentine. By 1887, Tilden, G. Bouchardat in France, and O. Wallach in Germany had all converted isoprene into an unsatisfactory rubberlike material. About 1900, several Russian scientists performed experiments with butadiene, a close relative of isoprene. Eventually, F. Hofman in Germany took out the world's first patent for synthetic rubber in 1909, after he was able to synthesize isoprene from certain mineral resources. In the meantime, a Russian chemist named I. Kondakov found that another hydrocarbon, dimethylbutadiene, could be converted into an elastic polymer (structured molecules) and was more easily obtainable than isoprene.

World War I stopped any further development of synthetic rubber in England. Germany was cut off from supplies of natural rubber and frantically sought a rubber substitute. The Germans, particularly Hofman, continued experimenting with dimethybutadiene and produced small quantities of "methyl rubbers" in two types: "W" for soft-rubber products, "H" for hard-rubber products. The Germans concentrated on the synthetic rubber, called *buna* (*bu* from butadiene, the main constituent; *Na*, the symbol for sodium, which was the catalyst). Tires made of buna developed flat sides when not in use, and the vehicles had to be jacked up. The total amount of methyl rubber produced from dimethylbutadiene during the war was about 2,500 tons.

Germany continued working on synthetic rubber in the 1920s and by 1929 two new types were developed. One was a copolymer of butadiene and styrene similar to the styrene-butadiene rubber (SBR) of today. The other was a copolymer of butadiene and acrylonitrile. Both were obtained as a latex (a liquid suspension of synthetic polymers) which could be coagulated to use in the dry rubber form or used in the liquid form. The development of synthetic rubber continued in Germany because of the need for the country to become self-sufficient and to meet the industrial demand for an oil-resistant rubber. Between 1934 and 1939, when World War II began, five styrene-butadiene rubber plants were built that were capable of producing 175,000 tons of synthetic rubber annually.

Russia's desire for self-sufficiency led to the development of a synthetic rubber industry that produced about 90,000 tons a year by 1939. The basic process was based on the polymerization of butadiene with a sodium catalyst — a process similar to that used by Germany.

The United States concentrated mainly on the production of oil-resistant rubbers such as polysulphide, chloroprene, and polychloropene early in the search for synthetic alternatives to natural rubber. In 1937, American chemists W.J. Sparks and R.M. Thomas developed butyl rubber. This led to the production of nitrile rubber in 1939.

Japan captured the major sources of natural rubber when it invaded Southeast Asia in 1942. The United States rubber industry was forced to undertake several crash programs to produce acceptable synthetics for multiple uses. Production went from 10,000 tons a year at the beginning of 1942 to more than 700,000 tons at the end of World War II. During this time, several new types of synthetics were developed.

Styrene butadiene rubber was further developed with much improved properties. It was called "cold rubber" because it polymerized, or allowed the combination of two smaller molecules (styrene and butadiene) to form a larger molecule (styrene butadiene rubber), at a temperature of about 4 to 5 degrees Celsius instead of 49 to 50 degrees Celsius. It was better than natural rubber in some ways and ceased to be a substitute. For example, tire treads made of it were better than those made from natural rubber. In the late 1940s the expansion of natural rubber could not keep up with the world demand, and synthetic rubbers filled the needs of industry.

Synthetic rubber produced in the United States has many advantages over natural rubber. Synthetic material is purer than natural rubber material and is adaptable to a wide range of products by changing the compounding ingredients. A disadvantage of synthetic rubber is that it has a fossil-fuel base and obtaining fossil fuel may vary due to political and economic crises in the country of origin.

Continued political unrest, the Korean War of 1951, the Suez Canal crisis in 1956, the Viet Nam War, and the pressing problems of dollar exchange led to the establishment of the synthetic rubber industry on a worldwide basis. New plants were built in Europe, Japan, Latin America, Africa, and Australia to serve the various need of the world's industry.

Types of Synthetic Rubber

Synthetic rubber is the name given to synthetic polymers with properties similar to those of natural rubber. There are many types of synthetic rubber—each with its own advantages and disadvantages, its own specific properties, and its own area of application. About twenty distinct chemical types are in commercial use today. Within each type there are usually many different grades distinguished by different methods of production, different molecular chain lengths, different relations of monomers in copolymers, different arrangements of the repeating units; from these differences emerge different properties and different applications. There is no single property in which higher performance cannot be obtained by using one or another of the synthetics. First choice would depend on what properties are essential for each particular application; the second choice, where more than one rubber can meet the requirements, would depend on price and convenience.

Isoprene Rubber (IR)

This rubber has the same chemical composition as natural rubber, but there are differences in their properties. The synthetic material is purer than natural rubber. IR is used mostly in tires. Other applications include footwear, sponge rubber, and sheeting. The dry rubber has advantages in injection molding, whereas the latex is used for foam rubber, adhesive, extruded thread, and dipped products.

Styrene-Butadiene Rubber (SBR)

This rubber accounts for about 60 percent of the synthetic rubber production in the world. It is produced in hundreds of different grades, a large proportion using a combination of oil and carbon black. This combination increases wear resistance and is superior to many other tire tread materials. Similar in properties to natural rubber, SBR has proved to be a good substitute in tires and similar products. It is less resilient than natural rubber. SBR is also used for heels and soles in footwear, flooring, conveyor belting. In latex form, SBR is used for adhesives, carpet backing, paper coating, and latex foam.

Polybutadiene Rubber (BR)

This rubber is produced in different forms. In general, all the forms have a higher resilience than natural rubber. Resistance to abrasion is outstanding, and the low temperature flexibility is excellent. BR can take oil extensions and heavy amounts of carbon black without serious loss in physical properties. A disadvantage is that tear strength is poor. Approximately 90 percent of BR is usually blended with other rubber for use in tires. The other 10 percent is used as an additive in rigid plastics—like polystyrene—to make them tougher and less brittle.

Chloroprene Rubber (CR)

This rubber offers considerably greater resistance to oils and solvents than natural rubber or SBR. It is also resistant to the destructive effects of sunlight, oxidation, and aging. Its heat, strength, and abrasion resistance are good. CR has valuable adhesive properties and is effectively flame-proof. These properties have created a demand for its use in a wide range of products other than tires. CR is used for seals, oil hoses, glazing strips, and roofing sheet in buildings. It is also used for lining and coating chemical products; waterproofing textiles for tents, tarpaulins, and life rafts; and manufacturing adhesives and paints.

Nitrile Rubber (NBR)

This rubber is more resistant to oil and heat than chloroprene rubber, but it is not very resistant to sunlight. NBR is used for many kinds of oil, gasoline, and solvent hose, for brake linings, and for industrial adhesives. Blends of nitrile rubber and the plastic polyvinyl chloride (PVC) produce an extremely tough oil- and abrasion-resistant material for heavy-duty cable covering and for the soles on industrial footwear. Other blends of NBR and certain plastics are used in paper making and coating; in manufacturing nonwoven fabrics, artificial leather, suedette, etc.; and in finishing and waterproofing real leather.

Butyl Rubber (IIR)

This rubber has a very low permeability to air and other gases. Its resilience is low, and it has very good resistance to sunlight, ozone, and aging, and relatively high temperature resistance. Its main use is in inner tubes and linings for tubeless tires. Other uses include steam hoses, roofing membranes, reservoir sheeting, and anticorrosion linings.

Ethylene-Propylene Rubbers (EPM and EPDM)

These rubbers have high resistance to ozone, sunlight, and all kinds of weathering and aging. Their use in tires has been limited mainly by processing difficulties; however, they have been used successfully in some tires through blending. Uses for EPDM include automobile components, acid hoses, roller coverings, reservoir linings, roofing sheets, and general building applications. There are important applications for EPM and EPDM in electric cable insulation.

Polysulphide Rubber (TM)

This rubber was introduced in 1931 as an oil-resistant rubber. It resists all kinds of oils and solvents. It is used for roller coverings, for hoses that handle paint and agricultural sprays, as a sealant for fuel tanks, and for high-rise and curtain-wall buildings.

Silicone Rubbers (SI)

These rubbers have many physical properties that are relatively poor at room temperatures; they retain their strength and elasticity over a much wider range of temperatures than organic rubbers. They have good electrical properties; their resistance to aging, ozone, and weathering is good; and their color consistency excellent. Common to most silicones is their valuable nonstick property. Important uses are in the aerospace industry, for conveyor belting in the food processing and confectionary industries, and in surgical applications.

Polyurethane Rubbers (Ue)

These rubbers have great strength and abrasion resistance as solid rubbers. They also have good resistance to oil and to all forms of oxidation. They are used for solid tires, roller coverings, fabric coatings, and synthetic leathers, and for the elastic thread called Spandex.

The main use of Ue is in foam. The flexible type of foam is used for upholstery, both in vehicles and furniture, and in foam-backed textiles. Foams that are semirigid are used for safety padding in motor vehicles. Rigid foams provide heat insulation in buildings and core material for sandwich construction.

Chlorosulphonated Polyethylene Rubber (CSM)

This rubber has a very high resistance to oxidation. It is used in linings for hoses to handle acids. It is also used as an elastic coating in outdoor and anticorrosive applications.

Acrylate Rubbers (ACM)

These rubbers have a good resistance to hot oils and aggressive lubricants. Dry rubber is used mostly in the vehicle industry for O-rings, oil seals, gaskets, etc. Other uses include textile coating, leather finishing, and paper making.

Fluororubbers (CFM)

These are among the most expensive rubbers on the market. Their main function is to provide oil seals and hose that will withstand hot lubricants and hydraulic fluids at temperatures of 200 degrees Celsius and beyond. Fluororubbers are mostly used by the aerospace industry.

Thermoplastic Rubbers (TR)

These rubbers are capable of melting when heated and solidifying when cooled, with their elastic properties unimpaired. This enables thermoplastic rubbers to be shaped by a simple molding process.

Ethylene-Vinyl Acetate Rubbers (EVAC)

This rubber is highly resistant to weather, oxygen, ozone, and heat. It is used primarily for insulating heat-resistant cables, cable coverings, oil seals, and waterproofing.

Table 10.1 compares the properties of natural rubbers to those of synthetic rubbers. Table 10.2 lists the various uses of natural and synthetic rubbers.

METHODS OF PROCESSING RUBBER

The processes of converting natural rubber (Figure 10.3) and synthetic rubber (Figure 10.4) into useful consumer or industrial goods are complicated and necessitate the use of massive equipment, many operations, and a large amount of power. Rubber, natural or synthetic, arrives at the factory in a hard and dry or liquid latex state. In general, four methods of processing must occur to make rubber products: (1) masticating the rubber compound, (2) mixing ingredients into the rubber, (3) shaping the mixture, and (4) vulcanizing.

Masticating

Before it can be mixed, hard natural or synthetic rubber has to be broken up (masticated) by a machine called a *plasticator*. This machine chews up the rubber and makes the material softer and more malleable. This process reduces the size of the large organic molecules in natural rubber, thus facilitating mixing. In general, synthetic rubber has shorter molecular structures that take little mastication. Mastication may be accomplished in several ways depending upon the condition or type of rubber.

TABLE 10.1 PROPERTIES OF NATURAL RUBBER (NR) AND SYNTHETIC RUBBERS

PROPERTIES	NR	IR	SBR	BR	CR	NBR	IIR	EPDM	EVAC	SI	Ue	CSM	ACM	CFM	TR
Tensile strength vulcanized without reinforcing fillers	1	2	5	6	3	5	4	5	5	6	2	5	6	5	3
Tensile strength vulcanized with reinforcing fillers	1	2	2	4	2	2	3	3	3	4	1	3	3	3	1
Elongation at break (maximum stretch at the breaking point) to achieve high elongation	1	1	2	3	2	2	2	3	3	4	2	3	3	3	1
Abrasion resistance with reinforcing fillers	4	4	3	1	3	2	4	3	2	5	1	3	4	4	5
Resistance to tear propogation	2	2	3	5	2	3	3	3	3	4	1	3	4	4	3
Shock elasticity optimal values	2	2	3	1	3	3	6	3	3	3	3	4	5	5	4
Flexibility at low temperature	2	2	3	2	3	3	2	2	4	1	4	5	6	5	2
Heat resistance	4	4	3	3	2	2	3	2	2	1	4	3	2	1	6
Oxidation resistance	4	4	3	2	2	3	2	1	1	1	1	2	2	1	5
Light resistance (resistance to ultra-violet radiation)	4	4	3	3	2	3	2	1	1	1	2	2	2	1	5
Weather and ozone resistance	4	4	4	3	2	3	2	1	1	1	2	2	2	1	5
Oil resistance	6	6	5	6	2	3	6	4	4	1	1	2	1	1	6
Resistance to gasoline	6	6	4	5	2	1	6	5	5	6	1	2	1	1	6
Resistance to acids and bases	3	3	3	3	2	4	2	1	3	5	5	2	5	1	2
Flame resistance	6	6	6	6	2	6	6	6	6	6	6	3	6	3	6
Electrical volume resistance	1	1	2	2	4	5	2	2	3	1	4	4	5	4	2
Permeability to gases	5	5	4	4	3	2	1	4	2	6	2	3	3	3	4
Compression set															
−40°C (−40°F)	3	3	3	3	5	3	5	4	6	3	5	6	4	6	4
+20°C (+68°F)	2	2	3	3	3	2	4	3	5	2	3	5	3	4	5
+100°C (+212°F)	6	6	5	5	4	3	2	2	1	1	5	6	5	3	6

High = 1; low = 6.

TABLE 10.2 APPLICATIONS OF NATURAL RUBBER (NR) AND SYNTHETIC RUBBERS

APPLICATIONS	NR	IR	SBR	BR	CR	NBR	IIR	EPDM	EVAC	SI	Ue	CSM	ACM	CFM	TR
Adhesives	1	1	1		1	2					1				
Air-rail-sea traffic	2	2	2		1	1				2	1	2			
Automobile components (except engine and tires)	1	2			1	1	2	1	1		1				
Automobile engines															
Automobile tires	1	1	1		1	1		2		1	1	1	1	1	1
Building industry	2	2	1	1	2		2	2		2	1	1			2
Clothing, leather, paper, textiles	1		1		1	1	2	1	2		1	1	1		
Construction engineering	1	1	1		1	1	2	2	1		1	1			
Electrical industry	2	2	1		1	2	1	1	1	1	1	1			
Food, dairy industry	1	2	1		2	1		2	2	1	2				
Footwear	1	1	1		1	1			1		1				
Leisure, recreation	1	1	1		1	1		2	1		2	1			
Machines, apparatus, equipment	1	1	1	2	1	1		1	1	1	1		1		
Pharmaceutical industry	1	1			1	1	1			1				1	
Transportation, belting	2	2	1	1	1	2	2	2		2					

Primary application = 1; secondary application = 2.

203

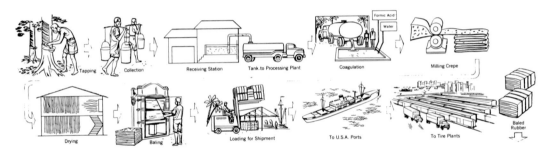

Figure 10.3
Production of natural rubber.
Courtesy of the Firestone Tire and Rubber Company.

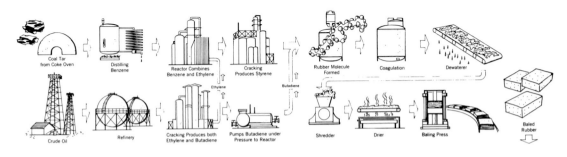

Figure 10.4
Production of synthetic rubber.
Courtesy of the Firestone Tire and Rubber Company.

Unvulcanized rubber displays certain characteristics that are preferred in products such as electrical insulating tape to wrap around copper wires, rubber cement, and adhesive tape. However, due to the shortening of the molecules in the masticating process, the wear-life of the product is shortened.

Mixing

Compound ingredients are mixed with the rubber to add certain color and characteristics such as durability, hardness, and toughness. Special mixing machinery may kneed, squeeze, and compress the mixture.

Different kinds of rubber articles call for the use of different chemical ingredients. Carbon black, a reinforcing filler, increases the strength of the rubber, making it much less liable to tear or to wear out from the effects of abrasion. Barites, chalk, clay, lithopone, talc, and whiting are inert fillers which reduce cost and increase the hardness of the rubber without affecting the strength. Antioxidants and antiozonants help to protect the rubber from the deteriorating effects of aging and exposure to sunlight and ozone. Peptizers, such as ammonia, organic sulphur compounds, or mineral oils, soften the rubber and make it easier to break down by mastication. Blowing agents are added to produce cellular rubbers (foam). Other ingredients used in mixing to vary the properties of rubber before vulcanization may include pigments, odorants, hardeners, tackifiers (to make sticky), extender oils, reinforcing resins, reclaims, crumbs, abrasives, and fungicides. There are thousands of ingredients from which to select, and as many as twenty or thirty may be used in any one mix. One outstanding feature of rubber technology is that the characteristics of the final product can be varied by changing the compounding ingredients. After rubber is mixed with the compounding ingredients, the substance is like putty.

Reclaimed rubber obtained from worn-out rubber materials is often used as a filler by mixing it with crude rubber. The reclaimed rubber aids the reprocessing and manufacturing of various rubber items. The wearing qualities of items may be impaired with excessive amounts of reclaimed rubbers. Tires, rubber apparel, and shoe soles are examples of articles which may be made of reclaimed rubber.

Foam rubber is made by mixing latex with sulphur, soap, and other ingredients such as mineral oil, pigments, and fillers, and then foaming mechanically. This lightweight, resilient material may be used for mattresses, pillows, upholstery, underlays, and packing.

Shaping

Once rubber and the compounding ingredients have been mixed, shaping is ready to take place. Shaping can be done in a number of ways such as extrusion, calendering, and molding.

The *extrusion* method forces the rubber through apertures in shaped metal dies to produce flat strips or round cords, tubes, cable coverings, tube linings, or more elaborate items like automobile window gaskets. A rubber thread trademarked Lastex is made by pouring liquid natural or synthetic latex through a nozzle and coagulating the thread as it is extruded. Later, it is vulcanized. Lastex is more durable and elastic than rubber that has been masticated.

A sheeting of rubber is produced on a *calender*. Calender machines are made with two, three, and four rolls which may be heated and are capable of accurate adjustments. Textiles may be impregnated with rubber by running the rolls at different speeds (frictioning) to force the rubber into the textile fabric. Products combining rubber with textile or steel wire reinforcement such as belting and plies of tires are laminated by calendering.

Rubber may be forced into *molds* under heat and pressure to form products like water bottles, footwear, rubber ball halves, and tires. Dip-molding may be done by dipping certain forms into a liquid natural or synthetic latex mixed with selected ingredients to produce thin rubber items like rubber gloves and balloons.

Once the forms have received their deposit of latex they are vulcanized by heat, then taken off, and packed.

Vulcanizing

The original method of *vulcanization* (or curing), and still by far the most common, is to mix sulphur with the rubber, place the mixture in a mold, and apply heat. Sulphur is added in proportions of up to 3 percent for soft rubbers and as much as 32 percent for hard rubber. It is inexpensive, effective, and relatively free from problems. If sulphur is used alone, vulcanizing may take several hours at temperatures up to 150 degrees Celsius. Adding other ingredients in the mix before vulcanizing helps to control the vulcanizing process.

The physical properties of rubber are changed when it is vulcanized to give it the following advantages:

1. It gives it greater elasticity (the ability to return to its original shape after it has been stretched).
2. It increases the ability to absorb shock or vibration.
3. It improves its resistance to extreme temperature changes.
4. It increases in plasticity use as a nonconductor of electricity and gases.
5. It is waterproof.
6. It is not soluble in ordinary solvents, such as chloroform and gasoline.

Liquid Latex

Many consumer goods we use are produced directly from either liquid or synthetic latex. It is easy to mix the required ingredients while the latex is in a liquid state, thus increasing the life of the rubber because it eliminates the plasticating process. A thin layer of liquid latex adheres to a dipped mold to make products such as balloons and gloves.

An electrodeposition process may also be used with liquid latex. An electric current runs through the liquid and causes negatively charged rubber particles to adhere to the metal molds. Rubber gloves and bathing slippers may be made using this process. Liquid latex may be attached to backs of carpets and rugs to make them nonskid (see Figure 10.5).

CARE OF RUBBER

Natural rubber articles need special care because they are affected by heat, sunlight, and oil. Avoid oiling rubber floors and rubber mats. Never dry rubber articles near heaters or expose them excessively to the sun as this may cause them to harden and crack. Excessive oil tends to soften vulcanized rubber. Stickiness may be prevented by sprinkling talcum powder on the rubber surface. Constant bending of hoses may cause them to crack.

Materials made with elasticized threads, such as Spandex, deteriorate with age and use. These materials should be kept away from sunlight and oil in order to increase their wear life.

Figure 10.5
Liquid latex is used to coat the back of carpets.
Courtesy of the Firestone Tire and Rubber Company.

KEY TERMS

1. Foam rubber
2. Hard rubber
3. *Hevea brasilienses*
4. Latex
5. Masticating

6. Natural rubber
7. Reclaimed rubber
8. Styrene butadiene rubber
9. Synthetic rubber
10. Vulcanization

STUDY QUESTIONS

1. Define latex.
2. What process is used to make rubber products from latex?
3. Define synthetic rubber.
4. Compare the advantages and disadvantages of natural rubber and synthetic rubber.
5. Describe the process used to make foam rubber.
6. What is the difference between vulcanized rubber and unvulcanized rubber?
7. How is rubber reclaimed?
8. How are hard rubber articles manufactured?
9. What are ten uses for rubber in the home?
10. What kind of care should be given to articles made of rubber?

STUDY ACTIVITIES

1. Visit a local business (hardware, housewares, or discount store), or obtain a catalog and look through it. List some products that are made from natural and/or synthetic rubber. Beside each listed product write down the selling points pertaining to its rubber content. Compare price ranges.

2. Obtain a world map and locate the countries listed below, where most of the natural rubber is grown. Explain why their location affects the rubber trade.

Brazil	Madagascar	Sri Lanka
Burma	Malaysia	Thailand
India	Mexico	Viet Nam
Indonesia	Nigeria	Zimbabwe
Liberia		

3. A customer looking at a men's waterproof rainwear unlined jacket made of PVC (polyvinyl chloride) with rayon backing was undecided whether to buy it or the vulcanized, heavy-duty jacket made of heavy rubber with rayon backing. Which jacket would you recommend that the customer purchase? Explain the reasons for your choice.

CHAPTER 11

Glassware

OBJECTIVES

After completing this chapter, you should be able to:

1. Identify three major types of glass and the materials used in making each.

2. Describe the manufacturing processes used for making hand-blown glass, mold-blown glass, and pressed glass.

3. Give five methods of decorating glassware using surface designs without color.

4. Give a typical classification of glassware and tell how it is bought and sold.

5. Describe the best methods of caring for glassware.

Glassware may be beautifully formed by hand-blowing to form fine, delicate pieces, or it may be mass produced to be durable and heat-resistant. Glass items are available in a variety of designs and colors to satisfy the needs of any home at almost any cost level.

It is important that the buyer and salesperson recognize glassware as a merchandise category which may be promoted as a fashion product. A basic knowledge of the production and care of glassware will enable the merchant to develop the proper assortment of glass in order to meet consumer needs.

HISTORY OF GLASSMAKING

The art of glassmaking goes back thousands of years. Archaeologists have discovered evidence that decorative glass bottles were used in Egypt more than 4000 years ago. The same two basic elements that were used in ancient times are used today to make glass: silica (sand) and an alkali (soda ash, potash, or lime). The difference is that other raw materials are now added and special furnaces are built for the heat needed for glassmaking. The ancient glassmakers made bottles by winding threads of molten glass around a core of sand or dipping a core of sand right into a pot of molten glass. When the glass coating had cooled and hardened, the core was extracted. The early glass items were opaque because the secret of adding other raw materials to make the transparent glass of present times was not known.

Around the third century B.C., it was discovered that a small amount of glass could be gathered on the end of a metal tube or *blowpipe* by dipping the pipe into a pot of molten glass. When the glassworker blew his breath through the tube, the glass at the other end expanded to form a hollow item. The end of the item attached to the tube could be broken off. This principle of the blowpipe was used for many centuries before bottles were produced by machine.

Once the glass blowers became skillful with the blowpipe, they were able to blow glass items into molds. Every glass container blown in a single mold was exactly alike in size and shape to all containers formed in the same mold. This principle of making glass is used to mass produce glass containers in today's factories.

The famous Venetian glassmaking guilds reached their peak by the fifteenth century. European countries added new developments to glassmaking during the sixteenth and seventeenth centuries. The secret of making colorless glass, called *flint* or lead, by adding lead to the glass mix, was discovered in England. The sixteenth century Venetian *cristallo* became the first totally colorless and transparent glass that could be blown and worked into various shapes.

The art of etching glass, using hydrochloric acid to decorate the surface, came about in the early eighteenth century. In Germany, decorating lead glass by cutting it came into prominence. About this time furnaces were developed in England which used coal instead of wood for heating and fusing glass. This development caused the glassmaking industry to expand rapidly.

Today's multimillion dollar glass industry in the United States began when glassmakers from Europe established a glass factory at Jamestown, Virginia, in 1608. The first important glass house was established in 1739 by Casper Wistar in Glassboro, New Jersey. It produced high quality glassware for forty-two years. The next great name in glass production was Henry William Stiegel of Manheim, Pennsylvania. His plant was established in 1785 and for nine years produced some of the finest flint glass artware this country had yet seen.

The third big name in early American glass was the Boston and Sandwich Company, founded in 1825 by Deming Jarves. This was the first American glass company that operated on a big scale. A method of shaping glass by pressing it into iron molds with a plunger instead of blowing the glass to shape the inside was invented; this method produced inexpensive pressed ware and made it available to the public.

Lenox was the first American manufacturer to produce fine crystal stemware, dating back to 1841.

In 1903 Michael J. Owens perfected his automatic bottling machine which began to produce containers with such uniformity, speed, and economy that it almost immediately put this part of the glass industry on an efficient mass-production basis.

Most glassware today is manufactured in the United States, although European countries and particularly Japan have made huge gains in exporting glassware to this country.

TYPE OF GLASS

Glass is a mixture of sand (silica) and alkali (such as soda ash, potash, lime, or all three) which has been melted, shaped, and cooled until it is a hard, nonporous, usually transparent material. The sand contains needed silica, and the alkali is added to help melt the sand. Other ingredients such as lead oxide, boric oxide, manganese oxide, and various minerals may be added to give glass certain characteristics such as brightness, hardness or softness, color, sound tone, or resistance to temperature changes. To every batch of raw ingredients, a certain amount of old glass is added. This is called *cullet* and must be the same type of glass as the new batch to be made. Cullet is used because it remelts quickly, helping to produce uniformity and to speed the melting of the new raw materials.

Quality glassware is made of 50 to 75 percent silica sand. Almost 90 percent of all glass sand used in the United States comes from West Virginia, Illinois, Pennsylvania, New Jersey, Missouri, Michigan, and Ohio. These areas have deposits of rich silica sand consisting of uniquely shaped grains that have proven satisfactory in the manufacture of every type of glass for which they have been employed.

The following are the basic kinds of glass: lime-soda glass, lead glass, and heat-resistant glass.

Lime-Soda Glass

Lime-soda glass is the least expensive of the basic kinds of glass because it is produced by using the basic ingredients used in glassmaking. These basic ingredients are commonly found in the earth as silica sand, soda, potash, and lime. Although inexpensive, lime-soda glass is very durable and is used to make drinking glasses, jars, dishes, bottles, mirrors, and windowpanes. It is the type most used in the home. Due to its characteristic brittle nature, lime-soda glass may not take machine-cut designs. However, it may be shaped and designed by pressing the molten glass into a mold. When tapped, the lime-soda glass will give a dull tone.

A typical commercial composition for a clear container glass batch is as follows:

Sand—1000 lbs.

Soda ash—340 lbs.

Limestone—380 lbs.

Feldspar—320 lbs.

Old glass (cullet) may be mixed in the batch to help in producing uniformity and aid in melting it.

Lead Glass

Lead glass, also known as flint glass or lead crystal, is a special type of glass that contains high levels of lead oxide. According to International Standards, lead crystal must contain no less than 24 percent lead (see Figure 11.1). The use of lead oxide instead of lime and the amount of care taken during production and shipment make lead glass more expensive than lime-soda glass.

Lead glass has unique characteristics which can help you easily distinguish it from other glasses. Lead glass has a unique, resonant, lasting ring when gently tapped. There may be varying tones due to the size, shape, and weight of the glassware. It also is brighter than other glasses because of the intricate techniques used during production to insure absolute colorlessness. The lead oxide content adds a unique sparkle to lead glass that is comparable to the sparkle of a diamond. The lead oxide creates a light refraction in the glass (crystal) which gives it this unique sparkle; the more lead oxide used, the greater the sparkle. Lead oxide also makes lead glass heavier than other glasses of comparable shape and size.

Figure 11.1
Lead crystal vase.
Courtesy of J.G. Durand International.

Lead glass also has a softer surface than other glasses, which enables machine-cut as well as hand-cut designs to be applied.

Lead glass, due to its unique properties and cost of production, is used mostly to make such items as optical lenses, imitation jewelry, and expensive table glassware.

In the United States, the term *crystal* is used, by definition, to denote the absence of color, such as crystal glassware compared with colored glassware. To most people today, *crystal* means fine glassware, both colored and clear. When used in connection with art and table glassware, the term *crystal* means a transparent lead or lime-soda glass as nearly colorless as possible. In Europe the amount of lead in the mixture of ingredients determines whether or not that glass item can be called *crystal*.

Heat-Resistant Glass

Borosilicate Glass

This is a heat-resistant glass containing a small amount of boric oxide, which helps prevent expansion and contraction when exposed to extremes of temperature. It is used for baking dishes and cookware and can be transferred from freezer or refrigerator to oven without cracking. Three familiar trademarks are Fire King, Glassbake, and Pyrex.

Glass-Ceramic

This is a heat-resistant, crystalline glass-ceramic substance made so that it is part glass and part ceramic (see Figure 11.2). It is durable and has the ability to withstand extreme temperatures. It has an opaque white appearance which resembles china, and it is used primarily for cook-and-serve ware in the home. The trademark names are Pyroceram and Centura.

Laminated Glass

This is a heat-resistant material made of two glasses: a dense, white, opal glass core covered on both sides by a thin coating of clear glass. It is called Corelle by trademark (see Figure 11.3). It resembles chinaware. Because of its special structure, this glassware and another heat-resistant glass called Flameware can be used to cook over an open gas flame or an electric burner. They are easily cleaned, and food may be observed in them while cooking. The advantage is that they hold heat better than metal cookware for baking. They may also be used for dinnerware or placed directly in the freezer.

FORMING THE GLASS

Once the materials for the glass have been prepared and heated, the resulting molten glass is ready to be formed into the desired shape. The finished glassware may be formed by three processes: hand-blowing, mold-blowing, and pressing.

Figure 11.2
A microwave covered, divided, heat-resistant dish. This Pyroceram dish is glass ceramic. The cover is made of tempered lime glass.
Courtesy of Corning Glass Works.

Figure 11.3
A set of laminated, heat-resistant glassware trademarked Corelle.
Courtesy of Corning Glass Works.

Hand-Blown Glass

This method of shaping glass, also known as the free-blown method, was used about the third century B.C. and is still used today.

Depending on style, size, and other design characteristics, a team of skilled craftsmen is needed to form a single piece of glassware. The gatherer begins the glass shaping by inserting the pear-shaped, porous end of a steel blowpipe into the molten glass (Figure 11.4). The right amount of molten glass to be shaped into the bowl is gathered on the end of the blowpipe. The gatherer then blows a bubble inside the piece being shaped. The blower works the bubbled glass into a desired shape by skillfully blowing and rotating the pipe (see Figure 11.5). Tools may be used against the surface of the glass bottle to make various forms. These impressed marks against the glass will remain permanent.

The glass cools and hardens while it is being worked and often must be re-softened by putting it back into a small furnace, called the *glory hole*. After it is softened, it can be shaped or other pieces of glass, such as handles, can be joined permanently.

The top part of the glass still attached to the blowpipe can be cut off. The rim is then shaped and smoothed by softening again in the glory hole or by grinding and polishing.

One of the most intricate methods of forming a stem is the draw stem (see Figure 11.6). The base of the blown bowl is reheated in the glory hole, then carefully drawn by craftsmen's fine tools to form the stem to just the right length and thickness.

The foot is formed in another intricate step. Using special tools, such as shears, the footcaster changes a mass of molten glass into the foot (Figure 11.7). The footcaster gradually shapes the mass by applying pressure on water-soaked wooden tools while rotating the blowpipe (Figure 11.8). The finisher then gauges the completed glass for correct size, straightens the still hot piece, and while it cools, removes it from the blowpipe.

The glassware must be *annealed* or cooled gradually to prevent uneven external and internal strain and to assure maximum durability. The glass must be tempered, like steel, for strength. This is done by sending the glassware through a long tunnellike structure called the *annealing lehr*. In the lehr, a moving belt slowly transports the glassware through gradually diminishing temperatures until it is cooled to room temperature. This cooling varies from several hours to several days, depending upon the size of the piece and the thickness of the glass.

Each crystal glass is inspected closely; then it is sent to the finishing department, where the *moil*, any excess glass found around the top, is removed by using a sharp diamond. Moil is any excess glass left at the end of an article in contact with the blowing mechanism during the manufacture of blown glass. Then the glass is placed in a *glazing* machine where needlelike gas flames slightly melt the edge of the glass to make it round and smooth. It is now ready for the decorating department.

Hand-blown glass is expensive because of the number of skilled craftsmen, special techniques, and amount of care necessary for production. It is for these

Figure 11.4
The gatherer collects molten glass on the end of a blowing tube.
Courtesy of Lenox, Inc.

Figure 11.5
The glass blower quickly blows the molten glass to the right size.
Courtesy of Lenox, Inc.

Figure 11.6
Shaping the stem attached to the glass bowl.
Courtesy of Lenox, Inc.

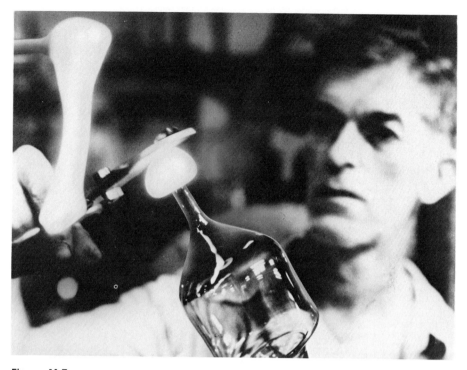

Figure 11.7
Placing molten glass on the stem to be shaped into the foot.
Courtesy of Lenox, Inc.

reasons that the hand-blown method is used only to produce fine quality glassware such as crystal glassware.

Mold-Blown Glass

As artisans became skillful with the blowpipe, glass pieces were blown into molds. Using molds enabled glassmakers to produce items that were identical in size and shape to every other object formed in the same mold. This method of shaping glass is less costly than hand-blowing and is widely used today in glass container factories (see Figure 11.9).

In the molding process, the glass is gathered on the blowpipe and a bubble of air is blown into the molten glass. Then the bubble of glass is put in a cast iron mold. By blowing through the blowpipe, the glassmaker forces the glass to expand and fill all parts of the mold. The inside of the glassware is shaped by the air. The outside form is shaped when the molten glass chills as it comes in contact with the mold. The iron mold may have designs cut into it that make a raised design on the outside of the piece being molded, making it resemble cut glass. The

Figure 11.8
Hand-shaping a goblet foot.
Courtesy of Lenox, Inc.

forming mold with its finished glassware opens and mechanical arms shove the finished glassware, still hot, into a delivery chute ready to go into the annealing lehr.

All bottles were mold-blown separately until the bottle-making machine was developed. In the nineteenth century, events such as the Napoleonic Wars and the American Civil War demanded the development of glass containers for preserving foods. This demand, along with Louis Pasteur's pasteurization techniques for killing harmful bacteria in foods, gave impetus to the development of the first bottle-making machine.

At the turn of the twentieth century, Michael J. Owens' fully automatic bottle-making machine was the most startling development in all the 5000 years of the history of glass. It made possible mass production of glass containers of uniform shape, size, and capacity and in the quantity needed to mass package drugs, food, household products, beverages, and other items necessary to modern living.

Figure 11.9
Production of mold-blown glass. Blowing through and revolving the blowpipe after placing glass in the mold.
Courtesy of Woods Glass, Inc.

Pressed Glass

Glass can be pressed into shape by hand, machine, or a combination of both. Most of the pressed glass is mass produced by machine.

The forming of pressed glass begins at the furnace. The mixture of raw materials, called a *batch,* is melted, blended, tested, and cooled to 2000 degrees Fahrenheit. The batch for pressed glass contains lime-soda as a basic ingredient because it cools more rapidly than lead. Heat-resistant and lime-soda glass pieces are often made this way.

A gatherer picks up the necessary amount of molten glass on the end of a long metal rod called a *punty* or *puntil.* (This process may be done by machine.) He hands the punty with its blob of glass to a presser. The gatherer must move fast because the blob of glass begins cooling rapidly. He places the molten glass over the mold. The glass drops into the mold, and the presser uses shears to cut off the amount needed. During the pressing method, the presser exerts just enough pressure on the plunger to make the glass fill every crevice of the mold. The amount of pressure and time will vary with different pieces. The Coca-Cola bottle with its seams and shape is a product of a mold bottle machine.

Molds must be reheated in an oven before each use and carefully cleaned after each four hours of use. They are among the most valuable items in a glass factory.

When the glass has been pressed into the shape of the mold, the presser releases the plunger. Then another worker, called the *warm-in boy,* sticks the hot glass from the mold on the punty and places it into an oven for reheating. The temperature is about 300 degrees Fahrenheit less in this smaller oven. This oven is called the *glory hole* because its temperature not only keeps the piece at the necessary working temperature but also gives the pressed glass its extra sparkly and permanent luster.

The piece is soft but still in form when it is taken from the glory hole to the finisher. The finisher uses a wooden paddle or stick to spin, turn, and twist the piece until it has been coaxed toward the finished shape. The finisher's hands never cease the constant rhythmic motion until the work is completed. Any sudden stop could cause the piece to sag out of shape.

The finisher may create different pieces from the same molded shape. Bowls and plates with the same diameter base are pressed in the same mold. If the finished glassware is to be a plate, it is twirled rapidly as it is taken from the glory hole, and this motion flattens out the sides. Stems of glassware may be pressed and then attached to the base of free-blown or mold-blown glass pieces.

After the finisher is done, he puts the piece into an annealing lehr where it is cooled gradually and evenly so that the glass will retain its shape, toughness, and durability.

A sample of each batch of glass is inspected many times to insure quality. In the polariscope test, polarized light is directed through the glass. If the image remains clear, the piece is free from strain and stress. Stresses are indicated by sharp bands of colors, causing the entire batch to be retempered. Another test involves immersing the pressed pieces in boiling water, then quickly plunging them into cold water. Fine pressed glassware which has been properly annealed will pass this test without cracking. Much glassware that appears perfect is rejected during the many inspections and tests and is reprocessed.

Finally, pressed glass needs smoothing and polishing. The bottom may have rough edges left by the punty to which it was stuck during the reheating and finishing operations. These rough edges are ground and polished to leave a smooth surface.

HOW GLASSWARE IS DECORATED

There are various methods used to decorate glassware; some are more expensive than others. Buyers, salespeople, and customers should become aware of these methods used to decorate colorless and colored glass.

Decorating Colorless Glass

Designs may be applied to the surface of colorless glass in several different ways: copper-wheel engraving, cutting, etching, decalcomania, embossing, and frosting.

Copper-Wheel Engraving

The finest glassware pieces may be chosen to have intricate designs or monograms engraved on them. The glassware is held against small copper discs impregnated with oil and emery that revolve on a lathe as the artisan creates complex, delicate-looking designs that vary in depth. The varying depth creates attractive illusions when viewed from the other side of the glass. The unpolished cut that is left gives contrasting beauty to the rest of the clear glass. Most modern masterpieces in glass are engraved.

Cutting Glass

Cut glass is cut by machine or hand on moving small metal or sandstone wheels (see Figure 11.10). Different sizes and shapes of wheels are used to cut the desired designs that are sketched on the glass. The abrasive action of the stone wheel gives glass a frosted look. Some designs are left in this state and are called *gray cuttings*. The amount and depth of cutting and the design determine whether the glass is expensive or inexpensive. Less expensive lime-soda glass may be cut by machine. A diamond wheel using diamond dust as an abrasive may also be used to cut glass.

Glass must be polished after it has been cut to bring out the luster. Polishing is done by dipping the glass in acid or by buffing it with felt, cork, or brush wheels. The acid technique is faster and less expensive than the buffing technique; however, buff-polished cut glass is marketed as *hand-polished glass* and has a more brilliant sparkle.

Etching

Etched glass is produced by a series of operations with strong hydrofluoric acid which eats the designs into the glass. The design pattern is applied to blank glassware, and the parts not to be etched are coated with wax. The hydrofluoric acid decomposes the glass wherever it touches it, leaving an indented, grayed surface. This process is called *etching*.

A transparent wax may be sprayed on the inside of the goblet or the underside of the plate. The wax makes the design show up clearly. An artisan then

Figure 11.10
Handcutting a design into a glass.
Courtesy of Lenox, Inc.

covers the entire piece with a heavier acid-resistant wax, leaving the lines of the pattern exposed. The crystal glass is now set aside for several hours, so the wax can harden.

Next, the glass is put into a bath of hydrofluoric acid which gradually eats into the exposed areas of glass, etching the pattern deeply and permanently so that it will last as long as the glass itself. This acidizing process takes about six minutes. After this, the glass is thoroughly rinsed to remove all the acid and then placed in scalding water to melt away the wax coating. A *frosted* look can be created by dipping a glass in acid for a few minutes.

About fifteen hand operations are used in the etching of each goblet or plate. These operations, and many inspections, are needed to turn out a master etching. This is the reason goblets are so expensive.

Decalcomania

Decalcomania is the process of transferring designs permanently onto specially prepared glass. The desired decal design is stenciled on the glass and fired. This transfer design imitates hand painting and is used for inexpensive glassware.

Embossing

A raised or molded decoration produced either in the mold or formed separately and applied to a piece before firing produces an embossed piece. Embossing is the opposite of etching: the design may be made in relief by etching out the rest of the glass surface. This is usually an inexpensive way of decorating glass.

Frosting

A frosted effect on glass is accomplished by exposing all or part of the glass surface to the action of acids. A frosted look may be produced by applying adhesives to all or part of the glass surface to which powdered glass grains stick. The piece is then fired so that the glass grains are permanently affixed. *Sandblasting frosting* may also be used. Sand is blown against glass by compressed air, pitting it and leaving a frosted look. A rubber or metal stencil may protect the glass except for the cut-out parts which give the desired design or monogram. Glassware decorated with a design that is deeply cut by sandblasting is called *carved glass*. The treated areas take on a soft gray color.

COLORING GLASS

Any glassware that is not clear has impurities in the sand, or certain mineral salts have been added to give the ware the desired color. Transparent or opal glass is sometimes covered with a layer or layers of colored glass which can be cut through to the level of the base glass. This two-colored or multicolored effect is called *case glass*.

Applying Colors on Glassware

Gold or platinum may be applied to glassware by brushing, stamping, or other means. The decoration is fired on to ensure permanence and may be polished. Occasionally, it comes out of the firing process dull and must be rubbed or burnished to produce a luster. When gold is applied on an etched surface, the process is called *encrusting*. The gold is then fired and polished.

Silver is applied to glassware by electroplating silver to a base metal fired onto the glass. Glass decorated this way is called *silver depositware*. The silver will not wear off easily.

Ceramic enamels may be applied to glassware which is then fired to make the enamels permanent. Paint is brushed on by hand unless the ware is fired.

Glass may be colored by adding mineral substances such as copper or gold for red or ruby, cobalt for blue, sulphur for yellow, chromium or alumina for green, and iron for amber. Other common and effective colorants of glassware are titanium, vanadium, manganese, and nickel. Simulated color is sometimes produced by spraying the article with ceramic paint which is fired on for permanency.

BASIC STOCK LIST AND CLASSIFICATIONS OF GLASSWARE

The heart of any system for planned future buying of stock in a glassware department is a basic glass stock list. Such a list should include detailed breakdowns of all glassware offered in the department and the minimum quantities in each group to meet normal, day-to-day customer demand. The basic stock list will, of course, vary from one glassware department to another. Not all classifications on the list of one department will be stocked in another. Minimum quantities will differ, based on differing clientele and differing emphasis among departments. For each store the basic items are those which the glassware department must not sell out of, and those which the buyer, once the list is submitted and accepted by management, promises to maintain. It is important that the basic stock list be reviewed periodically to meet constantly changing needs.

Typical classifications include stemware, plain tableware, etched or decorated tableware, cut crystal tableware, barware, drinkware, and miscellaneous glassware. *Stemware* includes drinking glasses that have a bowl, stem, and foot. They are used for both formal and semiformal dining occasions. Cocktail glasses, water goblets, sherbet glasses, and wine glasses are part of this classification. *Plain tableware* consists of drinking glasses having no stem or foot which are used for formal and semiformal occasions. *Drinkware* includes plain, cut, or decorated tumblers having a foot but no stem and coming in various sizes. Miscellaneous glassware includes coffee carafes, candleholders, coupettes (for fruit cocktails), casserole dishes, as well as units (e.g., salad bowls or coasters) combined with brass or other metals, punch bowl sets, and other decorative items.

MERCHANDISING GLASSWARE

Glassware, just like chinaware, is bought and sold in sets and through open stock. Examples of glassware sets include beverage sets, cocktail sets, and punch bowl sets that may be used every day or for special events. Complete lines of glassware in matching designs or patterns are made by some companies. This enables stores to buy smaller amounts of glassware at a time and customers to buy matching pieces from open stock at a later time. Many customers buy fine crystal a few pieces at a time.

When stemware is purchased a piece at a time, start with the water goblets first, then add sherbets, then the wines. Remember the selling point that glassware adds the dimension of height to the place setting at the dinner table.

Accessories are usually coordinated around china. Too much patterning in china, silver, glass, and linen should be avoided. Two patterned accessories with two plain accessories is a good rule to follow. If china and silver are richly patterned, keep the glassware plain. Also, colored glassware that emphasizes a note in the china pattern is always in good taste.

Prepackaged glassware is marketed in a wide range of businesses from small stores to large discount stores. Sets of four, six, and eight glasses are attractively packaged to save packing time, extra handling and money.

Buyers and salespeople who learn and use the following points will be prepared to promote an understanding of quality glassware items.

1. A pinpoint size *seed or bubble* may be observed in glassware, but it will not affect the quality or beauty of glass.

2. Slight variations in the diameter, height, and dimensions in articles of blown glass are the marks of fine hand craftsmanship.

3. An almost invisible difference in the density of the glass is called a *cord.* It occurs during the fusing of the molten glass. In a goblet, it is visible because it reflects light.

4. Unless overly prominent, a *mold mark* is merely a ridge on a molded glassware product and is not considered an imperfection.

5. A *shear mark* is a normal characteristic of glass and is not considered a flaw. It is a slight puckering of the glass caused when the artisan snips off excess molten glass while shaping the article, such as the end of the handle of a pitcher.

6. Fine crystal may or may not have a resonant *tone or ring.* Fine hand-blown glass often contains lead which improves its clarity and resonant tone, and increases its weight. The resonant tone of lead glass depends upon its shape and thinness. Most pressed glass utilizes lime-soda, which adds to its toughness and strength. It generally has no ring, but that does not lessen its value. Potash crystal may have a fine resonant tone and is much less expensive than lead crystal.

7. Look for clarity and luster by holding the item against a white background. Another mark of quality is the permanent polish or luster that results from fine polishing.

8. Look for smooth edges in glassware, never rough or scratchy ones. The design in hand-cut pieces should be accurate and sharp. Each detail in etched ware should be clearly defined and distinct.

9. Check the base of glassware for proportionate breadth and weight. Remember that the shape or symmetry has a vital place in the artistry of glassware.

CARE OF GLASSWARE

The following procedures should be followed in order to preserve glassware.

1. Remove grease and other dirt with mild soap suds or commercial detergents.

2. Wash glassware in hot sudsy water (as hot as the hands can stand). Do not crowd them in the dishpan.

3. Rinse with warm water, sliding edges into the water first.

4. Rinse out glasses and teacups that have held milk, coffee, or tea as soon as possible.

5. Do not use scalding water for gold-, silver-, platinum-, or enamel-decorated pieces.

6. A few drops of ammonia or bluing in the wash water will add luster to glassware.

7. Cut glass should be washed with a soft brush, wiped, then allowed to dry on a terry cloth towel if all crevices cannot be polished.

8. Wipe the glasses with a lint-free linen towel.

9. If two glasses stick together, put cold water in the inner one and hold the outer one in warm water. The slight expansion of the outer glass and the contraction of the inner one will make it easy to separate them.

10. Store glass carefully. Store fine quality glasses upright and never stack them.

11. When storing glassware use hooks for cups and racks to hold plates.

KEY TERMS

1. Crystal
2. Cut glass
3. Engraved
4. Etching
5. Frosted glass
6. Heat-resistant glass
7. Lead glass
8. Lime-soda glass
9. Mold-blown glass
10. Pressed glass

STUDY QUESTIONS

1. What are the properties of lime-soda glass and borosilicate glass? For what purpose is each used?
2. Explain various methods of decorating glassware.
3. Describe how glassware is shaped or formed.
4. Explain the two methods used to make glass durable.
5. What are the differences between chinaware and glassware? Describe glass.
6. What materials are used in making glass? How do the different materials affect the different glassware?
7. What glassware would you suggest for formal service? Informal service?
8. What advice should a customer be given about the care of glassware, such as washing, drying, and storing?
9. What two basic ingredients are always required to make glass?
10. What definitions are used for *crystal* in the United States and Europe?

STUDY ACTIVITIES

1. Locate glassware advertisements in newspapers and magazines. Copy the technical terms or selling points from the advertisements. Be prepared to discuss the terms.

2. Select an expensive goblet in the glassware department of a large store. Identify its parts, the pattern name, the name of the company that made it, and the price. Write down information which you could use in justifying the price of the goblet.

3. Find out the names and addresses of the companies which supply the glassware handled in the glassware department of a local department store or gift shop. Obtain information on the history of each company from the business or through correspondence with the company.

CHAPTER **12**

Wood and Furniture

OBJECTIVES

After completing this chapter, you should be able to:

1. Diagram a cross section of a tree trunk, identifying the different parts and pointing out how plain-sawn lumber and quarter-sawn lumber differ when sawed from the log.

2. Describe the different methods used in joining, decorating, and finishing wood furniture.

3. Give the four major furniture classifications presented in the chapter, and identify pictures of furniture within those classifications by major period or style.

4. Describe how upholstered furniture is constructed and how governmental regulations for the furniture industry protect customers.

5. Define the furniture term **bedding** correctly.

Wood has always been the basic material from which furniture is made. The widespread growth of wood and the relative ease of getting it in needed quantities have made it an important material. Although manufacturing techniques have improved, no substitute has ever been found for wood. Wood has a pleasing grain structure, variety of color, beauty of texture, strength, and lightness of weight. These natural qualities of wood can be further enhanced by carving, turning, staining, and polishing it. (Turnings are round wood pieces made on a lathe and used for such items as legs of furniture and stair railings.) The greatest problem in handling wood is that it expands and contracts across the grain as it absorbs or loses moisture. This means that furniture manufacturers must take appropriate actions to offset this expansion or contraction to ensure that the wood will not split or warp.

THE TREE

A tree is a perennial plant consisting of roots, trunk, and leaves. In a cross section of a tree trunk, the following parts will be found (see Figure 12.1):

1. *Bark* is the outer covering of the tree that protects it from internal damage. It is also a means of identification. Its by-products include cascara, cork, eucalypus, quinine, and tannin.

2. The *cambium layer* is located between the bark and the sapwood. It is a sticky substance that changes into cells to form new wood, usually in the late summer, to form a line called the *annual ring*. This is where the grain pattern appears and where you can tell the age of the tree by counting the lines or rings.

3. The *sapwood* is the newly formed living outer wood. It is lighter in color and contains more moisture nutrients than the heartwood.

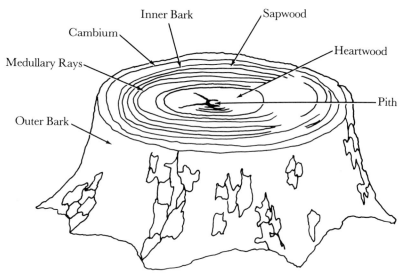

Figure 12.1
Components of a tree trunk.
Adapted from "How a Tree Grows," U.S. Department of Agriculture, Forest Service, May 1970, FS-32, p. 7.

4. *Heartwood* is the inactive center part of the tree which was once sap-wood. It is darker in color, takes longer to season, contains less water, and takes longer to absorb wood preservatives than sapwood.

From the center, or *pith,* of the tree trunk, thin cellular lines extend to the outside of the wood. These lines are called *medullary rays.*

The grain is the result of the pattern of the annual rings in relationship with the medullary rays. The beauty and value of the wood depend on the grain pattern and the method of sawing the wood. A pecularity of the annual rings creates *bird's-eye maple.*

Tree Classifications

Trees can be classified as hardwoods or softwoods. Each category is discussed below.

Hardwoods or Deciduous Trees

Hardwood trees are known as *deciduous* because they shed their broad, flat leaves during the fall season. The southern oak is one exception. The term *hardwood* applies strictly to the botanical characteristics. The term is deceptive, because basswood, a hardwood, is softer than the softwood southern yellow pine. Hardwoods have a more beautiful grain and are more durable than the softwoods because of their thicker cell walls. The great majority of the woods used for furniture are the hardwoods.

Softwoods or Coniferous Trees

The softwood trees do not shed their needlelike leaves in the fall, with the exception of the cypress and the larch. Their cells are thin and uniform in size compared with those of the hardwoods. Softwoods are used primarily in the construction of buildings. Some inexpensive furniture is made from softwoods.

Methods of Sawing Lumber

There are two principal methods used in sawing trees into lumber. These are plain-sawing and quarter-sawing. Each has distinctive advantages. The two types can be used to fit specific needs in lumber. In plain-sawn lumber (see Figure 12.2), the annular rings are at a slight angle to the face of the lumber. The annular rings are perpendicular to the face of the lumber when it is quarter-sawn (Figure 12.3). The advantages of plain-sawn lumber are as follows:

1. It is possible to obtain more lumber from the tree.
2. It is easier to cut at a less expensive price.
3. It is easier to season and dry.

The advantages of quarter-sawn lumber are as follows:

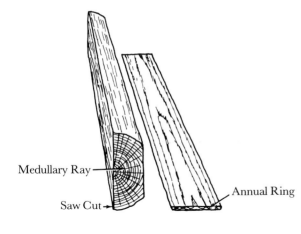

Figure 12.2
Plain-sawn lumber. Annual rings are at an angle to the face of the wood.
Courtesy of U.S. Department of Agriculture.

Medullary Ray
Saw Cut
Annual Ring

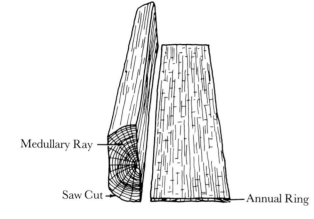

Figure 12.3
Quarter-sawn lumber. Annual rings are perpendicular to the face of the wood.
Courtesy of U.S. Department of Agriculture.

Medullary Ray
Saw Cut
Annual Ring

1. The wood does not cup, twist, or wind as easily.
2. There is less shrinking and warping.
3. The wood does not wear as much because the hard annular rings are exposed and protect the softer part of the summer growth.
4. During seasoning, fewer checks and surface blemishes will appear.

LUMBER

Before lumber can be used, the logs must be debarked and prepared for sawing. After debarking, the logs are cut into lumber, veneer, or timber. The first cutting leaves rough saw marks on the lumber. It is then seasoned and finished into smooth pieces.

Drying and Curing Lumber

Hardwoods and softwoods are usually cured before they are marketed. The curing process is known as *seasoning,* which causes the wood to lose its moisture and shrink before it is used. The lumber loses 5 to 10 percent of its moisture during seasoning. This loss of moisture reduces checking, cracking, twisting, and warping of the boards. Seasoning may take place by *air-drying* or *kiln-drying.* Air-drying is stacking the lumber in the open air. For most furniture uses, the hardwoods must be kiln-dried. Kiln-drying means that large ovens are used to control the removal of moisture for the lumber in one or two days. After the lumber is dried, it is surfaced (planed smooth) and straightened. Some softwoods, such as cedar, fir, and pine, are surfaced before seasoning and allowed to shrink to the correct size.

Sizing and Grading

Lumber can be classified according to size and grade. Each category is discussed below.

Sizing

Solid wood lumber sawed for use in the general building construction and furniture business is *sized* according to strips, boards, dimension, and timbers. *Strips* measure less than two inches thick and less than six inches wide. *Boards* measure less than two inches thick and two inches or more wide. *Dimension* includes all lumber measuring from two inches up to, but not including, five inches in thickness and of any width. *Timbers* are measured five inches or more in their smallest dimension (thick or wide). Finished lumber, planed and sanded, is always fractions of an inch less in thickness and in width than it was in its rough sawed state.

Grading

The highest grade of lumber has the fewest imperfections and is more costly than the poorer grades. Poorer grades have knots, splits, spots, and discolorations that reduce their value and desirability. Yet, they are still usable.

Veneer and Plywood

Veneers were used by the Egyptian Pharaohs over four thousand years ago. They had very little wood available for making furniture; therefore, they veneered the solid wood that they could find. *Veneering* is a method of placing a thin, beautiful piece of wood over a piece of wood of lesser beauty or quality. Present-day adhesives make veneering more satisfactory than in the historical past. Since some wood is no longer easy to obtain, man has been forced to use the tree more efficiently and to make more veneered wood and plywood.

Plywood is made by gluing together successive layers of thin veneer slices to form a thicker piece of wood. The layers are placed at right angles to avoid any weakness in the plywood that might result from grain direction. Common plywood is made from the inexpensive fir and pine trees, and may be used in the un-exposed, flat surfaces of inexpensive furniture. Interior or exterior plywood is used extensively in the building construction business. It is generally measured by width, length, and thickness.

Woods used for veneers, often called *cabinet woods,* come from around the world. Thin slices of an attractive wood are glued to a core of less desirable wood, usually hardwood. Veneer or plywood is extremely strong. The cabinet veneers most used include Philippine and Honduras mahoganies, ash, birch, maple, pecan, rosewood, and walnut. High quality furniture has always included ven-eered pieces. Modern trends in making furniture include using veneers more ex-tensively; using more laminated plastics; and combining wood and veneers with materials such as cloth, metal, molded-wood fibers, particle boards, and fiber-glass.

Veneer strips may be as thick as $\frac{3}{16}$ inch or as thin as $\frac{1}{200}$ inch. The $\frac{1}{28}$ inch veneers are used the most often for surfaces of furniture. There are six grades of veneer plywood, designated N, A, B, C, C plugged, and D. Grade A is for spe-cial order; it has a natural finish of select, all heartwood; and it is free from open defects. Grade A is the highest quality veneer that can be obtained as a standard plywood, although the veneer face can be joined or repaired. The lesser grades have increasing imperfections. Veneer patterns come from certain locations on a tree (see Figure 12.4). They are called *crotch* grain, *burl* grain, *trunk* grain, and *stump* grain.

HARDBOARD AND PARTICLE BOARD

Hardboard and particle board are both made from wood fibers, such as wood chips and sawdust. Hardboard is bonded with its own lignin, which is a natural bonding in wood that holds the wood cells together. Hardboard is made by heat and pressure into standard widths, thicknesses, and lengths. Hardboard has the following advantages: (1) being free from defects, not needing to be patched, and (2) not having a grain so that it does not chip, peel, or warp. The first hardboard process was discovered by William Mason in Mississippi in 1924. Its trade name is Masonite. It is used as a base for bonding veneers and plastic laminates. Dec-orative patterns of hardboard are used for room dividers, screens, and paneling. It is often perforated and used in inexpensive cabinets.

In particle board, adhesives have been added to hold the particles together. The wood chips used in particle board can be of any size, not uniform in size, and made from different woods. Particle board is made by the heat and pressure process, or it can be extruded. It can be used almost any place that a smooth, stable panel is needed, and it is available in many textures and strengths. Its ma-jor uses are for the cores in veneered furniture, paneling, shelving, and for the in-terior core in sink tops and cabinets. Particle board has about the same advan-tages as hardboard. Additional advantages are that it can be painted, finished, covered, or veneered with plastics, paper, or wood.

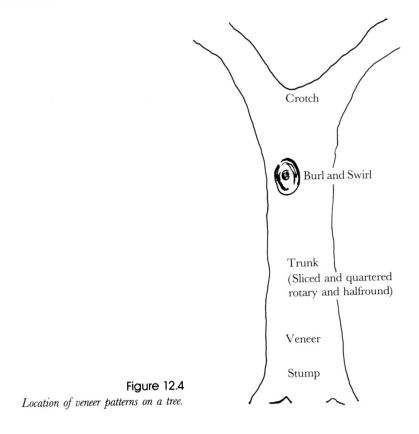

Crotch

Burl and Swirl

Trunk
(Sliced and quartered
rotary and halfround)

Veneer

Stump

Figure 12.4
Location of veneer patterns on a tree.

WOODS

Hardwoods

Most hardwoods used for furniture are native to this country. The salesperson should become familiar with the most popular hardwoods used in making furniture. The most popular hardwoods are briefly described below.

Beech
This wood is very strong; but because the grain is not distinctive, it is used for inner constructions such as frameworks and dowels. The wood is easily identified by the small, but very conspicuous, rag marks which appear as short dark dashes up to one-eighth of an inch in length. The pores are very small and cannot be seen without a lens, making the wood moisture-resistant. A wooden tray on a child's highchair made of beech would be highly resistant to moisture.

Birch
This is one of the most important woods used in the manufacture of furniture. There is no pronounced grain pattern. Naturally creamy white, it takes stains

very well, thus making it easy to match with other woods. Birch is one of the strongest and hardest woods. It has great shock-resisting ability and shrinks the least of any woods. Birch is used extensively for the structural (unexposed) parts of furniture and often for the exposed parts of upholstered pieces.

Cherry

This wood does not have as fine a grain and texture as birch, but its small, close pores give it a smooth look. It is used in harmony with reddish mahoganies as well as with birch and maple. Used on the formal side, cherry wood is also mixed with walnut. The reddish-brown finishes give it the effect of richness. It has a natural luster that makes it a valuable furniture wood. Cherry is used for veneers and solid pieces.

Gum

Gum has medium strength, weight, and shrinking qualities. There are two main kinds: *red gum* and *black gum* (tupelo). Red gum is one of the leading furniture woods. It is used for the unexposed parts of furniture and also in inexpensive furniture for the exposed parts to imitate mahogany and walnut. It is easily dented and has a rosy color and a smooth grain pattern. It splits easily and is a little brittle. Black gum (tupelo) has a whitish gray to gray-brown color. It is harder and heavier than red gum and has a tendency to warp badly. It takes a beautiful finish. Legs, frames, and unexposed parts are made from black gum.

Mahogany

Mahogany is an imported light brown wood with a slightly reddish cast which is generally darkened to look like other dark-colored woods. It has a smooth surface which is often marked with attractive patterns.

Mahogany veneered panels are often made by matching crotch patterns, ribbon strips, and mottles. It is resistant to warping, is very durable, and can be easily worked.

Most mahogany is imported from Central America, South America, and Africa. If it comes from Africa, it must be called *African mahogany.* Tanquile, called *Philippine mahogany,* is not a member of the mahogany family, nor is it considered to be as good a quality wood. Yet it has about the same color as mahogany. Tanquile is soft, lightweight, and its open grain is difficult to finish.

Ebony

This is a very dark brown hardwood imported from Asia and Africa. The wood is heavy and may possess lighter brown streaks. It is used for piano keys, ornamental work, handles, and paneling due to its pattern and shine when polished.

Teak

Teak is an extremely durable wood from Burma, India, Thailand, and Java. It is used for fine furniture and ship building. It has an oily appearance and is fairly rare and expensive.

Maple

This wood is light in color, does not dent easily, and generally has a smooth, close-grained, straight grain pattern, although several unusual grain patterns occur. One is called *bird's-eye* and is used in veneers. Other grain patterns available for veneer may be curly and wavy. Of the two main types of maple, the *hard* maple is the best for furniture. Hard maple may also be called *northern, rock,* or *sugar* maple. The other maple, called *silver* or *soft* maple, does not have the heaviness or strength to be used in furniture.

Oak

Oak is one of the most common woods used in furniture construction and is capable of receiving a greater variety of finishes than any other wood. White oak is preferred for natural and blonde finishes because it does not have the reddish color that red oak has.

Both oaks are used for darker pieces. Oak is a coarse-grained, rugged, sturdy-looking wood easily used for making heavy, masculine-looking pieces of furniture. Although it is durable and strong, it splinters easily. Oak may be carved and quarter-sawn to show its grain pattern.

Walnut

Walnut, called black or American walnut, varies in its natural color from light to dark, purplish brown. When it is plain sawn, the grain pattern may have irregular curves and stripes. Other unusual grain patterns may be developed by cutting veneer from stump wood, crotch, and burls. Walnut should be well-seasoned because of its high shrinkage. It is used for the construction of furniture because it warps very little, carves easily, and retains its color so well.

Softwoods

The following information about the softwoods, mostly native to this country, is important in the study of furniture making because of the role they play in its production.

Cedar

Cedar, especially the eastern or aromatic red cedar, is used to line closets and storage chests so that its oils will vaporize and kill moths. The knotty cedar contains more oil than the sheet cedar. The western cedar, grown in the Rocky Mountains and Pacific Northwest, is durable and takes paints and stains readily. It is a close-grained wood used for siding of houses, paneling in rooms, and some outdoor furniture.

Fir

Fir, especially white fir, grows in large numbers in the western part of this country. It is warp-resistant, has a light color, is lightweight, and is easy to use. It also has moderate strength and stiffness. The top-quality white fir is used for making bookcases, cabinets, and frames of upholstered furniture.

Pine

This wood, particularly sugar pine, northern white pine, and Pacific coast soft pine, may be used to make inexpensive furniture. Northern pine is easily worked, even-textured, lightweight, and soft. It is warp-resistant and contains less resin and turpentine than the other pine woods. It is used for light-colored, unpainted furniture and as a core for veneered furniture. Knotty pine is used for rustic-looking furniture. Pine may also be carved for decorative mounts.

Redwood

This wood is native to Northern California and Oregon. It is moderately strong. It has a fine, straight-grained pattern, with the heartwood varying from light red to a deep mahogany color. Resistant to insects and decay, it is used for rustic outdoor furniture.

PERIODS AND STYLES OF FURNITURE

A knowledge of the historical development of furniture styles and accessories is important to the buyer, the salesperson, and the consumer. The term *period* is used to denote an historical period of time. *Style* relates to design characteristics that identify the designer or school of designers. The terms are often used interchangably.

Each monarch in England and France in the sixteenth, seventeenth, and eighteenth centuries determined the lifestyle for his people as he ascended the throne. Specially designed furnishings were developed by skilled craftspeople for the monarch in power. Soon, many wealthy people had similar furniture and accessories.

Present-day furniture designers have built *reproductions* or *adaptations* of these styles. In general, designs are divided into three broad categories: (1) *traditional,* (2) *provincial,* and (3) *contemporary.* The traditional designs derive their major influence from the various historical periods. The provincial designs are adapted from the traditional styles, but they are less ornamented and are made from native woods. *Contemporary* relates to furniture designed and made in recent years that has a modernized form of classic design. With its simple, graceful lines, it depends on good design and finish rather than on artificial decoration.

Traditional Furniture

The traditional furniture designs can be broken into the following periods.

William and Mary Period, 1689-1702

The king and queen enjoyed the domestic life more than the ceremonial court life during this time, and it is reflected in the furniture that was built. This style of furniture was made mainly of walnut. Marquetry and veneers were used often. The most prominent features (Figure 12.5) were the following: serpentine curves and inverted cup—a bell-shaped detail found on the legs (see pieces number 4, 9, 12 in Figure 12.5). Trumpet-shaped (2) and octagonal legs (3) were common, as

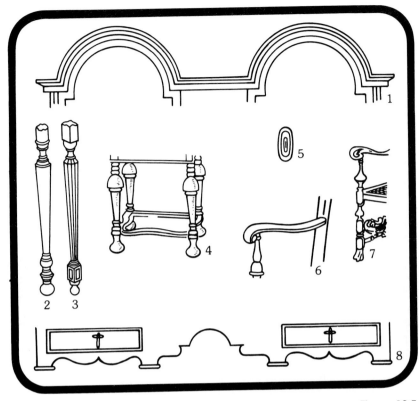

Figure 12.5
William and Mary Period furniture.
Courtesy of *Furniture Facts,* 26th Ed., Hoover Universal, Inc.

well as bun-, club-, hoof-, and pear-shaped feet (4, 7). All pieces were constructed with stretchers often set X-wise between the legs (12), with a finial at the conjunction. Chairs had the *cyma* curve and a half circle on the top of the back. Cabriole legs first appeared in this period. The cabinets were hooded with arched tops (1). The cabinets and desks were built with shaped aprons or skirts (8), and the drawers had drop handles (9). Six or eight connecting legs supported the highboys and cabinets. The upholstery fabrics were brocades, figured chintzes, cretonnes, damasks, embroidery, petit point, tapestry, and velvets. Chinese and Oriental rugs became popular because the English were trading in the Far East.

Figure 12.5
continued

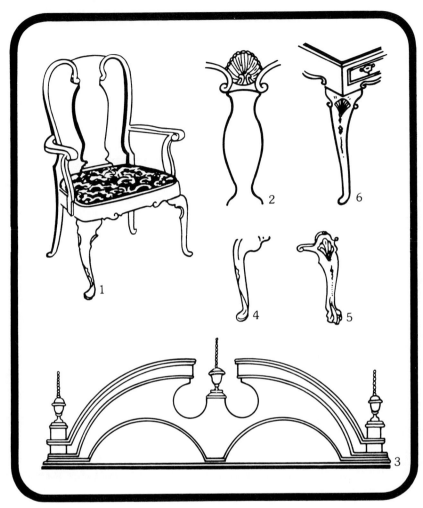

Figure 12.6
Queen Anne Period furniture.
Courtesy of *Furniture Facts,* 26th Ed., Hoover Universal, Inc.

Queen Anne Period, 1702–1715

The Queen Anne style of furniture was inspired from Holland (see Figure 12.6). It is recognizable by the cabriole leg (4, 5, 6), the ball-and-claw foot (5), the Dutch foot (4), and undulating lines. The principle motif for decoration was the scalloped shell (2, 10) which appeared at the knees of the cabriole legs (5, 6), at the top of the chair splat (2), or at the center of the seat frame. Acanthus and floral motifs were utilized. Brocades and embossed leather were the favored upholstering materials. The main woods used were ash, mahogany, oak, and walnut. Gilding and lacquer were used in this style.

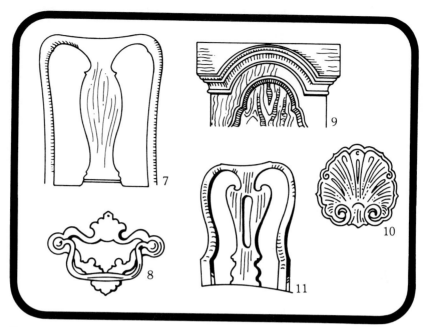

Figure 12.6
continued

Chairs usually had high rounded backs and cabriole legs (1). The splat was fiddle- or vase-shaped (7, 11). The bottom edge of the seat frame usually had a wavy shape (1).

The tops of the highboys were originally flat (9). In later pieces, highboys and tall cabinets had broken pediments (3) with shaped finials at the center and outer edges. Drawers in the case goods were usually equipped with plain brass ball handles. (Case goods are pieces of furniture made largely, but not wholly, of wood, and they have certain storage facilities.)

Figure 12.7
Georgian Period furniture.
Courtesy of *Furniture Facts,* 26th Ed., Hoover Universal, Inc.

Georgian Period, 1714-1795

The English kings George I, II, and III reigned during this period (see Figure 12.7). The mahogany furniture was curved with limited use of straight lines. French and Oriental influence was apparent. Casters were used on chairs and tables to distinguish them from Queen Anne pieces. Cabinets, bookcases, desks (2), and dressers had heavy lines with carving, columns, pilasters, and broken pediments (1). Carvings were elaborate (4) on cabriole legs and splats. The pieces were richly upholstered, and many were gilded.

This design period was dominated by the following craftsmen: the Adam brothers, Thomas Chippendale, George Hepplewhite, and Thomas Sheraton. Thomas Shearer invented the sideboard (5). Ince and Mayhew specialized in chairs (3).

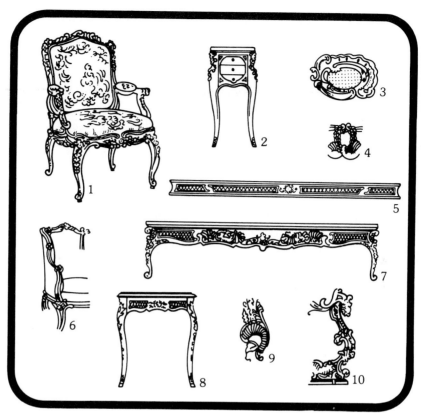

Figure 12.8
Louis XV Period furniture.
Courtesy of *Furniture Facts,* 26th Ed., Hoover Universal, Inc.

Louis XV Period, 1723-1774

The French king Louis XV encouraged new furniture designs (see Figure 12.8). This furniture included chairs with cabriole legs, carved knees, and scroll feet (1, 6). Tables had curved legs (2, 3, 7) and marble tops. Stretchers, when used, were elaborate (10). Characteristic furniture of this style included the commode, the console table, the cylinder desk, and the Louis XV chair. Decoration included carving (4, 5, 8, 9), metal inlays, ormolu mounts, and gilt. The woods used were chestnut, ebony, mahogany, oak, and walnut. Upholstery fabrics consisted of damasks, needlepoint (woolen threads on canvas), prints, and velvets.

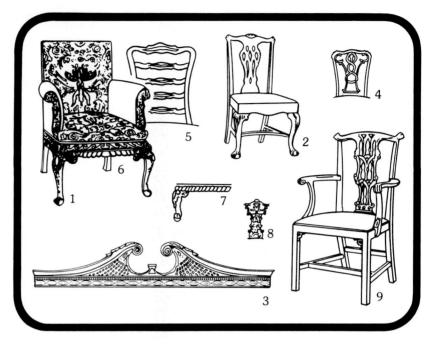

Figure 12.9
Chippendale furniture.
Courtesy of *Furniture Facts,* 26th Ed., Hoover Universal, Inc.

Chippendale Period, 1740–1779

Thomas Chippendale was a well-known English designer and master craftsman. His inspiration came from English, French, and Chinese sources. He was noted for his chairs, bookcases, beds, divans (11), settees (16), cabinets with pediments (3, 10), small tables, desks, clock cases, screens, and many other pieces (see Figure 12.9). His designs revealed a combination of strength and grace. Chippendale was influenced by and improved on three styles—the Chinese, the Gothic, and the French.

Chinese Chippendale furniture is characterized by lattice work, fretwork, reeding, straight legs (9, 12), stretchers, carving for decoration (15), ribbon back (4, 9), ladder back chairs (5), and pagoda-roof tops on cabinets. Gothic Chippendale furniture features straight-leg decoration, with ornate carving, fingering, and the pointed Gothic arch. French Chippendale furniture is characterized by cabriole legs (2, 6), claw-and-ball feet (6), oxbox lines, c-curves, leaf carvings (13), scrolls (14), and shell carvings. Mahogany was the favored wood. Materials used for upholstering included colored leather, damask, linen, satin, taffeta, and velvet.

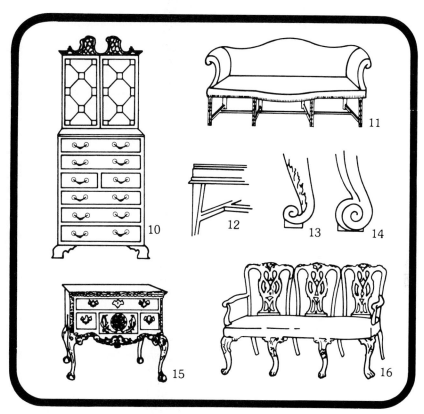

Figure 12.9
continued

Figure 12.10
Chinese Chippendale furniture.
Courtesy of *Furniture Facts,* 26th Ed., Hoover Universal, Inc.

Chinese Chippendale, 1750–1800

The Chinese influences were popular in England about 1740, and inspired Chippendale to design furniture styled after the original Chinese pieces.

Some characteristics of Chinese Chippendale pieces include open fretwork and all-over lattice work (see Figure 12.10). This work showed in chair backs (1, 2) and in the angles formed between the legs and seat of chairs (1) and the legs and top of tables (3). The legs of chairs and small tables were usually straight with Chinese designs that were of raised carving (1, 3, 5). Lacquer, gild, and enamel were used extensively.

Adam Brothers Period, 1760–1792

The four Adam brothers were English architects. Their interest in the excavations at Pompeii resulted in the use of classic designs in the furniture that they designed. The Italian influence in designing and decorating could be seen in the extended ceilings, walls, mantels, silverware, carpeting, upholsteries, and tapestries

Figure 12.11
Adam Brothers furniture.
Courtesy of *Furniture Facts,* 26th Ed., Hoover Universal, Inc.

used. Cool, delicate, pastel colors were used. Brocades, damasks, moires, figured and striped satins, and silks were the favored upholstery fabrics. The favored woods were mahogany and satinwood veneer, with ebony, sycamore, and other fancy wood used occasionally. Typical decorative designs were honeysuckle, fans, husks, ribbons, urns (2), and wreaths (see Figure 12.11). Classical motifs were used with the delicate carvings. Dominant motifs included acanthus, animal heads (6), drapery, human figures, floral swags and pendants (3, 8), disks and ovals, and spandrel fans. The most used feature was the classic urn. This style featured slim, tapered legs that were round or sqaure and sometimes fluted. The splats were designed to be square, curved, or open. Shield-shaped, solid backs were occasionally used. Adam pieces were known for carved moldings (4, 5). The Adam Brothers excelled in furniture such as bookcases, cabinets, and sideboards.

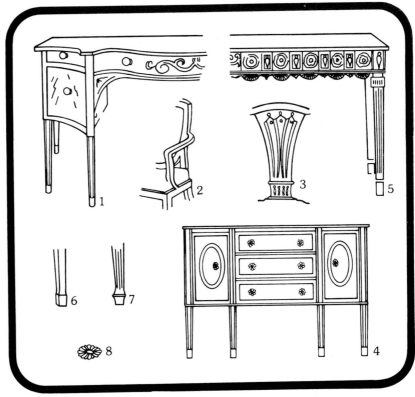

Figure 12.12
Hepplewhite Period furniture.
Courtesy of *Furniture Facts,* 26th Ed., Hoover Universal, Inc.

Hepplewhite Period, 1770-1786

George Hepplewhite was an English cabinetmaker who developed a unique style of furniture characterized by slender, fluted legs (1, 5, 7, 13) and low backs which gave the pieces a fragile appearance (see Figure 12.12). Delicate carving was used sparingly, using classical motifs such as ferns, husks, pendants, rosettes (8), urns, wheat ears, and the Prince of Wales feathers (14). The spade feet were also characteristic (4, 6, 7). The backs of the chairs were rarely upholstered and were nearly always open. The hoop (3), shield (9), and interlacing heart shapes (9, 10) were the most individual designs used. Hepplewhite kept the curve at the top unbroken in the shield back. Vase- or lyre-shaped back splats (12) were built into the oval backs. The backs never reached the seat frame. They were always supported above the seat by the back posts. The chair arms were usually short and serpentine or concave, curved, and carried down to the front legs (2). Upholstery consisted of striped damask, satin, linen, silk, and red and blue Moroccan leather used with horsehair stuffing. Mahogany was the favored wood; some birch, satinwood, sycamore, and imported woods were also used.

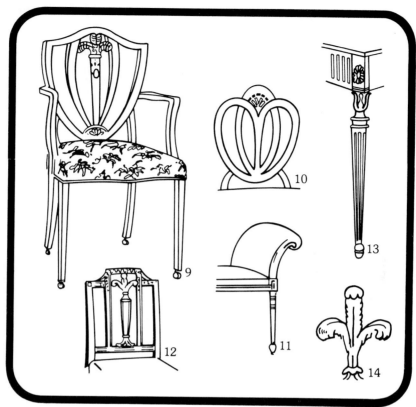

Figure 12.12
continued

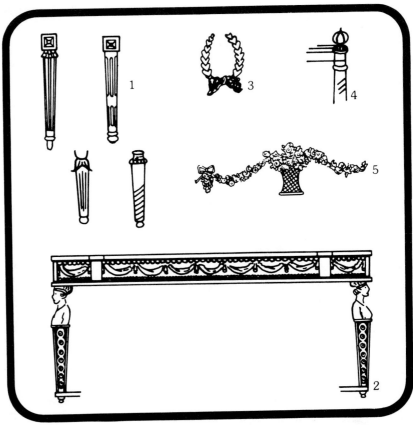

Figure 12.13
Louis XVI Period furniture.
Courtesy of *Furniture Facts,* 26th Ed., Hoover Universal, Inc.

Louis XVI Period, 1774–1793

Marie Antoinette of France influenced this furniture. It was dainty, delicate, and slender, with a few long curves (see Figure 12.13). This furniture had rectangular shapes, with right angles and straight tapered legs (8, 9), which were fluted and turned (1, 2) with carved aprons (2, 6, 7). Ornamentation included baskets of fruits and flowers (5), egg-and-dart, and ribbon motifs (2, 3). Damasks and brocades were used for upholstery textiles. Among the woods used were mahogany, rosewood, satinwood, and walnut.

Figure 12.13
continued

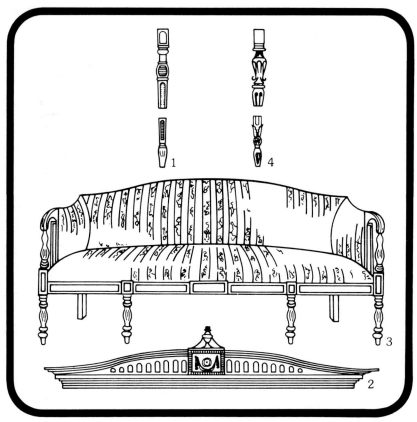

Figure 12.14
Sheraton Period furniture.
Courtesy of *Furniture Facts,* 26th Ed., Hoover Universal, Inc.

Sheraton Period, 1780-1806

Thomas Sheraton was a famous English designer, not a furniture maker. The woods he used were satinwood with mahogany inlay, tulipwood, rosewood, kingwood, and zebrawood. The upholstery was usually of fabrics such as gold or silver brocade, satin, and damask. In this style of furniture (see Figure 12.14), the bookcases were made with shaped pediments and curved traceries on glazed doors. The secretaries were delicate and well-proportioned. The sofas had light, slender legs and a graceful appearance. The backs of the chairs were square with delicately carved openwork in a variety of designs, including fretwork panels (6, 8), ferns, urns (5), lions' heads, lyre or turned posts (9), canes or shields (11). The splats never rested on the seat frame, but on cross-frames. The central panel generally rose above the top rail (5, 9, 10). Tapered, square, and reeded legs (1, 4) and spade feet were made in the early chairs. In chairs made later, the legs

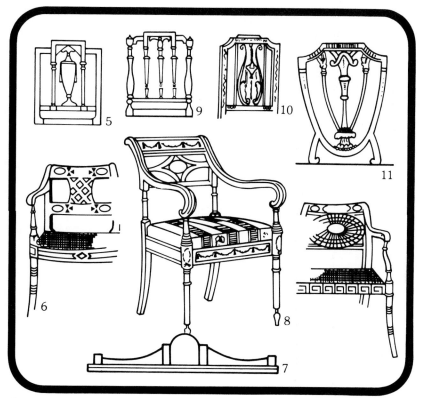

Figure 12.14
continued

were spiral turned. Present-day furniture pieces that originated from the Sheraton style are the sectional bookcases, drop-leaf Pembroke tables, and console extension tables. Sheraton shutter or tambour doors are used extensively in modern furniture.

Figure 12.15
English Regency Period furniture.
Courtesy of *Furniture Facts,* 26th Ed., Hoover Universal, Inc.

English Regency Period, 1793–1830

This English style featured chairs with both concave (4) and straight (5, 9) backs, ornamented with carving, fretwork, gilding, and relief (see Figure 12.15). The legs were generally straight without any underbracing (11); they were occasionally curved (4, 5), sometimes with classic double curves (1). The feet continued down from the legs (4, 5) with straight banding or collars (6) and sometimes lions' paws (1). The smaller tables were built with triangular bases (3). The tables were occasionally gilded, inlaid, and lacquered. The larger tables had straight legs. The bookcases and china cabinets were constructed with columns and grill-work doors (12). The sofas had a classic outline (10), sometimes with dogs' feet or lions' paws (1). Chairs with these feet styles were found in the tomb of King Tutankhamen (fourteenth century B.C.) in 1922.

Figure 12.15
continued

Figure 12.16
Biedermeier Period furniture.
Courtesy of *Furniture Facts,* 26th Ed., Hoover Universal, Inc.

Biedermeier Period, 1800–1850

Many German designers and craftsmen began producing simplified and sturdy furniture named after a fictitious character called "Papa Biedermeier," who represented middle-class Germans.

The furniture was designed to be functional and had very little ornamentation such as carvings, mountings, brass, or inlaid work (see Figure 12.16). Cabinets (1) and desks had square lines and efficient and simple designs. Chairs (3, 4,) were designed for comfort and strength, and they had thick cushioned seats. The legs of chairs were straight, tapered (3, 4), and sometimes curved (6). Table legs were usually round, straight (2, 5), and sometimes connected by heavy bases (2, 7). Ash, birch, fruitwoods, mahogany, and maple were the woods most commonly used. Native flowers or fruits and domestic animals were used as decorations.

Figure 12.17
Victorian Period furniture.
Courtesy of *Furniture Facts,* 26th Ed., Hoover Universal, Inc.

Victorian Period, 1830-1890

During this English period, furniture reflected an increasing utilization of machine methods, which led to the excessive use of decorative details. Prince Albert, consort of Queen Victoria, took the lead in the decorative arts. The Queen, conservative and sentimental, saved everything. Symbols of this period are knickknacks, elaborate floral patterns in carpets and wallpaper, and the horsehair-covered sofa. Decorations consisted of birds, flowers, and needlework (8). The woods used were mahogany, rosewood, and walnut. The favorite colors were black and dark green. The furniture was heavy and durable (see Figure 12.17). It was characterized by chairs with oval (1) or horseshoe-shaped (4, 5) backs. The backs were solid and upholstered, with some backs button-tufted. The upholstered seats were usually round or oval (1, 4, 5) and crowned in the center. If used, the arms were curved and low (1, 7), sometimes joining the rest rail near the back (7). This served more to brace the back than to support the arms of user. Marble tops (9) appeared on dressers and washstands. The beds were made with high headboards and footboards. The enormous dressers nearly reached the ceiling with their long beveled-edge mirrors. Other typical furniture

Figure 12.17
Victorian Period furniture, continued

pieces were whatnots designed for the display of objects, lacquered chairs, and sewing cabinets inlaid with mother-of-pearl. Enormous buffets and dressers were built later in the period.

Other Period Furniture Styles

Several period furniture styles have also influenced, to some extent, the designs of furniture over the years. Some representative examples are listed below.

Art Moderne (1925 to present)	French Regence (1715–1723)
Borax (about 1925 to present)	French Renaissance (1453–1610)
Carolean (1660–1688)	Gothic (1180–1509)
Chinese (1500–1800)	Italian Renaissance (1400–1600)
Commonwealth (1649–1660)	Jacobean (1603–1649)
Directoire (1795–1804)	L'Art Nouveau (1890–1905)
Dutch Renaissance (1500–1600)	Louis XIII (1610–1643)
Eastlake (1879–1895)	Louis XIV (1643–1715)

Egyptian (4000–300 B.C.)

Flemish (Seventeenth century)

French Classic (1760–1785)

French Empire (1804–1815)

Spanish Renaissance (1500–1700)

Tudor-Elizabethan (1509–1603)

Hitchcock Style (1820–1850)

Mission (1895–1910)

Directoire, 1795–1804

After the French Revolution, five directors ruled France. They eliminated all signs of aristocracy and royalty. A Jury of Arts and Manufactures controlled furniture design. The royal decorations were replaced with classic ornaments. The influence of Egyptian, Greek, and Roman designs is apparent. The furniture pieces had elegance, grace, simplicity, and a purity of line.

Tudor-Elizabethan Period, 1509–1603

The Tudors were the English royal family whose style of architecture and furniture prevailed during the reigns of four Tudor monarchs: Henry VII, Henry VIII, Edward VI, and Mary I. The furniture was heavy and cumbersome. It had the Tudor rose as a decoration and was massive and squat. Canopy beds were used. The most important woods employed were oak and walnut. The table legs were bulblike and there were low bars on the chairs. The rooms usually had beams. Wainscoting of simple rectangular panels with moldings was used on interior walls. Later in the period, geometric or scroll designs, using various woods, were inlaid in the panels. These designs also appeared, along with bold carving, on furniture.

Jacobean Period, 1603–1649

The English kings Charles I, Charles II, and James I maintained an active, ceremonial court life. The furniture made during this time showed the masculine in-

Figure 12.18
Modern rendition of a Jacobean gate-leg table.
Courtesy of Ethan Allen, Inc.

fluence. It was low, simply constructed, very durable, and massive. The principal woods used were oak and walnut. Table legs were straight or melon-shaped. The gate-leg table (Figure 12.18) was first developed during this period. Wood was extensively carved in low relief. Chairs had flat seats and low stretchers. Upholsteries were made from brocade, chenille, ribbon fabrics, leather, needlepoint, tapestry, and velvet.

French Empire Period, 1804–1815

This French-inspired furniture showed a masculine influence (see Figure 12.19). It was heavy, massive, and militaristic. Wreaths contained the letter N (for Napoleon). Ornamentation included honeysuckle, ivy, copies of Roman forms, and heroes of classical mythology. Principal woods used were ebony, mahogany, rosewood, and lots of veneer. Upholstery materials included heavy brocades, damasks, velvets, and leather.

Figure 12.19
French Empire Period arm-chair.

Provincial Furniture

The provincial furniture designs can be broken into the following periods.

French Provincial Period, 1650–1900

French Provincial includes a wide range of furniture made in France from the Middle Ages through the nineteenth century. The early pieces were made by craftsmen in the provinces to meet the needs of the peasant farmers. Later, in the eighteenth century, copies of the styles popular in the court at Paris were produced. Most current reproductions are simplified versions of Louis XIV and Louis XV styles. These pieces are comfortable, useful, and unpretentious (Figure 12.20).

Ladder-back chairs were developed in Normandy and Burgundy. Ladder-back settees (10) were produced in Provence. Straw-seated chairs were common in other provinces. Chairs were flat, with curved arms, resting on turned supports, and they were often upholstered (4, 5). Beds had canopies (12) and high posts. Armoires were found in all provinces.

Figure 12.20

French Provincial Period furniture.
Courtesy of *Furniture Facts,* 26th Ed., Hoover Universal, Inc.

Straight legs were found on nearly all early furniture (5, 10, 11, 12). Later pieces had cabriole legs (2, 3, 4, 7, 8). Stretchers appear on many pieces (5, 6, 10). Decoration was simple (4, 5, 7). Shaped aprons (1, 2, 7, 8) appeared on chests, cupboards, and tables. Trestle tables were made at first; then the cabriole legs (2, 3, 7, 8) became popular. Decorations were simple carvings. Modern styles are reproduced as sectional sofas, coffee and end tables, triple dressers, pianos, and TV sets.

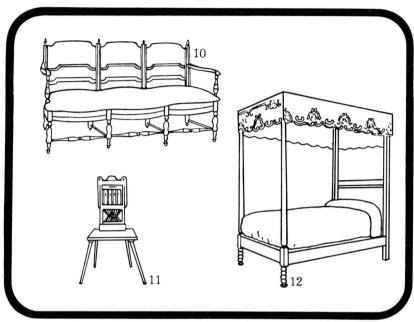

Figure 12.20
French Provincial Period furniture, continued

Figure 12.21
Italian Provincial Period furniture.
Courtesy of *Furniture Facts*, 26th Ed., Hoover Universal, Inc.

Italian Provincial Period, 1700–1850

The craftsmen in the Italian provinces simplified the lines of the elaborate furniture found in the major cities. They also eliminated the ornate decoration (see Figure 12.21).

Lines were predominately rectangular in cabinets (7), chests (6), desks (3), and sideboards (2). Those pieces had straight, square, tapered legs (4). Curves that appeared in occasional furniture (5), tables, and dining chairs (1) were graceful, smooth, and had few ornaments. Fruitwoods, mahogany, and walnut were the most commonly used woods.

Figure 12.22
American Colonial Period furniture.
Courtesy of *Furniture Facts,* 26th Ed., Hoover Universal, Inc.

American Colonial Period, 1620-1790

American Colonial is the name given to the furniture made by the first settlers. The lines were simple, straight, and sturdy (see Figure 12.22). This furniture was made of fruitwoods, maple, oak, and pine. The fabrics were simple homespuns, calicoes, chintzes, cretonnes, crewel embroideries, and rusks. Characteristic pieces were bannister back chairs (1), ladder-back chairs and rockers (5), gate-leg (3) and trestle tables (6), the cobbler's bench, highchests (4), and hutches (7). These pieces were infrequently decorated with carvings and metal work introduced by the Dutch.

Pennsylvania Dutch Period, 1680-1850

These furniture craftsmen made plain, solid Germanic pieces to meet the needs of a rural people in eastern Pennsylvania, southern New York, and New Jersey. Characteristic pieces (Figure 12.23) included the dower chest (4), generally square chest-on-chest cupboards (7), and hanging cabinets. The legs were usually round (2, 5) or square (3). Fruitwoods, maple, pine, and walnut were the native woods used. Sunbursts, medallions, geometric designs, and animal, floral, and fruit decorations were prevalent.

Figure 12.23
Pennsylvania Dutch Period furniture.
Courtesy of *Furniture Facts,* 26th Ed., Hoover Universal, Inc.

Late Colonial Period, 1700–1790

This American Provincial period applies to all American furniture made before the Revolution. This style of furniture ranges in design from complete simplicity to rich ornamentation as larger homes were built by increasing numbers of wealthy people. This brought about more sophisticated furniture adapted from English styles. At first lines were straight; later, curves were introduced. Maple, oak, and black walnut woods were used as well as damask, brocade, tapestry, taffeta, haircloth, and leather for upholstery. Ornamentation included carvings with acanthus-leaf, pendant, pineapple, and shell motifs. Characteristic furniture of the late colonial style included the ladder-back chair, the Windsor chair, the four-poster bed, and the butterfly table. Other furniture styles, adapted or imported from England, included the highboy, lowboy, tilt-top table, rocking chair, block-front desk, cedar storage chest, and the low-post bed. Adaptations of these pieces of furniture are still in demand today.

Figure 12.24
Windsor chairs.
Courtesy of *Furniture Facts,* 26th Ed., Hoover Universal, Inc.

Windsor Chairs Period, 1725–1800

Windsor chairs enjoyed their greatest popularity and most graceful styling in America even though they were named after Windsor Castle in England. They became the favorite chair in many American homes because they were attractive, comfortable, light, and sturdy. Wheelwrights originally made the chairs, which accounts for the use of the bentwood back frame, supported by spindles, and legs pegged into saddle seats. Many shapes (Figure 12.24) were common, such as hoop (1), fan (6), comb (4), and bow backs, rockers (5), and braced (3) backs.

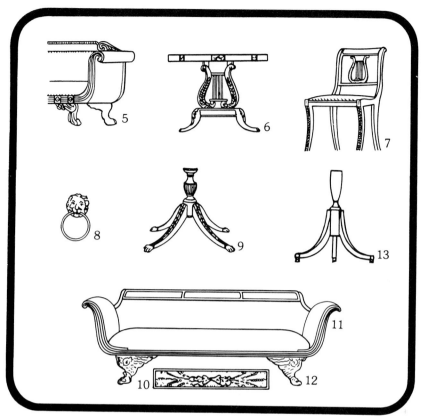

Figure 12.25
Duncan Phyfe Period furniture.
Courtesy of *Furniture Facts,* 26th Ed., Hoover Universal, Inc.

Varied woods were used including birch and pine for the seats; ash, birch, and hickory for the bent parts; and birch, maple, and oak for turned parts.

Shaker Period, 1776–1850

The Shakers were an American religious sect derived from the Quakers. They first appeared in New York before spreading over the East and establishing communal villages. Their craftsmen made everything they needed by hand. Religion prevailed in their daily life. The major characteristic was the lack of decoration. All pieces were designed to be functional. Legs of chairs and tables were round or square. Swivel chairs were produced. Slat-back construction showed up in early chairs. Later, spindles and sewing stands were used. Pedestal table and rockers were built. Native woods used were fruitwoods, maple, and pine.

Duncan Phyfe Period, 1790–1830

Although Duncan Phyfe was a person, not a time period, Duncan Phyfe Period is the term used to describe the first American furniture designer-maker's definite

Figure 12.26
Federal Period furniture.
Courtesy of *Furniture Facts,* 26th Ed., Hoover Universal, Inc.

furniture style. He utilized Adam, Hepplewhite, and Sheraton motifs. The motifs (see Figure 12.25) included the lyre (6, 7), acanthus, lion's head (8), wheat (10), and bunches of arrows. Many pieces were decorated with fluting, reeding, brass-tipped feet, and glass knobs. Symbols of the American independence, such as the eagle, horn of plenty, and the number 13, were characteristic of Duncan Phyfe furniture. Fabrics used were brocades, woolens, satins, silks, and horsehairs.

Furniture characteristically of Duncan Phyfe influence includes chairs with straight and curved legs (7); chairs with low backs and rolled-over top rails (7); tables with single lyre or column pedestals, flared legs, and curule feet (6, 9, 13). Other Phyfe furniture included drop-leaf tables, dressing tables, and sofas with "sleigh" front arms (5, 11).

Duncan Phyfe's furniture was influenced by the French and was curved, graceful, and slender. He favored dark mahogany wood, but also used cherry and walnut. During this time, about 1820, power was applied to woodworking and furniture manuacturing to add to the further sophistication of furniture.

Federal Period, 1795–1830

The Federal Period covered the time period beween late colonial and Victorian periods in America. Duncan Phyfe highly influenced the furniture. Other inspi-

Figure 12.27
Mediterranean Period furniture.
Courtesy of *Furniture Facts,* 26th Ed., Hoover Universal, Inc.

rations came from French Empire, eighteenth century, and colonial styles. Simple turnings (5) were used (see Figure 12.26). Irregular fronts and mirrors were used in chests. Sideboards were heavy and decorated with columns (6). Favored motifs were the acanthus, cornucopias, glass knobs, pineapples, and scrolls. Patriotic themes were also used (2, 4). Favorite woods were ash, fruitwoods, hickory, mahogany, and oak.

Mediterranean Period, 1500-1800

Mediterranean furniture began with local peasant craftsmen who used native materials and woods to build furniture for local use. The Moorish influence was adapted by Italian, Portuguese, and Spanish craftsmen. This style thrived after the sixteenth century, lost some interest in the nineteenth century, and returned to become popular today as the *Spanish Modern* style. The style usually has facades of turned spindles (6), geometric patterns (1), and deep carvings with decorations of fret and guilloches (3) (see Figure 12.27). The hardware is heavy and is often ornamented with brass nail heads, leather, and brass or iron hardware. The furniture is functional and has a masculine look. The woods used are mostly dark in color. The favorite woods are chestnut, mahogany, pecan, red pine, and walnut. Black, red, or brocaded upholstery is used.

Figure 12.28
Current Early American furniture.
Courtesy of *Furniture Facts,* 26th Ed., Hoover Universal, Inc.

Early American Current

Current Early American styles of furniture have come to us over a period of two centuries from the American Colonial period. Designers and manufacturers in California, New England, and the Southwest have redesigned the colonial styles to match casual and formal (provincial) living areas that people want today.

Decorative characteristics include the flourishes found in arms of the sofa (2), the hutch scrolls (3), and the ornately turned legs (1) (see Figure 12.28). Mechanical equipment is widely used for dual purpose furniture like the sofabed (2), the swivel chair (4), and the rocking chair. Naturally finished fruitwoods and maple are widely employed. Ash, hickory, and pine are used infrequently.

Contemporary Furniture

The word *contemporary* means the current designs of the day and describes furniture that has a modernized form of classic design. Contemporary furniture does not depend on artificial decoration but on beauty of good finish and design. It has simple and graceful lines.

Modern

The *art moderne* style of the French designers at the 1925 Paris Exposition inspired the American designers to create modern furniture. Until that date almost all American furniture was patterned after historical periods. The 1933 Exposition in Chicago also promoted modern furniture. At present, it is the most popular single style. This style is in a transitional state that may last for many years.

The clean, simple lines and the elimination of unnecessary decoration lead to mass production of modern furniture. Flat surfaces and straight lines are combined with graceful curves. Knobs and pulls are functional, and so is the furniture. Almost all types of cabinet woods are used. There is a broad use of veneer. Metals, plastics, and glass are sometimes employed. Plastic and plastic-coated fabrics are also used. Sectional assemblies are popular with this type of furniture. For example, sofas are available in individual piece sections.

Modern Metal Furniture

The post-World War II era has brought about the use of metal in furniture for the home as well as for patio, porch, or kitchen. Metal and part-metal furniture is made from brass; stainless, chrome-plated tubing; copper; aluminum; and wrought iron. Upholstered cushions are frequently tufted. Other materials utilized include plywood, glass, cloth, molded plastics, and plastic-coated wood.

Thin legs used in chairs are mostly straight lined. Chairs are shaped and formed. Metal ferrules or sleeves are commonly used. The flat surfaces are smooth, brightly colored, and highly polished. Coarsely woven, novelty fabrics, and washable plastics prevail.

Shaker Modern

Shaker Modern is a current interpretation of the original Shaker period furniture. It has simple, well-proportioned lines. The pegging and dovetailing generally show. Plane surfaces are unadorned.

The legs are usually straight-lined with a little tapering. Metal ferrules are not used. Native fruitwoods and maple with simple oil finishes are employed. This style furniture is rarely upholstered. It is usually placed in small rooms.

Ranch Styles—American

Furniture of the old West was plain, heavy, sturdy, and functional, often showing Spanish-Mexican influence. The furniture sold today is utilized throughout the home. Earlier pieces were originally designed for use in patios and sun rooms.

Ranch furniture has an informal, provincial style. It has a rustic and simple design. The pioneer western look is maintained through the use of leather, inter-

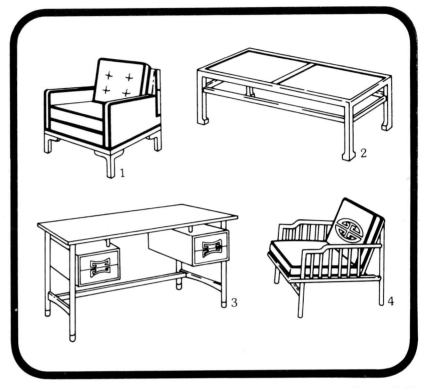

Figure 12.29
Oriental Modern furniture.
Courtesy of *Furniture Facts,* 26th Ed., Hoover Universal, Inc.

laced rawhide or plastic cord, and surfaces of joined boards with no attempt to conceal where they are joined. The wooden seats are flat. Decorative cushions are often used. The legs usually have square corners and are tapered. Ranch and western themes are used as decorative motifs. Native woods include birch, maple, oak, pine, and redwood.

Oriental Modern
Furniture designs from the Far East (China, India, Japan, and other countries) have contributed to contemporary styles in the United States. The sharp lines of Oriental Modern chests, tables, and chairs are prevalent in modern furniture (see Figure 12.29). Leg terminations (1, 4) and geometric treatment of upholstery and frames come from the Chinese culture. Bamboo, koa, and teak are widely used. Oversize hardware (3) and accents (beads, gold, and lacquer) are also widely used.

Scandinavian Modern

The Danish and Swedish designers marketed "modern" furniture during the 1930s. This furniture lacked decoration. The designers used plain woods like maple, oak, and walnut in simple curves and roundings, with tapered feet and flat turnings. The legs are round- or square-tapered. Chair seats use woven fibers, and plastics are employed as upholstery. This style of furniture is used in formal and informal living areas.

JOINING, DECORATING, AND FINISHING WOOD FURNITURE

Joining Furniture

Once the lumber and plywood pieces have been cut into the appropriate size and shape, they are ready to be joined together to make a piece of furniture. One of the earmarks of quality furniture is how it is fastened together. Because many of the joints cannot be seen, the salesperson may need to point them out as hidden values to the furniture customer.

Fasteners used to join furniture are nails, staples, screws, glue, and joints. Nails and staples are used mostly in low-priced furniture and occasionally in medium-priced furniture. Screws, because of their threads, give support to the furniture and hold the pieces together better than nails or staples. Quality pieces of furniture have screws securing backs and unexposed parts. Glue is used to connect most joints.

Basic Types of Joints

Furniture may be joined together by nine basic types of joints. They are butt, dado, rabbet, tongue-and-groove, miter, mortise-and-tenon, lap, dovetail, and dowel joints (Figure 12.30). Each of the joints may be adapted and combined in several ways.

The *plain butt* joint is made by placing one piece of wood against another piece of wood and gluing, nailing, or screwing them together. It is considered to be a poor joint because it needs additional reinforcement.

The *dado joint* connects one piece of wood with a groove into another piece of wood which fits. This joint is used in drawer fronts, to hold drawer bottoms to the sides of drawers, to hold shelves, and to secure the sides of furniture to front and back panels.

The *rabbet joint* joins two pieces of wood in which one piece fits into another which has been cut to the expected width of the first piece. This joint is used for a smooth continuous surface such as a drawer side. It may be *splined* for reinforcement by using a thin piece of metal or wood inserted in both pieces to prevent them from slipping.

The *tongue-and-groove joint* has a projection that fits into a groove. This joint keeps the pieces aligned and is often used for fitting bureau drawers or the side of a desk together.

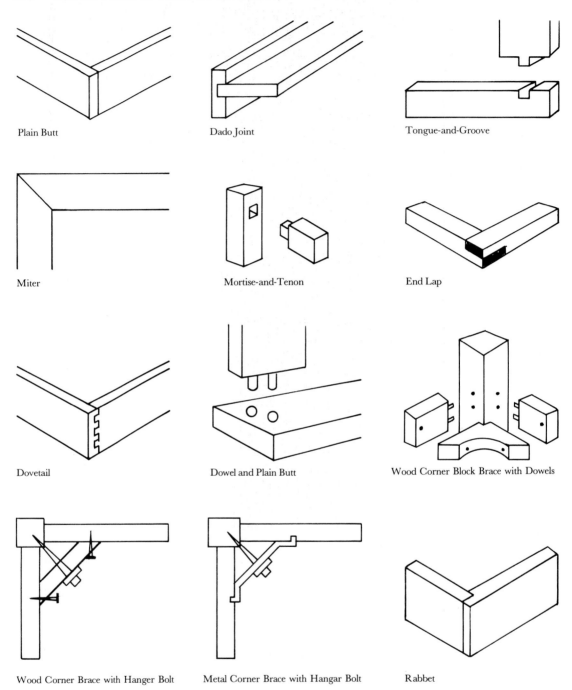

Plain Butt

Dado Joint

Tongue-and-Groove

Miter

Mortise-and-Tenon

End Lap

Dovetail

Dowel and Plain Butt

Wood Corner Block Brace with Dowels

Wood Corner Brace with Hanger Bolt

Metal Corner Brace with Hangar Bolt

Rabbet

Figure 12.30
Basic types of joints.

Miter joints fit two pieces of wood together at the ends to hide the ends for a smooth continous surface such as that found in picture frames. Since this joint is a weak joint, mechanical fasteners, splines, and other pieces of decorative hardware are used.

The *mortise-and-tenon joint* is made with a projection (tenon) which may be inserted into a rectangular hole (mortise). It is used for framing, bracing, and for rails.

Lap joints are made by cutting out equal amounts from two pieces of wood to be fitted together so that a smooth continuing surface remains. They are used to support brace legs and cabinet frames, and to join sections of chairs, couches, and beds.

The *dovetail joint* is one of the strongest joints used in woodworking because its pieces interlock. It offsets both pull and thrust stresses. Dovetail joints are often used in joining drawers and in top rail and leg construction in cabinetwork. These joints are the best for joining drawers because they cannot warp out of shape or come apart.

The *dowel joint* is made by fitting a chalk-size piece of kiln-dried hardwood, which may have spiral grooves into it so that air may escape, into a hole that is drilled in the two pieces of wood to be connected. Glue has been inserted into the holes. This is a butt joint that has been reinforced with dowels. Dowel joints are used for joining various parts of chairs, sofas, and the legs to the body of desks and tables.

Reinforced corner joints are corner braces used to strengthen joints and corners. Made of wood or metal, they prevent sway and loosening of joints. They are often used in units with legs, such as in the construction of desks and tables.

Decorating Furniture

Furniture can be decorated in many ways. Following is a description of some decorating methods.

Carving designs by hand is one of the ways detail may be achieved in solid wood. Machine carving (spindle carving) is often touched up by hand to add beauty to it after it has been turned on a lathe.

Fluting is a type of carving that is made by perpendicular grooves running parallel or in a funnel shape on legs or posts.

Reeding is the opposite of fluting. Convex or raised perpendicular lines with rounded edges are often used to decorate legs and posts.

Moldings give a raised outline. They are different wood sections fitted into grooves.

Inlay means to insert. Strips of wood or other materials may be inserted in channels that have been grooved in the wood. The strips are usually made from veneer that is $\frac{1}{28}$ inch thick. They may vary from $\frac{1}{8}$ to 4 inches in width.

Marquetry is a variety of inlay formed from woods or other materials. It is assembled in some design formation and glued to a paper background for ease in handling and applying to furniture. The design is fitted into grooves and made flush with the surface of the furniture.

Appliqué or *overlay* looks like a marquetry design except that this veneer panel form is glued on top of the wood surface to produce a raised design.

Decalcomania transfer designs are transferred from a lithographic stone to gummed paper that is strong and porous. They may be applied on a finished surface and waxed or they may be applied before varnishing. This is an imitation of hand painting.

Embossed or applied ornaments may be obtained by molding synthetic material and pasting it on inexpensive furniture.

Tooling designs may be effected by placing an adhesive coating on a leather surface, then pressing thin sheets of gold leaf with an embossing tool to form a design. Transparent finishes then bond the design to the leather.

Finishing Wood Furniture

Finishing may be defined as the process of coating or treating a wood surface for the purpose of protecting and/or decorating the piece of furniture. Almost all wood furniture should be finished.

The finish does a lot of things. It enhances the beauty of the color and grain of the wood. A good finish may bleach or darken the wood as desired, and it protects the wood against dirt, moisture, and wear. It may make less expensive woods look like better-quality woods. A finish that makes one wood appear to be another, must, by federal regulations, use the word *finish* in describing it. Thus "walnut veneer and walnut-finished gumwood" could be a correct description of a finish. Colors are used to make the furniture more attractive or to match or change the color of the wood. A finish may be *opaque* to hide the grain, change the color, or cover blemishes. Paint is an opaque finish used to cover lower-quality woods such as pine and fir. A finish like a stain may be transparent to change the color, but accent the beautiful grain patterns. This finish is used on more expensive woods like walnut and maple. New furniture may be finished to look like antique furniture by utilizing special techniques called *distressing* or *antiquing*. These finishes are usually applied after completion of the initial finishing process. Edges of furniture may be darkened to obtain the antique look, or painted with small marks over the surface that look like scars. *Specking* the entire piece may be accomplished by using dark-color paint, by scratching and denting the surface of the furniture with chains, or by boring small holes that look like worm holes.

Unfinished furniture may be purchased inexpensively so that it can be finished at home. There are many steps in finishing furniture. An excellent finish requires an orderly procedure. Most finishes are applied by:

1. Preparing the surface by sanding it.
2. Staining the surface coloring matter to raise the grain for sanding.
3. Filling and/or sealing the coarse-grained woods (ash and oak) and medium-grained woods (mahogany and walnut) with a paste, called a *filler*, that is rubbed into the pores of the wood. The filler is then sealed with a coat of shellac or lacquer and sanded again.

4.   Applying the top coats of finish such as shellac, varnish, lacquer, or paint.

5.   Waxing to give a sheen to the wood.

Common methods of applying the finishes are rubbing, rolling, brushing, dipping, and spraying. Special alcohol- and burn-resistant finishes may be applied to furniture at an extra expense.

FURNITURE CLASSIFICATIONS

Furniture manufacturers usually divide furniture into four major classifications: (1) occasional, (2) case goods, (3) upholstered, and (4) bedding. Furniture stores and departments usually arrange furniture into groups, based on these classifications. In addition to the four major classifications, there are minor classifications such as cedar chests, nursery furniture, kitchen furniture, summer furniture, and unpainted furniture.

Occasional Furniture

Small, nonmatching, accessory pieces such as coffee or lamp tables, television tables, whatnots, and étagères (variations of open shelves used for sundry items) are called occasional furniture.

Case Goods

China closets, desks, cabinets, chests of drawers, buffets, and other pieces of case-like or boxlike furniture are known as case goods. Because matching chairs, tables, beds, and other items are grouped and sold as sets or suites, the term *case goods* generally refers to dining room and bedroom furniture as a whole. Certain cabinet-like pieces in the living room such as buffet, desk, and china closet are also called case goods.

Construction of Case Goods

Outside Case.   Corner posts are made of solid wood; the panels are constructed of solid or veneered plywood. The outer frame is usually put together with mortise-and-tenon or dowel joints. The back of the case is set into the frame and screwed or nailed into place. The back is often finished to match the front and sides. The total case is finished so that there is evenness of color and no rough spots. Exposed surfaces of the wood are usually named on the label.

Inside Case.   The center or side drawer guides are fastened to the frame. Glued blocks are often used for additional strength. Metal glides may be used to provide easy action of drawers. Better cabinets have dustproof panels set into the frame to keep the dust from sifting through the drawers.

Drawer Construction. The sides and front and often the back are joined with dovetail construction (in better-quality cabinets). The bottom of the drawer is set into grooves in the back and sides. The inside of the drawer may be sanded smooth and finished to prevent snags and to clean it easily. The drawer bottom may be constructed of plywood or hardboard material. Small blocks may be glued underneath the drawer for additional strength and support.

Floating Construction. Solid wood furniture may be built in such a way that it can expand without buckling by placing the screws that hold the tops and sides together in slotted screwholes. This method allows the top and sides to expand or contract without damage to the furniture and is called *floating construction.*

Upholstered Furniture

Furniture made with filling materials and covered with a surface material (fabric, leather, or plastic) is known as upholstered furniture. Examples of upholstered furniture are barrel chairs, club chairs, love seats, and sofas.

Construction of Upholstered Furniture

Each part of upholstered furniture may be made from good-quality or poor-quality materials. Well-constructed upholstered furniture will remain comfortable for several years. Upholstered furniture made of inferior quality materials may become lumpy and uncomfortable within a short period of time.

Frame. The better-quality frame will be made of good-quality hardwood such as ash, birch, maple, or oak. It will not be made from gumwood, yellow poplar, or pine. The exposed parts of the frame should be made of walnut, mahogany, or other desired wood. The frame should be put together with mortise-and-tenon or dowel joints and reinforced for strength.

Bottom. The bottom may be made of various materials such as interwoven webbing, securely fastened, metal strapping, or a cover of heavy canvas. Sometimes wooden slats are used. The webbing or other material may be used on the back or on the sides.

Seat. The seat will be made of springs and filling. The springs may be single- or double-cone, high-tempered steel tied eight ways for the better-quality furniture and tied four ways for the lower-quality furniture. The number of springs used ranges from six to twelve according to the quality desired. The springs are put close together and covered with burlap, which supports the filling materials. Zigzag springs may be used instead of the cone type for lightweight furniture.

Filling. The filling may be moss, horsehair, hog's hair, cotton fibers, down, feather, foam rubber, or urethane foam. A muslin inner lining may be used to cover the filling. Layers of cotton padding are used over the filling.

Cushions.   The cushion is filled with down, foam rubber, feathers, polyurethane foam, or springs, covered with cotton padding and finishing fabric. Down and feathers come from birds and are often mixed together for softness in better-quality cushions. Foam rubber and polyurethane foam are used in less expensive cushions, especially in the cushions where the bottoms and seats of modern furniture are made of slats, webbing, or strap steel. Some cushions have zippers for easy cleaning and replacement of inner materials. *Tight seat construction* is where the cushions are attached to the bottom. Contents of cushions must be labeled accurately.

Roll-Edge.   The roll-edge is a thick fiber rope around the front edge of the seat or cushion that makes it more flexible and comfortable.

Back.   The back is constructed similar to the seat except that lighter coil springs are used.

Cover or Finishing Fabrics.   Almost any fabric may be used to cover upholstered furniture. The fabric will wear better if the weave is tight and a strong yarn is used. Carefully selected fabric should be carefully matched, hand-tailored, have good seams, and have roll edge or welting around the edges.
 Leather is a widely used, but expensive, material for upholstery purposes. Vinyl and urethane plastics, which resemble leather, are also widely used for upholstery materials.

Tufting.   Tufting used on the surface of the backs and seats of chairs and sofas adds to the cost of upholstered furniture. It takes time and skill to add this costly feature. Two types of tufting are generally used. One is *diamond tufting* and it is very deep and somewhat firm. A block-shaping tufting called *biscuit tufting* is used for modern furniture. In both methods of tufting, buttons are used to hold the material in shape. These buttons are fastened securely to the webbing so they will remain tight.

Bedding

Day beds, sofa beds, springs, and mattresses are all known as bedding.

GOVERNMENT REGULATIONS AND THE HOUSEHOLD FURNITURE INDUSTRY

The Federal Trade Commission issued Trade Practice Rules of the Household Furniture Industry that became effective March 18, 1964. These rules were established in order to protect the consumers, the retail trade, and members of the furniture industry. They require retailers and manufacturers to be truthful in making statements or claims about their furniture. Labeling by hang tags is required. Statements shown on labels and in advertising must be accurate, not deceiving. Information about woods, names of woods, imitation woods, leather and its imitations, surface coverings, filling materials, origin of styles, and other materials used to make furniture are covered by these rules. These rules also cover information about deceptive pricing and advertising practices in retailing. The following areas are covered by these ru es.

Woods

The exposed parts of furniture that are wood must be described accurately. If the wood is maple and it looks like birch, it cannot be labeled "birch." Veneer cannot be labeled "walnut"; it must be labeled "walnut veneer." Nor can it be called "solid wood."

Nonwood Materials

The label "wood" is to be used for wood materials only. Particle board or hardboard, both made of wood fibers, must be labeled "particle board" or "fiberboard." Any time a surface wood (veneer) imitates another wood grain, it has to be accurately labeled; for example, a "walnut veneer with imitation burl figures." Any surface material with a finish that looks like wood must be correctly labeled, such as "mahogany-grained plastic finish."

Place of Origin

Trade names must not be misleading as to the origin of furniture. "Asheville furniture" suggests that the furniture is made in Asheville, North Carolina. Any foreign-made furniture must indicate the country where it is produced. Swedish modern furniture not made in Sweden must be labeled or advertised as "Swedish modern style" or "Swedish style" if it is made in the United States. Because the term *French provincial* has been used so long and is generally known by the public, it may be used to describe a specific style of furniture rather than its place of origin.

Filling Materials

The filling materials used in upholstered furniture must be correctly described in advertising or on the labels. Reused materials must be described in detail on the label.

CARDBOARD AND FIBERBOARD FURNITURE

Some furniture is made from corrugated cardboard that may be laminated in several layers that alternate in direction. This strong, unusually styled furniture may have a textured surface. Its greatest advantage is that it is inexpensive. Other furniture may be made from fiberboard that has been formed into tubes and beams. The chairs, shelves, stools, and tables have a plasticized outer surface and are strong and inexpensive.

PLASTIC FURNITURE

Most plastic furniture is made from polyurethane and fiberglass-reinforced plastics. Polyurethane plastic may be molded into shells that make attractive and colorful chairs, chests, desks, and tables. *Rigid plastics,* like polyester and polystyrene, are often used as legs and exposed frames and for molded drawers with fronts made of wood. Metal or wood inserts are often placed in the mold so that nails or screws may be added later. Fiberglass-reinforced plastics, in shell form, may be joined with strong tubular metal to make lightweight chairs and other long-lasting furniture for businesses, homes, industries, and schools.

A *soft-type furniture* may be built of varying thicknesses or gauges of vinyl and filled with air. The thinner the vinyl, the less durable the furniture will be because it is easily torn. This also means it is less expensive than the thicker gauges of vinyl. The shapes of this furniture may be built to suit the user; shapes such as arms, backs, and seats may be filled with air. They may be inflated with air with a regular tire pump and may be deflated for easy storage or transporting. A beanbag chair is filled with small pieces of polyester to give buoyancy under the thick vinyl cover. When a person moves to a different position, the pieces of vinyl shift to the person's form and weight.

The greatest disadvantage of furniture made of plastic is the toxic smoke that the plastics emit if the plastic piece is in a fire.

Waterbeds

There are many variations of waterbeds, also called flotation systems, ranging from inexpensive to expensive. An inexpensive waterbed kit may include particle board and unfinished solid wood in the pedestal foundation and bed frame. The vinyl water mattress may have a middle- or top-heated lap seam, and fewer baffles built inside to cause little distribution of water to offset body weight and pressure. (A lap seam is made by overlapping two vinyl edges and sealing them together using a low density microwave. The heating unit is a flat metal grid system inside two pieces of vinyl. It is placed beneath the sides or middle of the water mattress. Several types of controls are made to be attached to the heating unit and are extended to the side or top of the bed.) A waterbed may require a heater, a custom-made quilted cover, and custom-made sheets. An expensive waterbed kit includes a solid wood pedestal foundation, a water mattress with a bottom-heated lap seam, sufficient baffles built inside the vinyl water mattress to provide even distribution of water, finished solid wood rails, and a headboard. It may not require a water heater and may use standard bed sheets. Another example of a flotation system that would come unassembled might include a steel bed frame with a center brace and plastic end caps; a polyurethane foam foundation several inches thick that rests on the bed frame; a five-inch-thick polyurethane border into which nests a vinyl water bag enclosed inside a vinyl liner; and a zip-on damask cover quilted to an inch or more of polyurethane foam for insulation to cover the water bag and border.

The unassembled system usually comes with instructions, a drain and fill kit, and an algae-killing solution. A regular water hose, like a garden hose, is used to fill the water bag. A queen-size flotation system will usually hold about sixty gallons of water weighing about 700 pounds when filled. It measures sixty inches in width and eighty inches in length. A king-size flotation system will usually hold about eighty-five gallons of water weighing over 900 pounds. It is about seventy-five inches wide and eighty inches long. Matching bedroom furniture may be sold with a flotation system. Some disadvantages include filling and draining of water, the weight, and potential puncturing.

BEDDING AND ITS CONSTRUCTION

Bedding is classified as springs, mattresses, chair beds, day beds, sofa beds, and ottoman beds. The furniture may be used to sleep on at night and to sit on during the day. These beds are constructed about the same way as upholstered furniture. Appropriate bedding is important to one's comfort and health. It is important that salespeople involved with bedding learn as much as they can about it.

Mattresses

There are two main types of mattresses: (1) *innerspring mattresses* that contain springs and (2) *solid* and *nonspring mattresses* made of filling materials such as foam and stuffed mattresses.

Innerspring Mattresses

Springs, varying in shape and made of tempered steel wire, are used in innerspring mattresses (Figure 12.31). Metal clips or wires generally hold these coils together. Muslin may be used to cover small, barrel-shaped springs to ensure that the springs will move evenly under someone's weight. The number of springs and the gauge of springs determine the amount of support given. A double-size mattress contains about 180 to 360 heavy-gauge springs. Or 500 to 850 smaller, thinner-gauge, muslin-pocketed springs may be used in the same space.

Layers of filling or padding materials are used to cover the bottom and top sides of the springs. Some filling materials used are cotton felt, kapok, animal hair, foam latex, or polyurethane foam. Imported horsehair gives the firmest support. Foam latex gives soft to firm support. More expensive mattresses contain preconstructed borders around the edges to help prevent sagging as with the less expensive roll-edges. Most innerspring mattresses have *ventilators,* small circular screen meshes placed along the sides, which allow air to circulate through the mattress. Better quality mattresses also have attached handles secured to the sides to aid in turning and handling.

Solid or Nonspring Mattresses

Stuffed mattresses utilize stuffing materials such as cotton felt, loose cotton, kapok, horsehair, and foam latex. *Cotton felt* and *loose cotton* make a less expensive, good quality solid mattress that tends to become lumpy with use. Imported *horsehair,* from South America, is used with cotton felt because of its durability and resilien-

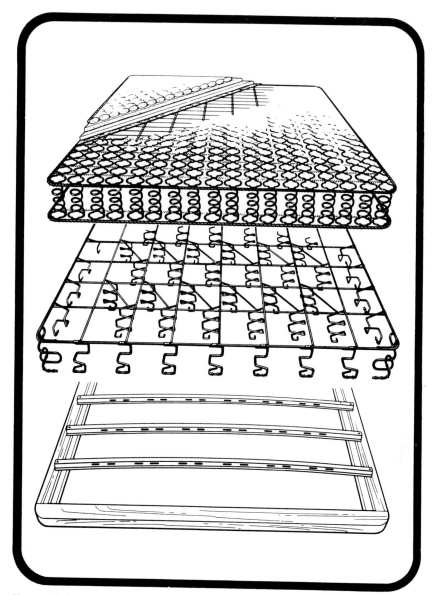

Figure 12.31
An innerspring mattress and foundation.
Courtesy of *Furniture Facts,* 26th Ed., Hoover Universal, Inc.

cy. It is used in better quality mattresses. Quality differs according to the amount and kind of hair used. Hair from the tail of a horse is the most expensive. *Kapok,* an imported vegetable fiber, is used in humid climates because it does not mildew or absorb moisture. It is not very resilient, pulverizes rather quickly, and is used in less expensive mattresses. *Foam latex* may be mixed with cotton felt for use in low- to medium-priced mattresses.

Foam mattresses may be made of natural foam latex, synthetic urethane foam, or both. Urethane foam is lighter than foam latex, less expensive, less resilient, but just as durable. Foam latex mattresses are marked on the side or on the container by a number that gives its firmness. The number "25 – 30" gives the compression resistance in pounds and indicates that the mattress is medium firm.

Fabric coverings enclose both innerspring and nonspring mattresses. A mattress will wear according to the heaviness of the cover. Good, durable covers are made of twill weave, heavy cotton tickings. They are not as attractive and do not have the feel of damasks and sateens. The filling materials are kept from moving by quilting to the outer materials. The better quality mattresses have tufting buttons attached with cords to other buttons on the opposite side.

Care of Mattresses

Cotton mattress covers or quilted pads should be used to keep mattresses clean and to protect them. Muslin pads that have a bonded foam-rubber back should be taken off and washed regularly. The mattress should be vacuumed for soil. Innerspring mattresses should be turned over at least three times a year. Mattresses made of foam should be turned frequently from side to side and end to end to prevent sagging. For the same reason, they should not be used as a chair.

Flammability Standards for Mattresses

The Consumer Product Safety Commission established flammability standards for all mattresses June 7, 1973. The Commission continues its testing and monitoring program regarding the established flammability standards.

Bed Springs

Bed springs are the foundation used to support the mattress and are as important to comfort as the mattress. There are many types and qualities of bed springs, and they vary in cost according to how they are built. The most common types of bed springs are the band, box, link, open-coil, and platform-top.

Band springs and *link springs* are the least expensive and the most space-saving. Strips of wire, bands, or twisted wire are interlaced and supported on the ends by small helical springs. This construction does not allow the resilience of other types of springs, and therefore the mattress may sag after a short period of usage. These springs are used for sofa beds, rollaway beds, children's beds, and cots.

The *box spring* is usually designed to sell with the innerspring mattress and is covered with a matching fabric. The base is made of steel slats or a wooden base to which coil springs are secured with metal braces. These springs are tied together by hand in quality constuctions or by small coil springs or metal clips in less expensive constructions. More springs will give better support for the mattress. Pads of filling materials, such as cotton, rubberized felt, or polyurethane foam, cover the springs to protect the mattress. An appropriate ticking then encases the spring, and a thin muslin is secured underneath the frame to cover it.

Platform-top springs have flat bands of metal that interlace across the top of the coil springs to lend support to the mattress to be used with them. These springs are not covered by fabric. They are constructed mostly for use with soft mattresses and may be firm.

Open-coil springs do not protect the mattress as well as the platform-top springs, but they are more resilient. The coils are secured to the steel slats across the bottom, and small helical springs hold them together on top to allow considerable flexibility.

Size of Beds

The sizes of mattresses are as follows:

1. Single (30 × 74 inches)
2. Twin (38 × 74–80 inches) usually sold in pairs
3. Three-quarter (48 × 74 inches)
4. Double (54 × 74–80 inches)
5. Queen (60 × 80 inches)
6. King (76 × 80–84 inches)

CARE OF FURNITURE

The following procedures should be followed in order to preserve furniture:

1. Wood surfaces should be dusted frequently with a soft, lint-free cloth.
2. Oily spots may be removed by dipping a soft cloth in lukewarm water and mild soap. After the spot is cleaned, wipe it with a clean, damp cloth; then dry it with a soft, dry cloth. Use a humidifier if the house is too dry, so the furniture will not check, crack, or warp.
3. A small amount of furniture polish or wax on a soft cloth should be applied with the grain of the wood. Excess polish or wax should be wiped off, as it collects dust.
4. Foggy streaks or white marks may be removed by rubbing them with a soft cloth dampened in a solution of one tablespoon of vinegar to one quart of water. If the white spot persists, an expert needs to be called to work on it. Turpentine may also be applied—if in doubt on how to use it, call an expert.
5. Use a vacuum cleaner with attachments on upholstered furniture. For spots, use a textile guide for removing spots or call an expert.
6. Polished brass may be cleaned occasionally with brass polish.
7. Except for minor repairs, furniture should be repaired by an expert craftsperson. Replacement of parts and refinishing takes special skill, especially spot finishing and repairs such as fixing dents, gouges, crushed corners, deep scratches, depressions, flaws, severe water rings, or stains; restoring grain finish damaged by cigarette burns or dents

and burns on leather; fixing dents and scratches on white appliances and bronze finishes; restoring antique furniture; restoring vinyl film; repairing cracks in table tops and chair seats; and restoring and maintaining marble.

KEY TERMS

1. Annual rings
2. Bedding
3. Bird's-eye maple
4. Case goods
5. Deciduous
6. Distressing
7. Étagères
8. Floating construction
9. Mediterranean furniture
10. Mortise-and-tenon joints
11. Side chair
12. Spindle
13. Traditional furniture
14. Veneer

STUDY QUESTIONS

1. What are names and approximate dates for each historical period of furniture?
2. Explain why all pieces of furniture in a set may not match perfectly in the appearance of the wood.
3. List the ways of decorating furniture.
4. Describe the difference between a softwood and a hardwood. Name and briefly describe five trees for each group.
5. List the different fasteners, other than joints, used in making furniture. Tell which is better and why.
6. Give the major classifications of furniture and the pieces of furniture included in each classification.
7. Explain the advantages and disadvantages of solid wood and veneer in constructing furniture.
8. What types of joints are used in making furniture?
9. Explain how federal regulations protect the purchasers of household products. Give two examples.
10. Describe the differences between the various finishes.

STUDY ACTIVITIES

1. Obtain a sample of hardwood and a sample of softwood. Examine both closely and write down your observations.
2. Examine a chair, chest of drawers, desk, or table. List the ways that the furniture is reinforced. How sturdy is it? Is the surface smooth? Do the drawers stick? Are they dustproof?
3. Analyze furniture advertisements. What construction, covering materials, finishes, and other technical phrases are featured?

CHAPTER 13

Paper

OBJECTIVES

After completing this chapter, you should be able to:

1. Relate the historical development of paper to the papermaking process.

2. Describe the main sources of fibers used in papermaking. Compare the eight natural fibers, other than wood, with at least two synthetic fibers.

3. Compare the three major types of wood pulp: (1) mechanical or groundwood pulp, (2) chemical wood pulp, and (3) semichemical pulp.

4. List, describe, and recognize seven special finishes given in this chapter.

5. Distinguish the seven grades of paper given in this chapter.

6. Describe four major properties of paper and products using these properties.

Papermaking, a process developed over hundreds of years, is a necessary topic of study for today's fashion merchandiser. Paper is considered a fashion item, as evidenced by the increased floor space retailers now devote to paper party and convenience items, paper by the pound, and other stationery items. Paper is produced from cellulosic fibers obtained from plants. Cellulose is a perfect choice for the composition of paper since cellulose such as wood pulp is strong when wet, relatively inexpensive, and available in large quantities. A basic knowledge of paper manufacturing and finishing will aid the merchant in dealing effectively with the suppliers of paper products.

HISTORICAL DEVELOPMENT

The word *paper* comes from *papyrus,* the plant that Egyptians used to make sheets upon which they could write. The paper substance was under the outer skin (reed) of the plant. These outer reeds were slit thin and laid lengthwise, side by side, with a moist second layer crosswise for reinforcement. The layers were then pressed and dried to form a sheet. Records written on sheets of papyrus are still legible over 4,000 years later.

Papermaking began about 105 A.D. in China when sheets of paper were created using pulp fibers from ground mulberry trees, bamboo stems, old fishnets, hemp waste, and silk rags. The art of papermaking slowly moved westward, reaching the Chinese city of Samarkand. In 704 the Arabians captured the city and with it the secret of making paper. The Arabians substituted linen fiber pulp for silk. The Moors brought the methods to Spain in the twelfth century. Papermaking methods then reached Europe. By the fourteenth century many paper mills existed in Europe, mostly in France, Germany, Italy, and Spain. The first paper factory was built in England about 1490. The first paper mill in America was built by William Rittenhouse in 1690 at Germantown, Pennsylvania.

Moveable type was invented about 1450, causing rapid development of the paper industry and increasing the need for adequate paper supplies. Paper mills later became plagued by shortages of paper because the supply of linen and old rags could not meet the demand. By the eighteenth century it was evident that a process using a more abundant material was needed. About 1719 a Frenchman discovered the value of wood, now the most common source of fiber, for papermaking.

Chlorine was discovered in 1774 and was eventually used for bleaching paper. Today, chlorine bleaching is a common papermaking technique.

Paper was made one sheet at a time until 1798. At that time a paper machine was invented in France with a moving screen belt that would receive a continuous flow of stock and deliver an unbroken sheet of wet paper to a pair of squeeze rolls.

Major pulping processes making large-scale production of paper possible were developed which decreased the dependency on cotton and linen rags. Prior to the nineteenth century, rags were boiled and then beaten into a mushy pulp using a stone mortar-and-pestle process. The Hollander beating machine came into use in the eighteenth century. Groundwood pulp was made by mechanical methods in 1844, and the process was used extensively around 1870. During this time the soda pulping and the sulfite pulping processes were also used.

Before 1800 paper sheets were sized by impregnating them with animal glues or vegetable gums. It was discovered in 1800 that paper could be sized in vats with alum and rosin, a process that became widespread twenty-five years later. Sizing retards moisture absorption by the fibers so that water-based inks will not penetrate and spread.

In 1803, Bryan Donkin, an engineer in England working for Henry and Sealy Fourdrinier, improved the printing machine, and it was patented in 1807.

Since 1803 all papermaking machines using an endless belt of wire cloth to form a continuous sheet have been named Fourdriniers. An English papermaker, John Dickinson, developed a cylinder paper machine in 1809. It is a common type of machine still in use today. By 1875 machinery was made to coat paper for use in printing halftones by the new photograving process. Carl Dahl invented sulfate (kraft) pulp in Germany in 1884. The invention of the Linotype machine in 1886 created an even greater demand for paper. Meeting the need for paper on a worldwide basis involves utilizing many sources of natural and synthetic fibers.

SOURCES OF FIBERS

All plants have cell walls containing cellulose fibers. Annual plants consist of about one-third of the structural material, while perennial plants consist of about one-half. Cellulose fibers are very durable and have high strength. They are easily wetted by water, showing considerable swelling when saturated, and are hydroscopic—that is, they absorb water when exposed to the atmosphere. Natural cellulose fibers show no loss in strength, even in the wet state. This combination of qualities with strength and flexibility makes cellulose uniquely valuable for the manufacture of paper.

Most plant materials also have nonfibrous matter or cells, and these may be found in pulp and paper. The nonfibrous cells are not as desirable as fibers for making paper but, when mixed with fiber, are useful in filling in the sheet. In all likelihood, paper of some kind can be made from any natural plant. The sources of supply would be limited by the requirements of the quality of paper and economic considerations.

Wood

Forest tree trunks that have been pulped are the predominant source of fiber for making paper. The tree trunk is made up of fibers with a minimum of nonfibrous materials such as pith and parenchyma cells.

Numerous species of trees are found in the forests of the world. These trees may be divided into two groups: (1) deciduous trees, usually called hardwoods, and (2) coniferous trees, or softwoods. The hardwood cellulose fibers are shorter than softwood fibers and fill in the paper sheet, giving it opacity and a smooth surface. The longer softwood fibers add strength to the paper.

The main method of pulping in the early days of the pulp industry was the sulfite process. (See page 295 for a discussion of this process.) The preferred species used were fir and spruce. Since then, technological advances, especially the introduction of the kraft process, have allowed almost all species of wood to be used, thus expanding the potential supply.

Concern has been expressed about the depletion of forest resources because of the enormous and rapidly growing consumption of wood for pulp. This concern exists even though annual growth often exceeds the yearly depletion. Almost half of the harvest goes into pulp. The public is demanding that forest land be withdrawn from timber production, so it can be used for recreational purposes and so ecological damage in specific areas can be prevented. Enormous increases in the productivity of forest lands in some regions have been brought about by the application of new techniques in fertilization and genetics.

Two major trends have occurred in the utilization of pulpwood. Lumbering and other wood-using industries have operated independently of the pulp industry until recently. Since the late 1940s, the waste from the wood-using industries has been used increasingly for pulp. More abundant hardwoods, even though they are less desirable, have been used as a source of pulp. Whereas the pulp mill formerly stored roundwood logs in the woodyard, it now generally stores chips, too.

Rags

Cotton and linen fibers, derived from textile and garment mill cuttings; cotton linters (the short fibers recovered from processing the cottonseed after the staple fiber has been separated); flax fibers; and clean sorted rags are used for those grades of paper in which durability, maximum strength, and permanence are required, as well as color, feel, fine formation, and texture. These properties are attributed to the greater fineness, length, and purity of rag fiber when compared with most wood pulp. Uses of rag papers include the following: life insurance policies and legal documents; bank note and security certificates for which permanence is a prime factor; technical papers, such as vellums, reproduction papers, and tracing paper; high grade bond letterheads, where texture and appearance are important; lightweight specialties such as Bible, carbon, and cigarette papers; and high grade stationery, in which beauty, softness, and fine texture are wanted.

Nonwood Natural Fibers

A large number of plants are potential sources of paper. Many of these plants have been pulped experimentally. Lots of plant sources have been used commercially, often on a small scale and at various times and places. Cereal straw was used long before wood pulp and is widely used now throughout the world on a low-production scale. Many parts of the world do not have forests; therefore, these areas must rely on annual plants and agricultural fibers to develop a paper industry.

Nonwoody plant stems are different from wood because they contain less total cellulose, less lignin, and more of other materials. Papers made from these pulps without the addition of other fibers tend to be dense and stiff, with low tear resistance and low opacity.

Cereal Straws

Straw pulp was used extensively in the United States for corrugating medium (the sheet fluted to form the inner ply of corrugated board). It has been replaced as a corrugating medium by semichemical hardwood pulp. Some Asiatic and European countries still make straw pulp on a small scale.

Bamboo
Botanically classified as a grass, bamboo has been used for pulp in papermaking for a long time. Bamboo pulp mills are located in India, the Philippines, and Thailand. There is an abundance of bamboo in Southeast Asia, where increased production of paper is needed and where much interest is shown in developing bamboo pulp. Bamboo fibers can be obtained without destroying the root system. An established stand of bamboo would produce more fiber per acre per year than any other plant if grown under ideal conditions of moisture and soil fertility. Wild bamboo is difficult to harvest and transport economically. Therefore, it will probably not be developed into large scale production.

Flax, Hemp, Jute, Kenaf
The fibers from these plants have been used for rope-making and for textiles for a long time. They have a high number of long, flexible fibers that are easily separated and purified from the other materials in the plants. The paper mills get most of the waste fiber. These fibers are highly sought after because of the durability and strength they give to products such as cover stock, tags, sandpaper, and other heavy-duty paper. They are used when an extremely light weight must be combined with unusual strength; for example, duplicating and manifold paper. High-grade cigarette paper is made from flax grown for that purpose. Various grades of paper are made from quantities of the kenaf plant fibers.

Bagasse
When sugar cane is crushed, the residue is called bagasse. It contains about 65 percent fiber, 25 percent pith cells, and 10 percent water solubles. Bagasse is used for paper in several Latin American countries and the Middle East because there are few forest resources.

Esparto
Esparto is a desert plant found in the Mediterranean area, especially in northern Africa and southern Spain. Esparto grass has a higher cellulose content then most nonwood plants, with greater uniformity of fiber size and shape. Its use for papermaking was developed in Great Britain in 1856. Consumption peaked in the mid-1950s and has declined since then.

In competition with wood, esparto held its own because of its papermaking properties. It has uniform fiber length compared with rag or wood pulp, which vary in fiber length. Printing papers possess good dimensional stability with moisture, resilience, opacity, and smoothness, and they are nearly lint-free.

Wastepaper and Paperboard

When greater quantities of wastepaper stock are used, the need for virgin fiber is reduced and the problem of disposing of solid waste is minimized. Expanding this source has been a complex problem because of the difficulties in gathering wastepaper from different sources, sorting mixed papers, and recovering the fiber from many types of coated and treated papers.

Wastepaper is generally classified into four main groups: (1) high-grade paper, (2) printed newspaper, (3) old corrugated boxes, and (4) mixed paper. High-grade and corrugated papers come mostly from mercantile and industrial firms. High-grade, white paper originates in envelope and printing plants. Tabulating cards come from large offices. Printed newspaper may originate from newsstand returns and home collections. Mixed paper comes from wastebaskets of office buildings and similar sources.

Recycled paper may be reprocessed to look like other paper, both unbleached and bleached. When paper is reprocessed, the fibers are usually broken down and become shorter. This weakens the paper. Paper made from rayon cellulose (such as bolt towels made with spray adhesives and no water) cannot be recycled as paper because the fibers break down totally. Recycled paper, in general, is less expensive to use than original fibers in producing paper. Some commonly recycled paper items include towels, sacks, bags, and greeting cards. Interest in wastepaper recycling continues to expand in the interest of ecology.

Synthetic Fibers

Widespread use of synthetic fibers may eventually occur in the paper industry. Fiber producers and paper manufacturers are showing an active interest in utilizing more synthetic fibers. Many specialty paper products are presently being made from synthetic fibers.

There are advantages of using man-made, or synthetic, fibers in papermaking. Synthetic fibers can be made uniform and of selected length and diameter, whereas natural cellulose fibers vary considerably in size and shape. Strong, durable papers require the use of long fibers. Papers made with synthetic fibers several times longer than those made of wood pulp have improved strength and softness properties. A limitation to the length of synthetic fibers is that when they are formed from suspension in water, they tend to tangle and rope together.

Synthetic fiber paper can be made resistant to strong acids; therefore, they are useful for chemical filtration. Fiberglass can be made into paper that is highly resistant to both chemicals and heat. Synthetic fibers can be used to produce dimensionally stable papers because they are not subject to the moisture problems of swelling and shrinking that take place with changes in atmospheric conditions.

Rayon is the least expensively made synthetic fiber; however, it costs over three times as much as an equal amount of wood pulp.

Synthetics such as polyamides (nylon), polyesters (Dacron, Dynel), acrylics (Acrilan, Creslan, Orlon), and fiberglass cost over ten times as much as wood pulp. This difference in cost does not preclude the use of existing synthetics, but it does limit their use to special products in which the additional qualities will justify the extra cost.

TYPES OF WOOD PULP

Wood is used for papermaking by reducing it to pulp. The three major types of pulp are (1) mechanical or groundwood pulp, (2) chemical pulp, and (3) semi-chemical pulp. Pulp made from rags and recycled paper are also discussed.

Mechanical or Groundwood Pulp

Once the logs arrive at the mill, the bark and the knots are removed. Through a mechanical or chemical process, the wood is altered to *pulp*. Mechanical or groundwood pulp is made by pressing the wood against a revolving grinding stone or by passing chips through a mill. The wood fibers are separated and fragmented. The pulp at this stage has discolorations and impurities in it and is called *groundwood*. At this point, paper made from the pulp would be grayish in color and speckled. Such paper is used for newspapers, building and insulation papers, and tissue papers. It will tend to yellow with age and become brittle.

Chemical Pulp

Chemical wood pulp is made by cooking wood chips in water or steam with various chemical solutions for eight to sixteen hours. Pure cellulose remains after noncellulose materials (about 50 percent) are dissolved and washed away. Further purification can be accomplished by bleaching and by alkaline extraction. This pulp is called alpha or dissolving pulp. It is used for specialty papers, for rayon and cellulose film production, and for cellulose derivatives, such as acetate and nitrate.

There are three chemical wood pulp processes: *sulphite, soda,* and *kraft.* The sulphite process employs soaking wood chips in solutions of a bisulfite mixed with either sulphuric acid or its normal salt. This pulp is much lighter in color than that derived from the kraft (sulphate) process and is more easily bleached. Since 1940, the kraft process has taken a prominent position in pulping. The soda process is not very prevalent now. In the soda process, hardwood pulp is cooked in caustic acid at high pressure and temperature. The high quantities of soda used have resulted in development of a recovery system for reuse. Usually this pulp is mixed with stronger fiber for printing paper. Many soda mills have been converted to the kraft process because of the greater strength of the pulp. The kraft (German/Swedish word for *strong*) process, also called the sulphate process, uses sodium sulfate (salt cake) in the chemical makeup. A water solution of sodium hydroxide and sodium sulfide is added to the wood pulp and is cooked at high pressure and temperature for one or more hours. The pulp is cooked carefully to keep the cellulose fiber undamaged. The resultant fiber is washed and sent directly to the paper mill if a dark color kraft board paper or kraft bag paper is wanted. Otherwise, it continues through a bleaching treatment process to make writing paper and to produce a base for rayon. The kraft process is the predominantly used wood pulping process. This pulp is usually combined with groundwood pulp to make newsprint paper, which is about 85 percent groundwood and 15 percent chemical pulp.

Semichemical Pulp

For semichemical pulping, wood preparation and chipping are basically the same as that for other wood-pulping processes. This process uses smaller amounts of inorganic chemical solutions under less severe conditions. The yield of semichemical pulp based on the amount of wood used is 66 to 90 percent. The fiber yield pulps are usually termed *semichemical pulps.* These pulps have chemical and strength properties between softwood, groundwood, and full chemical pulps. They are used in a wide range of low-cost printing papers and boards. Most of the semichemical pulp goes into the light board, called corrugating medium, which is fluted to serve as the inside layer of corrugated boxboard in heavy-duty containers. They also have the properties of strength and stiffness.

Rag Pulp

The longest-lasting papers are made from rags. The rags are received at the paper mill in bales weighing from 400 to 1,200 pounds. Upon arrival at the mill, the rags are sorted. Buttons, rubber, and metal are removed. Next, they are cut up into fine pieces. The rags are then cleaned and boiled in a solution of lime, caustic soda, and steam. All impurities are removed by thorough and repeated washings. When chemicals are not washed out, the paper may turn brown and become brittle later. The browning takes place because cellulose burns in the oxygen of the air (oxides) all the time. The next step involves chopping up the rags and pulling them apart to shorten the fibers. The rags are bleached and rinsed next to get an even white. For *pure rag paper,* sizing is added to the mix to close the pores and make ink stand on the surface. A little blue coloring is added for *pure white paper.* For colored paper, coloring material is added to the mix. Wood pulp is added in varying proportions for paper to have a "rag content." All the materials are now mixed and beaten. The pulp is now ready for the papermaking machines.

Recycled Paper

The scarcity of wood has brought about the use of recycled paper. Once obtained, it is reshredded, deinked (for making white paper), and made into pulp ready to be made into paper.

MANUFACTURING PAPER FROM PULP

Once the pulp has been prepared, it goes through a process called *beating* (see Figures 13.1 and 13.2). A machine called a Hollander beater further processes the cellulose fibers until they become separated and reduced to designated lengths.

Figure 13.1
The Kamyr Continuous Digester is used to convert wood chips into fiber.
Courtesy of *The Paper Trade Journal.*

Figure 13.2
A complete view of the Kamyr Continuous Digester shows how wood chips are carried into the
175-foot-tall digester tower by means of an enclosed conveyor system.
Courtesy of *The Paper Trade Journal.*

The kind and quality of paper wanted determines the amount of beating required. During this beating process, ingredients may be added for sizing, filling, coloring, and interfiber bonding to meet certain paper requirements. A *Jordan machine,* also called a conical or disk refiner, may be used to further refine the pulp. It tends to brush rather than cut the fibers.

When the beaten and refined pulp is ready, it will be formed into paper by a Fourdrinier or Verti-Forma papermaking machine.

The Fourdrinier Papermaking Machine

In a typical modern Fourdrinier papermaking machine, interlocking mechanisms operating in unison receive the paper stock from the beater or Jordan machine, form it horizontally into a sheet of the desired weight by filtration, press and consolidate the sheet by removing the excess water, dry the remaining water by evaporation, and wind the moving sheet into reels of paper (see Figure 13.3). The underside of the paper has a different texture from the upper side when the paper is formed horizontally on the Fourdrinier machine. This complicates its using printing. The paper machines may vary in width from about five to over twenty-five feet, in operating speed from a few hundred feet to over 3,000 feet per minute, and in production from a few tons per day to over 300 tons per day. Business papers and some printing papers must be cut, sorted, and packaged in lots of 500 or 1,000 sheets of some accepted trade size. Newsprint is shipped to printing plants in large rolls. Ledger and notebook papers must be ruled after cutting and before packaging. Magazine paper is shipped this way usually after a high gloss coating treatment before being finally rolled up for shipment.

The Verti-Forma Papermaking Machine

A papermaking machine named the Verti-Forma was developed in 1964 by the Black Clawson Corporation. Paper is formed on this papermaking machine on vertical wires instead of horizontal ones like those on the Fourdrinier machine. The upper and under sides of the paper have identical textures so that it will print the same on both sides. This paper machine is capable of producing paper faster than the Fourdrinier.

STATIONERY

Most stationery products are made in fashionable colors and designs. Business and formal use items generally come in white or off-white.

Envelopes

Envelopes first came into use during the 1840s. Until then letters were usually held together by folding them in a certain way, or they were folded and sealed with wax. Today, most customers want matching sets of envelopes and station-

Figure 13.3
The Fourdrinier Paper Machine. Pulp moving onto this machine is formed into a wet sheet on the wire screen.
Courtesy of *The Paper Trade Journal.*

ery in a certain size, color, and texture. Some envelopes are lined to add color and to help prevent the contents from being read from outside. The adhesives used for sealing the envelopes may come in different flavors.

In January 1963, the U.S. Post Office Department banned the mailing of envelopes smaller than 4¼ inches long and 3 inches wide. Also banned is mail of unusual shapes or materials, such as postcards made of leather or wood or shapes like animals or vehicles. These postal regulations became necessary with the mechanization needed to handle the large quantities of mail in post offices.

THE DIGESTER
Wood chips are converted into fibers.

THE WASHER
Cellulose fibers are washed to remove
chemicals and other impurities.

THE BEATER
Fibers are passed through metal bars which brush and fray the
cellulose fiber for ease of entangling. Bleaching, coloring, and
sizing are also accomplished in the beating process.

THE JORDAN MACHINE
Cellulose fibers are cut and frayed for better
cohesiveness in the final paper product.

THE FOURDRINIER MACHINE
The refined pulp (about 99 percent water) is moved onto a
vibrating wire mesh screen which serves to entangle the fibers
while removing most of the water.

DRYING
The paper is passed through rollers to remove
water and press entangled fibers together.

CALENDERING AND WINDING
The paper is polished with fast-moving smooth
rollers and wound into rolls.

Figure 13.4
The production of paper.

Sheet Sizes

Various sizes and shapes of stationery are needed to meet customer demand.
Some people like smaller single sheets or folded sheets that have more than one
sheet for corresponding. Other customers like large single sheets to meet their
writing needs. People use thank-you notes and different kinds of announcements
which are small, note-sized, and single, or they use folded sheets called *informals*.

Weight

Weight per unit area, called basis weight, is a fundamental property of paper and paperboard products. From the first use of paper in the printing trades, the paper manufacturers have measured paper by the ream and later sold it by standard size and weight. Standard book paper is 25 × 38 inches. Standard writing paper is 17 × 22 inches. Standard wrapping paper is 24 × 36 inches.

The manufacturer of writing paper may cut the sheet of standard paper into four pieces by folding it over once from top to bottom and then from left to right. There will be four sheets, each 8½ inches wide. This makes a good size of typing paper for business use. The manufacturer may fold in half the sheets that are 8½ × 11 inches and box them along with envelopes. Paper may be cut to any special size wanted.

The paper manufacturer sells paper by the *ream*, originally 480 sheets (20 quires) but now more commonly 500 sheets (long reams). Book papers and writing papers have 500 sheets to the ream and wrapping paper has 480 sheets. A *quire* contains 24 sheets but may occasionally contain 25. The term *ream weight* commonly signifies the weight of a lot or batch of paper. Since the printing trades use a variety of sheet sizes, there can be numerous ream weights for paper having the same basis weight. The higher the paper weight is in number, the heavier the paper. For example, a ream of writing paper, size 17 × 22 inches, may weigh 24 pounds. Even though it may be cut into smaller sizes (like 8½ × 11 inches), it is still called 24-pound paper.

Personalized Stationery

Personalized stationery usually is made by engraving, embossing, or printing it. People seem to like printed materials, such as announcements, calling cards, Christmas cards, invitations, and stationery, with their names or initials on them.

Engraving

The most costly but the best method of imprinting paper is done by *engraving*. The chosen lettering is applied to a copper plate. A longer-lasting steel plate may be used for large orders of a thousand or more. It also will give a clearer impression with quality production. Ink is placed on the plate, and then the inked plate is placed on the paper to transfer the ink. This leaves a raised impression. The customer maintains possession of the plate to be used again if desired.

Embossing

Special ink may be printed on paper. Then the paper is run over rollers that are heated in order to set the ink. This process is called imitation *engraving, raised lettering,* or *thermography.* This method is used on less expensive stationery, although it does not give as fine a detail as engraving.

Printing

Printing is the least expensive way of personalizing stationery. Once the raised letters are put into position, an inked roller is rubbed against them. Then the inked letters are transferred to the paper. This leaves a flat, smooth finish on the paper.

GRADES OF PAPER

Paper can be classified into the following grades.

Bond Paper

There are two kinds of bond papers: (1) those made from chemical wood pulp and (2) those made from rag content pulp. Rag content bond may range from 25 to 100 percent cotton fiber content. Bond paper is noted for its resistance to the penetration and spreading of ink, a degree of stiffness, its durability for repeated handling, its bright color, and cleanliness. The major uses of bond paper include the following: advertising pieces, announcements, certificates, currency, deeds, insurance policies, legal documents, letterhead stationery, leases, and writs.

Book Paper

Different combinations of chemical wood are used for most book papers. Lower priced grades of book paper are made from groundwood, semichemical, and de-inked wastepaper pulp. Besides the pulp, various quantities of dyes, fillers, and sizing may be used to make book paper.

Uncoated book paper is made in four finishes: (1) antique or egg shell finish, (2) machine finish, MF, (3) English finish, EF, and (4) supercalendered finish.

The antique finish is made from soda pulp or other high bulking pulps that are lightly beaten in stock preparation. The sheet is then lightly calendered to provide the roughest surface finish. Antique finished paper is used for stationery, book covers, and parchment.

Machine finished book paper has a medium-smooth surface acquired from a calender stock at the dry end of the calender. A relatively inexpensive general utility book paper, it is used for line etchings in books, catalogs, and circulars. Machine finish book paper is also used for halftones up to 100-line screen.

English finished book paper is considered smoother than machine finished paper. It is distinguished by a higher degree of beating by greater pressure going through the calender, and by calendering with greater moisture of the sheet (see Figure 13.5).

The smoothest surface that can be obtained without coating is called super-calendered finished paper. This finish is obtained by a special calendering pro-

Figure 13.5
Calendering is the process of pressing the paper through rollers to flatten the sheets in order to provide a smooth finish.
Courtesy of *The Paper Trade Journal.*

cess which presses the paper between successive sets of iron and compressed fiber rolls. The supercalendered finish is used for books, brochures, and magazines where halftone printing is required in the range of a 100- to 120-line screen.

Coated book papers are used for the printing of fine-screen halftones where certain surfaces are required. This paper must be receptive to printing inks, be uniformly smooth, have high brightness and gloss, and be folded without cracking.

Bible paper was developed for use in such books as Bibles, dictionaries, and encyclopedias which require minimum bulk. This paper's sheets are lightweight, thin, strong, and opaque. Pigments such as titanium dioxide and barium sulfate are used. The strength of the paper comes from the long fibers and artificial bonding agents that are used.

Kraft Wrapping Paper

Kraft wrapping paper is a heavy stock used to make paper bags. It is produced in greater volume than all the rest of the wrapping papers. The wood pulp is made of unbleached softwoods, mostly pine. Kraft wrapping paper has unusual tearing and tensile strength. Special resins give the paper wet stength for use in wrapping wet items. Bulk materials are shipped using multiwall layers of kraft paper.

Bristol

Bristol grades of paper are made from different combinations of chemical wood. They are heavy, stiff papers with thicknesses beginning from 0.006 inch (0.15 millimeter) and upward. Beaten a medium amount, the stock is generally well sized to keep moisture from penetrating. Bristol papers are used for punch cards used in tabulating and sorting equipment.

Groundwood and Newsprint Papers

These printing and converting grades of paper contain varying quantities of groundwood pulp, along with small amounts of chemical wood pulp for durability and strength. Groundwood pulp was used almost exclusively for newsprint for many years. Now, improvements in the pulping and bleaching processes have developed a broad class of paper usage. Large quantities of these papers go into making books, catalogs, directories, and magazines. Groundwood papers have an even, uniform formation and are highly opaque. Yet, they tend to be bulky and receive ink well. They do not have high whiteness, and they yellow in the light and with age.

Paperboards

Paperboard is made of fibrous materials on paper machines. It is 0.012 inch (0.30 millimeter) or more in thickness. Paperboard is generally made from wood pulp, straw, wastepaper, or a mixture of these fibrous materials.

The three major kinds of paperboard are (1) boxboards, used for items such as food boards, food trays, paper plates, and paper boxes; (2) container boards, used for making corrugated and solid fiber shipping cartons; and (3) paperboard specialties, used for products like binder board and building boards.

Sanitary Papers

This group includes facial tissues, napkins, toilet tissue, and toweling. Various amounts of bleached kraft pulps and sulfite with very little refining of the stock develop an absorbent, bulky, soft sheet of paper. Machine creping further softens the sheet when the wet sheet is pressed upon a smooth dry roll and is later removed by running against a flat stationary metal blade called a doctor blade. When the sheet is piled up upon itself, it develops a creped effect. Facial tissue is an example of dry-creping. Toweling is usually creped while still wet. Paper napkins may be embossed while the heavier paper is slightly moist. Resins are often added to sanitary papers to increase wet strength.

DISTINCTIVE PAPER FINISHES

Paper products have various distinctive finishes. Distinctive paper finishes include carbon and noncarbon papers, coated paper, borders and edges, embossed paper, grease-resistant and waxed paper, metal finishes, sandpaper, wallpaper, and watermarking. In order to sell them successfully, the salesperson and buyer need to become knowledgeable about them.

Carbon and Noncarbon Paper

Carbon paper was developed in England in 1803. One side of thin tissue paper is coated with lampblack mixed with oil or wax. In 1963, the Minnesota Mining and Manufacturing Company developed a noncarbon paper that is coated with microcapsules of a certain chemical. This noncarbon paper makes a blue impression on as many as six sheets under it when typed or written on.

Coated Paper

Coated paper has a high, glossy shine. Aluminim sulfate, casein, clay, and slaked lime are used to coat the paper. A high gloss is applied by running the paper through a calender.

Borders and Edges

Different processes are used to make the edges and borders of paper more attractive. *Beveled* or *sloping edges* are embossed or pressed on announcement or greeting cards. Characteristic of some handmade sheets of paper is a rough or uneven edge called *deckle edge*. Sometimes the edges of the paper are fanned out and the borders are colored by stenciling with an airbrush or by hand.

Embossed Paper

Often sheets of paper are placed against heavy linen fabric, then a hydraulic press is used to exert heavy pressure to give the paper a linenlike or ripple finish. A leatherlike texture is obtained by pressing the paper against smooth sheets of cardboard. This is called *vellum finish*.

Grease-Resistant and Waxed Paper

A grease-resistant paper is made by passing the paper through a bath of sulphuric acid and then washing and drying it. This translucent paper, also called *vegetable parchment,* is used for wrapping foods. Milk and butter cartons are made with paper that has been coated with wax.

Metal Finishes

Very thin sheets of metal are glued to the paper to create metal finishes. Aluminum paper, colored or not, is very popular and is used for wrapping food and tobacco products, and for decorative wrappings.

Plastic Finishes

Different types of plastics are used to coat paper to give it special properties. Plastics may give the paper colorful textures or make it more durable, and waterproof. Plastics that are prevalently used to coat papers are vinyl resins, silicones, melamines, cellulosics, and ethylenes. Papers with plastic finishes are used for waterproof coffee cups, placemats, products with leatherlike finishes, hot food plates, and playing cards.

Sandpaper

Sandpaper is made by covering one side with an adhesive and adding sand or other abrasive material. It is used for smoothing and polishing.

Wallpaper

Wallpaper is a paper that is usually printed and embossed. The weight of the paper, its fineness or coarseness, and the beauty of the design all affect its value.

Watermarking

Designs or lettering are impressed on wet paper by rollers which cause the paper to be thinner where these impressions (*watermarks*) are made. The wire roller has small raised wire letters or designs that press against the wet sheet and separate the fibers and cause an impression. If you hold a sheet of bond paper up to the light, you should see a watermark. Good-quality papers usually have watermarks. Paper that is watermarked by a few heavy wires that run vertically and many finer wires that run horizontally, leaving a fine-line design, is called *laid paper.*

KEY TERMS

1. Abrasive paper
2. Bond paper
3. Bristol
4. Corrugated board
5. Crepe paper
6. Currency paper
7. Deckle edge
8. Linen paper
9. Sizing
10. Stencil paper
11. Vegetable parchment (parchment finish)
12. Vellum finish
13. Watermark

STUDY QUESTIONS

1. How is the manufacturing process related to the quality of a paper?
2. Briefly explain the steps in making paper.
3. What are the fibers that are used in making paper?
4. What can we do to preserve our present supply of raw materials so that we may continue to have an adequate supply of paper?
5. Describe a watermark and how it is made.
6. Explain two processes used to make edges and borders more attractive.
7. Why do some greeting cards cost more than others?
8. Trace the historical development of papermaking.
9. Explain how rags are prepared for and used in making paper.
10. Name four special finishes used for paper.

STUDY ACTIVITIES

1. Visit a printing office supply business. Make a list of the different paper products with respect to uses, weights, sizes, finishes, edges, and textures.
2. List all the paper items located in your home and school.
3. Prepare a three-minute, illustrated sales presentation on stationery.

CHAPTER 14

Plastics

OBJECTIVES

After completing this chapter, you should be able to:

1. Explain how plastics have developed since the 1860s as a substitute for ivory to attain one of the major positions in the world's total materials business.

2. Differentiate between the two groups of plastics: (1) thermoplastics and (2) thermosetting plastics. Tell the important members of each group.

3. Explain how plastics are made from chemicals and additives, and how these can alter the appearance and working properties of a plastic material.

4. Describe the ways that manufacturers use plastics to produce or form the finished product for consumer use.

5. Explain how plastics, once formed, may be machined, finished, and decorated.

In a little over one hundred years, plastics have moved to fourth place in the world's total materials business. They are used less than raw steel, paperboard and paper, and lumber, respectively. In fact, this era could be called the Age of Plastics. No other industrial materials have the almost unlimited prospects that plastics have. They may be used alone, or they may be mixed with other materials. The production of plastics is projected to be almost three times that of other hard goods and dry goods combined by the year 2000. The basis of the American economy may rely on the production of plastics.

Plastics are versatile materials that may be called by their trade names or by their chemical names. Plastics come in a range of colors and may be as transparent as glass, as elastic as rubber, or as hard as stone. Plastic materials may also be light in weight, moisture- and chemical-resistant, nonporous or air-filled. They may be either flammable or flame-retardant.

HISTORICAL DEVELOPMENT

In 1862 an English chemist, Alexander Parkes, invented the first plastic, composed of nitrocellulose, certain vegetable oils, and small amount of camphor. This plastic was named Parkesine and was later called Xylonite. The ability of camphor to yield necessary plasticizing effects was discovered in 1869 by John W. Hyatt, a printer in the United States. John Hyatt improved upon Xylonite and patented his new synthetic plastic under the name of Celluloid. Celluloid was used for a variety of products such as billiard balls, carriage and automobile windshields, false dentures, combs, motion picture film, and many products formerly made from ivory and tortoise shells.

In 1910 Leo Hendrik Baekeland, a Belgian-born American chemist, commercially produced a heat-resistant synthetic plastic made from formaldehyde and phenol which he called Bakelite. Due to the new plastic's heat-resistant properties, it was primarily used in the electrical industry. It was the first of the plastics known as *thermosetting plastics,* which are virtually incapable of being melted. Thermoplastics may be melted and used again.

Colored plastic was formed in 1918 from urea-formaldehyde. The plastic absorbed moisture readily, but this problem was resolved in 1939 by the use of melamine in the place of urea.

During the same period of time, cellulose acetates were under experimentation and were first used as a waterproof coating for aircraft wings. Acetates were also used later for transparent packages, and beginning in 1935 they were used as a photographic film base.

Major advancements were seen in the plastics industry after 1920, mostly due to three key contributions. In 1922 Hermann Standinger, a German chemist, introduced the concept of polymerization, which stated that plastics were composed of a chain of macromolecules of various lengths. This key concept activated the experimentation and production of many new synthetic plastics. This research lead to the invention of nylon by DuPont de Nemours and Company.

In 1939 the British discovered polyethylene, which was to be the second key contribution to the plastics industry. This created a surge in the discovery of related plastics such as polyurethanes, epoxy resins, polyethylene terephthalates, and polycarbonates as purchased in retail stores.

The development of special machinery for the production and processing of plastics was the third major contribution to the development of the plastics industry. The first plastics were processed via rubber fabrication machinery. But as plastics developed, new machinery was designed especially for plastics production. Injection mold equipment was invented in 1921; detailed machinery for thermoplastics, in 1935; extrusion machines were designed for the production of plastic sheets, film, and blown bottles; automatic machinery, in 1937; and later there were improvements of certain feed mechanisms.

Ever since the invention of plastics in the 1800s, scientists have been developing and improving upon new and previously existing plastics. Due to the special properties exhibited by plastics, there has been a great demand for them in our everyday lives. As more versatile plastics are developed and as the demand for plastics increases, the importance of retail and consumer awareness also increases.

WHAT ARE PLASTICS?

Plastics refers to the name of synthetic materials composed of chains of atoms that are capable of being soft and moldable during production but that eventually become solidified. Plastics are used for a variety of products and are found in many forms. They may be combined to produce different effects. Effects may be greater due to different combinations of plastics rather than different types of plastics.

The definition for plastics accepted by both the Society of Plastics Engineers (SPE) and the Society of the Plastics Industry (SPI) is "a large and varied group of materials which consists of or contains as an essential ingredient a substance of high molecular weight which, while solid in the finished state, at some stage of its manufacture is soft enough to be formed into various shapes—most usually through the application (either singly or together) of heat and pressure."

MATERIALS USED FOR PLASTICS

Plastics are developed by the use of chemical reactions which actually unassemble and then rearrange natural materials into different molecular structures with the aid of heat, pressure, and chemical reactants. Plastics owe their special properties to the ingredients and combinations of those ingredients used in their manufacture. Natural substances such as wood, air, water, petroleum, natural gas, and halite are used to produce synthetic plastics. Ingredients used in the production of plastics are known as resins, fillers, solvents, lubricants, plasticizers, stabilizers, and colorants.

Resins

Resins are the principal ingredient of plastic. They are responsible for binding the plastic and the properties of the plastic together.

The resins are often used for identifying certain plastics. Resins determine whether a plastic will become thermoplastic or thermosetting.

Fillers

Fillers are utilized by most producers of plastics. They are either organic, inorganic, or a combination of the two. They help reduce the cost of the plastic by increasing the amount of the product. Fillers also help add to certain physical and chemical properties exhibited by the plastic. For example, wood flour (granulated waste wood) reduces brittleness, and gives excellent appearance and unique electrical properties to plastics. Asbestos aids plastics chemically by helping to reduce their deterioration due to heat or acid. Other fillers commonly used are fumed silica for use in paints; certain metals for added strength or electrical conductance in radios and other electronic equipment; and wax, graphite, bran, and glass for self-lubricating properties.

Solvents

Solvents are used to liquify, dissolve, or dilute resins. This is important because most resins are very thick and hard by nature. Therefore, they must be made more manageable in order to be processed effectively. For example, in solvent molding, the solvent maintains the resin in solution while it is being placed into the mold. The solvent is easily evaporated, therefore leaving only a plastic mold.

Lubricants

Lubricants are materials added to plastics to help reduce friction between plastic constituents and machinery, to aid in internal lubrication for plastic constituents, and to help add a nonadhering surface to the plastic during and after processing.

Although lubricants may be helpful in plastic production, they may also cause problems if not controlled. For example, excess lubricants may yield reduced polymerization and a "lubrication bloom" may occur on the plastic. This is an irregularly shaped cloudy area on the plastic.

Materials used as lubricants may include waxes, metallic soaps, and even other plastics that display nonstick self-lubrication properties such as fluorocarbons, polyamides, polyethylene, and silicone plastics.

Plasticizers

Plasticizers are very important in the formation of plastics. They are responsible for reducing the intermolecular attractive forces, van der Waal's bonds, that tend to make some resin too viscous (nonflowing) for proper use. Therefore, plasticizers help produce a more pliable and manageable polymer.

Plasticizers are often confused with solvents. Plasticizers and solvents both help to produce a less viscous resin and allow for ease of movement between molecules. However, plasticizers, unlike solvents, are not created to evaporate from the plastic during its normal life. Plasticizers are used to create a more pliable resin at increased processing temperatures, and to make a more moldable, less explosively reactive plastic.

Plasticizers are numerous—over 500 are used today. They are chosen for their compatibility with the resin with which they are used. They are also chosen due to the effects they have on certain polymers. They are used as major constituents in plastic coatings, extrusions, moldings, and adhesives.

Stabilizers

Plastics, although seemingly indestructible, have adverse reactions to certain conditions such as extreme heat and/or light. In order to protect plastics from these harmful conditions, stabilizers are added. Stabilizers are numerous and are added in different forms to the plastics to help curtail discoloration, reduced service life, and decreased storage life.

For example, liquid or powder stabilizers are employed in plastics for their capabilities to screen out or drastically reduce the harmful effects of ultraviolet light on plastics. Stabilizers are important to help prevent the breakdown of plastics during normal production due to the high temperatures involved, or to increase the storage life of the plastic by preventing degradation due to weathering. Plastic siding used on houses employs stabilizers.

Many stabilizers are used in the production of plastic, and each creates a special set of properties for plastics. For this reason, the type of stabilizer used must be taken into account when considering how the plastic is to be used. For example, the Food and Drug Administration (FDA) and the U.S. Department of Agriculture (USDA) have enforced laws to prevent the use of toxic stabilizers in the production of packagings for food.

Colorants

A wide range of colors (over 800) are found in plastics. This is a property that no other materials available can match. One of the reasons that plastics have become so widely used in products such as floor tiles, toys, and jewelry is because they are produced in a spectrum of colors. Many resins can assume hundreds of colors from clear transparent to opaque black.

There are four basic types of colorants used in making plastics: (1) dyes, (2) organic pigments, (3) inorganic pigments, and (4) special effect pigments.

Dye is mixed with the resin so that the color is consistent throughout the plastic. Resins which are a dark color in the natural state are usually restricted to opaque colors, but they produce brilliant colors. Solubility is one of the basic differences between dyes and pigments. Dyes are more complex and color the material by forming chemical linkages with molecules. They have excellent optical and clarity properties, but poor thermal and light stability. They are used in jewelry and umbrella handles.

Since pigments are not soluble in resin or solvents, they may be mixed in the resin. The colorants may cause surface color defects. They may stain or cause allergic reactions to the skin and therefore are seldom used in fabrics that touch the skin.

Organic pigments may produce the most brilliant and brightest opaque colors. Colors that are translucent and transparent are not as brilliant as dye-produced ones, but they are better than those produced with inorganic pigments.

Inorganic pigments are chemicals such as carbon (black), iron oxide (red), cobalt oxide (blue), cadmium sulfide (yellow), and lead sulfate (white). These chemicals are easily mixed into the resin but do not produce as brilliant a color as organic pigments and dyes. Most inorganic pigments are used in dense quantities to produce opaque colored plastics such as handles and bases on toasters and irons and housings for radio and television sets and telephones.

Special effect pigments may be organic or inorganic compounds. Colored glass is used, in a powdered form, as pigment for plastics. This powder is used for exterior applications because of its color stability and chemical resistance.

A metallic sheen may be developed by using metallic flakes of aluminum, brass, copper, and even gold. When metallic powders are mixed with colored finishes, they may even be used in many ways, for example, as the finish on an automobile.

Both natural and synthetic pearl essence may be used to develop a pearl luster in finishing jewelry, toilet seats, toys, fishing tackle, and other items. The *quanine crystals* are retrieved from the fatty skin of several species of fish to make natural pearl essence. The less expensive, synthetic, multifaceted quanine crystal is easily produced.

Luminescent materials are frequently added to plastics for special effects. Applications of these materials include hunting jackets, hard hats, gloves, raincoats, life preservers, warning signs, dolls, and paints. *Luminescent* is the radiation of light that takes place when chemical, electrical, or light energy excites electrons.

Because it is frequently necessary to mix colorants to achieve the desired shade of color, the use of a color chart of primary and secondary colors is extremely important in the plastics industry.

THERMOPLASTICS

Thermoplastics are those plastics which possess the unique characteristic of becoming soft and pliable when exposed to heat and becoming rigid when cooled regardless of how many times they go through the heating or cooling process. Therefore, they may be shaped and reshaped simply by heating, shaping, and then cooling. Thermoplastics display this quality due to their molecular structure. They are arranged in a chain-type structure independent from adjacent molecules which allows for easy slippage of the individual molecules when heated. When cooled, the thermoplastic again becomes hardened.

Too many repeated exposures to heat and cooling need to be avoided. Thermoplastics may lose their color or plasticizer with continued exposure to heat and cold, therefore affecting both appearance and desired qualities of the plastic.

Items made from thermoplastics include coated fabrics to make artificial leather, eyeglass frames, toothbrush handles, packaged cosmetic products, buttons, plastic furniture, shower curtains, toys, tableware, wastebaskets, and foamed cushioning.

Acrylic Plastics

The acrylic plastics, basically composed of carbon (C), oxygen (O), and hydrogen (H), are among the most common type of plastic encountered by the consumer. These plastics are extensions of the primary research of Dr. Otto Rhom in 1901. These plastics were first used as principal agents in the production of safety glass in 1931. They later became prominent in World War II as the material used for cockpit and other aircraft windows. Acrylic plastics are now desired for these same functions due to their high transparency, light weight, and ability to withstand various weather conditions. These characteristics also make acrylic plastics ideal for outdoor advertising signs and displays.

Due to other special properties of acrylic plastics, they are used for a variety of items in the marketplace, such as for automobile tail lights and television screens, due to their unique resistance to breakage. Acrylic plastics are also used for contact lenses because of their clarity and transparency; in toilet articles, due to their ease of care, sparkling finish, and increased inability to become scratched; and for food containers because they are odorless. Acrylic plastics are also used for dials, control panels, faucet handles, jewelry, paints, waterproof garments, combs, and certain articles of clothing.

Cellulosic Plastics

Cellulosic plastics contain cellulose material from wood and/or cotton. Five basic resins are in the cellulosic group: (1) cellulose acetate, (2) cellulose nitrate, (3) cellulose acetate butyrate, (4) ethyl cellulose, and (5) cellulose proprionate.

Cellulosic plastics got their start in 1869 when the Hyatt brothers of the United States first discovered cellulose nitrate. The cellulosic plastics were responsible for the rapid development of both the film and the plastics industries for their use in movie film.

Special properties exhibited by cellulosic plastic make it useful for a wide variety of products in today's market. The durability and pliability of cellulose plastic make it a very valuable ingredient for lacquers, and make it ideal in the production of pens and pencils. The ability of cellulose acetate to be easily worked with and shaped has made this material excellent in producing various indoor display racks, heels for ladies' shoes, and packages. Cellulose acetate has become important in the fabric industry due to its characteristic high tensile strength in material even in environments of extreme moisture. Other special properties of cellulose acetate such as increased resistance to detergents and scratching, resistance to weathering, light weight, and durability make it ideal for such articles as toothbrush handles, toilet supplies, steering wheels, eyeglass frames, and outdoor advertising.

Fluorocarbon Plastics

Fluorocarbon plastics were developed in 1943 and contain two main formulations: tetrafluorethylene (TFE) and chlorotrifluorethylene. Fluorocarbon plastics are costly to produce and contain a special combination of properties. For these reasons they are mainly used in industrial situations.

Fluorocarbon plastics are characterized by high heat tolerance, supreme dielectric qualities, resistance to chemical corrosion, low frictional coefficiency, and nonadhesiveness. These characteristics make them ideal for such products as wire insulation, pipeline for the transportation of chemicals, bearings for machinery, coatings for skis, and for the transportation of hot, adhesive glues.

Nylon Plastics

Nylon (polyamide) has become one of the industry's most widely used plastics. Nylon was introduced into the market in 1938 by the Du Pont Company as an alternative means for the production of hosiery. Since that time, due to nylon's unique properties, it has become a highly demanded material for use in today's market. However, due to the expense in making nylon and its difficulty in moldability, the use of nylon is limited to only certain materials. For example, nylon is excellent for use in lubricant-free machinery parts because of its low coefficient of friction, great strength, and damping qualities.

Nylon's durability and strength capacity make it especially good for use in fabrics. The light weight of nylon makes it very popular for parachute production. Nylon's resistance to chemicals, light weight, strength, and flexibility also make it especially good for the production of articles such as hammers, dies, chemical piping, and aerosol bottles.

Polyolefin Plastics

Polyethylene was first produced in 1933 and received special attention by the U.S. government during World War II because of its unique properties. Polyethylene has since received a major place in today's market. Polyolefins contain two major members: polyethylene and polypropylene.

Polyethylene, one of the simplest plastics, has unlimited storage capabilities and can be stored for extended periods of time without loss of its properties. Polypropylene is similar to polyethylene in property values except that it is somewhat more restrictive to heat and is stronger.

The properties of these two ingredients are what makes them so useful. For example, polyethylene's ability to allow gases such as oxygen and carbon dioxide to pass through it makes it an excellent food/produce packaging material. Polyolefins are also used in the building industry because of their resistance to the effects of aging. This property, as well as their resistance to breakage and pliability, makes them excellent for material in the manufacture of children's toys. Polyolefins also resist adhesion of water and are therefore used for making ice cube trays (see Figure 14.1). The unique properties of polyolefin plastics also make them usable for kitchen canisters, high frequency electrical wiring insulators, and waterproof packages.

Styrene Plastics

Styrene was developed by chemical experimentation in 1830, but it was rarely used until the 1930s. Although styrene has had a slow start, it is the second most used plastic produced today.

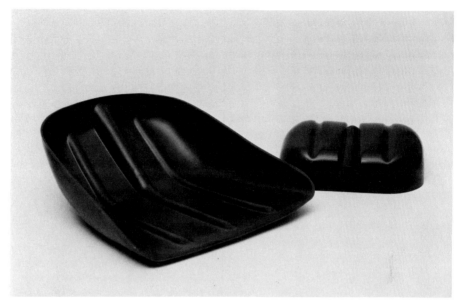

Figure 14.1
Lightweight snow shovels made of polyethlyene encourage ice and snow to slide off easily.
Courtesy of American Hoechst Corporation.

Styrene contains two basic groups: (1) general purpose styrene, and (2) styrene alloys, sometimes referred to as rubber blends. General purpose styrenes are lightweight, rigid, brittle, and show quality dimensional stability. Styrene alloys are brittle, have high impact strength, and resist chemicals. Styrene alloys are somewhat more expensive to produce than general purpose styrenes.

Styrene plastics can be found in a wide variety of products due to their characteristic properties. For example, styrene's low cost and ease of molding make it ideal for children's toys. Styrenes can be developed into a wide range of colors. They are employed for use in refrigerator doors, frozen food containers, and many other items which utilize styrene's low temperature qualities.

Styrene alloys are also desired for the production of carrying cases (Figure 14.2), automobile interiors, and appliance housings (Figure 14.3). Other uses of styrene are for tile pieces, lamp shades, serving trays, paints, washing machines, chemical piping, battery cases, display cases, and flotation devices. Properties of styrene include moisture resistance, the ability to diffuse light, odorlessness, light weight, resistance to alkalies, clarity, and buoyancy.

Vinyl Plastics

Vinyl plastics have been around for over seventy-five years; however, their pure resins are hard and easily broken. For these reasons, commercial uses of vinyl plastics came about with the development of plasticizers for suitable processing of the plastics.

Figure 14.2
Cassette carrier molded from polystyrene.
Courtesy of American Hoechst Corporation.

Figure 14.3
Smoke alarm housing molded from polystyrene.
Courtesy of American Hoechst Corporation.

Vinyl plastics were first produced commercially in 1925 in Germany, but they were not used on an increased scale until 1933 when the United States used these plastics primarily for lacquers for tin can linings.

Vinyl plastics contain at least seven family members with almost unlimited characteristics; therefore, they are more commonly referred to in respect to the properties exhibited by the entire family. Vinyls are lightweight, flexible, stretchable, and resistant to tearing. Vinyls employ certain properties such as their unique adhesive qualities in the manufacture of certain glues. They also are utilized in safety glass production due to their elastic quality and transparency. Vinyl's resistance to chemical effects makes it ideal for use as household containers for chemicals. Vinyls resist adherence of dirt, are easily cleaned, and are smooth but not slick; therefore, vinyls are often used for floor coverings (Figure 14.4), rainwear, packaging, toys, and fabrics.

Figure 14.4
Cushioned vinyl flooring.
Courtesy of Armstrong World Industries, Inc.

THERMOSET PLASTICS

Thermosets is the name given to the group of plastics that are fixed into a permanent shape or form by heat. After they have been fixed, they cannot be remelted and returned to their previous state. That is to say, even if the plastics are remelted they will not return to their previous flow state. Most of the plastics in the group are affected by heat exceeding 350 degrees Fahrenheit. The main members of this family are aminos, polyesters, epoxies, and phenolics.

The reason thermosets display the quality of not returning to their original state when heated is that their molecular structure does not allow them to do so. The thermosets are much like the thermoplastics at the beginning, but as they are heated their chainlike structures develop cross bridges between these chains; therefore, slipping of separate chains is prevented.

Amino Plastics

Amino plastics contain two major resin groups: urea and melamine. These two groups comprise a major part of the common forms of plastic used in consumer goods. For example, urea resin in powder form is utilized in the production of certain wood glues. Melamine is commonly used for dishware known as Melmac. However, it is also used to produce such common products as Formica and Texolite, which are two kinds of countertop coverings.

Properties displayed by these plastics make them ideal for a wide variety of products. For example, amino plastics are tough, hard to scratch, and resistant to heat and chemicals, which make them excellent for countertops. They are ideal for dishware due to their properties of resistance to heat and detergents, and their lustrous colors. They make great switch gear for electrical current due to their excellent resistance; however, they are mostly suitable for low frequency current. Other properties make them ideal for stove and refrigerator surface coatings and for soil and wrinkle-proof materials.

Polyester Plastics

Polyester plastics contain a number of different plastics which are used for a variety of products. Polyester resins are generally thermosetting. They are used in such products as enamels, paints, lacquers, and many other surface coats. However, one polyester resin, known as Dacron, is a thermoplastic and is used in the production of fabric.

The qualities of polyester plastics create specific uses for it in today's market. Some common products made with polyester plastics include auto bodies, boat hulls, and truck bodies because, unlike most plastics, polyester must not be molded under great heat and pressure but will cure at room temperature. Resilience to scratching and denting make polyester plastics ideal for appliance cabinets. Strength and chemical resistance are features that make polyester plastics ideal for chemical storage containers. Polyester plastics are also used for building panels, fishing rods, films, and laminating resins. Polyester is relatively inexpensive to produce and, therefore, is a favorite of most plastics producers.

Casein Plastics

Casein plastics have been used in a limited facet of production due to their absence of certain physical and chemical properties; however, casein plastics were very prominent around the time of World War I as an ingredient in waterproof adhesives. Casein plastics were brought to the United States from Europe around 1900.

Casein plastics today find their major use in the production of certain products which are not limited by casein plastics' undesirable physical and chemical properties, such as fading of color in sunlight, brittleness in cold weather, low chemical resistence, and low resistence to moisture. Items produced from casein plastics include novelty items which incorporate the brilliant color and surface finish properties of casein plastics. Knitting needles are also sometimes made from casein plastics due to the plastic's smooth surface and flexibility. Buttons and buckles are also created from casein plastics due to the plastic's ease of production and durability.

Epoxy Plastics

Epoxy plastics, though one of the newest plastics on the market, have been known for about one hundred years. They received commercial significance around 1947 as a metal-to-metal adhesive. Now epoxy plastics have a wide range of uses.

Some of the uses for epoxy plastics include adhesives used in areas where bonding is difficult. The epoxy has great adhesive qualities and is used in the production of aircraft, automobiles, mobile homes, and ceramics. Epoxy plastics are excellent for floor protectors, appliance surfaces, and athletic courts of various hard-to-protect surfaces due to the epoxy plastic's resistance to abrasion, chemical solvents, and outdoor environments.

Phenolic Plastics

Phenolic plastics are considered the forefather of plastics production. They were developed around 1909 and were the first plastics used in the production of consumer goods on a volume scale.

Today phenolic plastics can be used for a wide variety of products by simply substituting various fillers during the production of the plastic. Such products are molded furniture and frames due to phenolic plastic's desired strength, hardness, and rigidity necessary for compression molding. Phenolic plastics exhibit a high resistance to grease and oil, and they have a high insulating value necessary for such products as electrical supplies and switch gears in automobiles and distributor caps. Phenolic plastics also exhibit low conductance of heat which make them ideal for use as handles on irons and cooking wear.

Phenolic plastics are also used to create washing machine parts due to their high resistance to water and detergent-chemical products. Phenolic plastics are also suited for photographic developing equipment due to their high chemical resistance. Phenolic plastics are ideal for outdoor waterproofing material due to high water resistance and adhesiveness. The ability for phenolic plastics to be foamed greatly beyond their original volume makes them excellent for such products as flotation devices like buoys and life jackets as well as structural components for aircraft wings. Phenolic plastics display great adhesive qualities and resistance to heat, therefore making them especially ideal for metal and other plastics dies and molds.

Silicone Plastics

The invention of the resins for silicone plastics originated during the 1870s as the result of the works of German chemists. Silicones did not reach their important place in the market until about 1900 in England, when the basis for silicone plastic usage was developed. Commercial production of silicones arose in the United States as a result of cooperative efforts between the General Electric and Corning Glass corporations.

Silicones exhibit unique properties that create their place in the marketplace. Silicones are often used in combination with rubber. This combination with rubber allows for silicone's high resistance to loss of physical, electrical, and chemical properties. Silicones combined with rubber give antifoaming and nonflammability to combustibles such as oils and greases at high temperatures.

Also, they are valuable in the furniture and automobile industries for their unique ability to produce a cover for small scratches and as a stain-resistant polish. Due to their special properties such as chemical inertness and nonsticking, silicones can be used as mold release agents or additives for other products. Silicones are also used for electrical coverings due to their unique water resistance, electrical nonconductance, and production of foam at relatively low temperatures.

Urethane Plastics

The basic components of urethane plastics were discovered in Germany around 1848 due to the intense research of a French chemist named Charles A. Wurtz. Urethanes received little notice by the plastics industries until prior to World War II when they were utilized by the military. Urethanes have received much attention in the market of today as major constituents for foam materials, both flexible and rigid foams. Urethanes have received so much recognition as a major constituent for foams that the plastics industry has adopted the general name *urethane foam* for all kinds of foams originally developed from such materials as isocynate, polyurethane, and polyesters.

Urethanes are varied and so are their different properties, which creates a wide range of uses for them. For example, urethanes are excellent to use for cushioning materials for various articles due to their resistance and flexibility. Urethanes are also used in the construction of aircraft wings due to their light weight, compression strength, ability to adhere to lightweight metals, and foaming ability. Urethanes also hold heat well and are often used for the linings of many types of jackets. Urethanes have other unique uses such as linings in the helmets of space suits and service in parts of aircraft and missiles.

Urethanes are somewhat more expensive to produce than some other forms of plastics and for that reason are not as widely used as are other forms of less costly plastics. Urethanes, however, have won popularity in the market due to their varied properties and are thought of as a material of the future.

See Table 14.1 for a listing of the properties of various plastics.

SHAPING PLASTICS

A few large chemical companies make most of the plastics raw materials in the United States. No other family of materials has available to manufacturers as many variations of powder, sheet, tube, or liquid as plastics. The manufacturers then shape the plastics into desired shapes and package it ready for the consumers. Plastics may be blown (Figures 14.5 and 14.6), cast, extruded, foamed, laminated, molded, or thermoformed into shape. They may also be used as adhesives, coatings, and fibers and filaments.

Blow Molding

Blow molding of thermoplastics did not develop until the late 1950s. This technique was adopted and modified from the glass industry.

The basic principle of blow molding is simple. A hollow tube or balloon of molten thermoplastic is placed in a mold cavity and forced (blown) with air pressure against the walls of the mold. After a cooling period, the mold opens and ejects the finished product. Products that range in size from tiny toys to large barrels may be blow-molded.

There are two basic blow-molding methods: (1) injection blowing and (2) extrusion blowing. The main difference in the two methods is in the production of the hot, hollow tube.

A variation of blow molding, called *rotomolding,* is used for making deep, hollow, or large articles. Pellets or powders and a plasticizer are put into a heated hollow mold which can rotate rapidly. The finished article is taken out after cooling and opening the mold.

Injection blow molding is used because it can produce a more accurate thickness of the material in various areas of the object. No bottom weld or scrap needs to be reprocessed.

A thermoplastic tube (parison) is *extruded* between the halves of an open split mold. While the plastic is still soft from the extruder, the mold is closed, trapping the tube and sealing one end. Air pressure is forced through the other end, forcing the tube to stretch and follow the contours of the closed mold. The mold is kept cool, and the thermoplastic material becomes rigid as it contacts the mold surfaces. After cooling, the mold is opened and the part is ejected and trimmed. Various bottles are made this way.

TABLE 14.1 PROPERTIES OF PLASTICS

	EFFECTS OF SUNLIGHT	EFFECTS OF SOLVENTS	EFFECTS OF STRONG ALKALIES	EFFECTS OF WEAK ALKALIES	EFFECTS OF STRONG ACIDS	EFFECTS OF WEAK ACIDS	RATE OF BURNING	ELECTRICAL RESISTANCE
Thermoplastics								
1. Acetals	slight	none	harmful	harmful by some	harmful	harmful by some	slow	excellent
2. Acrylics	none	soluble in some	harmful by some	slight	harmful by some	slight	slow	good
3. Cellulosics	slight	soluble in many	decomposes	slight	decomposes	slight	slow to ST*	good
4. Fluorocarbons	none	none	none	none	none	none	none	excellent
5. Polyamides	slightly discolors	slight	none	none	harmful	slight	slow to ST	excellent
6. Polyolefins	discolors	soluble in some	slight	slight	harmful	slight	slight	excellent
7. Styrenes	discolors	soluble in some	none	none	harmful by some	none	slow	good
8. Vinyls	slight	slight	slight	slight	harmful by some	slight	slow to ST	good
Thermosets								
1. Aminos	discolors	none	harmful by some	slight	decomposes	slight	none to ST	good
2. Casein	discolors	slight	decomposes	decomposes	decomposes	slight	slow	fair
3. Epoxies	none	slight	slight	none	harmful by some	none	slow	excellent
4. Phenolics	discolors	slight	decomposes	none	harmful	slight	slow	good
5. Polyesters	discolors	harmful	harmful	harmful	harmful	slight	slow	good
6. Silicones	slight	harmful	slight	slight	slight	slight	slow	excellent
7. Urethanes	discolors	slight	slight	slight	slight	slight	slow	good

ST = Self-terminating

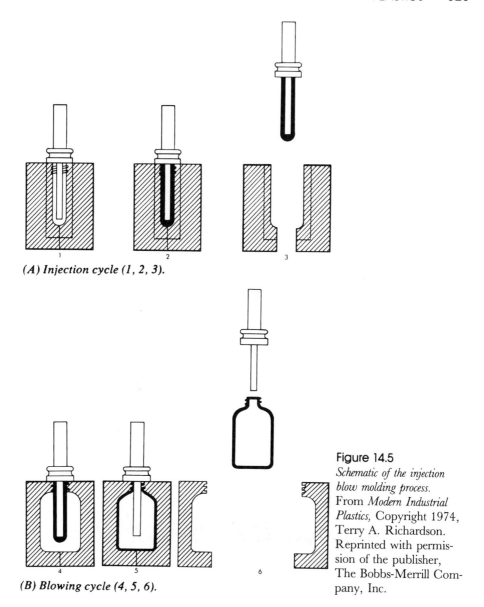

(A) Injection cycle (1, 2, 3).

(B) Blowing cycle (4, 5, 6).

Figure 14.5
Schematic of the injection blow molding process. From *Modern Industrial Plastics,* Copyright 1974, Terry A. Richardson. Reprinted with permission of the publisher, The Bobbs-Merrill Company, Inc.

Casting

Many plastics, both thermoplastic and thermoset, may come as liquids or solids for casting. Solids are melted and cast much like candle wax. Plastics may also be formed by pouring liquid plastics into molds which are baked in ovens until the

Figure 14.6
Blow molded drums made from polyethlene.
Courtesy of American Hoechst Corporation.

plastic hardens. Because these molds do not have to withstand any pressure like the compression or injection molds (Figure 14.7), the plastic produced in them is less expensive. Casting plastics is one of the simplest molding techniques and has become a very popular technique for hobby craft and art craft. Unusual and complicated shapes are possible by casting with glass, metal, plaster, or rubber molds. Most of these molds are used only once.

Some of the most important casting resins include acrylic epoxy, phenolics, polyester, and polystyrene. Cast phenolics have replaced many ivory and horn items and are used to produce most of the world's billiard balls. Polyester plastics are used as a binder of marble dust and reinforcements to make *cultured marble* which some people consider superior to marble; cultured marble is used in bathroom sinks. Clear polyester and acrylic resins are used to encase various objects in clear transparent plastics for the purposes of preservation, display, and study. For use in biological (including medical) sciences, animal and plant specimens may be imbedded in plastics to preserve the specimen and allow the most fragile sample to be handled. Other cast items include hangers, brush and mirror backs, jewelry stones, and inexpensive buttons.

Rotational casting takes place when polymerized casting compounds of small pellets or powders of plastics are placed in hollow metal molds and rotated in two planes at the same time. As the metal mold heats, the plastics melt on the walls of the molds. The rotation causes the plastics to flow over the surfaces of the mold.

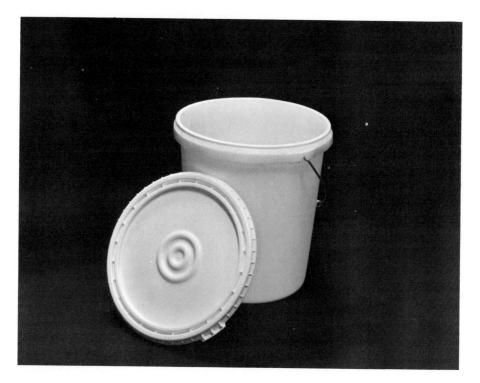

Figure 14.7
Polyethlyene pail made by the injection molding process.
Courtesy of Amèrican Hoechst Corporation.

Seamless, large, deep, hollow objects are possible with this process such as doll parts, toy balls, and one-piece modern chairs. The finished products are easily removed after chilling and opening the mold.

Dip casting is a simple process of dipping a heated mold into liquid dispersions of plastics. The plastics melt and adhere to the hot metal surface as the mold is withdrawn. Additional curing is done in ovens to assure proper fusion of the plastic particles. After the curing has taken place, the plastic is peeled from the mold. Certain gloves and hot water bottles are made this way.

Coating

Many plastics come in the form of coatings. Coatings are usually thin protective coatings applied to a material which are not removed. Plastic resins have replaced many of the natural resins as constituents of finishes. Plastic-based paint, varnish, and lacquers are generally far superior to those with natural resins as bases. Alkyd resins are used in the paint industry; cellulosics are used to coat paper; phenolics make tough varnishes; and epoxy resins make excellent metal coatings.

Plastisols are used as coating materials by dipping or submerging products in plastic dispersions. Examples of this process include dish drainers, tool handles, coated fabric gloves, and bobby pins.

Coating paper and textile fabric in plastics is generally accomplished by using the "knife" and roller method. In this method, a solvent mixture of plastics is spread on the item to be coated and afterwards it is dried.

Electrostatic spray methods are frequently used to eliminate overspray and to ensure even coatings without preheating the part. The bed process uses positively charged, heated, or preheated items that are placed into negatively charged dry plastic powders. When the powders touch the hot surface of the item, they melt and fuse to the item. Parts for dishwashers, refrigerators, washing machines, and automobiles are electrostatic bed-coated.

Extrusion

Softened thermoplastics may be shaped by continuously forcing them through a die or nozzle. This process is called *extrusion* (see Figure 14.8). Extrusion is ordinarily used with thermoplastics such as acrylics, cellulosics, fluorocarbons, nylon, styrenes, polyethylene, and vinyls.

The only shapes which can be extruded are those with consistent cross sections such as rods, tubes, flat sheets, moldings, and filaments of varying lengths and thicknesses. Many polyethylene bags are made by cutting thin extruded tubing and sealing the ends. Rayon and acetate filaments are made by extrusion through tiny holes in a spinneret. Monofilament fishing line is extruded nylon. This process produces a multifilament yarn or thread. Many carpets, ropes, and textiles are made from the threads and yarns. Other extruded products include water hoses and napkin rings.

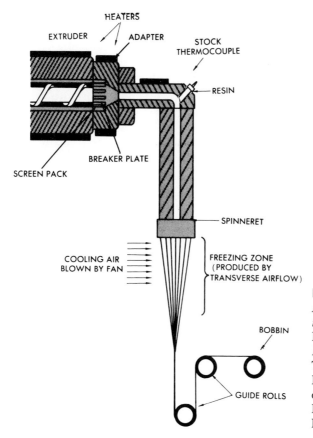

Figure 14.8
Multifilament extrusion through a spinneret.
From *Modern Industrial Plastics,* Copyright 1974, Terry A. Richardson. Reprinted with permission of the publisher, The Bobbs-Merrill Company, Inc.

Foam Molding or Casting

Most thermoplastic and thermosetting plastics may be processed into a cellular form (foam). Two of the most common foams are styrene (Figure 14.9) and urethane, but cellulosics, epoxies, phenolics, polyethylenes, silicones, and vinyls (imitation leather) are also expanded.

Two general types of foamed plastics relative to cellular structures are as follows: (1) *Open-celled* foams that resemble sponges. The cells are capable of holding liquids because they are interconnected. (2) *Closed-celled* foams occur when the cells are completely closed by the walls of plastic. The air may be mechanically whipped into many resins just before polymerization. Chemicals may also be used as foaming agents by causing gaseous bubbles to form in the resin. Items made of closed-celled foams include snowmen, plastic cups, and lightweight toys.

Any shape can be produced by either foam molding or foam casting. Many plastic foams may be obtained in rigid, semirigid, or flexible foams. Many may be made flame retardant (see Figure 14.10).

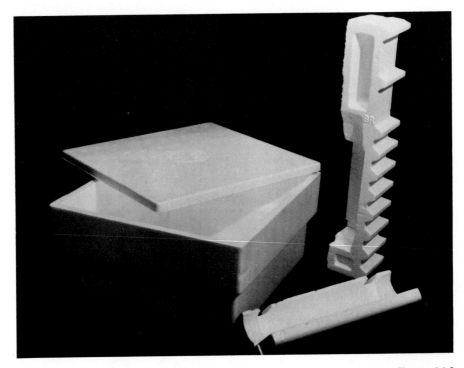

Figure 14.9
Packaging and cushioning applications made from expandable polystyrene.
Courtesy of American Hoechst Corporation.

Foamed products familiar to consumers are Christmas decorations, flotation toys and buoys, ceiling tiles, cushioning materials, mop heads, and imitation leather.

Laminating

When two or more layers of any material are bonded together, they are considered to be *laminated.* Lamination is the process of bonding layers of thermosetting resin-impregnated or resin-coated materials with heat and pressure. The thermosetting resins are usually phenolic, melamine, silicone, epoxy, and polyester. The base material used in laminating is often paper, cotton fibers, asbestos felts, mats and papers, fibrous glass, textiles, and wood. Laminates offer physical, chemical, and electrical properties superior to those of other materials. They may be tubes, rods, sheets, or other molded shapes. There are many applications of laminates in the textile industry, where layers of cloth, plastic film, and foam are bonded together to produce materials for special purposes.

Formica, Micarta, and Texolite are tradenames for laminates used as counter tops, wall panels, flooring and other applications where a decorative and dur-

Figure 14.10
This expandable polystyrene sheathing contains a chemical modifying agent which significantly alters its burning characteristics and complies with all federal, ASTM, and building code regulations.
Courtesy of American Hoechst Corporation.

able surface is needed. The surface may be patterned or textured by different methods, it may contain abrasives or metallic flakes, or it may be embossed to simulate fabric, stone, or wood grain. Other consumer goods where lamination is used include artificial leather, imitation veneers for furniture, raincoat materials, shower curtains, and safety glass.

Molding

Thermosetting plastics are molded into shape by pressure and heat. Compression molding is the simplest type of molding and the most common process. In molding methods, both sides of the object are shaped by pressure from a molding surface.

The *compression molding* process begins with the plastic pellet, powder, or preformed discs which are preheated to dry the plastic and raise its temperature. The plastic is then loaded into the mold cavity and held at selected temperatures depending on the materials. Next, the mold is partially closed; the heat and pressure cause the plastic to liquify and begin to flow in the farthest parts of the mold. The mold is then fully closed, making the plastic complete its flow and cure. After the cure is completed, the mold is opened for removing the part that was molded. Compression molded parts include dinnerware, buttons, buckles, knobs, handles, appliance housings, drawers, radio cases, and industrial parts (see Figure 14.11).

Thermoforming

Thermoforming processes are made possible because of the ability of thermoplastic sheet or film stock to soften and be reshaped when heated and to retain the new shape when cooled. This important process, of which there are several variations, is used to form most thermoplastic materials into finished products. The process of heating a thermoplastic material and forcing it to take a mold shape by air, mechanical, or vacuum pressure is in demand because tooling costs are usually low and parts with large surface areas may be produced economically.

Examples of articles made by thermoforming processes include ice cube trays, light fixtures, take-out food packaging, blister packages, children's wading pools, toys, disposable containers and lids, tote trays, and clear covers that protect and help display bakery goods.

MECHANICAL LINKAGE

There are two main ways of mechanically joining plastics: (1) using mechanical fasteners, and (2) by press-and-swag fitting.

Mechanical Fasteners

There is a wide variety of mechanical fasteners available for use with plastics. Most are also used with metals and woods.

Standard machine screws are available in metal or plastic. The plastic screws are not as strong as metal ones, and care must be used when screwing them into the tapped hole. Self-threading screws are used if the fastener is not removed very often. Standard bolts and nuts are used often, as with metal and wood. Many types of rivets are available in plastic and metal. Speed nuts are used for sheet metal screws for quick assembly. Spring clips, hinges, catches, knobs, dowels, and other devices are also used for the assembly of plastics.

Press-and-Swag Fitting

Press-and-swag fitting is a term used to indicate a pressure-type joint of like or dissimilar materials without any mechanical linkage. Parts may also be forced over a lip or into an undercut retaining ring. An example would be on some Tupperware plastic products.

JOINING AND FASTENING

It is often necessary to join plastic parts to other plastics or to other materials. Several of the methods used are similar to those used for metals and woods. There are only three basic methods by which plastics are joined together or with other materials: (1) adhesion, (2) cohesion, and (3) mechanical linkage.

Figure 14.11
Coal chute liner produced by compression molding.
Courtesy of American Hoechst Corporation.

Adhesion

Adhesion is a fast, effective way of bonding plastics by using a film which adheres to each of the materials being joined. The adhesive is a substance such as glue, paper, or metal that is different from either of the materials and remains in the joint.

Cohesion

Cohesion involves an intermingling of the molecules of the materials being joined. No foreign material is used; therefore, some means is used to cause the two materials to flow together and fuse. Cementing, hot gas welding, spin welding, heat joining, dielectric joining, induction welding, and ultrasonic heat sealing are methods of cohesive assembly.

The cementing method consists of applying a solvent or a mix of the solvent and the plastic being joined to soften the areas to be joined. Then the softened areas are pressed together in the proper position, and pressure is maintained until the solvent evaporates.

Hot gas welding consists of directing a heated gas (generally nitrogen) at temperatures of 400 to 800 degrees Fahrenheit onto the joints to be melted together.

Spin welding consists of frictionally joining circular thermoplastic parts. Frictional heat causes a cohesive melt at a certain point when one or two parts are rotated against each other. Joints may also be spin welded by rapidly rotating a filler rod on the joint.

The heat joining method involves heating like materials by different means and bringing the joints together while in the molten state. Specially designed heating tools are used to fuse or melt the plastic surfaces. The heated areas are quickly brought together under pressure until cooled.

Dielectric heat sealing is used to join plastics, fabrics, films, and foams. Only plastics that have a high dielectric loss characteristic (dissipation factor) may be joined by this method. Cellulose acetate, ABS (Acrylonitrile-Butadiene-Styrene), polyester, polyvinyl chloride epoxy, polyamide, and polyurethane are among the plastics that could be sealed electronically. One important application of this property is made in the electronic heat sealing of vegetable bags.

Induction welding takes place when heat is induced by a high-frequency electrodynamic field in a thin metallic insert placed between the plastics to be joined. The main advantage in using this method is speed. Almost any thermoplastic can be welded using this technique.

Mechanical Linkage

In ultrasonic heat-sealing, the plastics to be joined are held together between electrodes and vibrated together mechanically. The heat created by the vibration melts the thermoplastic. Ultrasonic methods are used to weld and assemble metal and plastic parts, to activate adhesives to a molten state, to spot weld, and to sew and stitch films and fabrics together, eliminating needles and threads.

FINISHED PLASTICS

Most articles made from plastics by any of the production methods require some extra work in the form of assembling, drilling, polishing, smoothing, tapping, or trimming. Few products are made in their entirety by fabrication, but many formed or molded parts are fabricated into finished products.

After the plastic is formed, it may be carved, drilled, polished, sanded, or sawed to finish the edges or to give a decorative effect. Plastics may also be metal plated, painted, printed, or stenciled to present an attractive appearance.

CARE OF PLASTICS

In order to maintain plastic products, the following guidelines should be followed:

1. Read the instructions about care on the labels and hangtags because there are many kinds of plastic materials.

2. Plastics products are generally easy to care for. Most have surfaces that may be washed or wiped with a damp cloth and then dried. Most plastics can be washed in mild soap suds or detergents. They may also be cleaned in ordinary glassware washing machines. Ultrasonic cleaners may be used if the products do not rest directly upon the transducer diaphragm.

3. Avoid abrasive cleaners, scouring pads, and strong oxidizing agents.

4. Furniture wax may be used on the plastic surfaces of furniture that may have fine scratches.

5. Most plastics should be handled carefully because they may chip or crack if abused.

6. Avoid exposing some plastics to high heat. Thermosetting plastics products will withstand fairly high heat. They generally char rather than burn in extremely hot situations. Thermoplastics products will deteriorate around heat unless specific directions state the appropriate temperatures to use.

7. Autoclavable (collapsible) items such as plastic baby milk or drinking water containers should be washed free of detergents or other cleaning agents before being sterilized. Closures on autoclaving plastic bottles must be loose during and after autoclaving until cool. If not, a partial vacuum will form inside the bottle and cause distortion or collapse of its walls.

SELLING POINTS

Following is a list of selling points that may help promote the use of plastics.

1. Knowledge of the properties of plastics will help the buyer who buys the products at market, the salesperson who sells them, and the customer who buys and uses them.

2. Most plastics are available in a wide range of colors. They are light-weight, easy to handle, and are available in beautiful designs, patterns, and shapes.

3. Most plastics take rugged use but require low maintenance and replacement. They will not break or scratch easily, and they will wear well. If plastics break or crack, most can be repaired with clear cement or with a matching colored plastic glue. For example, vinyl plastic glue can be used to repair cracked or torn vinyl auto seat covers.

4. Many plastics can be cleaned by hand, washing with mild soap and warm water. Others can be rubbed clean with a dry cloth. Some plastics are dishwasher-safe with hot water.

5. Most plastics are nontoxic, odorless, and tasteless. Many are not affected by freezing temperature but should be kept away from high heat and direct flame. Most plastics are water-resistant and are not water-absorbent. Abrasives and strong acids are harmful to many plastics. The electrical resistance of many plastics is good.

KEY TERMS

1. Amino
2. Cellulosics
3. Compression molding
4. Filler
5. Plasticizers

6. Resin or binder
7. Silicones
8. Thermoforming
9. Thermosetting
10. Ultrasonic bonding

STUDY QUESTIONS

1. What are plastics?
2. Explain how the two basic types of plastics differ.
3. What are the general ingredients of most plastics? What does each ingredient do?
4. What are the major differences between reinforcements and fillers?
5. What is the most important source for the production of synthetic plastics? What are some other sources of hydrocarbons for the production of plastics?
6. List eight plastics belonging to the family of thermoplastics and give a product application of each.
7. List four plastics belonging to the family of thermosetting plastics and give a product application of each.
8. Why is it necessary to identify plastics?
9. What are the four types of colorants used in plastics?
10. What are four basic ways plastics are joined together?
11. Explain the differences in the following ways of shaping plastics: molding, extrusion, casting, laminating, blowing, and foaming.
12. Describe the following decorating processes: coloring, painting, hot stamping, plating, engraving, printing, and heat transfer.

13. Name ten operations of machining and finishing plastic products that give a decorative effect or an attractive appearance.
14. Why are plastics used for handles for pots, pans, and other appliances?
15. How would you care for plastics?

STUDY ACTIVITIES

1. Make a list of the plastics belonging to the families of thermoplastics and thermosetting plastics. After each plastic list two advantages and disadvantages of its properties.
2. What three properties would you consider in making the following plastic products: raincoat, ice chest, fishing rod, counter top, washing machine agitator, furniture covers, and canoe?
3. Visit a dinnerwear department, a housewares department, or a toy department. List the different merchandise made from plastics. Check those in which plastic materials may have replaced natural materials in making the product. Which material would be used more effectively in making each product?

CHAPTER 15

Furs

OBJECTIVES

After completing this chapter, you should be able to:

1. Differentiate between the families of fur-bearing animals and give distinguishing facts about each fur belonging to each family.

2. Describe how furs are obtained from wild animals and fur farms. Explain the facts that affect price.

3. Explain how furs are dressed and dyed.

4. Trace the process of constructing fur garments. Explain why each step must be taken.

5. Explain the different ways to care for furs to maintain their serviceability and beauty.

Furs add an exciting dimension to the fashion apparel world. They provide a visual and tactile luxury unequalled by any other apparel. Knowledge of furs is a must for anyone aspiring to sell, buy, or wear garments made from them. It takes a great amount of knowledge about furs to interpret this information in terms of what the garment will do for the fashion-conscious customer.

Fashion trends often dictate which furs are popular and which are not. Furs may be purchased more for their beauty than for their warmth and serviceability. If a specific kind of fur is in fashion, it may cost far more than a fur that will give more warmth and be more durable. Supply, demand, and price may vary greatly for different colors of furs; flat furs; bulky, fluffy furs; short-haired and long-haired furs.

HISTORY

The history of people's use of furs is even older than recorded history. Prehistoric people used fur-bearing animals for food and their fur as an apparel for warmth. The early civilizations of China, Greece, and the Roman Empire used furs lavishly, as did the pharaohs and high priests of Egypt, who wore leopard and lion skins.

The fur trade developed rapidly in medieval Europe, and it played an important role in the exploration and settlement of North America. Russian fur trappers and hunters surged eastward in the early eighteenth century from the Kamchatka region in eastern Siberia to the southern edge of present-day Alaska. American fur traders moved westward across the Mississippi River into the Louisiana Purchase territory and the Rocky Mountain region early in the nineteenth century. During this period the fur trade was first organized commercially when John Jacob Astor, a famous name in American corporate history, established the American Fur Company.

Former trading posts or fur collection centers which have become cities include Albany, New York; Chicago, Illinois; Detroit, Michigan; New Orleans, Louisiana; Pittsburgh, Pennsylvania; Spokane, Washington; St. Louis, Missouri; and St. Paul, Minnesota. Indeed, the processing, distribution, and marketing of furs have become major factors in the sophisticated economy of America.

PELT CHARACTERISTICS

The term *fur* is derived from the old French words *forre* ("sheath") and *vair* ("red squirrel"). Furs have been defined by the Fur Products Labeling Act of 1952 (amended in 1961 and 1969) as any animal skin or part thereof with hair, fleece, or fur fibers attached, either in its raw skin or processed state; but it shall not include skins that are to be converted into leather. The fine, soft, hairy covering (coat) of a mammal, usually consists of a layer of relatively short, soft, barbed hairs next to the skin, called *ground hair, underhair, underwool,* or *fur fibers.* These fur fibers help to maintain the body temperature. A top layer of longer, stiff, smooth hairs growing up through the underlying layer serves as protection and sheds rain (Figure 15.1). These hairs are called *top hair* or *guard hairs,* and they may be *sheared* in beaver or fur seal to give a pile texture, or picked out to leave the sheared fur.

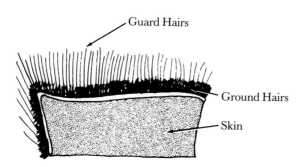

Guard Hairs

Ground Hairs

Skin

Figure 15.1
Sample of fur showing guard hairs, ground hairs, and skin.

The guard hairs give the fox and mink furs their beauty. The pelts of certain animals, lacking either fur fibers or guard hairs, are not considered to be true furs although they are sold commercially as furs. Monkey furs have guard hairs but no underhair. Persian lamb is sold as fur, but it has only underwool and no guard hairs. Mink is called the true fur because it has dense underhair and long, glossy guard hair.

If a fur garment has been worn and the fur has been cut up to make another garment, it has to be labeled as *used fur*. A label that says that the garment is made of *waste fur* means that the leftover pieces, the necks, and ears of new furs have been used. Inexpensive or fur-trimmed garments are sometimes made with waste fur.

Parts of a Pelt

The term *dorsal* is used to identify the center back strip of the pelt (see Figure 15.2). It is the largest and best part of the pelt, with few exceptions, and is used for the basic parts of expensive fur coats and jackets. The dorsal generally is darker than the other parts and divides the pelt into two major sections. However, the leftover parts of the whole skin, including the rump and flank, are used in making less expensive fur garments. The paws, gills, sides, and parts of the belly may be used as *waste fur* and sewn in a patchwork pattern to make inexpensive fur garments.

THE EFFECT OF ENVIRONMENT ON FUR

Effects of Temperature

Fur-bearing animals in northern regions produce their fullest coats in the prewinter period when days become shorter. It is in this way that nature prepares them

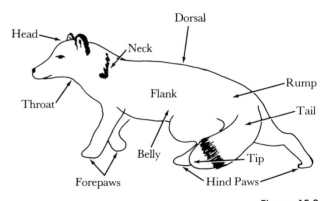

Figure 15.2
Sections of pelt used in the fur industry.

for protection from the cold. The fur becomes glossier and thicker so that it reaches its peak quality by the time heavy frosts arrive. Fur-bearing animals in the colder regions produce long lustrous hair and thin, somewhat weak skins; the warmer climates result in coarser, shorter, less dense hair and a stiffer, thicker skin. Since nature provides animals with a certain degree of protection against enemies by giving them the color of the environment (protective coloration), the fur may become lighter in color. An ermine is pale brown or brown-streaked in the spring and summer and white in winter. An animal of the same species will be somewhat smaller in a warmer climate than in a cold climate. A marsh animal will have a dark-colored fur.

When an animal begins to shed its hair, the skin becomes sinewy and later turns bluish on the flesh side. The hair roots come through and are lost when the fur is dressed. The skin has little value. In cold weather the skin becomes cream-colored and elastic; it is desirable as a *prime skin* with abundant fur fibers, guard hairs, and a rich color and gloss. Good fur fibers are produced by a cold, dry winter. A wet winter will produce lighter and better guard hairs, but poorer fur fibers.

Effects of Water

Animals living in the water develop their best fur in spring because the water is coldest in the first part of spring. Because the water is cold, the animal needs the thickest fur fibers and guard hairs. Dark hair is developed in dark swamps. Salt water tends to cause the hair to become pale.

Effects of Hibernation

Many wild animals hibernate during part of the winter. To keep alive during hibernation an animal eats more food that usual in the fall. The animal thins down during hibernation until it emerges in the spring. Therefore, a fur skin is not as valuable after hibernation.

SOURCES OF FURS

Furs traded commercially originate from both wild sources and fur farms (ranches), with the greatest proportion obtained by fur farming.

Wild Sources

Over eighty countries located on all six continents contribute wild furs for commercial use. Most of the wild furs come from the cold climates where the temperature ensures the growth of luxuriantly thick fur. North America has the greatest variety of fur-bearing animals, with forty different kinds.

Wild furs are obtained by trapping, shooting, clubbing, or snaring. The most commonly used trap is the steel-jaw spring trap. It is generally set baited, using lures of special scents or food. Muskrat, beaver, and mink are generally trapped underwater and drowned. Trapping in most of the world is licensed by, and subject to, control of state, provincial, or other governmental agencies. In order to preserve the resources of the animal, the trapping season and the numbers that can be taken are usually controlled. Fur seals are usually clubbed or shot. Muskrat, raccoon, and beaver, in that order, are the most numerous wild furs caught annually in the United States. Other wild furs trapped in smaller numbers in this country include fox, mink, nutria, opossum, seal, and skunk.

Individual governments and international organizations, in the late 1960s and early 1970s, realized the possibility that certain animal species were in danger of becoming extinct. Some countries passed legislation that prohibited or restricted commercial use of specific fur-bearing animals. These animals included the northern kit fox from Canada; the giant otter from the Amazon Basin; the spider monkeys from Costa Rica and Guatemala; the southern fur seal of Argentina, Ecuador, and Peru; the Spanish lynx; the Asiatic cheetah; the Sinai leopard; the Sumatran tiger; the Caspian tiger; and the Barbary leopard.

Fur Farming

Fur farming, an ancient practice, is the keeping and breeding of animals for their pelts. In 1880, scientific fur farming began in eastern Canada on Prince Edward Island. Livestock practices were generally adapted, but certain problems pertaining to the raising of wild species under confinement required special research. The fur farmers began breeding the colored silver fox, a black color phase of the red fox having white-tipped hairs. This breeding project was becoming very successful when World War I caused an economic setback in the fur industry. In 1920 the fur became popular again and the Canadian government in cooperation with the Canadian National Silver Fox Breeders Association established an early research station at Prince Edward Island.

The first United States experimental station began at Saratoga Springs, New York, in 1923. Later, in 1953, it moved to Ithaca, New York, where it operated cooperatively with Cornell University. By 1940 the U.S government cooperated with several universities in research programs; some of these programs concentrated on diseases of fur-bearing animals. A government fur fiber laboratory at Beltsville, Maryland, concentrated on fur fiber origin, development, and growth.

Other Canadian provinces began fur-bearing animal research stations. Other countries that began fur-bearing animal research programs include Denmark, Norway, and Sweden.

The research eventually resulted in better techniques of breeding, feeding, and management, producing the finest quality furs available. *Mutation* takes place when an animal is domesticated. Such an animal differs, especially in coat color, from typical animals of the wild type. These differences are maintained by selective breeding in chinchilla, mink, fox, and nutria fur farms. When an animal is born with an unusual color of fur, it is carefully bred to close relatives (*inbreeding*) and to other animals from nonrelated families (*cross breeding*). This results in unusual colors in furs of an adequate number of animals to be made into garments.

Mink Farming

Minks have been raised on fur farms since 1866. Quantity production has taken place since the early 1930s, and mink furs have remained in fashion. Mink has accounted for the large majority of the fur trade since the early 1960s. Minks are usually mated in March and pelted the last of November. The development of mutant colors has increased the popularity of mink fur. The pale brown, medium brown, dark brown, black, and white colors are costly because of the scarcity of numbers of mutation minks being bred to meet the demand. Examples of mutation minks are the Silverblu mink (grey blue) and the Samink (sable mink), which are mutations that were developed in 1972. Figure 15.3 illustrates one mink farm.

Fox Farming

Silver fox fur was in great demand during the 1930s and early 1940s. The silvery effect was a result of a controlled mating (mutation) of a red fox with the reddish-orange color replaced by black and the outstanding white band on the guard hairs. The mating of black or silver foxes always results in silver-black foxes. This is a rarity among wild foxes. In the early years, odd-colored fox pups were destroyed. Later, they were mated in certain ways to produce the mutant colors like blue, pearl, platinum, and white.

Figure 15.3
A mink farm. Mink are raised in cages within large well-lighted sheds. Fine pelts are produced with scientific feeding and controlled conditions.
Courtesy of National Board of Fur Farm Organizations, Inc.

The United States, Canada, and the Scandinavian countries reached peak production of silver and mutation fox pelts about 1939. In the 1950s, fox farms declined in number due to the fact that fashion demanded less fox fur and more mink. The 1970s brought about a renewed interest in fox as a fashion item.

Chinchilla Farming

The chinchilla is a squirrel-like rodent, native to the mountains of South America. So many were trapped during the early 1900s that they almost became extinct. Fur farming began about that time in the United States, Canada, and other countries. For fifty years breeding stock was primarily sold and few pelts entered the market. In June of 1954, the first auction of a large quantity of pelts from farm-raised chinchillas took place.

Today chinchilla associations, such as Emba Mink Breeders Association, market the furs. This luxury fur is extremely fine, silky, and soft. The fur fibers are blue-gray. The short to medium length guard hairs are white with dark tips.

Marten Farming

Martens are found in northern wooded areas and closely resemble sables. They weigh one and one-half to three pounds when mature. Martens have been difficult to raise in fur farms because controlled breeding is unmanageable. About 15 to 20 percent of the females reproduce. They naturally breed in July and August under the effects of artificial light, which simulates early spring conditions, causing the animals to whelp in December rather than in April.

Farming of Other Fur Animals

Karakul sheep and similar breeds of sheep have been raised for hundreds of years in Middle Eastern countries. The black Persian lambskins and similar kinds are popular. Newborn lambs produce the best pelts because the tight, small curl is in its prime at that age. Several million Persian lambskins are produced annually in South Africa. It takes many years of selective mating of Karakul rams to produce offspring that come from white sheep. *Mouton* is the select skin from the white lamb that is sheared, generally dyed, and marketed.

Other fur animals have been farmed, but not on a large scale commercially, because there has been an adequate supply from wild animals. These animals include beaver, fisher, fitch, muskrat, nutria, raccoon, and skunk. Fashion trends have not created a demand for these particular furs to be farmed in large quantities.

Rabbits are raised in hutches primarily for their meat, not their fur. Some natural or sheared and dyed rabbit fur skins from Europe have been made into fur garments. Garments made from rabbit pelts have been popular in the late 1970s and 1980s in this country.

CLASSIFYING FUR-BEARING ANIMALS

There are a number of ways to classify fur-bearing animals. Some of these classifications are by (1) color, (2) general characteristics, (3) type of fur, or (4) family groups.

The animals may be classified roughly into the following family groups: weasel, rodent, cat, canine, hoofed animals, and miscellaneous animals. Information not found within the discussion of each group may be located in Table 15.1, which compares characteristics and origins of animals. See Figure 15.4 for photos of two of these fur-bearing animals.

The Weasel Family

Included in the weasel family of fur-bearing animals are the badger, ermine, fisher, fitch, kolinsky, marten (American, baum, or stone), mink, otter, sable (Russian or American), skunk, spotted skunk (misnamed "civet cat"), and wolverine.

Most of the expensive furs have come from this family, like the ermine, mink, and sable. The *sable,* native to Russia (Siberia), has been held in renown for many years. The best quality sables have shiny short, dark brown, fluffy guard hair and dark, bluish brown fur fiber.

The finest *ermine,* which comes from Russia (Siberia), is pure white in its winter color. It is also well-known for its lustrous natural brown summer color. The ermine living in North America is known as the *American weasel.* It stays a brown color all year long and is a less expensive fur than the sable from Russia.

Mink fur has retained its popularity for many years as an attractive and durable fur. The qualities of mink vary greatly among the wild and ranched ones, which include the different mutation minks. Other furs that are dyed to resemble or imitate mink fur come from other animals including fitch, marmot, muskrat, rabbit, and squirrel.

Ermine, mink, and sable furs are made into coats, capes, strollers, jackets, scarves, hats, cuffs, and other trimmings. *Stoles* are short fur capes that fit across the back and shoulders and extend in long panels down the front. They may be worn over coats, gowns, or suits. Currently, they are not in fashion. *Strollers* are coats that are about knee-length.

Skunks have long fur fibers that are brown. Two white stripes run along the animal's back. These stripes may vary in length and width among the animals. The white stripes do not absorb dye well and are sometimes cut out of the pelt and placed together to make inexpensive *dyed skunk stripe* coats. *Natural skunk* coats have had the skin side dipped into dye so that the white skin would not show through the dark fur. Color has been applied to both the fur and skin in *tip-dyed skunk* coats. *Dyed skunk* indicates that the white stripe was left in and that the total coat was dipped in dyestuff strong enough to make all the fur look alike in color. Dresswear and sportswear are made of skunk fur. The skins are sometimes let out to lengthen them and leathered to keep them from looking so bulky. (These processes are described below.)

The *spotted skunk* (often misnamed "civet cat") is about the size of a skunk, and the fur has many of its characteristics. Against a dark black-brown fur background, lyrelike-shaped, white markings appear. The quality of the fur depends on the clearness of the coloring and the attractiveness of the markings. The fur is made into inexpensive sportswear and jackets and is used for trimmings.

TABLE 15.1
continued

FAMILY	COUNTRIES OF ORIGIN	CHARACTERISTICS OF PELTS
The Rodent Family		
Beaver	North America	Glossy tan to dark brown; dense, silky, medium length fur fiber; guard hair is coarse and often removed; medium weight; good wearing qualities. Glazing gives a smooth appearance. Best quality from eastern Canada.
Chinchilla	South America, fur farms in United States	Fine, soft, lustrous, bluish-gray fur fiber; short to medium length guard hairs that are white with dark tips; fragile, lightweight; luxury fur.
Marmot	USSR, Mongolia	Brownish to black; fur fiber is thick and short; guard hair is long; often dyed brown with darker tips to resemble mink; poor to fair wearing qualities; less durable than muskrat.
Muskrat	North America, USSR	Soft, dense, even, gray fur fiber; long, lustrous, stiff, dark brown guard hair; fair to good wearing qualities; medium weight; belly section inexpensive, side sections medium quality.
Nutria (Coypus)	U.S., South America	Short, dense, dark bluish-brown fur fiber is best quality; long and coarse guard hairs are generally plucked; fair wearing qualities. Belly section is best quality. Less durable than beaver but may be of equal cost.
Rabbit (Coney, Lapin)	Throughout the world	Fur fiber is blue-gray; guard hair is dark; spots indicate season in which pelt was taken; often sheared, plucked, and dyed in novelty colors to resemble other furs; poor to fair wearing qualities.
Squirrel	USSR (Siberia)	Lustrous, fluffy steel-blue fur; sometimes with red streaks; often dyed; long, dense fur fiber; slightly longer, silky guard hair; poor to fair wearing qualities; lightweight. Imitates more costly furs.
The Cat Family		
Leopard	Africa, Ceylon	Very little fur fiber; short, flat, silky guard hair; buff color with black or dark brown rosettes; good wearing qualities. Best quality comes from Somaliland. *Endangered species.*
Lynx	Canada, Northern Europe, Asia	Long, silky guard hair; dense fur fiber colored grayish-buff to tawny color with darker markings; sometimes dyed black, pale blue, or pale brown. Best quality from Canada. Requires great care because it sheds easily.
Ocelot	Mexico, Central America, South America	Flat fur with short guard hair; little fur fiber; black markings on tawny-yellow or gray ground hair; poor to fair wearing qualities; less valuable than leopard fur; best quality has flat, silky hair. *Endangered species.*
The Canine Family		
Fox	Mostly Northern Hemisphere; fur farms in Canada, United States and Scandinavia	Soft, dense, fine fur fiber; long guard hair; lower grades have coarser hair. Light-colored furs are less expensive and are mostly dyed. Poor to fair wearing qualities; expensive

TABLE 15.1   MAJOR FUR PELTS AND THEIR COUNTRIES OF ORIGIN

FAMILY	COUNTRIES OF ORIGIN	CHARACTERISTICS OF PELTS
The Weasel Family		
Badger	Asia, Europe, North America	Long, soft, silky white, pale cream, or yellow fur fiber; coarse, black, white-tipped guard hair of different wearing qualities. Best quality from North America.
Ermine	Asia, Europe, USSR	White in winter, red-brown in summer; sometimes bleached or dyed brown; fur fiber and guard hair about the same length; lightweight; poor to fair wearing qualities; fur from USSR is densest and commands the highest price.
Fisher	Canada, United States	Rich dark brown fur fiber; long, coarse, glossy black guard hairs; full tail; good wearing qualities; expensive fur used for coats. Best quality from eastern Canada.
Fitch	Canada, USSR (Siberia)	Fur fiber and guard hair longer than that of other weasel family members. Soft, lustrous; natural color yellow to white; fine, open fur fiber contrasts with black guard hair; durable wearing qualities. Best quality from Siberia.
Kolinsky	USSR (Siberia), China, Korea, Japan	Yellow brown, fairly lightweight with short fine fur fiber and long, silky guard hair; dyed soft brown to resemble better quality mink or sable; fair to good wearing qualities. Best quality from Siberia.
Marten, American	Alaska and Canada	Blue-black to various brown shades to a pale yellow that is generally dyed; medium length fur; fair wearing qualities.
Marten, Baum	Europe, Asia	Yellow-brown guard hairs are longer and slightly coarser than those of sable; frequently dyed deep brown to match the sable color; fair wearing qualities. Best quality from USSR are soft, silky, and fully furred.
Marten, Stone	Asia, Asia Minor, Europe	Whitish fur fiber and ashy-gray or brown guard hair; mostly used natural; good wearing qualities; less expensive than baum marten.
Mink	North America, Europe, fur farming in Canada, United States	Color ranges from very dark brown to reddish-brown and includes various mutant colors; dense, short, fine fur fiber; lustrous guard hair; fairly lightweight; luxury fur with good wearing qualities.
Otter	Throughout the world	Dense, fine, short fur fiber is gray, medium brown, or dark brown. Stiff long, silvery guard hairs with lighter tips are frequently plucked and dyed; medium weight; excellent wearing qualities. *Endangered species.*
Sable	USSR (Siberia)	Best quality has dense, bluish-black, or brown fur fiber and long, silky, lustrous short dark brown guard hair; medium weight; fair wearing qualities; finish type is called crown sable; luxury fur.
Skunk	North America, South America	Dense, bluish-black fur fiber; long, glossy guard hair; two white stripes extend down the pelt back; often plucked and dyed; good wearing qualities; heavy weight; often let out and leathered to give less bulky look.
Wolverine	North America, USSR (Siberia)	Black or bluish-brown with tan stripe on sides; long guard hair with coarse texture; very good wearing qualities; the only fur on which moisture does not congeal.

TABLE 15.1 MAJOR FUR PELTS AND THEIR COUNTRIES OF ORIGIN
continued

FAMILY	COUNTRIES OF ORIGIN	CHARACTERISTICS OF PELTS
Wolf	Throughout Northern Hemisphere	Long, silky guard hair; dense fur fiber; colors are off-white, yellowish, brownish-gray, or black; heavyweight; fair to good wearing qualities; finest fur comes from timber wolves of the Arctic area. Less costly and less attractive fur is called *Canadian* and *prairie*.

Hoofed Animals (The Ungulate Family)

Guanaco	Southern South America	Fur fiber is short, not too thin or woolly; guard hair is coarse; soft, yellow-red fur. Only the young are used for fur. Fair wearing quality.
Kangaroo	Australia	Medium short fur fiber; medium length guard hair; gray color; fair wearing quality.
Kidskin	Asia, Africa	Short, black, gray, or white hair generally curly or wavy; no fur fiber; mostly dyed; thin leather; sheared, pressed, and dyed to resemble broadtail. Poor wearing quality.
Lamb, Caracul	USSR, China	Short to long, glossy, curled, or wavy hair; white, brown, or black; poor to fair wearing qualities.
Lamb, Mouton—processed	North America, South Africa, South America	Unkinked, dyed, and sheared to resemble beaver fur; also dyed novelty colors.
Lamb, Persian Broadtail	Afghanistan, Southwest Africa	Fur of very young lambs; lustrous and tightly curled; gray, brown, or black; may be dyed for uniformity; poor to good wearing qualities.
Pony Skins	Europe, South America	Lustrous, flat guard hair; no fur fiber; best quality have a moirélike pattern; often dyed black or bleached and dyed tan; poor to fair wearing qualities.
Wallaby	Australia, Tasmania	Fur fiber is thick and long; guard hair is silky; fair wearing qualities.

Miscellaneous Animals

Opossum	North America, South America, Australia	Natural grayish white with long fur fiber; long silvery tipped guard hair; tends to mat and shed; quality of fur and skin may vary in a pelt; fair to good wearing qualities; often dyed to resemble beaver fur; more expensive and serviceable than American opossum.
Raccoon	North America, South America	Long and silky hair, gray to black color with black-tipped long guard hair; sometimes a dark brown color; better quality furs are darker, more densely furred, and may be sheared, let out, and dyed to resemble beaver or nutria fur. Good wearing qualities.
Seal, Fur	United States (Alaska), South Africa, South America, Japan, USSR (Siberia)	Often dyed black, brown, or gray-black; guard hairs are coarse and generally removed; good wearing qualities. Each skin is stamped with U.S. government label. *Endangered species.*

Figure 15.4
A kangaroo and a fitch, two fur-bearing animals.
Courtesy of the Columbus (Ohio) zoo. Kangaroo photo by Lyle Holbrook.

Badger fur has pale yellow fur fibers with long guard hairs that have brown and white tips. Sometimes the guard hairs are glued to a black fox skin to imitate silver fox fur. This process is called *pointing*. Badger fur is used as collars on women's sport coats.

The Rodent Family

This family is distinguished from the others by the presence of sharp incisor teeth, used for gnawing. The members vary in size from a mouse to a beaver. One group lives on land; the other group lives in the water. The land rodents used for furs are the chinchilla, marmot, rabbit, and squirrel. The water rodents used for furs are the beaver, nutria, and muskrat.

Muskrat fur is dyed, sheared, and made to resemble baum, marten, mink, sable, and seal. It is also used to make natural brown center back sections. The medium quality fur comes from the sides of the animal and is a golden color. The inexpensive quality fur comes from the silver-colored belly.

Nutria originated in South America and is related to the northern beaver. It is raised on fur farms to some extent and is mated with the nutria from Louisiana. Its belly section contains the best quality fur, and the fur fibers are not plucked as in the beaver. The fur tends to mat, but this problem is easily corrected by carefully brushing it. Sportswear or casual wear is made from nutria fur.

Beaver fur has become more popular since 1935 when a new method was developed to lessen its weight and bulk by thinning the skin, plucking the guard hairs, and shearing the fur fibers. When wet, sheared beaver has a tendency to mat, but this is easily corrected. It is made into sportswear and dresswear.

The best quality *squirrel* furs are used to make natural squirrel coats, although they are not very durable. This fur is also used to make inexpensive capes, jackets, and scarves.

Marmots are animals that burrow under the surface of the ground. Their fur is coarser in appearance than that of other brown furs, such as mink, which it imitates. The luster of the fur appears glassylike. Its wearing qualities are inferior to those of the muskrat. Marmot fur is made into inexpensive dresswear.

Rabbit fur can be blended, spotted, or dyed to imitate beaver, chinchilla, ermine, leopard, mink, and sable. The French word *lapin,* meaning rabbit, may not be used now. The Federal Trade Commission regulations state that rabbit must be called *dyed rabbit* or *natural rabbit.* Rabbit furs from France are the finest quality pelts. Furs from male rabbits (bucks) give better service than fur from females (does). The furs may be made into all types of garments.

The Cat Family

Among the animals in the cat family that have spotted furs are the leopard, lynx, and ocelot. These animals are on the endangered species list. In order to use the furs, a certificate must accompany them. The finest quality and most valuable *leopard* fur comes from Somaliland in Africa. This fur is considered more attractive when the markings are small. Expensive jackets and sportswear are made from leopard fur. It is often imitated in other furs and fabrics. *Ocelot* fur is considered less valuable than leopard fur. It has markings that are elongated and oval-shaped rather than rosette-shaped like those of the leopard. The finest quality *lynx* fur comes from Canada. The fur has a tendency to shed. It is used for trim on dress coats and sports coats, and for jackets.

Other fur-bearing animals in the cat family are the cheetahs, jaguars, and wild cats. The wild cat fur is hard to dye and is not considered attractive.

The Canine Family

The most popular and attractive furs come from the *fox* and *wolf* animals of the canine family. Furs from foxes are made into scarves, collars, dresswear, and capes and jackets for evening wear. Most fox furs come from fur farms or ranches. The fluffier and richer the appearance of the fox fur, the better the quality. Fox fur has a tendency to shed. The *swift or kit* (young) foxes are considered the least valuable of fox furs. The offspring of the red fox may be black fox, cross fox, red fox, or silver fox. Garments made of fox fur fluctuate in popularity.

Blue foxes are usually not blue at all but are a combination of dark grey, brown, and misty blue colors; some have a purple tinge and others are brown with gray fur fibers. The *Norwegian blue fox* is an expensive mutation fox that is actually blue and was developed on a fox fur ranch. The *cross fox* resembles either red fox or silver fox (the better quality). It has a distinct black cross at the neck and across the shoulders and down the back of the skin. Fur from the *gray fox* is among the inexpensive, less attractive fox furs. It is almost always dyed to imitate silver fox, and the tips of the guard hair are left silvery white. The *platinum fox* is a mutation of the silver fox. It was developed in Norway in 1933 and marketed in 1940 as scarves. The name platinum comes from the fur, which is a shaded cream to light blue with a silverlike hue.

The better quality wolf furs come from the *timber wolves* that live in the arctic region. There is a wide variety in species and texture. They are used in natural color or dyed. The furs shed a lot. Garments of wolf, mainly sportswear, fluctuate in popularity. *Coyotes* are a member of the canine family whose fur is less valuable than that of the fox group. *Coyote* fur is usually dyed and made into garments for sportswear.

Hoofed Animals (The Ungulate Family)

The fur-bearing animals that have hoofs and belong to this family include the lamb, kid, guanaco, and pony. *Persian lamb* does not come from former Persia (Iran), but from Afghanistan, South Africa, and Central Asia. Special permission was given to use the term *Persian* by the Federal Trade Commission because of the time-honored reference to that type of fur. It has naturally gray, brown, or black hair. The finest type of lamb has silky complete curls of firm-bodied, lustrous character which vary in size from small to large, and is made into better quality coats and trimming on fabric coats. *Persian paw, Persian head,* and *pieced Persian* are plated garments made from sections left over from whole-skin coats. They are not as expensive as the whole-skin garments. Persian lamb ranges from low to good wearing qualities.

Broadtail lamb is the pelt from a prematurely born or newborn Persian lamb. The hair has a moiré pattern because it is not long enough to curl, but it does have more curl than the regular broadtail lamb. The skin is thin, and the hair is flat with a firm texture. It has low to fair wearing qualities, depending on the natural sheen and design of the fur. The fur is expensive and is made into capes, dress coats, jackets, and trimmings.

Caracul lamb is the fur pelt of a newborn lamb of the karakul sheep, after the curl begins to loosen. The pelts come from Russia and China. These furs have short to long hairs of various colors and textures. The fur is usually white, but may be brown or black. The skins are graded according to curl and luster. The wearing qualities are low to fair. The fur is used mostly for dresswear. There is a wide price range for this fur.

Mouton-processed lamb pelts come from the South American sheep group. This fur is known for its warmth and durability. This short-pile fur is sheared, processed to straighten the hair, and dyed. One process, called *plasticizing,* straightens the kinky hair using a plastic chemical that also makes the fur water-repellent and moth-resistant. Another chemical process, called *electrifying,* also straightens the kinky hair. Mouton-processed lamb fur is fairly low in price and is made into sportswear.

Broadtail-processed lamb fur comes from a certain South American sheep that is selected and processed to imitate the more expensive broadtail lamb fur.

Kidskin comes from goats living mostly in China, western India, and Africa. It is an expensive fur and has poor wearing qualities.

Guanaco is related to the camel family and is from South America. The guard hair is coarse and the fur fiber is short, not too scanty or too woolly. The medium-priced fur of the young guanaco has a reddish-brown color and may be used in its natural color or dyed to imitate the blue fox.

Pony skins mostly come from Poland and Russia. The flat, short-haired fur usually has a natural brown and tan color, or is dyed. It is not durable. Some pony skins have attractive moiré markings. These low- to medium-priced furs are usually made into sportswear.

Miscellaneous Animals

Some fur-bearing animals, such as the American opossum, Australian opossum, raccoon, and fur seal, cannot be classified into any of the families or groups already given.

The *American opossum* is part of the pouch family group. It is found in North America, especially in the central part of the United States. It has guard hair that is dense, long, straight, and evenly distributed. Its natural color is gray-white with black-tipped guard hair. The fur is inclined to mat and shed. The quality of skin and fur may vary in a single pelt. The fur is frequently dyed to resemble that of the skunk. Its wearing qualities are fair to good. This inexpensive fur is used in making sportswear.

The *Australian opossum* comes from Australia and Tasmania. The color of fur ranges from natural to yellowish muddy gray. The more bluish the color, the better the quality. The guard hair is fairly short and is softer than that of the American opossum fur. The fur may be sheared and dyed to imitate beaver fur. It is usually more serviceable and more expensive than American opossum. This fur is used mostly for sport coats.

Raccoons are part of the bear-raccoon family that live in certain regions of North America. The long guard hair is black-tipped, silver-gray, long, and silky. The fur fiber is of medium length, dense, and woolly. Its color varies from light silver to dark brown. The better quality furs are darker, more densely furred, and may be sheared. Raccoon may be sheared, let out, and dyed to resemble beaver or nutria fur. Even sheared raccoon gives good serviceable wear. Inexpensive to medium-priced sportswear garments are made from this fur.

Fur seal comes from the Pribolof islands near Alaska. This animal, whose fur is called the *Alaska fur seal,* is hunted under the supervision of the United States government. The young male seals, under six years of age, are caught for their peltries when the mating season begins each year. The United States government label is stamped on each skin that is caught. The guard hairs are plucked from the peltries, leaving the deep, soft, lustrous fur fibers. Seal skins are dyed black, dark-brown, or gray-black. Extra effort is need to dye the fur side of these seals. They have good wearing qualities and are used to make moderate to expensive coats, capes, and trimmings. Other seals come from Japan, Siberia, South Africa, and South America.

MARKETING FURS

The system of fur trading companies and collection agencies has disappeared. In their place are highly organized marketing systems in which fur-farming breeder associations ship members' pelts to auction houses on a cooperative basis. The fur crop each year begins about December 1, when pelt shipments begin. In the case of mink, auctions are held at least once a month from December through July, and then periodically until the entire fur crop has been sold. The wild animal pelts that reach the auction houses come from a few collection agencies.

Most of the furs are auctioned in the raw form of pelts that were stripped from the bodies of the animals and dried. Those pelts stripped off inside out, with the fur turned in, are known as *case-handled* (see Figure 15.5). Most of the smaller animals, such as foxes, minks, muskrats, rabbits, and sables, are skinned this way. Larger furs, such as beavers, lambs, and seals, are slit down the belly and removed with both fur and pelt sides exposed. These pelts are called *open-handled.* Trappers stretch and dry such skins on frames. The skins are assorted and graded into lots according to color, size, texture, and quality. Then they are put into bundles.

The bundles of wild and ranched furs are sent to auction houses, where they are bought by commission agents, retail and wholesale fur manufacturers, and skin merchants.

Commission agents are professional fur buyers representing international fur businesses. They buy on request and receive a commission for each purchase they make. The retail and wholesale fur manufacturers who attend the auctions generally are from large businesses that can afford to send their own representatives. Skin merchants are dealers who buy fur skins in order to resell them to small manufacturing retailers or small manufacturers. The auction houses receive fees based on the prices paid at auction.

Major fur centers are located in New York City, Montreal, Leningrad, and London. Regular auctions of secondary importance are held in Greensville, South Carolina, where dressed fur seal skins are sold semiannually; Minneapolis, Minnesota; Seattle, Washington; Edmonton, Alberta; Winnipeg, Manitoba; Vancouver, British Columbia; Regina, Saskatchewan; Stockholm, Sweden; Copenhagen, Denmark; Helsinki, Finland; and Oslo, Norway. Melbourne and

Figure 15.5
Raw peltries. Mink pelts are sorted by color, size, and quality with skin sides out.
Courtesy of The American Fur Industry, Inc.

Sydney, Australia, are the main centers for rabbit skin auctions, which are also held in London. The dominant fur-collecting organization and marketing agent in the world is the Hudson Bay Company, which has auction houses in London, Montreal, and New York City. Major auctions are held by London Public Sales in the autumn, spring, and winter.

The major fur auctions in London, Montreal, and New York City usually last a week or longer and draw international buyers. The Leningrad, USSR, sales are held in January, July, and October. They are conducted by Soyush-pushnina, an official Soviet agency, which buys the fur skin from state and collective farms and controls domestic and foreign marketing.

Millions of skins worth millions of dollars may be sold in a single day's auction. The closeness of the international market is such that buyers may travel from country to country just for sales.

FUR PROCESSING

Fur Dressing

Fur skins that are purchased raw (peltries) are sent to a specialized dressing firm for cleaning and tanning. *Dressing* is the treatment of the skins so that they will not disintegrate or putrify, yet leaving the hair covering on the skins. The skins are washed in salt water to get out the dirt. Revolving sharp knives are used to scrape off the excess fat and flesh from the skin side, leaving the hair side intact. After the skins have been soaked in salt water, chemical tanning solutions such as mineral salt, acid salt, synthetic tannins, or oil are applied to the skin side. The chemical solutions convert most stacked skins to leather overnight. Because most fur-bearing animals have thin skins, this leathering process only takes a few hours to a few days. Oils and fat liquors are then applied to the skins. Then *kickers* (large wooden blocks) are used to beat the furs against each other to work the oils into the skin fibers to make them supple. Any excess oil and grease that cling to the hair and fur fiber are removed by tumbling the skins in large revolving vats containing hardwood sawdust. This process leaves the fur clean and shiny. Another separate process that may take place in dressing is to shave the leather side to decrease weight, impart suppleness, and improve draping qualities.

Plucking and Shearing

This is a separate process that takes place during the dressing of certain animals to make the fur more attractive. The guard hairs of Alaska fur seals and beavers are generally plucked by taking the wetted skin and bending it on a machine or block of wood, so that the long guard hairs can be grasped and pulled out. No stubble of coarse guard hair is left among the velvety-textured fur fibers. Sometimes, when guard hairs are less coarse, a rotary razorlike device is used to cut the hair. The fur fiber is blown aside during the cutting. This process, used on the fur of animals like the rabbit and muskrat, reveals a shiny stubble of guard hair on close examination of the fur. Shearing of the fur fibers of such furs as beaver, fur seal, muskrat, and raccoon may take place to achieve a desired depth.

Fur Dyeing

Dyeing pertains to changing or darkening the color of fur. Furs have a *natural* color resulting from the pigments present in the animal's skin. It is long-lasting, and when rich-looking, it is the most desireable color. Many fur skins, however, are not attractive in their natural colors. Dyeing furs to make them look like better furs is an ancient art. For thousands of years furs have been dyed with vegetable or mineral coloring matters. The modern development of dyeing began in the latter part of the nineteenth century with the development of chemical compounds known as fur bases. The use of synthetic compounds has simplified the application of dyes and has enabled fur dyers to produce a wide variety of colors.

Full Dyeing

Dyeing is achieved by complete immersion of the skins in dye solutions or by rolling dye onto the surface until the hair and fur fiber are penetrated. The immersion process is called *full dyeing* and is somewhat damaging to the hair because it removes the oils so that dyes will penetrate the hair. The ancient dyes (made from minerals or vegetables) are still used for such furs as lamb and broadtail, as well as fox.

Tip Dyeing

Stenciling or top blending is executed by lightly brushing the guard hairs and sometimes the fur fibers with a dyestuff. This may give the fur a more even tint or a darker cast.

Stencil Dyeing

Stencil dyeing takes place when an inexpensive fur is dyed to imitate a more expensive one. A stenciling process is used to apply a design. Rabbit fur, for example, may be spotted to look like leopard fur.

Bleaching

Furs may go through a bleaching process that removes the color from the hair and fur. This is done to achieve color contrast in areas of fur such as the tip ends, to imitate stripes in furs, or to make off-colored yellowish furs appear whiter. Chemicals such as salts of strong acids, peroxides, or potassium permanganate tend to dry out the leather of the pelts. This has a tendency to reduce the wearing qualities of the furs. The exposure of the sun may cause bleached furs to yellow or tan. Chinchilla furs, for example, may be lightened to make them more appealing.

Glazing

This glamorizing process may be achieved in a number of different ways to give a lustrous sheen to the surface of the fur. The furrier also glazes a customer's fur after cleaning it. The fur is dampened, combed, stroked, and ironed by running a padded iron over it to draw the oils to the surface. Some furs may be blown with air. Others may be brushed with a glazing chemical to produce the luster desired on the surface.

MANUFACTURING FUR GARMENTS

After skins are processed, they are ready to be made into fur garments. The furrier may buy pelts in assorted bundles ready for manufacturing. The sorting is done according to the quality and type of garment planned.

The manufacture of fur garments is still basically a hand craft. Fur skins require individual handling and, in effect, every garment is almost entirely handmade. The manufacturer usually specializes in a particular fur or garment on a wholesale basis, then distributes the garments through department and speciality stores. The furrier maintains a custom business, making a garment to the customer's order. Most retail firms combine the sale of custom order work with ready-made garments.

A muslin garment is made, fitted on a form, and analyzed before a fur garment is started. Each style of garment is planned by a designer or stylist who is knowledgeable about fashion, fur characteristics, and the potential of each type of fur (see Figure 15.6). The outline of the garment and its overall specifications are determined on the designer's drawing board. This design is then translated into heavy paper patterns by patternmakers who determine the exact placement of

Figure 15.6
A designer using muslin coats on a dress form and a live model to plan the construction of fur coats.
Courtesy of The American Fur Industry, Inc.

pelts, the number of pelts to be used, and the way that the pelts are to be used for that style of garment. The patterns are then used to guide the fur cutters and sewers in cutting and arranging the furs. The patterns will be graded for size variations if the fur garment is to be mass produced.

Matching Furs

Furs are matched for color, size of pelt, texture, thickness, and length and markings of guard hairs. Individual pelts are selected to fit the pattern and where they are to be placed on the pattern. The best quality pelts are placed where they will show off their beauty. The poorer quality pelts are placed where they will be seen the least; for example, under the sleeve. Once the fur matcher places the furs on the pattern, it moves on to the fur cutter.

Cutting Furs

The fur cutter is one of the most skilled and highest paid of all the fur craftsmen. Work tools consist of a ruler and a razorbladelike knife with an attached handle. The fur skins are arranged to fit the various parts of the pattern. Once the markings of the fur are matched perfectly, the cutter cuts the skins to match the color and pattern of the adjoining fur.

Fur skins may be cut in various ways, according to the way in which the skins are attached together. The two main cutting methods used by the cutter are the letting-out method and the skin-on-skin method. Other methods include using the whole fur skin for the length of the garment, the semi-letting-out construction method, and the split-skin process.

Letting-Out Method

This costly method of constructing fur garments eliminates the horizontal markings by cutting the skin into narrow diagonal strips, one-eighth to one-fourth inch in width, and sewing them together end to end to make one long strip of fur the full length of the garment without the seams showing on the fur side.

These long narrow strips are joined to give lengthwise grace to a garment, minimize width, and improve draping qualities, especially with mink skins. This process is also used with muskrat, silver fox, platinum fox, sable, beaver, ermine, chinchilla, raccoon, and gray Persian lamb. This method of construction is also known as a *fully let-out* fur garment. Figure 15.7 illustrates this process.

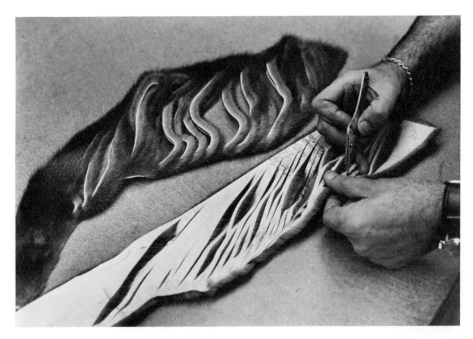

Figure 15.7

Letting out. The one-eighth to one-fourth inch wide slivers of skin will be sewn end to end to form long strips of fur. These long strips will then be joined lengthwise to fashion a full-length garment without horizontal markings and obvious seams.
Courtesy of The American Fur Industry, Inc.

Skin-on-Skin Method

The skin-on-skin method is less costly than the letting-out method and consists of sewing one full skin adjacent to another in a uniform alignment. The seams are difficult to conceal except with curly or wavy haired furs. The straight seam is the least expensive and easiest to cut and sew. It is also the least durable. This seam is often used in making rabbit and squirrel fur coats.

Another seam used in the skin-on-skin construction is the wavy seam used in making better quality kidskins, spotted fur, and patterned fur garments. These seams are a little more expensive than the straight seam and are more difficult to cut and sew, but they secure the skins better.

The strongest seam is the zig-zag seam used in making flat-haired fur garments from animal skins like the marmot, muskrat, and squirrel. The tail section is cut into a "V" shape and the head section of the fur skin to be placed below it is cut into a "V." Then the skin sections are secured with zig-zag seams.

Skin-on-skin seams will have horizontal markings that make some wearers appear to be shorter in height.

Whole Skin Construction

Certain lambskins, and a few other pelts, are large enough to be used for making a fur garment without having to add another skin for length or width.

Semi-Let-Out Construction

Some skins that are broad and short, like chinchilla or squirrel, are lengthened and narrowed by cutting them two or three times in each half skin. This provides lines that are more attractive to the fur garment, and it is not a costly process.

Split-Skin Construction

This method of manufacturing short fur garments, such as jackets and stoles, cuts the cost greatly in working with mink skins. In the early 1950s some furriers introduced a method of cutting skins to look like let-out skins. Instead of leaving the center dark mark of the mink skin in the center of each strip that is narrowed by cutting and restitching, the skin is cut in half right through the dark stripe. The dark stripe at the bottom of the pelt is made to run horizontally across the back of the garment by turning the halves on end and placing them side by side.

Finishing Operations

After the skins are prepared by the cutter, they are made up into sections that are dampened, then stretched and nailed to fit a pattern (the exact shape required for the finished garment) on a wooden nailing board. The skins are then dried on the form. After the skins dry, they are sewn together.

The glazing process follows, whereby the fur is dampened and arranged in a certain way by mechanical methods. Gums and related substances are applied to hold the hairs in position; then the fur is dried. The setting substances often increase the luster of the fur.

After the glazing treatment, the lining is sewn in, and buttons, loops, and snaps are attached.

A piece of fabric may be stitched or glued to the skin of some thin-skinned furs to reinforce them. Kolinsky, rabbit, and broadtail lamb have thin skins that may be need to be strengthened. This reinforcement process is called *staying*.

Plates

Waste fur or leftovers after cutting, such as the flanks, bellies, gills, and paws, are used in making inexpensive garments. These parts are sewn together in an oblong shape known as a *plate*. Most furriers prefer to sell waste fur and have a specialist stitch the pieces into the forms for manufacturers of inexpensive garments. Grecian furriers specialize in assembling these odds and ends into plates.

Labels must be attached to fur garments that indicate to the buyer the source of waste fur, such as muskrat flank and Persian paw.

Resetting

Resetting shortens the length of the fur skin but makes it wider. The skin is cut lengthwise in half along the dark center stripe and each half is then cut into vertical strips about one-fourth inch in width. These parts are rearranged and sewn together to produce two dark strips on the single skin. This is done in mink to create herringbone and diagonal effects and increase the number of dark stripes in the fur. This process is expensive.

Leathering

Thick, full-haired pelts may be cut in strips and then resewn with leather inserted between the strips to thin out the natural woolly appearance, to prevent matting, and to make the fur fluffy and beautiful (see Figure 15.8). Certain species of European white fox, as well as raccoon and skunk, are leathered. For example, fox, raccoon, and skunk are such bulky furs that strips of leather or ribbon may be sewn at intervals between strips of fur. This process may be detected by blowing or pushing the hair to the side and examining the skin.

Pointing

Sometimes red fox peltries are processed to simulate the aristocratic and expensive silver fox. The peltries are dyed black and "pointed" by cutting white badger hairs to the right length, dipping one end in glue, blowing the fox fur to the side, and attaching the badger hairs as near the leather as possible. Pointing is even done to an inferior natural silver fox peltry to make it look like a better quality fur. If this is done, it is called "pointed silver fox" and is described as such. When cleaned, some of the inserted hairs may shed or come out, but on the whole they remain secure. Pointing may be detected by the examination of badger hairs glued in groups of two or three to the natural foxhairs and to the leather. Also,

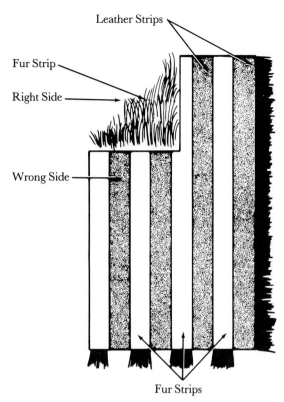

Leather Strips

Fur Strip

Right Side

Wrong Side

Fur Strips

Figure 15.8
Leathering. This technique is often used to lighten a heavy or bulky fur or simply to add style to a fur garment.

badger hairs are all white rather than alternatively black, white, black from bottom to tip as are the natural silvery hairs of silver fox.

Damaging Out

A small piece of poor quality fur may be cut out and replaced by a better quality piece of fur. This process may be seen on the skin side where the seams and stitches show (see Figure 15.9).

Scarves

A fur scarf means a scarf made of one or more full skins. A full skin, original peltry with paws, tail, and head still attached, makes up a *scarf*. The *boa*, a rounded, plain fur neckpiece, became fashionable in the 1960s and replaced the scarf. Boas are worn with coats, dresses, and suits.

Some furs that are used in making boas or scarves are mink, fox, sable, stone marten, and squirrel. Certain manufacturing companies specialize in mounting or attaching the heads on pelts. Sometimes boas or scarves are made from pieced skins or mixed combinations of animal fur skins and tail, such as

Figure 15.9

Damaging Out. A long pointed oval cut is used to remove the damage from the skin; it is then stitched together. The natural elasticity of the skin will accommodate for the lost area. Only lamb skins may be patched because of the difficulty of matching other furs.

Wrong Side of Skin

dark brown-dyed squirrel with a mink tail. Materials used must be specified on the label. Generally, pieced skin boas or scarves are less expensive and less durable than those made of full skins.

FUR LABELS AND SKINS

The Fur Products Labeling Act, which became effective on August 9, 1952, and was amended on May 19, 1961, and January 10, 1969, was designed to protect the American consumer. This act prohibited any fur advertising that was misleading or contained false claims, including those related to comparative prices. These regulations, and also regulations in force in other countries, further require that the true fur name appear in advertising as well as on labels attached to the garment. Prior to this act, there were over 200 trade names in common use, most of them misleading and confusing to the consumer. It was common practice in the fur trade to use descriptive trade names to describe a fur treated and dyed to resemble or imitate some other fur. Rabbit fur was rarely called rabbit. It was described as lapin, chinchillette, northern seal, coney, or ermeline. "Hudson seal" was a trade name used to describe muskrat fur treated and dyed to resemble Alaska seal. Now those practices have been eliminated. Manufacturers must describe accurately on the labels the name of the fur, as well as its dye or treatment; for example, "dyed muskrat," "dyed rabbit," "black-dyed muskrat," or "tip-dyed sable." No other animal's name may be used. The treatments also include those whereby the fur has been shaded, blended, tipped, or pointed.

The country or geographic origin of the fur must be described accurately on the label; for example, "American opossum." If waste fur or used fur is used, it must be noted on the label.

CARE OF FURS

The life of good quality furs depends upon the care given to them and the service demanded of them. More care is required of the less durable furs. Proper care will lengthen the life of the most perishable furs. Friction, heat, moths, and strong sunlight are very injurious to furs. Improper care is the major problem experienced with most furs rather than quality or workmanship. Proper care of furs will extend their life as luxurious garments.

Knowledge of the following rules is essential in order to get better and longer service from fur garments.

1. Read the hang tags attached to every fur garment. They outline the care requirements.

2. Keep furs clean. Dirt, dust, and grime invite moths, which destroy the fur and pelt. Select a reputable, responsible furrier or dry cleaner specializing in furs to clean and glaze the furs or fur-trimmed garments once a year. Never dry clean furs because it removes the oils from the skin, causing it to crack and dry.

3. Avoid friction wear. Normal wear will take place where jewelry rubs against fur. Carrying bags or packages under the arms will cause premature wear. Wearing the fur high and close to the neck will cause the movements of the head to wear the fur. The front and bottom edges, at the wrists, and under the sleeves will show wear from friction. Friction wear also occurs at the elbows, shoulders, and lower part of the fur coat from riding in an automobile.

4. Certain parts of the lining of any fur coat will show signs of wear from constant rubbing. Prolong the wear of the lining by handling very carefully.

5. Care should be taken to avoid exposing dyed or undyed furs to strong sunlight in order to prevent discoloring or singeing.

6. Attend to wet furs. If the leather has been soaked with water, send the garment immediately to the furrier or dry cleaner specializing in cleaning furs. The wet fur should be combed lightly with the flow of the fur and then brushed in the same direction. Next dry the fur slowly in well-circulated, cool air. Then beat and shake it lightly.

7. Shaking is good for fur, if it is carefully done so that it does not break the leather or split the seams. Wide-end coat hangers should be used to hang fur coats so the skin is not pierced from the coat's weight.

8. To protect against moths, fur garments should be properly cleaned and then stored in a cool closet to increase their life. A fur should not be crushed in a small area or covered with plastic. Cold storage vaults are available for a moderate charge. Moths are such an ever-present danger that they may deposit their eggs in the fur within a few weeks after the fur is put away in a closet.

9. Fur garments that are torn, that have opened seams, that are noticeably worn or otherwise damaged, should be repaired immediately so that the repair cost may be minimized and the maximum service obtained from the garments.

10. A fur garment may be restyled to keep up with fashion changes if the cost of the work does not exceed one-fourth the original cost of the garment.

SELLING POINTS

Salespersons who sell furs should become familiar with the following selling points.

1. Find out the purpose for which the fur is desired, then select two, and not more than three, appropriate garments so that the customer gets a choice. For example, ask if the garment is to be worn as dresswear or sportswear.

2. Consider the height and weight of the customer when showing a fur garment. Show the short, stout consumer a flat-haired lustrous fur coat rather than a short, bulky fur jacket. A tall, thin person may wear a bulky jacket or a full-length fur coat.

3. Point out the luxurious color, beauty, and pattern of the fur.

4. Stroke against the course of the fur, when the pile is deep and rich, to show the luxury of the fur fiber.

5. Direct the customer's attention to how the richness of the fur shows off her face and matches her skin tone.

6. Assist the person in trying on the garment. Point out its suitability for certain occasions, how becoming it is, its fashionable style, and how serviceable it will be.

7. While the customer is walking and looking at the garment in the mirror, call attention to the luster and sheen of the fur.

8. Show how well the garment fits across the shoulders and in the sleeves.

9. Explain how warm and comfortable the garment is to wear. Point out that a serviceable fur is inexpensive when one considers the length of wear and the comfort. Consider the fun of wearing it.

10. Turn the fur garment inside out and show the facings and the linings.

11. Point out that good quality fur has been used at the points of wear such as the cuffs, the outer sections of the sleeves, the back of the garment, and the back of the neck.

12. Explain that fur garments should be purchased from reputable firms that buy only from manufacturers who make standard sizes. This may save expensive alterations later.

KEY TERMS

1. Boa	8. Nutria
2. Dressing	9. Peltry
3. Dyeing	10. Prime fur
4. Fur	11. Resetting
5. Guard	12. Stole
6. Leathering	13. Tip dyeing
7. Mutation	14. Waste fur

STUDY QUESTIONS

1. What role did furs play in the history of the United States?
2. Why are fur garments made from altered whole skins instead of from the whole skins?
3. Explain the effect that environment has on furs.
4. What would cause the prices of furs to fluctuate?
5. Tell how fur farming has developed to the extent it has with specific fur-bearing animals.
6. Explain the various methods used to change and improve the coloring of furs.
7. Describe the process used in constructing or manufacturing fur garments.
8. How does the Fur Products Labeling Act help the customer? Explain three parts of the Act.
9. Name three fur-bearing animals from each of the five families and miscellaneous group given in the chapter. Then give as many identifying facts and characteristics as you can about each fur.
10. List at least five considerations in caring for a fur garment.

STUDY ACTIVITIES

1. Obtain from catalogs, magazines, and newspapers ten advertisements of women dressed in fur coats. Analyze each advertisement in regard to the name of the fur, color of the fur, source of animal (wild, fur farm, and country), construction terms mentioned, and comparison of prices.
2. Visit a fur department and look at the labels on ten garments. Copy the name of each fur. How many are dyed? What colors are indicated?
3. Obtain a map of North America and indicate the areas where fur-bearing animals are found. Develop a key for the map.

CHAPTER 16

Jewelry

OBJECTIVES

After completing this chapter, you should be able to:

1. Describe the role that jewelry has played historically and still plays in our lives.

2. Explain how different metals are used in making fine jewelry and fashion jewelry.

3. List the precious gemstones and tell how quality is determined.

4. Compare and contrast the semiprecious stones and materials used in making fashion jewelry.

5. Describe how costume, or fashion, jewelry is decorated and manufactured.

6. Explain how to care for fine jewelry and fashion jewelry.

The salesperson who sells jewelry should know the fundamentals about gemstones and precious metals as well as other jewelry merchandise in stock. He or she should also know the fashion trends.

The study of jewelry concerns expensive *fine jewelry* and inexpensive *costume,* or *fashion, jewelry.* Precious metals and precious gemstones are used in making fine jewelry. Base metals, used in making fashion jewelry, are plated with precious metals or may be used with other materials, such as ceramic, plastic, or wood. Fashion jewelry may be set with imitation or semiprecious stones.

TYPES OF JEWELRY

Jewelry consists of necklaces, bracelets, earrings, brooches, rings, and other ornamental pieces made of materials that may or may not be precious metals. Jewelry is often set with genuine or imitation stones, and is worn for personal adornment. Costume jewelry comes in a wide range of qualities and styles and varies in price.

Necklaces

Many types of necklaces are popular. Their nomenclature and description vary as fashion and manufacturers vary. Several basic types of necklaces are as follows (see Figure 16.1):

1. Collar—a flat design fitting close to the base of the neck. It also designates a sixteen- to eighteen-inch length.
2. Choker—a short necklace with graduated or uniform beads that fits the neck closely.
3. Lavaliere—a chain from which an ornament or pendant hangs.
4. Locket—a chain or cord from which a small case carrying small pictures or mementos hangs like a pendant.
5. Matinee length—a single-row necklace about twenty-four inches long, mostly used for pearl necklaces (Figure 16.2).
6. Opera length—a single-row necklace about thirty inches long; mostly used for pearls.

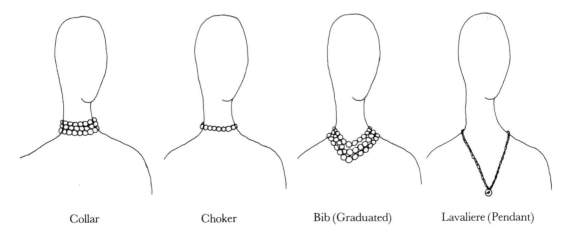

Collar   Choker   Bib (Graduated)   Lavaliere (Pendant)

Figure 16.1
Necklace variations.

Figure 16.2
Model is wearing double strand of matinee length pearls and pearl button earrings.
Courtesy of Jewelers of America.

7. Graduated—a necklace of varied length, usually with pearls or gold beads in graduated sizes, the largest being in front.
8. Princess length—a single-strand necklace of beads, pearls, or chain about eighteen inches in length.

Bracelets

The salesperson should know the various types of bracelets because customers often ask for them by name. Basic types of bracelets are as follows (see Figure 16.3):

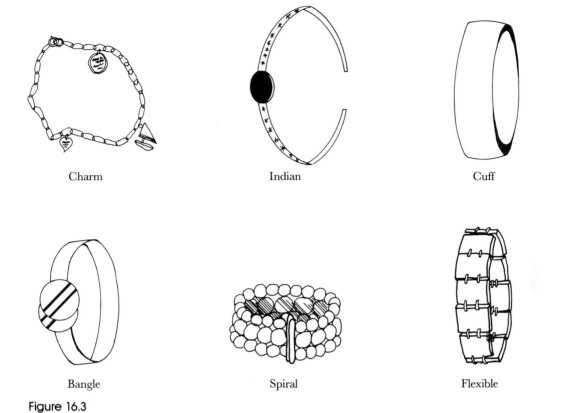

Charm   Indian   Cuff

Bangle   Spiral   Flexible

Figure 16.3
Bracelet variations.

1. Bangle—a rigid round circle with no opening that slips over the hand.
2. Charm—a link bracelet with many charms or motifs hanging from it. Each charm may represent something different.
3. Cuff—a wide-hinged circle that opens on a hinge to make it easier to slip on and off the hand.
4. Flexible—a number of metal or stone pieces linked and fastened together in a straight line. These bracelets are held together by rubber-like strings.
5. Indian—a rigid oval bracelet that circles three-fourths of the wrist, leaving the bottom side open.
6. Spiral—a bracelet made of two or more lengths of beads or metal circled on a spring.

Earrings

The most important jewelry for enhancing a woman's face is earrings. They can be elegant, exciting, and flattering. Earrings come in many styles and shapes (Figure 16.4), including the following basic types:

1. Button—a single, domed or flat, round earring made from various materials.

2. Clip back—a hinged adjustment is used for fit.

3. Disc—Round but larger than a button earring.

4. Drop—Earrings suspended from a button or cluster, also called chandelier or pendant. Pairs may look alike or come in left or right earrings.

5. Friction back—a post that pierces the ear hole and contains a notch which helps hold the back on.

6. Hoop—a round metal ring that clips to the ear or is suspended from small buttons. Also called wedding band earrings. Hoops can be found in pierced and clipped earrings.

7. Pierced ear screw—a straight post that goes through the ear hole. It is similar to the screwback.

8. Pierced ear wire—a metal thread worn in pierced ears.

9. Screwback—a post screw which adjusts the earring to the individual ear size.

10. Stud—a small ball or a single stone on a post, which is worn in a pierced ear.

Button

Clip-Back

Screw-Back

Hoop

Drop

Figure 16.4
Earring variations.

Brooches, Clips, and Pins

Brooches are made in a great variety of patterns and sizes. They may come in metal alone or set with gems. A pin is usually attached to the back for pinning to a garment.

Clips are similar to brooches, but they have a prong held shut by a spring for fastening. They are often worn on the edge of a garment.

A *chatelaine* may be a single large brooch with chains that loop below to two brooches connected by one or more chains.

A *stickpin* is a straight pin with an ornament on top. The point of the stickpin is protected by a guard.

Rings

Rings have probably been the most universally worn items of jewelry. They may be used as ornaments or as symbols. They are worn on the fingers. The styles and designs are almost limitless. Men's and women's rings may be made of metal alone or set with precious, semiprecious, or imitation stones. The parts of the rings are the shank, the head, and the shoulder. The *shank* is the plain part of the ring at the back. The *shoulder* is the section of the ring on either side of the central ornament. The part displayed on the finger is called the *head, front, shield,* or *table.* Some types of rings include *engagement* and *wedding, birthstone, religious, fraternal, signet* (utilizes initials or crest), *personal signature, cocktail, cluster* (stones set in groups), *dinner* (long, narrow rings worn on a little finger), and *solitaire* (ring with a single stone).

Watches

There is a vast selection of watches on the market. Much variation in prices, styles, mechanism types, and quality can be observed.

Mechanical Watches

Mechanical watch movements need daily winding by hand. The coiled mainspring is tightened; then as the mainspring unwinds, it powers the wheels in the movement. The self-wound models use a weight that moves back and forth as the wearer's arm moves. The movement of the weight winds the mainspring. Small wafer-shaped batteries are used to power the wheels in electric watches.

Inexpensive mechanical watches with nonjewel movements are called *pin-lever watches.* The movements are often mass produced using inexpensive metal that revolves against metal. These watches soon become inaccurate, have a short life span, and are not worth fixing once they break.

Most precision-made watches are called *jeweled-lever watches.* The moving parts revolve in jeweled bearings to resist friction and wear, to reduce noise, and to be more accurate. The less expensive jeweled watches should have at least a seven-jewel movement. The better movements have fourteen, fifteen, seventeen, twenty-one, or twenty-three jewels. Synthetic jewels have replaced most of the natural rubies or sapphires once used for bearings. Certain watches have calendars, timers, and other devices. Some watches are shock- and water-resistant.

Electronic Tuning Fork Watches

These watches were developed during the 1950s. They do not use a mainspring and balance wheels; instead, a tuning fork is the regulating mechanism. They are powered by a tiny battery, using electromagnets that transmit power to the gears that drive the watch. These watches have fewer parts to wear out than the jewel-level watches and keep better time.

Electronic Quartz Watches

Electronic quartz watches, developed in the 1970s, have become extremely popular because they never need winding. They also keep more precise time than mechanical watches; they offer many optional features (alarms, calculators, and calendars); and they give years of trouble-free service for reasonable prices. Each watch is powered by tiny batteries that cause a quartz crystal to vibrate and energize electromagnets that provide the power for the gears to move.

Some quartz watches are digitals (with the time displayed in numerals); others are analogs (with hands that point to numbers). The early digital models that flashed the numbers at the push of a button are in the process of being phased out. Quartz digital watches now have numbers that show continually. The numerals stand out and can be read easily.

The case may be the most expensive part of the watch. Inexpensive cases may be made from anodized aluminim, plastic, plated brass, or stainless steel. More expensive cases may be made from karat gold or platinum, and may have settings of precious stones. The important part about a case is that it should be strong enough to protect the sensitive movements inside it.

Care of Watches

Because quartz watches are affected by detergents and moisture, they should have water-resistant cases. They need servicing every five years. The batteries last about one year.

A man's mechanical watch should be serviced once every three years; a woman's watch every two years.

Many of the low-priced, off-brand foreign imported watches run only a short time and cannot be repaired. You should buy a watch from a reputable business.

Jewelry for Men

Men's jewelry is sensitive to fashion and new ideas. Designers use every opportunity to create jewelry from lustrous metals in most types of finishes and set with colorful stones and other metals. Useful and decorative staple jewelry items may include cuff links, belt buckles, tie accessories, key rings, money clips, watch bands, and identification bracelets. Purely ornamental items may include bracelets, earrings, lapel pins, necklaces, and rings. The trend in men's jewelry continues to be susceptible to the dictates of fashion.

HOW JEWELRY IS MADE

Metal jewelry may be cut from a thin sheet of selected metal and then shaped by pounding it by hand. It may also be shaped by exerting pressure from a die that may also imprint any selected pattern onto the surface. Some jewelry may be made by melting the metal, then pouring it onto a textured or smooth casting mold. All the parts are then assembled and soldered together.

Costume jewelry begins on the designer's drawing board. The model-maker then makes a model, analyzes it, and sends it to the production model department. A master rubber mold is made from the model. Several pieces of jewelry are rushed through the factory on a trial manufacturing basis. These finished pieces are sent to the design office for review. When a finished sample piece receives approval, the factory is notified.

A mold is made of the finished model. The empty mold is filled with liquid white alloy metal which is forced into every crevice by centrifugal force. The castings are then removed, the edges filed, and the pieces cleaned and polished.

The final finish is applied by electroplating methods, copper plating, and nickel plating. This final coat may be of gold, silver, or rhodium for a bright finish. Some pieces are then lacquered for protection. The stones are then set, using prongs or cement. The final process involves attaching the findings (pins, earring backs, and clasps). Making fashion jewelry requires many steps of hand work.

VARIETIES OF METALS

Metals are elements that are usually found in ores. Metal-bearing rocks contain one or more minerals called *ores*. *Minerals* are crystalline elements of two or more *elements*. An element is a basic substance that alone or together with other elements makes up all other substances. Each metal has different characteristics or properties for special uses such as malleability, ductility, conductivity, and sheen or luster. Metal is removed from ore by chemical means or by heating the ore in a smelter. Metals are then formed into shapes called pigs, ingots, or bars which are ready to be used in making jewelry.

Precious Metals

Gold, silver, platinum, and its kindred metals palladium, rhodium, iridium, ruthenium, and osmium are the *precious metals* which craftsmen use in making jewelry. These metals have unusual beauty, unique qualities, rarity, and working properties that make them expensive and precious.

Gold

Jewelry has been made of gold and gold alloys for thousands of years. In ancient times some jewelry that was 90 percent pure gold was formed by hand. Gold, in its original state, is so soft that it must be alloyed, or combined, with other metals such as copper, silver, or zinc to increase its strength and durability. Today gold is manufactured into *karat* gold jewelry using gold alloys which are stronger than pure gold. The term *karat* refers to the amount of pure gold an item contains.

In the karat system of labeling, solid gold is marked 24k or 24 parts (100 percent) gold, but it is not used commercially. The finest quality of gold used in jewelry is 22 karat. This means 22/24 of the item is gold and 2/24 is composed of some other metal to give the necessary hardness. The proportionate quality of gold contained in the metal alloy is indicated by the number preceding the "k." The content of pure gold by weight is 18/24, 14/24, 10/24 or 75 percent, 58.5 percent, and 42 percent respectively. *Plumb gold* means an accurate measurement or full measure of gold. The higher the gold content in a piece of jewelry, the yellower the color, and the higher the price. In the United States, any metal containing less than 10 parts gold may not be stamped with the karat mark for consumer protection.

Gold is a yellow color with a bright luster which does not change color or tarnish. Gold is not affected by acids. Therefore, it won't turn the wearer's skin green unless it has been combined with an excess of copper.

When mixed proportionally with other metals, gold takes on variations of color. Copper gives gold a pinkish tint; silver makes it greenish; copper and silver combined produce a different shade of yellow; and nickel used by itself or with copper or zinc produces white gold. These alloys, or karat golds, wear well and hold their shape. They are less expensive than pure gold, but they are still expensive to produce. Therefore, manufacturers have learned rolled gold plating methods. This causes limitations in styling.

Finishes can also change the appearance of gold. Various finishes include brushed, faceted, textured, satin grain, dull matte, or Florentine with tiny lines cross-hatched on the surface. A filigree, or fine gold wire, worked into intricate patterns may also be used to change the appearance of a gold piece.

Gold Plating Methods. Gold may be bonded to a base metal with a sheet of alloyed metal as in the case of gold filled or rolled gold plated jewelry. Gold may also be bonded to a base metal by coating the base metal with gold through electroplating to produce gold electroplated jewelry.

Gold filled indicates that a thin layer of gold has been fused to a base metal such as copper, brass, or nickel silver. The layer of karat gold must weigh at least 1/20 of the weight of the entire metal used in order for an article to be called gold filled. Such jewelry is stamped "gold filled" and is preceded by the karat designation, such as 1/20 14k gold filled. The finest quality of gold-filled jewelry is 1/10. There may be problems engraving and wearing certain gold-filled articles if the wearer is allergic to the base metals.

Rolled gold plating is the process by which a specific thickness of gold is bonded to the base metal by being rolled together into a desired thickness and then shaped. This is similar to the process of creating gold-filled jewelry, the difference being a thinner gold layer of only 1/30 to 1/40 the total weight of the base metal. Therefore, rolled gold plated jewelry is less expensive and less durable. Articles made of low karat alloys tend to tarnish where the raw edges of base metal are exposed. During pressing or forming operations, the base metal may shift, causing differences in the thickness of the gold layer. In most rolled gold pieces, the thicker the metal, the thicker the gold plate. Uniformity of color is made possible by using an electroplating process.

Gold electroplating is the process by which gold is more evenly distributed over the entire surface of the base metal regardless of its shape or pattern. An electroplating process is used to apply a thinner layer of gold to the articles than in filled or rolled gold methods. In this process a base metal is dipped or bathed in an electrolytic solution containing gold. The gold contained in the solution is deposited in a very thin layer on top of the base metal by electrolysis. The base metal used is generally one that can readily be shaped, punched, or polished.

The quality of gold plate depends on the thickness of the coating. Thin electroplate is inexpensive but is less durable; it is used only in cheaper jewelry pieces due to its limitations. The thin electroplating process of less than .0015 inch is referred to as *gold wash* or *gold flash* in most cases although neither of these terms is stamped on the jewelry. Watchcases are commonly less than .0015 inch thick; therefore, no quality mark indicting the presence of karat gold can be applied.

Heavy gold electroplating has more advantages such as greater wearability, less chance of tarnish, and more freedom of design and finishing; and it is more economical than the thinner electroplating. Gold that is 18k to 24k may be used under heavy gold electrolytic processes. The greatest advantage of the heavy electroplating process is that an even coating of heavy karat gold is applied to the total surface of the article regardless of its shape, pattern, or ornamentation to ensure durability (see Figure 16.5).

Silver

Silver will be discussed in this chapter only as its use applies to jewelry making. Silver is used less than any of the other metals in jewelry because of its tendency to tarnish; however, cleaning and polishing restores its original beauty. Jewelry made of silver was used as long ago as 4500 B.C. It has been found in Chaldean tombs. Called the "Queen of Metals," silver jewelry was worn by women around the neck, on headdresses, as earrings, bracelets, charms, pins, clasps, and rings.

In addition to its beauty and usefulness, silver has considerable religious significance. Up until the Middle Ages only the very rich and royalty could afford jewelry. The Spanish found the Aztecs in Mexico and the Incas in Peru using silver for jewelry.

Silver is the most lustrous and whitest of metals. It is ductile, has great reflectivity, and is an excellent conductor of heat. It is one of the easiest metals with which to work because of its versatility. Silver can be burned, cast, chased, damascened, electroplated, embroidered, engraved, filigreed, hammered, inlayed, pierced, stamped, and wired. Silver can be hammered into sheets so thin it would take 100,000 of them to make a pile an inch high. It can also be drawn into wires finer than human hair.

Pure silver melts at temperatures above 1700 degrees Fahrenheit. A cubic inch of silver weighs 0.379 pounds or less than 6 ounces. The world's largest single producer of silver is Mexico, outranking other leading producers such as the United States, Canada, and Peru.

In jewelry making, silver is alloyed with copper for durability. The term *sterling,* which dates back to 1300, assures the subjects of England's King Edward I that objects contained a degree of pure silver. Today's sterling silver is 92.5 percent pure and is weighed in troy ounces. The remaining 7.5 percent is usually

Figure 16.5
Gold electroplated jewelry.
Courtesy of Engelhard Corporation.

copper. Any article meeting this standard must be marked sterling. The official stamp placed on a piece of silver to indicate its purity is known as a *hallmark*. Like gold, silver can be chemically tested, rather easily, to make sure that it is not base metal or, as is common in folk or ethnic jewelry, of very low grade. *Silverplate* refers to a base metal electroplated with silver. Although silverplate is not as durable as sterling, it may last a lifetime.

The term *coin silver* sometimes appears on the backs of silver pieces of jewelry, and is usually a sign of age. Most of the old Navajo Indian jewelry was actually made from silver coins up until 1965 when the mints in this country stopped minting silver coins. The old coin silver is about 90 percent silver and 10 percent copper. Indian-made jewelry with dull, hammered finish is popular, and it is not as expensive as other types of hand-wrought jewelry. Hand-wrought jewelry in silver is in demand, although rare and expensive. Most of the silver jewelry that looks handmade is expert machine-made imitations of handwork. Just as in gold, *filigree* refers to fine silver wire worked into intricate patterns.

Vermeil is a gold finish electroplated on silver plate or sterling. A 14k finish is generally used.

The Platinum Metals

The platinum family of precious and rare metals is composed of platinum, palladium, rhodium, ruthenium, iridium, and osmium. Each year the free world markets receive 10,000 tons of silver, 1,000 tons of gold, and 70 to 80 tons each of platinum and palladium. All of the platinum ever mined would fill a cube 14 feet square.

Platinum and its allied metals come from the Sudbury Basin of eastern Canada, Colombia, the Bushveld Compex of South Africa, and the Soviet Arctic. The United States buys nearly half of the world's supply of the metal.

Platinum and its five kindred metals usually are found together in nature. Gold-seeking conquistadores called it *platina* (little silver), picked it out of their pans and tossed it back into rivers, believing it would ripen into gold. Pre-Columbian Indians forged jewelry from platinum alloys found mixed with gold in the rivers of the Choco region of Colombia. The Spanish reported their discovery to Europe in the mid-sixteenth century.

Two centuries passed before sizable samples of platinum were smuggled into Europe. Craftsmen found that platinum would blend with other metals but resisted being refined into its pure state. Eventually they learned that by adding arsenic, platinum would melt at a lower temperature. This process rendered the metal malleable enough to be intricately worked. All six of the platinum metals have some common characteristics—a high melting point and resistance to most acids. Adding a small amount of iridium to platinum creates an alloy with a higher melting point, increased ability to combat corrosion, and increased electrical resistance. Combining platinum with cobalt makes an alloy with unusually high magnetic qualities. Platinum serves as a catalyst that directs a chemical conversion to form a new product, perhaps a million times faster than the conversion would take place on its own. Rugged, yet malleable, platinum can be rolled into a sheet a thousandth of an inch thick. It may be used to coat the edges of razor blades a thickness of approximately 100 atoms. Platinum's melting point, 1769 degrees Celsius (3216 degrees Fahrenheit), exceeds that of iron by 230 degrees.

In the United States the consumption of platinum for jewelry accounts for only 2 percent of the total imported. The Japanese craftsmen use more than half of their imported platinum for making jewelry. They especially value its suppleness and strength for delicate looking jewelry.

The royal heads of Europe chose platinum jewelry. King Edward VII, son of Queen Victoria, had a platinum crown set with twenty-seven diamonds for his coronation.

Jewelers entrust their most valuable gems to platinum settings, because platinum is stronger than gold or silver. And it provides a setting that is safer for emeralds, diamonds, rubies, and sapphires in addition to showing them to their best advantage. Platinum has other attributes that make it nontarnishing, ductile, able to develop a satiny finish with age, and nonallergenic.

Palladium is a white, ductile metal that melts at 2829 degrees Fahrenheit. It is lighter than gold and all other platinum metals. Jewelry craftsmen use palladium to eliminate extra weight from brooches, earrings, and other jewelry. An alloy of palladium (95.5 percent) hardened with ruthenium (4.5 percent) is generally used to make fine jewelry. This alloy, called *jewelry palladium,* has the ductility necessary to make intricate parts, to make it easier to set gems, and to lessen the risk of chipping gems during the setting operation. Settings made of the alloy hold precious gems securely and complement diamonds by showing them to their best advantage in a white background. Palladium-filled or rolled palladium plated articles should be described and marked the same as gold-filled or rolled gold plate items. The word *palladium* or the abbreviation *pall.* is substituted for the word *gold* and the karat mark.

Rhodium is a shiny white element much harder than palladium and platinum. It melts at 3571 degrees Fahrenheit. Rhodium can be wrought, but it is used mostly as an electroplating or alloying metal. Extensive use is made of rhodium plating to obtain a brilliant finish on fine jewelry, costume or fashion jewelry, and novelty items where this type of finish is desired. A hard, nontarnishing finish can be obtained with a "flash" coating less than 0.00001 inch thick; however, thicker coats will provide greater wearability.

Ruthenium is a hard, white, metallic element that melts at approximately 4530 degrees Fahrenheit. Practically unworkable by itself, ruthenium is used to harden palladium or platinum. It is considered to be two times more effective than iridium.

Iridium is a very heavy white element with an extemely high melting point of 4449 degrees Fahrenheit. It is used mostly as an alloying material, generally to harden platinum. An iridium-platinum alloy containing 10 percent iridium is used to make fine jewelry. The jewelry item is marked inside with *10 percent Irid. Plat.*

Osmium is a white metal which is very hard, unworkable, and has the greatest density of all the elements. Due to these characteristics, osmium is rarely used by jewelers even though it is considered a precious metal.

Metal Alloys

Metals are seldom used in their pure form because they do not have the necessary characteristics to make different products. *Alloy* metal is made by melting two or more metals and mixing them together while they are in a liquid state. An alloy is obtained when the mixture returns to the solid state. This combination generally improves the characteristics and usefulness of the metals. The advantages of alloys include:

1. *Color.* Mixing certain metals may result in remarkable color changes. *Brass,* resembling gold, is made by combining copper with zinc. Russet-colored *bronze* is usually made from copper and tin. *Imitation gold* is made by combining copper with aluminum and nickel. *Britannia metal,* also called *white metal,* is made from copper, tin, and antimony (lead was used in ancient times). *German silver* looks like silver but is made from copper, nickel, and zinc. *Pewter* is comprised of mostly tin mixed with copper and small quantities of the whitish metals antimony and bismuth. Sometimes lead is used as a constituent of pewter. *Solder* is made from metals like tin and lead having low melting temperatures

that are mixed with metals having high melting temperatures such as gold and silver. *Steel* is made from a mixture of varying quantities of carbon and refined iron. *Stainless steel* includes certain mixtures of chromium and nickel added to steel.

2. *Characteristics.* In general, an alloy is harder than the metals that went into it. Gold, silver, and zinc, when mixed with copper, make a metal harder than any of them used separately. Breaking point, elasticity, melting point, strength, and workability may be changed by alloying different metals.

3. *Value.* Inexpensive metals may increase in value by adding small quantities of expensive metals. On the other hand, expensive metal may be decreased in value by adding less expensive metals.

PLATING METALS

The plating of jewelry is a process of applying a thin layer of one metal upon the other. The desirable characteristics of the base metal are maintained while putting a better looking or more protective metal on the surface. Plating may take place in three ways: (1) by using heat and pressure to bond two or more metals together, (2) by dipping one metal into a molten metal, and (3) by electroplating.

Bonding was first used to apply silver to a copper surface by using heat and pressure. This process is now used to make jewelry articles that are rolled gold plated and gold filled.

Dipping metal in molten metal is used to plate some products. Iron and steel articles are dipped into molten zinc to galvanize them to protect them from rust. Brass is used in making less expensive costume jewelry items. When brass is dipped in sulfuric acid and finished with clear lacquer, it is called *bright-dipped brass.* Its lasting quality is much less than that of plated jewelry.

Electroplating is used to plate chromium, gold, nickel, rhodium, and silver onto base metals. It is a commonly used and relatively inexpensive plating method. The item to be electroplated is called the *cathode* or negative terminal and the plating metal is called the *anode* or positive terminal. Both terminals are immersed in a salt solution of the plating metal. An electric current passing through the plating solution dissolves the plating metal and coats the item to be plated. The length of time the item is in the solution determines the amount of metal coated on the item. Very quick plating is usually called *wash* or *flash,* and this thinness of plating affects the wearing quality of the item. Aluminum can be *anodized* by reversing the electroplating process to place an oxide film on the surface, thus sealing in the chosen color and making the item wear-resistant.

Finishes

Jewelry may be finished in numerous ways. Chemicals may be used to darken the surface of the metal, usually gold or silver, in a technique called *antiquing.*

Using the hands or special equipment, metal may be *engraved* by scratching a design into it. Tapping designs into the surface of the metal object is called *chasing. Florentine finishes* are made by engraving a series of fine scratches into metal surfaces. When a machine is used to engrave geometric designs into the surface, the process is called *engine turning.* Acids may be used to eat away the metal in specific places to make a design on brass, copper, and silver. This method is known as *etching.* Colored enamel paint may be used as a surface finish on inexpensive jewelry, or it may be baked on permanently at an added expense.

BASE METALS USED IN JEWELRY

Base metals are nonprecious metals that are readily available. They are not as attractive or as expensive as the precious metals. Some of the base metals that are most used in making fashion jewelry include aluminum, chromium, copper, lead, nickel, tin, and zinc.

Aluminum is silver-colored, ductile, lightweight, and malleable. It loses its shape easily unless it is thick. It may be anodized to give it certain colors. Aluminum is used in making inexpensive novelty jewelry.

Chromium is used to plate brass, copper, and steel metals. It has a bluish white color and metallic sheen. Stainless steel is made from alloying chromium with steel.

Copper is a common reddish metallic metal that is ductile and malleable. The outside will change color rapidly by oxidation to a black-green coating. It is used in alloys such as brass, bronze, karat gold, and sterling silver.

Lead is a soft, malleable metal of low tensile strength. It is a heavy, dark gray metal. It is used in some *solders* (alloys used to hold together metal pieces) because it melts at a low temperature.

Nickel is a silver-white, hard, malleable, ductile metal capable of a high polish and resistant to corrosion. It is used chiefly in alloys. It gives a hardness to karat gold, nickel silver, and stainless steel. Sometimes nickel is used to add durability beneath a chromium plating or to add a silvery colored plating to certain metals.

Tin is white, soft, malleable metal that will not tarnish. It prevents rust from forming on steel. Bronze, white metal, pewter, and soft solder are made from tin.

Zinc is a bluish-white metal that is used in small amounts in alloys like brass, white gold, pewter, German silver, and nickel silver. Zinc is used as a plating on steel to help prevent rust.

SELECTION OF GEMSTONES

The purchasing of gemstones is a very tricky and complicated business. It takes experience to select the best gems. Gems are rated according to certain properties possessed by the gem. These properties can be either natural or synthetic. Ratings of gems are based on the four C's process according to clarity, color, cut, and carat weight. The expense of the gemstone depends on a combination of these properties. For example, a smaller carat weight gemstone may be more expensive than a larger carat weight gemstone simply because it contains fewer flaws than the larger.

Clarity

Clarity is the term used to denote the perfection in the structure of the gemstone. The clarity is dependent upon the presence or absence of flaws called *inclusions*. Inclusions are imperfections found in the stone, such as bubbles, specks, carbon spots, and blemishes. Certain inclusions are desired in gemstones, such as the star in a star sapphire. But as a general rule, the number of inclusions has a direct influence on the price of the gemstone. The Federal Trade Commission has set a regulation which indicates the requirement necessary in order to label a gemstone *flawless*. The gemstone must appear flawless when viewed under a ten-power magnification. More flaws will be present in colored gemstones; therefore, clarity is less important in these gemstones.

Color

Color is probably the most significant quality possessed by a gemstone. No one color is superior to another as long as the color present in the gem is sufficiently intense. Gems that have been color treated to attain a desired color are less expensive than those that are naturally colored. Certain gems, such as the diamond, are desired for their absence of color.

Gemstones are varied in color, with gems of the same family also varying in degrees of color. The color of gemstones can occur naturally through processes such as the presence of certain foreign chemical components in the gemstone, trapped moisture in tiny cracks in the gemstone, the absence of certain chemical components in a gemstone, or the color reflected from surrounding gemstones.

Cut

The shape into which a rough stone is cut is also extremely important. The *cut* can increase the beauty of an inferior stone, reduce or eliminate imperfections, and emphasize the color. Opaque or translucent stones, such as turquoise or opal, are usually cut into the *cabochon* dome shape, with a curved surface and flat bottom. Transparent stones are *faceted* (see Figure 16.6). The lapidary, or precious stone cutter, creates a series of tiny flat surfaces cut at different angles to catch and reflect light. The shape called *round brilliant* (see Figure 16.7) contains fifty-eight facets and is ideal for displaying the icy beauty of diamonds. It is used to flatter many other gems. Other shapes include emerald, a cut in which the contour of the gem is square or rectangular (Figure 16.8); heart; marquise (Figure 16.9), oval, and pear (Figure 16.10). Baguettes, long and rectangular in shape, are used alongside a larger stone in a setting.

Figure 16.6

The precious stone cutter expertly cuts transparent stones to create facets which will show off the natural beauty of the stone while eliminating imperfections. The basic parts of a faceted stone are the table, crown, girdle, pavilion, and cutlet.

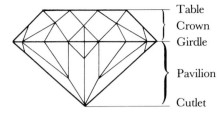

Table
Crown
Girdle

Pavilion

Cutlet

Figure 16.7
Round brilliant cut diamond.
Courtesy of Diamond Information Center.

Figure 16.8
Emerald cut diamond.
Courtesy of Diamond Information Center.

Figure 16.9
Marquise cut diamond.
Courtesy of Diamond Information Center.

Figure 16.10
Pear cut diamond.
Courtesy of Diamond Information Center.

Carat Weight

The weight and size of the finished diamond are important factors in the gem's value. The *carat* is the standard unit of weight for gemstones. The term stems from the small carob seeds that were originally placed on a scale to weigh the gems.

The carat is 3.165 grains troy weight if using the jeweler's scale and 4 grains avoirdupois weight using the scale for many consumer goods. A scale that shows troy weight would read:

$$1 \text{ pound } = 12 \text{ ounces}$$
$$1 \text{ ounce } = 20 \text{ pennyweight}$$
$$1 \text{ pennyweight } = 24 \text{ grains}$$
$$3.165 \text{ grains } = 1 \text{ carat}$$
$$1 \text{ carat } = 100 \text{ points}$$

One carat also equals 200 milligrams, or one-fifth of a gram. Carats are subdivided into 100 points—a half-carat stone weighs 50 points. Carat weight is unimportant if a stone rates poorly in the other three C's. Jewelry experts suggest investing in the best, rather than the biggest, gem one can afford.

The value of a gem of good quality increases with the size of the gem. A one-carat stone is worth many times that of a half-carat stone of the same quality, color, and cut. Carat weight is a measurement of *weight,* not *size.* Stones weighing two carats or more are becoming increasingly rare.

Another dimension in the measurement of diamonds is the size. For example, a one-carat brilliant would appear a different size when compared with a one-carat marquise or one-carat emerald cut. Jewelers use gauges to measure size.

Three gauges are commonly used by jewelers, the least complex being the millimeter gauge. This gauge simply measures the length and diameter of the stone in millimeters.

The second gauge is the Moe gauge, which is about three times more precise than the millimeter gauge. The Moe gauge measures the stone at the girdle and then its depth, translating these measurements into weight estimates. For example, one millimeter is equivalent to $3\frac{1}{3}$ units of the Moe gauge. The Moe gauge is mainly used as a measurement for round stones that are mounted.

The Leveridge gauge is the most versatile because it allows for the weight estimation of mounted gems as well as for marquise and emerald cut gems. This gauge is three times more precise than the Moe gauge and ten times more accurate than the millimeter gauge, allowing for a more precise identification of stones by jewelers.

Settings

All fine jewelry is hand set. The purpose of the setting is to hold the stone securely in place. Precious-metal settings are carefully prepared to hold fine quality gemstones safely and securely. In most costume jewelry the inexpensive stones may be glued into a depression in the metal. Prongs (long projections) are used in some settings to press against the stone to hold it in place. *Tiffany settings* utilize high-prong settings for round stones. When right-angled corner prongs hold a stone they are known as *square* settings. Very small rolls of metal are raised up from the metal (gold or platinum alloys) and pressed against the stone to make the *bead settings* that hold small diamonds called *melees* or *chips. Flush settings,* used for inexpensive and medium expensive stones, encircle the stone with a band of metal. A *pavé setting* is a bed of gems set in the manner of cobblestones. A *bezel setting* is the top part of a ring that holds a stone in place or is used for ornamentation. An *illusion setting* extends the metal around the side of a small stone to increase the apparent size.

PRECIOUS GEMS

To qualify as a precious gem, the gem must exhibit a super degree of *beauty, color, hardness,* and *rarity.* Traditionally, four precious gems have met these standards of quality; they are diamonds, emeralds, sapphires, and rubies. All of them come from minerals in the earth. The other precious gemstone to be mentioned is developed under water within the bodies of mollusks, usually oysters. It is the pearl. Each pearl, like each mineral gemstone, is unique. They are judged by size, shape, color, luster, and purity.

Diamonds

The diamond is the best known and the most popular of the precious stones, especially in its colorless state. Diamond is the hardest substance known. Hardness tests show that a diamond is up to 150 times as hard as corundum, which ranks second to diamond on the Moh scale of hardness. History and tradition have proved that the diamond is the most enduring of all gems.

Chemically, the diamond is pure carbon, a common element found in coal, graphite, and soot. Diamond differs, however, in that it is crystalline carbon, formed deep in the earth millions of years ago through tremendous volcanic heat and pressure. When molten lava cooled, it formed the basic igneous rock that is the source of diamonds.

Diamonds were first found in India about 800 B.C. In 1726 they were discovered and later mined in Brazil. The discovery of diamonds in South Africa, in the 1800s, created the new mass market for diamonds compared to the "class" market that existed until that time. Today, diamonds are available to everyone at popular prices.

The value of diamonds is judged by their color, size, perfection, and the quality of cutting. A *perfect* diamond is one that shows no flaws (to a jeweler) when magnified ten times its size. Diamonds may be white (colorless) or they may come in black, yellow, blue, green, pink, or red-orange colors that are called *fancies.* Colored diamonds can cost four times more than a flawless white diamond (Figure 16.11).

Of all the diamonds found, only about 20 percent are of gem quality and can be used for jewelry (Figure 16.12). It is estimated that only one diamond out of a million is the size of one carat. The synthetic diamond look-alike, cubic zirconia, caused gem-testing equipment to be built especially to identify it. It is estimated that artificial diamonds are sold under at least seventy-five names, such as diamelle and cubic zirconia.

Figure 16.11
Natural uncut diamonds may come in black, yellow, blue, green, pink, red-orange, or most commonly, white.
Courtesy of Diamond Information Center.

Figure 16.12
The traditional diamond engagement ring is shown with matching wedding band.
Courtesy of Diamond Information Center.

Emeralds

The emerald belongs to the beryl family and is the only stone of that family that is considered a precious stone. Only medium-light to dark shades of green beryl are labeled as emeralds. It is chromium oxide that makes the emerald green.

Most emeralds contain an elaborate network of veinlike cracks that are haphazardly crossed throughout the stone. The cracks or "jardins" and cloudy portions of emeralds take a skilled lapidary to avoid. Although flawless emeralds do exist, there are few in today's market. A large flawless emerald is so rare that carat for carat it is probably more expensive than a fine diamond.

Emeralds are not heavily faceted because they fracture more easily than diamonds and are likely to split if they receive a sharp blow. Emeralds are usually engraved or carved with the step cutting being the most desired cutting method of emeralds. Step cutting results in an oblong- or square-shaped stone with facets diagonally across the corners. Emeralds cut in the cabochon (dome-shaped) cut perhaps achieve their greatest beauty. This cut is incorporated when there are a great number of inclusions to be worked on. Step cutting is incorporated for more flawless gems.

Emeralds display less brilliance than most gems and rely upon beauty and distribution of color as prime factors for their worth. Usually the better the color, the less flawless the stone. Ironically, it is the fine green color, transparency, soft brilliance, and velvety texture that creates the worth of the emerald regardless of flaws.

The emerald is the birthstone for the month of May. It has had many mystical and magical qualities attributed to it. The emerald was known as the gem of spring and earth's guardian of generation and ripening. It was said to give a stronger memory, eloquence, and insight to its wearers. The emerald also could measure a lover's favor and warrant honesty. Emeralds have been a favorite gemstone of royalty. Emeralds are found in Colombia, Siberia, Brazil, and South Africa.

Sapphires

Sapphires are formed from the same materials as are rubies. The stones differ only in color. Like diamonds, sapphires come in a wide range of colors such as yellow, orange, green, violet, pink, and white. Each color can be attributed to a different trace mineral found in the chemical composition of the stone. The blue color of sapphires has been attributed to a small amount of titanium and iron oxide. Pink sapphires receive their color from small amounts of manganese. Yellow sapphires receive their color from traces of iron oxide.

Sapphires vary in price and are similar to diamonds in color grading values. Up to a certain shade of yellow, the grade is considered rather poor and has a small value. In general, the most sought-after sapphires are the "cornflower" blue tone type which are quite rare. Violet sapphires are more costly than yellow ones, with large sizes being rare. Blue sapphires that change to violet under artificial light are called *alexandrite* type sapphires. Orange sapphires are scarcely seen in the United States and are prized in Eastern countries. Australian sapphires are dark—almost black, dark blue, and golden colored. Montana sapphires are a steely blue color and of high quality. They are less expensive than other types of sapphires, however. Sapphires displaying asterisms are known as star sapphires. This effect is caused by a fibrous content called silk in the crystalline structure of the stone. This phenomenon may occur in all colors of sapphires; however, it rarely occurs in the yellow and green stones.

When the star sapphire is cut in the cabochon dome shape creating an arch of the structured layers of silk, it reflects light to create a star shape. The value of the star sapphire depends upon its transparency and the definition of the star. Cloudiness decreases the value. Depth and centering of the star are also prime considerations for the worth of the star sapphire.

Fraudulent methods are sometimes used to increase the apparent price of star sapphires; for example, pencil leads may be used to increase definition of the star, or oil, wax, nail polish, or silica compounds may be used to conceal cracks. Care should be taken when choosing the star sapphire. A star stone that exhibits no defects under ten-power magnification is quite rare and expensive.

Sapphires have had many mystical qualities attributed to them, such as wisdom, divine power, and clear thinking. Sapphire is the birthstone for the month of September.

The sapphire is second only to diamonds in hardness. It is found in Thailand, India, Burma, Ceylon, Australia, and the United States.

Rubies

The *ruby* is the birthstone for July and is one of the rarest and most valuable gems in the world. The ruby is prized mostly for its color and is considered to be primarily a gem of the Orient.

Many legends surround the history of the ruby. For example, the ruby was believed to contain a glowing spark from the planet Mars, a spark that could not be dimmed until the world itself grew cold, thus giving the ruby its various red hues. The ruby was also thought to make its wearer invulnerable and to cure inflammations, hemorrhages, and skin ailments.

The Eastern cultures have placed much religious and monetary significance in the ruby; therefore, few rubies found their way to Western markets in the earlier years. Rubies are found primarily in Burma, Thailand, and Sri Lanka. The finest varieties come from Burma. These rubies are generally a bright, clear red, and are the most valuable type found. Rubies with such characteristics are called *pigeon blood* rubies and are very rare.

Rubies are tough and possess exceptional wearing qualities, making them suitable for rings, bracelets, pendants, and brooches. They enhance jewelry designs when combined with other gems such as diamonds, emeralds, and sapphires.

Gems such as garnets and tourmalines may be confused with the ruby at first appearances. However, the ruby can be distinguished from these gems due to the inspection of the hexagonal crystal system possessed by the ruby in comparison to the cubic crystal systems of other stones.

Pearls

Pearls have long been the subject of fascination, admiration, and legend. Pearls were considered among one of the most precious items in the early days before the processes of polishing gems and stones arose. Royalty found the pearl to their liking and incorporated it into their most treasured royal possessions.

Various legends abound about the origin and magical qualities of pearls. However, today the processes of how pearls are produced have been researched, and the production of fine pearls and pearl articles has become somewhat of a science. All pearls are sorted according to grade and size. Pearls fall into one of four categories: (1) natural, (2) cultured, (3) freshwater, or (4) simulated.

Natural pearls, also called oriental pearls, are pearls produced directly by nacreous mollusks, such as pearl oysters, abalones, mussels, and others. Pearl in the mass is regarded as mother-of-pearl, but when detached it is known as a pearl and is considered a gem. Natural pearls are formed when a tiny irritant, commonly a sand grain, enters the mollusk shell and ledges itself somewhere near the body or inner shell of the mollusk. The mollusk secretes a carbonate of lime solution, commonly called a nacreous solution, which coats the irritant and creates the pearl in a complex and lengthy process.

A pearl can exhibit a variety of shapes and colors, depending upon the site of formation and the chemical composition of the surrounding water. For example, pearls formed near the shell of a mollusk are considered less precious due to their somewhat flattened shape, whereas pearls formed near the body of the mollusk are more precious due to their rounded and smoother appearance. The chemical composition of the surrounding water may create many variations of colors in pearls. As a result, pearls may come in shades of white, yellow, pink, red, blue, brown, green, or black. Natural pearls are very rare and therefore are very expensive. The best sites for natural pearls are found in the Persian Gulf.

Cultured pearls are the result of man's attempt to duplicate the natural processes involved in pearl production. Cultured pearls were first produced around the thirteenth century in China and later became one of the most valuable industries in Japan during the twentieth century due to Japan's mass production of pearls.

Cultured pearls are produced by embedding an irritant, usually a small piece of mother-of-pearl, in the mollusk. Mostly oysters are used for this method. The mollusk is then placed into a cage and lowered into the water, where the mollusk is allowed to coat the irritant with its nacreous substance. By varying the amount of time allowed for coating of the irritant, the chemical composition of the water, and the temperature of the water, the pearl farmer can achieve a varying quality of pearl. The mollusks are usually allowed from eighteen months to three years to form the pearl before they are harvested. Even under these constant conditions, of course, the pearl farmer is never really sure of the outcome of the final pearl. The longer the mollusk is allowed to form the pearl, the more expensive the pearl becomes. Cultured pearls are so unique and well-developed that only an X-ray can detect the difference between the cultured and the natural pearl.

Freshwater pearls can be either natural or cultured. They are produced by the same methods mentioned previously, with the exception of being produced in fresh water as opposed to salt water.

Freshwater pearls are usually more elongated than other types of pearls. They are a dull white in color. Due to their characteristic shapes and to shorter growing time required, freshwater pearls are less expensive than natural or cultured pearls. The mollusks primarily used for making freshwater pearls are mussels and clams. Freshwater pearls are incorporated in many natural-looking jewelry designs.

Simulated pearls, or imitation pearls, are man-made reproductions of pearls produced by coating beads of glass, plastic, or other materials with a substance produced to give a pearly glow. The substance used to produce this radiant appearance is sometimes composed of fish scales and adhesive plastics melted together. Other coating material, however, can be produced depending upon the properties desired.

Price ranges and qualities of simulated pearls vary, depending upon the number of layers of coating material used and the base material being coated. More expensive simulated pearls are carefully produced under controlled conditions. The more expensive simulated pearls are thoroughly dried between each dipping under ideal conditions to acquire maximum drying, and they are usually polished after every dipping to ensure smoothness by using chamois and polishing powders.

Properties of Pearls

Pearls display many unique properties that make them a desired item for the jewelry market. Jewelers classify and discriminate pearls according to several properties such as the following:

1. *Shape.* Pearls differ in shape with no two pearls being exactly alike. Pearls come in all shapes such as spherical, pear, mabe (hemispherical), button, drop, irregular, baroque, or biwa (long and oval).

2. *Cleanliness.* Cleanliness refers to the absence of blemishes on the pearls. The cleaner the pearl, the more expensive it will be.

3. *Color.* Pearls come in various colors depending on the chemical composition of the water the mollusk inhabits. Pearls are selected according to which color best compliments its wearer. For example, pearls with a rose tone may look better on a person with a fair complexion, whereas pearls with a golden or cream tone would be more complimentary to a person with a darker, olive complexion.

4. *Size.* Pearls come in all sizes, and as might be expected, the larger the pearl the more expensive, all other qualities being equal. Pearls are

measured diametrically using the millimeter as the scale of measurement. The measurement of weight for pearls is the grain, one grain equal to fifty milligrams or one carat. However, in the cultured pearl industry, the weight measurement is the Japanese momme, one momme weighing about three-quarters of an ounce.

5. *Luster.* The luster of a pearl depends on the reflection of light from the surface of the pearl. Generally, the more coatings of nacre, the deeper and more brilliant the luster of the pearl and the more expensive it becomes.

6. *Orient.* The orient refers to the luster characteristic of pearls. This luster results from the refraction of light from the translucency of the surface of the pearl through the different layers of nacre material. The greater the orient, the greater the luster and the more valuable the pearl (see Figure 16.13).

Care of Pearls

Pearls may be kept beautiful by following a few simple rules.

1. Put on pearls after makeup and perfume have been applied because the chemicals used in makeup and perfume can be harmful to pearls. Pearls should never be immersed in an acid or chemical solution.

2. After each wearing, wipe pearls off with a chamois, soft cloth, or tissue. Perspiration, body oils, and hair spray can eat away at pearls, eroding layers of nacre and dimming the luster.

3. Handle your pearls with care and try to prevent them from striking any hard surfaces that may cause them to chip or crack. Pearls should be stored in a soft lined box when not in use.

4. Pearls need to be strung on silk threads with a knot tied between each pearl. This prevents the pearls from touching one another and becoming damaged. The string used should not be allowed to become wet. It is advisable to have your pearls restrung at least once a year to ensure maximum protection.

5. Pearls should be worn often to enhance their luster and beauty because body contact is believed to enhance a pearl's glow.

SEMIPRECIOUS GEMS

Amethysts

The amethyst belongs to the quartz family and comes in varied shades of purple from pale violet to deep purple. The most valuable amethysts are purplish-red and are evenly colored. Delicate brilliance, transparency, and beautiful color ranges are qualities that help make the amethyst the most valuable gem of the quartz family.

Figure 16.13
This model wears pearl button earrings; opera, matinee, and princess pearl necklaces; pearl spiral bracelet; and pearl rings.
Courtesy of Jewelers of America.

In ancient times the amethyst was thought to bring the owner success in business, to prevent contagious diseases, and to help the wearer maintain sound judgment. Many bishops in the Roman Catholic Church have followed the tradition of wearing amethyst rings as a symbol of ecclesiastical status. Today the amethyst also denotes sincerity.

Amethysts are found chiefly in the Ural Mountains, Brazil, and Uruguay, although many are found in the United States, South Africa, Japan, Madagascar, Iran, Sri Lanka, and Mexico. The more expensive shades are commonly found in volcanic rocks and basalt.

The ability of the amethyst to complement every skin tone has helped to make it a very popular gem in today's jewelry market. The amethyst is the birthstone for February.

Aquamarines

The aquamarine is structurally classified as a beryl, which is the same mineral structure found in the emerald. The aquamarine will deepen in color when subjected to heat. This deepened color will also add to the value of the stone.

Colors of aquamarine vary from deep blue to a transparent greenish blue. The meaning of the word *aquamarine* is a combination of the words *aqua* and *marine* meaning "sea water."

The larger specimens of aquamarine are more striking than are the smaller due to their light color. The color in aquamarine is the result of a very small amount of iron compound. Aquamarines many times are found in very large crystals and are mainly mined in Brazil, although others are found in Russia, Madagascar, and the United States.

Aquamarine is used to create beautiful solitaire necklace gems, brooches, pendants, bracelets, and are often used with diamond jewelry. The more transparent and brilliant the aquamarine, the more valuable it is. Aquamarine was a favorite of many ancient cultures due to its versatility in jewelry design. Aquamarine is the birthstone for the month of March.

Topaz

Topaz was considered the supreme golden stone during the Middle Ages. At one time, all yellow stones were given the name topaz. Topaz comes in a great array of colors; however, the yellow-colored stone is the most familiar and originates in Brazil.

The rarest and most expensive topaz are those in the violet-red color range which exhibit a velvety texture and an intense luster. In general, the darker the color, the more expensive the topaz. Blue topaz is comparable to aquamarine in color. Light colorations are exhibited in most topaz, except for the yellow- and brown-colored. Topaz quartz is sometimes sold for original topaz; however, topaz is a separate mineralogical species from the quartz variety and any reputable jeweler can distinguish between the two.

Topaz received its name from the Sanskrit word *topas,* meaning "fire." Topaz was attributed as a magical stone that could cure such ailments as asthma, insomnia, burns, and bleeding. Besides being noted for its medical qualities, topaz was believed to have held mystical properties which would ensure its wearer's long life, intelligence, and beauty.

Topaz is chemically composed of aluminum fluosilicate, and it originates in cavities of igneous rocks where the crystals are created by the action of the rich fluoride acid vapors acting upon the aluminum silicate of the surrounding rocks. Topaz and topaz quartz usually come from Brazil, the Urals, Sri Lanka, and the United States. Topaz is the hardest of the semiprecious stones and therefore is adaptable to every variety of facet cutting or engraving. For this reason and the magnificent color range of topaz, it is a very desired gem used in rings, necklaces, and bracelets. Topaz is the birthstone for the month of November.

Garnets

Garnets come in various colors such as pale orange, dark red, violet, purple-red, and green. Green garnets, referred to as demantoid or diamondlike, are the most expensive. These rare garnets, found in the Ural Mountains, are very close in color to the emerald and exceed the diamond in dispersion. Other garnets are mined in Brazil, Madagascar, Sri Lanka, India, Siberia, Africa, and the United States.

Garnets are very durable gemstones chemically composed of magnesium, silicates of calcium, iron, and manganese, which explains the most commonly found red gemstone. The hessonite, a garnet ranging from orange to brown, is often used in cameos.

Garnets are attributed with such mythical qualities as assurance of constancy, friendship, and fidelity. They were also considered as an incomparable cure for many blood disorders. Garnets were also considered as a deterrent of anger. Garnets are relatively inexpensive and therefore are widely used in today's jewelry market. Garnet is the birthstone for the month of January.

Tourmalines

Tourmaline is an alternate birthstone for October, and is a relative newcomer to the family of gemstones.

This gemstone is a complex silicate combined with various metallic elements which contribute different colors, therefore making the stone available in many colors. These colors range from shades of red, green, blue, brown, and black to cat's-eye varieties which are gems containing two or more different hues. The color is usually determined by the chemical composition of the surroundings from which it is found. Brazilian stones are deep blue, green, yellow, and pink. Madagascar produces brown shades of tourmaline, and various shades are found in the United States.

The value of tourmaline is usually determined by the beauty of the stone, but the cut plays a major role in price. Tourmaline is one of the least expensive gemstones and is used for cuff links, studs, tacks, and rings.

Peridots

Peridot is a transparent rich olive green gem which has been popular for centuries. The peridot may vary in shade but will always display a green color. More valuable peridot are slightly yellow-green; the less expensive forms are yellow or brownish green. Peridot will vary in price according to its color, absence of flaws, and size.

Peridot has the unique quality of being able to be flashy even under dim lighting. For this reason peridot received much acclaim as a mystical gem in early times. It was believed to have been a deterrent of evil, a cure for asthma, an agent to lessen the thirst caused by fever, and as an assurance of married happiness. If worn on earrings, peridot was believed to have given its wearer an increased sense of hearing. Peridot was called the "gem of the sun" by the ancients and was brought back to Europe in great quantities during the crusades in the Mediterranean area.

Today peridot gems are designed with gold to create jewelry pieces suitable for most occasions. Peridot is found in Burma, New Mexico, Arizona, Australia, and St. John's Island in the Red Sea. It is the birthstone for August.

Alexandrites

Alexandrite was discovered in 1839 on the birthday of Alexander II, czar of Russia. For this reason Alexandrite received its name. The discovery happened in the Ural Mountains. Miners discovered the stones and first believed them to be emeralds due to their green appearance. When the miners brought the stones down near their campfires, the stones gave off a red color. In the morning the stones were green again, and the miners realized they had found a new gem.

Alexandrite displays a unique quality which makes it a very desirable gemstone. Under the influence of natural lighting the stones appear to be green in color; however, under the influence of artificial lighting, the stones appear to be red in color. This explains the phenomenon experienced by the early miners of Alexandrite.

Alexandrite is a composite of the mineral chrysoberyl and is a fairly new member of the gem family. It is usually found in small sizes but occasionally a few large specimens are found. Alexandrite is found mainly in Sri Lanka and Russia. It is the alternate birthstone for the month of June.

Opals

The opal is the birthstone for October and is considered to be one of the most lovely, most fragile, and most desirable of all gems. The flashes of color from an opal, called "play of color," create a unique appearance that has fascinated collectors for centuries.

The opal was believed by ancients to have fallen from the sky in flashes of lightening, thus creating its unique coloring. The opal was believed to bring its wearers good fortune, exempt them from evil, make them clairvoyant, soothe their eyes and nerves, cure kidney diseases, and protect them from lightning.

The opal is chemically composed of hydrated silica. Background colors of the opal are black, white, and red. The black background opal is very expensive. The white background opal is somewhat less expensive than the black, but it is more expensive than the reddish background opal.

The play of color is produced by the light interference in layers or cracks filled with material of varying optical densities. This produces an effect similar to that seen when a film of oil is on the surface of water.

The opal is a fragile gemstone and may crack when fashioned as a thin stone. If the opal is carefully mounted so that it receives protection from the mounting, it will work satisfactorily for jewelry pieces that do not receive much abuse, such as rings, scarf pins, and pendants.

Most opals originate in Australia. They work beautifully in combination with other gemstones to create lovely jewelry pieces.

Moonstones

Moonstone is a form of feldspar and is so named due to its ability to produce the optical illusion of a color similar to that of the moon. This internal reflection can vary in color to include shades of green, yellow, and blue. The more evident the silvery light color produced by this illusion, the more valuable the gemstone. This misty light diffusion is referred to as adularescence. Moonstone that has the cabochon cut is said to appear as a raindrop viewed in an early morning mist. Moonstones are very unusual and received early popularity which has since declined.

The moonstone is believed to arouse passion in lovers. It is also able to allow lovers to have the power to see their future together, so legend goes. The Orientals gave moonstone its name, which means "no tear." This is because the moonstone has no sharp edges and is sometimes compared to the appearance of a raindrop or tear.

Moonstones have been found in such places as India, Switzerland, and Sri Lanka. Most moonstones found are small with larger unflawed gems being quite rare. This gem is appealing to people wanting the unusual. Moonstone is the alternate birthstone for the month of June.

Jade

Jade is perhaps the oldest gemstone and is generally associated with the eastern cultures such as China and Japan, perhaps due to the large numbers of jade articles discovered in both of these countries which date back for many centuries. Jade was even used by primitive man as a source of working tools. For centuries, jade has been used to create a wide variety of articles such as bowls, utensils, and amulets. Today, however, jade is more widely used in the creation of jewelry pieces.

Jade is a chemical composition of jadeite and nephrite minerals found in ordinary looking rocks along streams and hillsides. Jade, a very durable stone, is found in a wide variety of colors ranging from white, various shades of green, black, to blue. Blue jade is very rare and is found in only a few collector's pieces. Green jade is the most common and is found to be readily available.

The jade center of the world is Hong Kong. Top-grade jade is mined in Burma. Some jade has been discovered in Wyoming, New Zealand, Alaska, Germany, and Siberia.

Jade is used in the jewelry market because of its luster, sheen, and durability. Jade mixes well in setting with other gems such as diamonds, pearls, and rubies. Some jade requires a high degree of polishing to achieve its beautiful luster. Once it has attained its magnificent luster, however, jade is one of the most spectacular gemstones.

Bloodstone

Bloodstone is the alternative birthstone for the month of March. It is quite popular as an item for men's jewelry due to its dark green color with contrasting red flecks.

Bloodstone is a member of the quartz family. It has less durability than aquamarine. The opaque qualities and color of bloodstone make it especially suited for such men's jewelry items as signets, cuff links, and tie tacks. The bloodstone is also often carved with monograms, initials, or crests.

Sardonyx

Sardonyx is a multilayered gem that comes in a variety of colors such as white, brown, and red. However, sardonyx is most commonly known for its burnt orange color. It is an alternate birthstone for August.

Many mythical and magical qualities were attributed to sardonyx in early times. It was used as a charm against warts and cramps, and it was also a gem of courage for orators and shy lovers. It is found in many Roman and Greek artifacts.

Sardonyx is prized for use in men's jewelry and is most often used for intaglios and cameos. It can be cut for crests or initials. An intaglio is a small carved figure or design cut or incised below the surface of a stone. A cameo is a small carved sculpture on a raised surface of a stone.

Turquoise

Turquoise was a gem much desired by the ancients, such as the Incas, Aztecs, Egyptians, Persians, and American Indians of the southwestern United States. The ancients manifest a multitude of legendary power and superstitious ability to the gem. Not only was turquoise used for its perceived magical qualities such as a means to insure victory or a means to increase wealth, but turquoise was also employed simply for its desired beauty as a decorative item such as jewelry. Turquoise was also used as a medium of exchange. The oldest known pieces of jewelry, which were discovered in the tomb of Queen Zer, Egypt's ancient monarch some 7,500 years ago, were composed of gold and turquoise.

Today turquoise is primarily used for jewelry. The gem is light to medium in color. It is opaque. Sometimes turquoise will appear greenish in color. This is the result of the stone being highly porous. The porous stones allow certain acids and oils, such as those secreted by the skin, to be readily absorbed. This creates the green color in the stone. Greenish turquoise is not considered to be gem quality.

The finest quality turquoise is a medium blue color which is evenly distributed throughout the stone. Some turquoise may exhibit an even distribution of color and also contain a fine evenly distributed series of lines. This kind of turquoise is referred to as *spiderweb turquoise*. The price of turquoise may vary widely depending upon the quality of the gems. Turquoise is the birthstone for December.

Turquoise is a fairly tough gem; however, it cannot withstand high temperatures. To improve the appearance and reduce the harmful effects of acids and oils, turquoise is sometimes dipped in blue paraffin, sodium silicate, or plastics.

The best quality turquoise gems come from Persia. However, most of the turquoise used today comes from the southwestern United States, such as Arizona, New Mexico, Colorado, California, and Nevada.

Amber

Amber was one of the first materials used by the ancients for both decorative and mystical purposes. Amber was employed for such things as a cure for goiter, a medium of exchange, a sweet-smelling incense, boxes, bottles, figurines, and jewelry.

Amber is not a mineral but rather a fossilized organic resin produced from the sap of ancient trees. Amber may vary in colors ranging from pale yellow to brown, orange, red, and even shades of blue and green. Amber will turn a whitish color with age. Some samples of amber may contain fossils of ancient insects which were trapped in the resin.

Today amber is used primarily for such articles as beads, ornamental objects, brooches, pendants, earrings, bracelets, rings, and rosaries. Amber is desired as a material in jewelry due to its light weight and ease of cutting. Amber is desired most in its transparent varieties.

Major sources of amber come from the Baltic Sea area in Poland. Other sources of amber are found in East Germany, Sicily, Burma, and Rumania.

Ivory

Creamy white ivory has been used as ornaments and carvings since early times. Ivory refers to the material of African and Asian elephant tusks. The color of ivory varies from translucent to opaque, the most valued being a pale, rosy white. Its pure color has made it especially appropriate as an ornament of royalty, and in the past, it was often a symbol of powerful monarchy.

Coral

Coral is produced by a small sea organism called *coral polyp*. This gem was believed by the ancients to have the power to ward off evil, alleviate fear, impart wisdom, and cure sterility.

Some sources of coral are along the coasts off Morocco, Sardinia, Italy, and Japan, but it is found throughout the world in tropical and subtropical waters. Coral usually grows in shallow water, and the color of coral generally lightens with the depth.

Coral has a vitreous luster and a branchlike shape. Hundreds of shades of red coral exist, and its value varies according to its color and size.

Coral is mostly carved into round or egg-shaped beads for necklaces, rosaries, bracelets, cameos, intaglios, and figurines.

Onyx

Onyx is similar to agate except that the layers in onyx are in parallel planes. Gem onyx, with layers of contrasting colors, can be carved into cameos and similar ornaments with light figures on a dark background. Both onyx and agate belong to the group of quartz minerals called chalcedony. Common kinds of onyx are black and white or gray, red to brownish red, and white and red to brownish red. Black onyx is usually a deep, glossy black that is often artificially colored.

Jet

Jet, brown coal known as lignite, is found in shale formations in England, Colorado, Canada, France, Germany, and Spain. The hard shale rock was formed as a result of the compaction of driftwood that sank to the bottom of the sea, became embedded in fine-grained mud, and later transformed into shale.

The opaque, lustrous black mineral was widely used as mourning jewelry in the nineteenth century. Today, jet is used in beads, rosaries, bracelets, pendants, and brooches. The value of jet depends on its polish, its freedom of other mineral particles, and its lack of fine cracks.

BIRTHSTONES

Birthstones have been worn since 1562. The choice of gems is traced to the twelve precious stones in the breastplate of Aaron, the High Priest. The twelve gems represented the twelve tribes of Israel and were also the foundation stones for each of the twelve apostles in the temple at New Jerusalem. Later the twelve gems were linked with twelve signs of the zodiac and eventually came to be associated with the months of the year.

Birthstones were valued at first for their special mystical powers as talismans of good luck. As lapidary arts and skills developed to enhance their natural beauty, they were worn also as attractive gems and jewels.

The following list of birthstones is the official one adopted by the jewelers in the United States.

MONTH	STONE	SIGNIFICANCE
January	Garnet	Constancy
February	Amethyst	Sincerity
March	Aquamarine or bloodstone	Courage
April	Diamond	Innocence
May	Emerald	Love
June	Pearl, alexandrite, or moonstone	Health
July	Ruby or star ruby	Contentment
August	Periodot or sardonyx	Married happiness
September	Sapphire or star sapphire	Clear thinking
October	Opal or tourmaline	Hope
November	Topaz	Fidelity
December	Turquoise or zircon	Prosperity

SYNTHETIC AND IMITATION STONES

Synthetic stones are copies of original natural stones having the same chemical, optical, and physical properties as the ones created by nature. They have the same crystal formation, same coloring, same atomic arrangement, and they are as nearly identical to the natural ones as physically possible. The mixed ingredients also had either heat or pressure applied to them using the Verneuil furnace process. (The Verneuil oxyhydrogen furnace was hot enough to melt small ruby crystals to create new larger masses, or synthetic rubies. Later, purer synthetic ruby stones were developed by mixing pure aluminum powder with chromium oxide added for color. Blue sapphires were produced synthetically by adding titanium oxide.) Special equipment and great skill are needed to tell the difference between natural stones and the "too perfect" synthetic ones. Synthetic stones are inexpensive compared with the natural stones. Diamonds, rubies, emeralds, sapphires, and garnets are among the stones that are made synthetically.

Treated or *altered* stones are natural gems whose color has been changed by heat treatment, atomic radiation, or X-ray. *Reconstructed* stones are made by fusing worthless bits of real gems into a bigger, better gem that may be cut and polished into a more valuable stone.

Assembled stones are made by using pieces of real gems cemented together in order to create a better looking stone. Pieces of colored glass may be sandwiched around the assembled stones to improve their coloring.

Imitation stones are made from materials that simulate a genuine, natural gem. The materials may include glass, plastics, and amorphous substances. Diamonds, amber, topaz, turquoise, tourmaline, and peridot are stones that are imitated. Rhinestones are among the best known imitation stones made from glass and other materials.

CARE OF JEWELRY

In regard to jewelry, better care means longer wear. Hints on lengthening the life and preserving the "new look" beauty of jewelry are beneficial. Follow the suggestions below.

1. Place jewelry in a plush-lined, plain or tiered, jewelry box to help prevent scratching of metal and stones.

2. Polish the metal when it gets dull with a good silver or metal polish.

3. Clean the stones by boiling in two parts of water to one part of ammonia to loosen the dirt.

4. Keep colognes and perfumes from contacting jewelry whenever possible. The alcohol discolors pearls and may affect stones and metal finishes.

5. Mechanical defects, such as pin guards, are usually easy to repair. It only takes a little time and money to keep the items useful.

6. Take rings off before washing your hands, and put the rings in a safe place.

7. Check ring settings to make sure that the stones are held securely by the prong; otherwise, they may be easily lost.

8. Check the thread on which beads are strung to see if it needs to be replaced.

SELLING POINTS

Jewelry salespersons should observe the following selling points.

1. Call jewelry items, metals, and stone cuts by their correct names.

2. Determine the item of interest to the prospective customer. Then show as few types as possible. Point out the workmanship, fine detail, and the uniqueness of the color, cut, or sparkle of the stone or other item.

3. Encourage the prospective customer to try on the item or model it yourself. Suggest a related piece of jewelry to match, such as earrings to match a necklace. Earrings should be tried on, as their shape accents the shape of the face, and their color reflects skin tone.

4. Show higher priced items first. You can always trade down.

5. Handle jewelry gracefully. Use the jewelry pad under bright lights. Hold flat pieces from the side to prevent finger marks on the stones or metal.

6. Help the customer to know and appreciate the fashion, becomingness, use, value, suitability, and care of the piece of jewelry. Jewelry color may contrast or blend with the wearer's apparel, but it should always dramatize the entire clothing look.

KEY TERMS

1. Base metals
2. Carat
3. Cultured pearls
4. Facet
5. Gold filled
6. Gold plated
7. Karat
8. Moh's scale
9. Precious stones
10. Semiprecious stones
11. Settings

STUDY QUESTIONS

1. Describe the ways gold can be used with other metals in making jewelry.
2. Differentiate between precious and semiprecious stones. How do synthetic and imitation stones differ?
3. What stones are used in place of diamonds?
4. What materials are used in making costume jewelry?
5. How do freshwater, saltwater, cultured, and imitation pearls differ?
6. Describe six types of surface decorations that may be used on costume jewelry.
7. What is the origin and significance of the birthstone ring?
8. What determines the color, size, and shape of the natural or oriental pearl?
9. What qualities does the pearl have that are not found in other gemstones?
10. Describe five types of inclusions found in diamonds.

STUDY ACTIVITIES

1. List at least ten jewelry stones that are available for your examination. For each one, chart (a) the name of the stone, (b) approximate size, (c) color, (d) whether it is transparent, translucent, or opaque, and (e) the type of cutting.
2. Obtain the current market price for the following (preferably not mounted) stones:
   - 1-carat perfect white diamond
   - 1-carat nearly flawless emerald
   - 1-carat nearly flawless ruby
   - 1-carat nearly flawless sapphire
   - 7 mm. natural pearl
   - 7 mm. cultured pearl
3. Select five jewelry advertisements and list, define, and describe technical terms that are used regarding jewelry.

CHAPTER **17**

Flatware and Hollowware

OBJECTIVES

After completing this chapter, you should be able to:

1. List the steps in making sterling silver flatware and hollowware. Tell why some items are stamped and cast. Tell why others are shaped through a spinning process.

2. Describe the pieces of flatware that are included in a basic minimum place setting and how the essential pieces are sold.

3. Identify five different methods of decorating flatware and hollowware, and describe each method.

4. Describe how finishes are applied to flatware and hollowware, and how each may affect a customer's choice of item.

5. Tell why and how the various metal flatware and hollowware pieces should be given proper care when they are in use and when they are not in use.

Sterling silverware was used by royalty for centuries before a method of plating silver on base metals was discovered about 1742. In 1840, mass production methods in the production of electroplated ware on copper or base metal alloys (brass, nickel silver, or steel) were discovered. These methods have made plated silverware so inexpensive that it is readily available to the majority of families. Any plated or sterling silverware made more than 100 years ago is called *antique*

403

silver. Recent trends show that articles made of quality stainless steel and other alloyed metals are readily accepted by consumers. For purposes of study, tableware is divided into two parts: flatware and hollowware. *Flatware* consists of small table utensils used for serving and eating food, such as forks, knives, and spoons. *Hollowware* consists of deep, hollow items such as bowls, candlesticks, cups, sugar bowls and creamers, and vases. These may be handmade or machine made.

STERLING SILVER FLATWARE

In its pure state, silver is too soft to be practical for ordinary use. Therefore, it is alloyed with other metals to strengthen it. In sterling silver the metal used to strengthen the silver is copper. Legal requirements state that sterling silver must contain 92.5 percent silver and 7.5 percent copper. The term *sterling silver* does not refer to the thickness of the article but to the fineness of the silver. *Sterling* is the word used in the United States to indicate purity of silver and is accompanied by the name or mark of the manufacturer. In England, the official mark stamped on articles of gold or silver to indicate purity is called *hallmark.*

Sterling silver flatware is chosen by customers for its quality, beauty, and long life (see Figure 17.1). Its thickness and weight vary according to the manufacturer. The heavier and more ornate the sterling silver item, the more expen-

Figure 17.1
Sterling silver flatware.
Courtesy of Oneida Silversmiths.

sive and longer its life. Sterling silver often is elaborately designed because the metal is easier to work with than other kinds. However, the more hand finishing and polishing required, the more sterling silver pieces will cost.

Manufacturing Sterling Flatware

Between the drawing board and the dinner table, flatware goes through a series of operations demanding the greatest skill of many specialized craftsmen. It may take years for a design that has been created for a flatware service to then be accepted. The process of manufacturing sterling flatware is described in the following steps:

1. A series of three-dimensional models are made based on the design.

2. Experienced craftsmen work on the ornamental details before the final steel dies are made.

3. Sheets of silver are then stamped into individual blanks to shape the outline (see Figure 17.2). The silver blanks consist of 925 parts silver and 75 parts copper in the correct thickness or gauge for the items produced.

4. Next, the rolling process forms the actual thickness of the piece throughout the cut blank.

Figure 17.2
Blanking.
Courtesy of The Gorham Company.

5. The decoration is stamped in with two blows from a thousand pound hammer (see Figure 17.3).

6. A series of hand operations follows to insure perfection and uniformity (see Figure 17.4). For example, the rough edges are removed on a belt grinder in the grinding department.

7. Polishing on cotton-wheeled buffers brings out the shine of the silver.

8. Oxidation follows if the pattern requires it. This method darkens certain surface areas. Special liquid formulas are applied to give contrast and strong accents to the raised surfaces.

9. Each piece is polished by jeweler's rouge on a fast-turning wheel that puts on the final mirrorlike sheen or *bright finish*. Another finish that may be given to the sterling flatware is called *butler finish*. This distinctive surface luster is now produced by mechanical buffing and polishing with abrasives instead of being done by hand rubbing (see Figure 17.5).

10. After a steam bath and a dry bath (sawdust process of drying), each item is given a final inspection and weighing before being packed and shipped.

Knife handles are hollow in most sterling flatware and, thus, require special handling in manufacturing. The handle is stamped in two separate halves, which are then rounded and soldered together. Some knives that are hollow-handled are made by drawing the metal into a form like a tube rather than being sol-

Figure 17.3
Die stamping.
Courtesy of The Gorham
Company.

Figure 17.4
Perfecting details of handles.
Courtesy of The Gorham
Company.

Figure 17.5
Sandbobbing.
Courtesy of The Gorham
Company.

dered. The forged stainless steel blade is anchored in place by soldering. *Forging* means that the metal is pounded to the desired thickness.

Sterling silver flatware is usually manufactured in different weights or with varying thicknesses of metal to shape the different blanks. The heavier the weight, the more the item costs and the longer it will last. Knives which are hollow-handled usually have more weighting. Elegant and elaborate designs may be used on sterling silver flatware because sterling is so easily worked.

SILVERPLATED FLATWARE

The quality of silverplated flatware is determined by the workmanship, the amount of silver used to cover the base metal, and the thickness of the base metal itself.

Nickel silver, an alloy composed of nickel, zinc, and copper, is used for the blanks that form the finished spoons, forks, and knife handles. The nickel silver pieces are cleaned and polished to get rid of oil and dust which would make the silverplating imperfect. The silverplating bath takes place next, when the pieces are attached to a rack and are left in the bath until the desired amount of silver has adhered to the base metal. The pieces that get more use, such as spoons and forks, have an extra layer of pure silver plated on the areas that get the most wear. Then the pieces are removed from the bath, polished, inspected, and wrapped.

The amount of silver coating on the flatware determines whether it is single plated (A1), double plated (XX), triple plated (XXX), or quadruple plated (XXXX), which refers to the thickness of the plate. Quadruple plated indicates that the silver coating is four times as thick as single plate.

Sheffield plate was made by heat rolling together sheets of copper, brass, or other metal and silver of the desired proportions. The process, discovered in 1742, was virtually abandoned around 1840 with the introduction of electroplating.

Silverplated flatware (Figure 17.6) is less expensive than sterling silver, but the higher priced silverplate looks and feels like sterling, and there are just as many different patterns from which to choose.

STAINLESS STEEL TABLEWARE

Knife blades made from stainless steel have been used successfully for silverware since the early 1930s. In the late 1930s, stainless steel was used to make inexpensive, thin, ungraded, and almost undesigned flatware for restaurants. New formulas and processing methods were developed in the late 1950s to produce the necessary shapes, varying thicknesses, correct weight, good balance, and intricate designs.

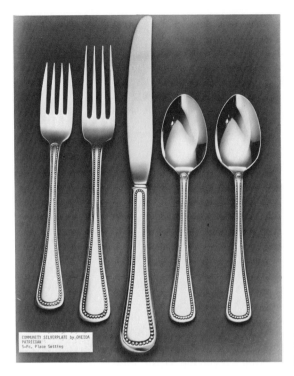

Figure 17.6
Silverplated flatware.
Courtesy of Oneida
Silversmiths.

Characteristics of Stainless Steel Flatware

Five characteristics may be used to determine the quality of stainless flatware.

1.   The *chemical content* of the metal can vary in its composition to increase or decrease the stainless property of the final product. Stainless steel is composed of iron to which chrome and nickel have been added to make a metal that resists rust and most other stain-producing elements. Quality stainless should be care free.

2.   Certain *types of patterns* take more effort and expense to manufacture than plain patterns. More attention is given to details in quality flatware patterns.

3.   The care given to *finishing operations* can affect the cost and quality of flatware patterns. Higher inspection standards are applied to the more expensive patterns.

4.   Stainless steel metal is *solid* and the same throughout. It resists chipping, corrosion, peeling, and rusting. It does not need to be polished to stay bright.

5.   The *weight and thickness* vary greatly according to the quality of the flat-ware and whether or not the pieces are "graded." Fine stainless is grad-ed so that it is graceful and has strength where it is needed. The less ex-pensive types often do not have any variation of thickness from one end of the piece to the other.

Manufacturing Stainless Steel Flatware

Many processes are used to make a spoon from the raw material. A special stain-less steel alloy is used to make flatware such as forks, knives, and spoons. This special alloy is composed of iron to which chrome and nickel have been added to help create a more rust- and stain-resistant metal. There are many different com-binations of these metals alloyed in accordance with the type of product desired. The metal comes from mills in sheets from one-eighth to five-sixteenth of an inch in thickness, four to twelve inches in width, and from eight to sixteen feet in length.

The first process involves feeding a sheet of metal into a machine which cuts out a spade-shaped rough blank a little smaller than a finished spoon. Both ends of the flat blank (bowl and handle parts) must be thinner than the stem and are rolled out to the required thickness and proper length.

The rolled flat blank goes to a machine which cuts out the spoon form and pattern outline, and removes the surplus metal from the outer edges. The blank is now annealed to make it pliable. It is then placed under a drop hammer which hollows out the bowl and curves the handle in one operation. This is done by two solid hard steel dies, one mounted on a rigid base and the other mounted in the drop, which weighs about 1,000 pounds. The drop falls about twenty inches to the spoon blank.

The pattern design is now ready to be placed on the spoon handle. The two steel dies have the design embossed or engraved upon them in reverse, one for the front and one for the back. When the drop hammer falls it imprints the "posi-tive" pattern. Some ornamental pattern designs require weeks of careful chiseling by craftsmen to make the dies.

The patterned spoon is now trimmed, washed to remove all traces of dirt and grease, and polished ready for the final finishing. Next, the edges and sur-faces are carefully polished to bring about a bright or satin luster. The spoon is now ready for inspection and shipment.

The hollow knife handles are produced in halves, lengthwise. The halves are machine-soldered together, and the forged blade is then inserted and ce-mented to the hollow handle.

GOLD-COLORED FLATWARE AND HOLLOWWARE

Vermeil

The Vermeil gold-plating process was developed in France in the mid-1700s. Ex-travagant French kings would confiscate gold objects belonging to their subjects to help bolster the economy. The Frenchmen began to plate objects made with less expensive metal with gold. Thus, the gold-plated items were safe from seizure. The finest craftsmen of that time began creating fashionable table service and other pieces from sterling silver coated lavishly with a layer of gold.

The production of Vermeil was banned by France early in the nineteenth century because the process used mercury, which blinded many workers. This ban lasted until a safer process was discovered.

Vermeil is now a process whereby 24-karat gold is electroplated to sterling silver. Unlike former processes, it has an extremely hard surface which will give many years of service.

Jacqueline Kennedy gave the use of Vermeil impetus in this country when she began using the Vermeil table service that had been made for the White House several years before. Vermeil pieces such as bowls, boxes, candelabras, goblets, and flatware give decorators greater opportunities in coordinating table settings. Some customers prefer Vermeil for its beauty and nontarnishing characteristics.

Dirilyte

Dirilyte is a gold-colored alloy invented by two Swedish engineers in the 1920s. It is a solid yellow-colored metal and is not plated. The metal is made in the company's foundry, where it is cast into billets. Once processed into sheets, it is formed through die-hydraulic operations into various articles. Some of the articles are forged, such as dinner knives, and some are cast, such as salt and pepper shakers.

In 1950, Dirilyte hollowware was first marketed with a tarnish-resistant finish. It needed to be cared for with systematic cleaning and polishing just as does all fine tableware. In 1961 a bonded protectant was developed for Dirilyte. The protectant is transparent and actually bonds to the articles to keep them tarnish-free for a period of two to seven years before needing to be reapplied. Dirilyte patterns are permanent and can always be matched by the customer.

Gold-Plated Stainless Steel

Stainless flatware is being gold-plated in the United States for sale in certain department stores, jewelry stores, and gift shops. A minimum of 22-karat gold is electroplated on the flatware. A coat of nickel is applied to the stainless steel flatware before it is plated with gold. The thicker the gold-plating, the longer it will last. Gold-plated merchandise must be carefully handled. Items should not be placed in dishwashers, nor should abrasive materials be used on them.

PEWTER

Pewter, a favorite metal of Americans since Colonial days, is enjoying an unprecedented return to prominence. Items made of pewter fit with most decors, but they are especially appropriate with Early American and Colonial home furnishings. Pewter is popular for the manufacture of a wide variety of decorative service articles.

Characteristics

Pewter is a blend of several metals, but it is mostly tin. When tin is properly blended with lead-free metals, it will not tarnish and is ideal for use with foods. Pewter, used in the production of most hollowware and flatware, is an alloy composed of 91–93 percent tin, 6–7 percent antimony, and 1–3 percent copper. It has a dull gray color, is soft and easily shaped, and melts at a low temperature. It has some limitations which should be understood in order to appreciate its nature. It is soft; therefore it is easily dented. It should be kept away from hot stoves or other sources of heat because of its low melting point. For this reason, pewter is used for decorative purposes or with serving unheated foods of all kinds. Utensils made of modern pewter have a high resistance to almost all weak acids, and they can be used to serve food and beverages without fear of chemical action. It requires a minimum of care to keep it looking attractive, since it is non-tarnishing and does not need polishing.

Manufacturing Pewter

When pewter is properly blended, it is an expensive metal. It is about four times as expensive as brass or copper and twelve times as expensive as steel. Because of its unique characteristics, it is not well adapted to automatic production. It is best made by the hand methods of casting and spinning. Pewter gets softer as it is worked and hardens when it is heated to specific temperatures.

Finishes

Finishes available on pewter range from the highly polished bright finish (Figure 17.7) to the lead-bearing metal that turns black from oxidation on contact with the air. Many old pewter items contained some lead that required polishing to maintain a finish. Modern pewter does not need frequent polishing under normal usage. Fruit acids such as citrus juices and vinegar tend to darken pewter. Most experts suggest that pewter may need to be polished twice a year to restore the original luster to the finish.

Some people prefer a low-luster finish which shows the nature of the metal (Figure 17.8). An easy finish to live with, it does not show finger marks, yet it brings out the warmth and beauty of the metal.

Types of Modern Pewter

A wide variety of well-constructed and well-designed items are available, including coffee and tea service, bowls, candelabra, ashtrays, trays, spoons, plates, pitchers, salt and pepper shakers, tankards, and vases. For persons who prefer the American Colonial period antique design, many reproductions are available.

Figure 17.7
Pewter may be polished to create a bright luster as illustrated in this pewter coffee service.
Courtesy of The Gorham Company.

Figure 17.8
Pewter coffee and tea service with traditional low-luster finish.
Courtesy of The Gorham Company.

A wide variety of articles of contemporary design are also available. Decorative articles are also being manufactured that combine pewter with hand-rubbed woods in antique pine tones.

Cleaning Modern Pewter

Although modern pewter is tarnish-resistant, the exposed surfaces may become dusty and show fingerprints. It can be cleaned by washing in warm, soapy water or in regular household detergents using a soft bristle brush or a soft flannel cloth. Clear hot water should be used to rinse the articles well. The articles should be dried immediately with a clean soft cloth to prevent water spotting. A pewter polish or a good silver polish may be used when a pewter article with a high polish needs to be cleaned.

Displaying Pewter

Pewter articles are usually decorative accessories and should be effectively displayed as such in settings that relate to the period for which they are styled. They may be displayed in an Early American or a contemporary theme.

SELECTING AND SELLING FLATWARE

For most people, buying flatware represents a substantial investment in both time and money. It should be selected wisely so that it harmonizes with dinnerware, crystal, and table linens. Flatware can create a gracious and hospitable mood to make dining a pleasure. Depending on the style of living and budget, the customer may have a choice of sterling silver, silverplate, gold-electroplate, or stainless steel.

Flatware is sold in sets and open stock. Sets come in several sizes and adapt to various numbers of people. Basic place setting units are usually made up of six, eight, and ten pieces. The basic six-piece setting consists of the knife and fork (luncheon or small-sized), cream-soup spoon, teaspoon, salad fork, and butter spreader (see Figure 17.9). Anything but a formal dinner table may be set with these pieces. Other pieces which may be added include the dinner knife or other large-sized knife, dinner fork, dessert or cereal spoon (also used as a soup spoon), cocktail or oyster fork, and iced tea spoon. It is always wise to be practical and suggest getting the basic place settings first. The basic four-piece place setting consists of a place knife, place fork, teaspoon, and salad fork. The five-piece place setting has a cream-soup or place spoon in addition.

After the size has been selected, the salesperson may suggest the purchase of as many place settings as the customer can afford. Other pieces may be added gradually as time goes on. The consumer may wish to supplement place settings with additional pieces such as demitasse and iced beverage spoons, cocktail forks, and an assortment of serving pieces (see Figure 17.10). The serving pieces do not have to be in the same pattern as the place settings.

Figure 17.9
Basic six-piece place setting.
Courtesy of The Gorham
Company.

Figure 17.10
Serving pieces.
Courtesy of The Gorham
Company.

How to Display Flatware

A store's display arrangement of flatware items should be displayed just as they might be used in a home. The salesperson must remember that meal times may be the only times of the day when the whole family is together as a group with a common interest. A gracefully and correctly set table makes the meal more enjoyable by pleasing the eye and improving a person's sense of well-being.

Certain rules of table setting, such as where the flatware is placed, are usually based on convenience for the people dining. It is best to have the right knives, spoons, and forks arranged where they can be picked up easily rather than have them placed in disarray on the table. Arrangements should also follow a certain pattern on every table, so that people become familiar with them and can use them simply and easily (see Figure 17.11). Salespeople should be fully aware of the reasons why correct table settings are used. Here are some basic rules of table setting to consider.

1. A well-balanced table is a must. No area should be overcrowded with items. Allow twenty-four inches for each place setting. Place each setting about one inch from the table's edge.

2. Maintain orderliness by keeping all the lines on the table at right angles or parallel to the edge of the table (place mats, pieces of silver, etc.).

3. Arrange flatware at each place in the order of its use so the individual may use outside items on each side first.

4. Knives and spoons are placed at the right edge of the plate with the handles even and with the sharp edge of a knife always turned toward the plate. Soup spoons should be placed on the outside at the right.

5. All forks should be placed at the left of the plate. The salad fork is placed next to the plate, then the meat fork, and fish fork on the outside left, if needed. The exception would be the placement of the cock-

Figure 17.11
The proper placement of flatware at the table.
Courtesy of Lenox China•Crystal.

tail or oyster fork, which should be placed at the extreme right of the spoons, if needed. Both outside pieces may be brought in separately, if needed.

6.   The bread-and-butter plate is placed above the tip of the fork in a breakfast or luncheon place setting, but is not used in a formal dinner setting. The butter spreader is always placed across the top or on the right side of the bread-and-butter plate with the edge facing the center of the plate.

7.   Place the water glass or goblet above the tip of the knife blade. The cup and saucer are placed correctly to the right, in line with the middle of the plate.

8.   A napkin is generally placed to the left of the forks, open corner to the left or next to the plate. The folded napkin may be placed on the empty plate if no food has been served.

9.   Use centerpieces and decorations low enough so that diners can see over them easily. Use candles that are tall enough that the flame is above eye level.

10.   Place serving pieces on or near the dishes with which they will be used.

STERLING SILVER HOLLOWWARE

Sterling silver bowls, bonbon dishes, bread trays, coffee pots, cream pitchers, gravy boats and trays, sugar bowls, vases, and vegetable dishes are made by one of the following processes: (1) spinning, (2) stamping, or (3) casting.

Spinning Process

Flat, circle-shaped silver blanks are placed on spinning lathes against a wooden mold called a *chuck*. The rotation of the chuck stretches the silver blanks to form the rounded items. This is a difficult process which takes skill. When the item has been spun into its final shape, the silversmith department then assembles it, which may include soldering a spout or handle into place. A finish may then be applied, and the item is polished and inspected. The spinning process is costly because it is a hand-guided operation. A large percentage of round work (bowls, tureens, gravy boats, etc.) is spun.

After the hollow bowl has been formed, it is decorated by hand using a process called *hand-chasing* in which small tools, a pitch, and a canvas-covered cushion filled with lead shot are used. The silver design is impressed into the surface of each item by tappings with a hammer, which push the silver from side to side to create a sign.

Engraving may also be done after the spinning process. Sharp tools, rather than a hammer, are used in engraving to carve out the silver and to perfect ornamental design.

Stamping Process

Silver blanks are stamped into the desired shape by huge steel dies that press and pound against the metal until an item is formed. Items with unusual contours such as spouts on teapots are made using this process. This process is also used to make such pieces as bowls, plates, creamers, and sugar bowls. Stamping is the most common process for shaping hollowware.

Casting Process

Casting is used for intricate shapes such as handles, ornate borders, and trophies. The silver, or other metal with a low melting point, is melted and poured into a mold.

HOW FLATWARE AND HOLLOWWARE ARE DECORATED

Silverware may be plain, or it may be ornately decorated. People seem to prefer some sort of design on their silver because decorations often disguise minute scratches. Few designs are put on articles made of stainless steel and gold-colored alloys because of their hard surfaces (see Figure 17.12). Fancy designs usually mean that the articles will cost more, according to the method of application (Figure 17.13).

Methods of Applying Decorations

Decoration is applied to silverware in many different ways. Some of these methods are discussed below.

1. *Applied borders*—These borders or strips of metal have been precast or prestamped and may be soldered onto the edge of silverware articles such as a teapot or vegetable dish. The borders may vary from a plain line or a thread to elaborate shell and flower motifs.

2. *Chasing*—special tools are used to tap indented designs on sterling silver or the copper base of plated articles. The metal is pushed in from the front to form the design, which is raised from the background. Machines may also be used to stamp the design on the metal.

3. *Embossing*—most flatware designs are applied by using this method. Designs to be embossed on metal are first carved into steel dies or plates. Then the dies impress the pattern onto the object. The design has alternately raised and lowered surfaces. Soft metals take more attractive and deeper impressions.

4. *Engine turning*—metal is decorated by a hand-controlled cutting machine which is made to follow the design of a master pattern or stencil.

5. *Engraving*—this expensive hand process differs from chasing in that metal is scratched off the surface by the engraver's tool. This process may apply motifs ranging from initials to very elaborate scrolls.

Figure 17.12
Plain hollowware bowls.
Courtesy of Oneida Silversmiths.

6. *Etching*—sterling silver or base metal may be coated with wax. Then the desired design is cut through the wax. The article is then immersed in a nitric acid bath. The acid eats into the exposed portions of the design not covered by the wax. The acid is washed off and the wax removed. Articles needing to be plated are then immersed in a plating bath.

7. *Hammering*—a bumpy textured surface on metal can be produced with a hammer, either by hand or machine. Pitchers, sugar bowls, and creamers made from plated silver may have this textured surface.

8. *Piercing*—small holes may be punched into the metal (either plated or sterling) with cutting dies.

9. *Repoussé*—this most expensive method of ornamenting sterling is done by hand. The design is beat out from the inside of the ware and on top with hammers, punches, and other tools. The term is popularly used to mean a combination of repoussé and chasing. This method may be applied on expensive coffee sets, tea sets, bowls, and other items.

Figure 17.13
Intricately decorated hollowware tea and coffee set.
Courtesy of Oneida Silversmiths.

CARE OF FLATWARE AND HOLLOWWARE

When caring for flatware and hollowware, remember the following points.

1. When silver is used often, it is less likely to tarnish as quickly as silver that is not in regular use. A point should be made to use all of the pieces of a silver collection.

2. Each silver piece should be separated before being packed in felt bags or airtight chests to prevent deep scratches.

3. Silver should be washed promptly and thoroughly with hot, soapy water and rinsed with hot water after each use. If food particles are left on silver too long, tarnishing and black spots may result.

4. Silver should be dried with a clean, soft cloth or chamois immediately after washing. It is important that the silver be completely dry before being put away to prevent tarnishing.

5. Tarnishing is caused by sulfur in the air or in food such as salad dressing which contains eggs. If tarnishing occurs, a good quality silver pol-

ish which is quick and easy to use should be rubbed on the silver pieces lengthwise with a very soft cloth. Use a soft brush to clean small crevices of ornate silver items.

6. As silver flatware is used, tiny scratches will appear, adding to its beauty. These tiny scratches, or *patina,* are desirable and add what is called a *butler finish.*

7. Silverplated flatware requires the same care as sterling silver.

8. Stainless steel flatware is widely accepted today because it requires little care. It is dishwasher safe and does not tarnish or stain. If discoloration occurs, a stainless polish may be used.

9. Gold-electroplated flatware is becoming increasingly popular because it is dishwasher safe and is highly resistant to tarnish and wear.

SELLING POINTS

Salespersons should observe the following points when selling silverware.

1. Stress the beauty, usefulness, popularity, versatility, balance, weight, and manufacturer of the sterling silver before giving the price.

2. Sell the pleasure of living with beautiful things; the excitement of entertaining with the best flatware and hollowware; the training of children in good manners through the use of sterling silver; and the legacy of a family's lifetime symbolized by its most precious possession.

3. Show the expensive pieces and let the customer decide if they are affordable.

4. Instill confidence in the customer that the pattern selected is right or that the gift selected is appropriate. When a customer is selecting a flatware pattern, show a few pieces of hollowware, too.

5. Let the customer hold each item he favors to give him the feeling of ownership. Remove the patterns the customer doesn't like. Ask questions to find out why the customer likes or dislikes specific patterns. Learn as much as possible about the customer's background, home, and way of entertaining.

6. Selling points may vary with each prospective customer, but some include the name of the pattern, name of the manufacturer, period of design, principal motif, recency of pattern (some customers like the latest; others prefer the traditional), appropriateness of the pattern to the customer's home, shape of the individual pieces, multiple uses, and availability of a complete service. Make a suggestion at this point.

KEY TERMS

1. Antique silver
2. Electroplating
3. Engine turning
4. Hallmark
5. Nickel silver
6. Open stock
7. Oxidizing
8. Pewter
9. Repoussé
10. Sheffield plate
11. Silver plate
12. Sterling silver
13. Triple plate
14. Vermeil

STUDY QUESTIONS

1. What is the difference between flatware and hollowware?
2. What is meant by single-plated? Double-plated?
3. Why does one sterling silver flatware pattern cost more than another?
4. What is meant by a table setting of silverware? What pieces are usually included?
5. What are five characteristics which determine the quality of stainless steel tableware?
6. What metal is most used as a base metal for hollowware? Why?
7. List the steps in the manufacture of hollowware.
8. What does a monogram do for each piece of silver?
9. Explain the uses of the following: candelabra, compotes, console sticks, and waiters.
10. How are silver flatware and hollowware cleaned, polished, and stored?

STUDY ACTIVITIES

1. Select four patterns in silverplated flatware: one in classical, one in contemporary, one in plain, and one in traditional design. Locate and place illustrations of each selected pattern in your notebook. Identify each design.
2. Visit a fine jewelry store in your area. Make a list of the hollowware and flatware that you see. Note the finish and metals used. Also determine what may be used for everyday and for special occasions.
3. Prepare a short discussion to be held with new salespeople about the care of flatware and hollowware.

CHAPTER **18**

Dinnerware

OBJECTIVES

After completing this chapter, you should be able to:

1. Identify pottery, semivitreous, and vitreous dinnerware.
2. Explain how ceramic and plastic dishes are manufactured.
3. Explain how ceramic and plastic dinnerware are decorated.
4. Classify the basic shapes, sizes, and types of dishes.
5. Explain how to care for ceramic and plastic dishes.
6. Explain how the types of dinnerware may be purchased.

Attractive dinnerware can create a gracious and hospitable mood whether it is a hurry-up breakfast with family members or a formal sit-down dinner for guests. Manufacturers and designers have anticipated dining desires by producing selections of dinnerware in all types, designs, colors, and prices for indoor and outdoor usage. Dinnerware is available in different weights and shapes. There is dinnerware that is durable, break-resistant, crack- and chip-resistant, microwave oven safe. Some is fragile and has to be hand-washed. Chinaware, earthenware, glassware, and stoneware that are used for food are known as *dinnerware*. Salespeople and buyers need to be well-acquainted with dinnerware in order to help customers select dinnerware to meet their personal tastes, budgets, lifestyles, types of entertaining, and number of family members.

EARTHENWARE

Earthenware dishes are made from clay and other materials found in the earth. Most dinnerware departments stock two kinds of earthenware dishes: (1) pottery and (2) semivitreous. *Pottery* dishes are not a very durable form of clayware because they are composed of crude, porous clay and are fired at low temperatures. The actual color is red or brown. Either transparent or opaque glazes, when applied and fired at high temperatures, will make the pottery sanitary, but if the pottery is chipped, it will absorb any liquid touching it. The transparent glaze is sometimes preferred to the opaque when the actual color of the clay is desired. Pottery dishes are handmade in many countries, and they may be heavy, colorful, informally decorated, and simply shaped.

Fine earthenware or *semivitreous* dishes are found in many homes because they are fired at higher temperatures than pottery ware. Therefore, the clay under the glaze is ss porous and more sanitary. *Ironstone* is an example. It wears better than pottery dishes. It does not chip readily, but it does absorb moisture because of its porosity. Ironstone is sometimes confused with stoneware, which is vitrified ware.

STONEWARE

This dinnerware was widely used in Europe for centuries and has become popular in the United States in the last two decades. It is a mixture of different clays that can withstand high firing temperatures and thereby obtain the highly desirable qualities of the hard, nonporous *(vitrified)* china finish. At the same time, it may provide a more casual pottery look when the color finishes are opaque. It is thicker than fine china. Stoneware may be left unglazed and uncolored because it is vitrified.

Some manufacturers glaze only the inside surface where the food contacts the ware. The high firing temperature makes stoneware especially durable. It is dishwasher and microwave oven safe. Stoneware can be taken from the oven, used on the table, and placed in the freezer. The exceptions that may not be placed in the freezer are high-walled pieces filled with liquid. This is because the liquid may expand when frozen and cause the stoneware to crack.

CHINAWARE

Chinaware is the finest, most expensive, durable, and most fragile-looking ceramic ware. It is so translucent that shadows of the fingers can be seen through a piece of dinnerware when held to the light. It imparts a clear, bell-like tone when a dish, held carefully at the base, is tapped gently on the edge with a pencil or the fingertip. China is fired at such a high temperature that the clay particles meet and fuse to make it completely nonporous. It is *vitrified* to make it look glossy by heat and fusion.

Chinaware was first made in China about 1000 A.D. from a fine, white clay called *kaolin* (silicate of alumina). It was exported to Europe, where it became known as *chinaware*. In the United States it is generally known as *china*, while the Europeans generally call it *porcelain*. Various experiments in England by Josiah Spode led to the development of *bone china*, where bone ash was pulzerized and added to kaolin instead of feldspar. This process increases translucency and whiteness.

Most chinaware sold in the United States today, when not made domestically, is imported from England, France, Japan, Germany, and Scandinavia.

MAKING CERAMIC WARE

In making fine chinaware and earthenware, all the impurities must be removed. The clays are washed, filtered, and mixed with water to form *slip,* a mixture the consistency of thick cream. The slip is further refined by screening and agitation, and in the case of fine chinaware or earthenware, it is poured over magnets to attract all iron particles, which might leave red or dark brown marks on the ware.

The slip then flows into filter cloths where excess water is removed. The slabs of moist clay are stored for several weeks for aging to improve their plasticity; this makes the clay easier to work. The air bubbles are removed from the clay and the clay is blended with a pug mill. This machine minces, squeezes, and compresses the clay, then extrudes it from various shaped openings ready to be shaped.

Table 18.1 lists various materials used to make ceramic dishes, and the reasons for using each one.

Forming the Clay

The most expensive way to form clay is by hand. A piece of moist clay is placed on a fast-revolving turntable called the *potter's wheel.* The person who shapes the clay by hand as the wheel revolves is called a *potter* (see Figure 18.1). Articles shaped by the hand of the potter are considered to represent the highest form of potter's art.

Machines called *jollies* or *jiggers* are used in factories to press the outside or inside of the clay against a mold while the clay is revolving on the turntable (see Figure 18.2). This shapes the inside and outside of the ware at the same time. Jiggering is the word used to describe the shaping of flat and oval pieces of ceramic ware such as plates, platters, and saucers. This method utilizes the moist clay form called *plug.* Jollying is the term used to describe the shaping of hollowware such as bowls, cups, coffeepots, and vases. This method incorporates the use of the liquid clay slip.

Handles or spouts may be made by adding pieces of clay to be squeezed between the bottom and top half of a mold. Another ware may be cast by pouring slip into a porous plaster of paris mold and letting it set. Once the outer edges set, the center liquid is poured out, leaving a hollow center in a ware. Drying shrinks the clay in the mold so that it can be easily removed.

TABLE 18.1 MATERIALS USED IN CERAMIC DISHES

MATERIALS	REASONS FOR USE
Clay, common china clay, or kaolin	It is the basic material used in making pottery. Mixed with water, it gives plasticity to the paste. The ware will keep its form during the firing. It is the whitest, purest, finest, strongest clay used for fine china.
Ball clay or blue clay	Semivitreous ware is made from a mixture of china clay and ball or blue clay which adds moldability and strength to the body.
Feldspar	It is a crystalline mineral which melts at a low temperature and is used, in powder form, as a flux to hold the clay particles together. When the materials are combined and heated at a certain temperature, feldspar gives translucency to chinaware.
Flint	It is a hard stone that is heated until it becomes white. It is ground and mixed with clay to help hold the body of the ware in shape and to add strength.
Bone ash	Animal bones are burned and crushed into powder. Bone ash replaces flint in making bone china. Bone ash helps fuse the clay particles together. It adds whiteness and strength to the body of bone china.
Nephelene syenite	This material is used as flux and has a long and flexible firing range. It makes a body so strong that it is possible to make extremely thin pieces to stand hard use. Example: Franciscan china.
Beryllium	Used as a salt in the glaze on Franciscan china, giving it an extremely hard and brilliant surface.
Tin	Used in glazes in English delftware and in tin-enamel glaze coatings on majolica ware.
Silica	An abundant mineral used in ceramic glazes and high quality clayware bodies.
Salt	A glaze obtained by injecting salt into the kiln during the glaze firing. It has a semimat or half-glossy pitted look.
Cobalt	A silver-white metallic oxide used to produce the ceramic color cobalt blue, which is a deep, rich blue.
Silver	A type of decoration in which silver is applied to the clayware in the desired design by an electrolytic process and then bonded to the ware by firing.
Platinum	Using an etched design to decorate dishes. The raised design may be covered with platinum paint; then it is fired.
Gold	An etched design is used to decorate dishes. The raised design may be covered with gold paint; then it is fired.

Figure 18.1
A potter forming the shape of a vase on a potter's wheel.
Courtesy of Lenox, Inc.

Attaching Handles, Spouts, and Ornaments

Slip acts as a bond between the damp, but not soft, greenware body and the handle or spout to be affixed. After trimming or smoothing the handle or other piece, the ends to be attached to the body are dipped into slip and then pressed against the cup or pot. The excess slip is wiped away (Figure 18.3). This bonding pro-

Figure 18.2
Jigger machine is used to shape the ceramic ware.
Courtesy of Lenox, Inc.

cess has proved to be so strong that a handle or spout will rarely break at the bonding point.

FIRING THE WARE

Ware that is fired once and has no glaze is called *bisque* or *biscuit*. Greenware, or clay that has never been fired, will shrink up to one-fifth its original size during the first firing process.

Figure 18.3
After the slip has dried, the excess is removed by hand.
Courtesy of Lenox, Inc.

Crude pottery, fine earthenware, and finer chinaware are fired at temperatures that range from low for crude pottery to very high for chinaware. Better materials and workmanship are needed in a ceramic ware as the degree of heat is increased. Temperatures range from about 1000 degrees Celsius (about 1800 degrees Fahrenheit) or lower for pottery to 1150 degrees Celsius for earthenware and 1250 to 1600 degrees Celsius (about 2280 to 2900 degrees Fahrenheit) for hard paste porcelain china.

The specialized *tunnel* kiln is used for firing ceramic ware. Greenware is placed in the bisque kiln in fired clay boxes. The kiln is about 200 feet long. About seventy to ninety hours are required in this first biscuit fire. Beginning with a temperature of 300 degrees Fahrenheit, cars move mechanically through temperatures which gradually reach a peak of 2300 degrees Fahrenheit. Then the heat drops gradually. When the product leaves the kiln, it has been transformed from clay to china and is called biscuit. The body is completely vitrified; all particles have melted and fused together.

GLAZE APPLICATION

The glaze, or glassy coating, is applied to earthenware to make it nonporous and to add a luster to it. The glaze on chinaware gives it beauty, makes it pleasant to eat from, and makes it easy to clean. Various formulas for glaze are used. It usually contains finely ground glass. If a glaze is made dull-looking, it is called a *mat* glaze. Glaze may be painted or sprayed on, or the product may be dipped into it.

The glazed ware is readied for a second firing *(glost firing)* at a lower temperature than the biscuit firing. The pieces of ware are kept separate so that the glaze will not melt and weld them together. Usually the marks where the ware rested during the second firing are ground away so they do not show on fine chinaware. *Crazing* may be a problem with earthenware when minute cracks form on the glaze or enamel due to uneven expansion of the clay and shrinkage. Crazing does not occur with chinaware because the body of the ware and glaze are both nonporous and therefore contract and expand at the same time.

Decorating Ceramic Ware

The difference in the prices of different sets of ceramic ware may be due to the countries where they are made, the raw materials used, the kind of care given to making the ware (Figure 18.4), but especially the difference in the quantity and kind of decoration used. It is important that buyers and salespeople in the chinaware department know why decorations greatly affect the price of ceramic ware.

There are specific times during the making of ceramics that ceramic ware may be decorated. Decorations are usually applied while the ware is being shaped, after the biscuit firing, during the coloring of the glaze, or after the overglaze has been put on. The more handwork and costly materials used in decorating, the more expensive the ware becomes.

Moist Clay Decorations

One of the oldest methods of decorating is incising, cutting, or scratching designs into the moist clay ware. *Lattice work effects* are made by cutting out areas of clay. *Rice patterns* are made by small holes glazed over to make transparent spots in the ware.

Relief (raised) motifs are done in several ways. The mold may be grooved to make slightly raised or lowered designs. Separate clay designs may be molded

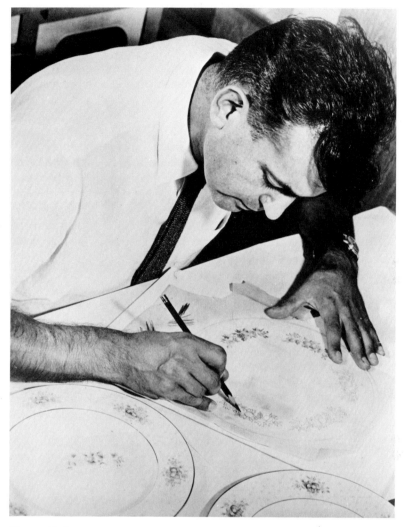

Figure 18.4
Designer is working on minute pattern detail. Hundreds of such sketches will be made and many hundreds of hours spent before a design concept will become a pattern reality.
Courtesy of Lenox, Inc.

and applied to the ware, using slip to keep them in place. Wedgewood jasperware is made using slip decoration formed in a mold.

Graffito, or *sgraffito,* is a process by which a design is made when two layers of different colored clay are stacked together, and the top layer is scratched away until the lower layer of clay is revealed and a design is formed.

Resist designs may be made by placing a sizing over the clay to protect certain areas. The whole surface is then coated with the desired enamel color or luster. The sizing is removed by scraping or washing, leaving the protected areas white.

Slip decoration means decorating ware with raised motifs of liquid clay of different heights or painting with colored slip. The ware must be fired after decoration has been applied.

Underglaze Decorations

Color motifs are applied on the biscuit ware after the first firing. Dishes are usually decorated this way because the colors and design details will be protected by the glaze that will be applied later. The intense heat needed to melt the glaze limits the colors that are used; however, research is increasing the number of underglaze colors. Cobalt blue is a much used color that was developed early by the Chinese. Precious metals, such as gold and platinum, are never used as underglaze decorations because they burn away. The glaze gives permanency to the colors and designs.

In-the-Glaze Decorations

The transparent glazes allow the clay to show through the glaze. Opaque glazes cover the color of the clay. Colored glazes give a solid-color look to clay ware such as earthenware sets and ornaments.

Varicolored glazes may be given to clay ware. One part of the ware may be given a transparent glaze and another part given a colored or opaque glaze, imparting a banded-design look.

Lusterware has a metallike look and has been made for many centuries. Metallic powder is added to the glaze, and this thin metal deposit covers part or all of the surface with a mirrorlike sheen.

Crackle glaze is caused by quickly cooling the glazed ware after it has been fired. Fine crazed lines appear over the surface of ware. The Chinese developed this design centuries ago.

Overglaze Decorations

Overglaze decorations, applied after the wares have been glazed, add to the cost of the ware. Gold and platinum are applied during overglaze; otherwise, they will burn away. Certain color tints and shades are applied as an overglaze. The overglaze decorations may rub off in time or if improperly handled.

Overglaze decorations can usually be identified by a slight dullness in texture when fingertips are passed over them. Light that is reflected along the ware's surface will show a dullness of design if it is an overglaze design. A glazed surface will reflect the light smoothly over the entire area.

METHODS OF APPLYING DESIGNS TO CERAMICS

Handpainting is one of the oldest methods used to apply designs to ceramics (Figure 18.5). However, it is expensive and requires great skill. *Engraved lines* may be

Figure 18.5
A jewel-like effect is created by hand-applied, raised enamel dots.
Courtesy of Lenox, Inc.

made in clay for designs. Holes may be carved into the clay as patterns. A slip may be used to build *raised decorations* into the clay. A low, raised design, called *low bas relief,* may be formed in a mold that has a carved-out design which gives a dish a different pattern.

Multicolored clays are used to make *colored designs* by putting them over the glaze or on the bisque, or by coloring the glaze. Other methods besides hand-painting may be used to apply designs to ceramics.

Transfer printing, or *copperplate decoration,* is an expensive method of applying designs on ceramic ware because handwork is used. The design is engraved or printed on a copper plate and then filled with the desired color and transferred to tissue paper. The tissue paper is pressed against the ware and rubbed until the design has been transferred. The paper is then removed by washing, leaving the design, which is fired onto the dish. This method requires much handwork, particularly in adding color, because only one color can be put on at a time.

Stamping the design on the ware is similar to the transfer printing method, but it is less expensive. The desired design is cut into a rubber stamp. The stamp is dipped into the color material and pressed against the dish. This design is used for lacelike border designs or one-color patterns on inexpensive dishes. If *liquid bright gold* is used, it may be fused to the ware in the final firing, then later carefully polished using fine silver sand or an agate stone to burnish it. Its shiny finish does not need polish. Care should be used in washing and storing these dishes.

Decalcomania (often called *decal*) is a transfer design method that resembles handpainting. The design is printed on an especially prepared tissue paper. The paper is pressed against the ware, which has received a coat of varnishlike material. The design is rubbed carefully and transferred from the paper onto the dish or ware. The paper is washed off and the dish is fired, causing the design to be permanent. Dishes can be given colorful designs at lower costs than if they were done by hand.

Silk-screen printing uses color designs that are put on silk screens and then applied to the dish. Colors are put on one at a time. It is an inexpensive method of decorating china.

Etched design is a method of applying a design on the glazed surface of a dish or on glass dinnerware to give a design effect. The pattern is put on the dish with an acid-resistant wax substance covering the parts not to be etched; the rest of the dish is left uncovered. The dish is given an acid bath. The wax is washed off, leaving the design on the surface. The raised design may be covered with gold or platinum paint. This decoration is called *encrusted* ware. It is then fired.

PLASTIC DINNERWARE

Materials Used in Manufacturing

Melamine, the raw base material used for nearly all plastic dinnerware, was discovered in Europe in 1834. Over a hundred years passed before this chemical oddity was rediscovered.

The United States Navy entered into a joint venture with two plastic molding companies during World War II and developed grayish colored melamine plastic dishes that could be used on ships. They were break-resistant, light in weight, and sanitary to use. In 1946, manufacturers introduced melamine dishes to restaurants, hospitals, and institutions. Immediately thereafter, the consumer market boomed, even though the first dishes were durable, heavy, institutional in appearance, and produced only in solid colors. Gradually, new shapes were developed and dishes became more delicate, more graceful, less institutional-looking, but still durable.

In 1952 the first plastic melamine line to feature a bas-relief or raised decoration was introduced. The next major improvement in decoration was the multi-color overlay, a printed paper sheet that has been impregnated with melamine resin. It is similar to the decal used in decorating ceramic ware.

Melamine plastic dinnerware was originally sold through housewares departments and specialty stores. As styling improved and with the introduction of a variety of patterns, colors, and shapes, the dinnerware was upgraded. The higher styled melamine ware is now merchandised through china and glassware departments and the more utilitarian ware through housewares.

Plastic melamine dinnerware is popular for today's casual living (see Figure 18.6). It is mar-, heat-, and break-resistant and will not crack or chip in normal household use. It may be washed in a dishwasher, and the colors and patterns are offered in many combinations. It is ideal for families with young children and for

Figure 18.6
Plastic melamine dinnerware is practical because of its crack and chip resistance.
Courtesy of Bootonware Dinnerware.

using on picnics or while camping because it is lightweight and nearly unbreakable. Its disadvantages are that stains from coffee and tea may need special cleaning; it can be scratched by sharp knives; and it will char if exposed to flames. Plastic dinnerware should not be placed near a fire or in an oven hotter than 270 degrees Fahrenheit.

Decorating Plastic Dishes

Plastic dishes may come in white, colors, and in various patterns. Colors and patterns must be added before the dishes are shaped in the mold. During the forming of the dish, two layers of different colors of plastic may be fused together; for example, a white layer may be inside and a colored layer outside. Each new step in the manufacturing process adds to the manufacturing costs.

The first decorative patterns were applied to plastic dishes in 1955. The patterns are applied by using a sheet of melamine with the pattern design imprinted on it. This sheet of melamine is called a *foil*. The foil is placed in the mold, and the whole dish is fused in one operation that becomes a permanent pattern. The patterns do not rub off or wash away.

HOW DISHES ARE CLASSIFIED

The classification of dishes may be made in several ways. The shape, type, and size of dishes are commonly used classifications.

Basic Shapes of Flat Dishes

There are two basic shapes for flat dishes and plates. They are *coupe* and *rim*. A dish that has no flat edge for holding while serving is called a *coupe* dish. A dish that has a flat edge for holding while serving is known as a *rim* dish. The rim is often decorated.

Types of Dishes

The different types of dishes that have different kinds of uses and may be found in the chinaware department include those listed below:

Plates
Dinner, 10-inch
Luncheon, 9-inch
Salad or Tea (also used for dessert), 8-inch
Bread and Butter, 6-inch

Soup Dishes
Cream Soup Bowl and Stand
Soup/Cereal Bowl

Bouillon—a cup with two side handles.

Coupe—a large bowl with no rim.

Rimmed—a large bowl with rim.

Miscellaneous Dishes

Teacup

After-Dinner Cup (Demitasse)—a small cup used for after-dinner coffee.

After-Dinner Saucer

Coffee Pot with Cover

Teapot with Cover

Fruit Bowl—small individual bowls used for serving fruits, vegetables, puddings at the side of the dinner plates.

Gravy Boat or Sauce Boat—an oblong or rounded bowl with a separate or an attached saucer. They may have handles and spouts.

Gravy Boat Stand

Platter, Large—a flat serving plate that may be any sized and may be round, oval, or square. It might not have handles. Used for serving meats and other food.

Vegetable Dish with Cover

Vegetable Dish, Round (Nappy)—An open dish that comes in varying sizes.

Vegetable Dish, Oval (Baker)—An open dish that comes in varying sizes.

Sugar with Cover

Cream Pitcher

Tureen Serving Bowl—a large serving bowl with two side handles and a cover. It is used for serving beans, soup, or stew.

Casserole, Individual (Ramekin) Dish—Round, covered vegetable dish.

Egg Cup—an hourglass cup made to hold an egg that is to be eaten from the shell.

Salt and Pepper Shakers—they may be small for individual service or large for use in the center of the table.

Familiar names of United States-made dinnerware are as follows:

Trade Name	Dinnerware Made
Anchor-Hocking	Commercial weight china
Corning	Ironstone and glass (Corelle)
Fostoria	Glass
Frankoma	Earthenware
Gorham	Fine china
Haviland	Fine china
Hull Pottery	Earthenware
Iron Mountain	Stoneware
Lenox	Fine china
Lexington	Plastic
Libby-Owens-Illinois	Glass
Melamine	Plastic
Metlox	Plastic
Pickard	Fine china

Plastic Manufacturing	Plastic
Royal China (Jeannette Corp.)	Ironstone and plastic
Salem China	China, stoneware, and ironstone
Syracuse	China
Western	Stoneware
Zanesville	Stoneware

Familiar names of foreign-made dinnerware are as follows:

Trade Names	Country	Dinnerware Made
Ceralene-Raynaud	France (Limoge)	Fine china
Dansk	Denmark	Fine china and stoneware
Delft (House of Goebel)	England	Fine china
Derby	England	Stoneware
Haviland	France	Fine china
Herend	Hungary	Fine china
Jenson	Denmark	Stoneware
Johnson Brothers	England	Stoneware
Lipper	Japan	Fine china
M.E. International	England	Fine china and earthenware
Mikasa	Japan	Fine china, ironstone, and stoneware
Noritake	Japan	Fine china
Rosenthal	West Germany	Fine china
Royal Albert	England	Fine china
Royal Worchester-Spode	England	Fine china
Staffordshire	England	Fine china
Tienshan	China	Fine china
Villeroy and Boch	Western Germany	Fine china
Wedgewood (Royal Doulton)	England	Fine china, earthenware, and stoneware

DETERMINING SIZES OF DISHES

Flat dinnerware (plates, platters, and saucers) are measured in two ways, overall and well-to-edge measurement (see Figure 18.7). The easiest measurement is called the *overall measurement*. The diameter of the dish is measured from one edge to the other. This way of measurement is used by manufacturers of coupe-shaped dishes. *Well-to-edge measurement* is another way to measure dishes. It is also called the *trade measurement*. The dish is measured from the inside rim across the dish to the outside of the rim. Most older dinnerware manufacturers measure this way as shown in their price lists. Some price lists also show round vegetable bowls measured by diameter of opening and oval bowls measured by length of opening. Oval platters and gravy boats may be measured by length.

BUYING AND SELLING DISHES

Dishes are bought and sold in various combinations. Chinaware departments offer combination sets, place settings, and open stock.

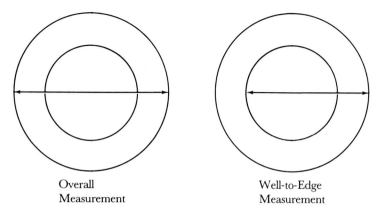

Overall
Measurement

Well-to-Edge
Measurement

Figure 18.7
Two methods of determining dish size.

Sets

Original purchases of dishes may be made in sets. There is usually a price advantage when purchasing the whole set. Also, a few serving pieces may be included. The size of sets may vary according to the number of dishes desired for each serving and the number of persons to be served.

Sets of dishes are assembled and may be purchased in groups sufficient to serve four or more people with the basic pieces needed for a meal. The most common sets are four, six, eight, and twelve persons. The number of dishes (pieces) in a given set (service) vary. For example, sets may be as follows:

12 piece set for 4	47 piece set for 8
16 piece set for 4	60 piece set for 12
20 piece set for 4	67 piece set for 12
32 piece set for 6	105 piece set for 12
40 piece set for 6	

Place Settings

Higher priced chinaware is generally puchased by the *place setting* to keep the price at a comparatively popular level. This enables a person on a budget to purchase expensive dishes a few at a time. Purchases of one or more pieces of a place setting are also popular wedding gifts arranged through selected retail stores. A place setting is a complete service for one person composed of three, four, five, and infrequently six pieces. The number of pieces is often determined by the local business according to its clientele. A buffet place setting of three pieces includes one dinner plate, one tea cup, and one saucer. A four-piece place setting includes one dinner plate, one salad plate, one tea cup, and one saucer. A five-piece dinner place setting includes one dinner plate, one salad plate, one bread and butter plate, one tea cup, and one saucer. Sometimes a sixth piece is added to place settings; it is a soup/cereal bowl. Because some place settings are becoming so expensive, salespeople are recommending to customers that they can mix and match other dinnerware patterns and materials. As long as they go together, you may use two decorated pieces with one plain or two plain with one decorated. Stainless steel, brassware, and pewter pieces may go with various patterns of flatware, stemware, and dinnerware.

A typical 20-piece setting for four (often called a "basic service" or "starter set") includes:

4 dinner plates	4 tea cups
4 salad plates	4 saucers
4 bread and butter plates	

A typical 47-piece set for eight includes:

8 dinner plates	1 large platter
8 salad plates	1 rounded open vegetable dish
8 bread and butter plates	1 oval open vegetable dish
8 tea cups	1 gravy boat
8 saucers	1 sugar bowl with cover (2 pieces)
	1 creamer

All of the pieces in a set are counted, including the sugar bowl with cover (two pieces). A salt and pepper set also counts as two separate pieces.

Open Stock

Open stock dinnerware is sold in individual pieces or small groups rather than in complete, predetermined combinations such as place settings or sets. A dish is in open stock only so long as the manufacturer continues to make that particular design. Customers often mistake the term to mean available for an indefinite period of time. When buying expensive dinnerware that will be used for several years, customers should make sure that they can purchase matching dishes to offset breakage or to add more pieces or place settings.

Closed stock means that particular dinnerware is available only in the sets that the retailer has for sale because the manufactuer did not make extra pieces in that particular pattern.

HOW TO STORE DINNERWARE

Dinnerware may be enjoyed more if storage problems are minimized or eliminated by doing a little planning and organizing.

Use separate pads or paper napkins between fine china plates when storing them. Fine china that is seldom used should be stored in zipped, quilted cases of padded plastic with protector pads. These will protect dinnerware from dust and breakage. Cups should not be stacked. Place them on shelves individually or hang them on a rack or on hooks.

Stack ceramic, earthenware, glass, ironstone, and plastic dinnerware one on top of another with no pads between each one. Place them one at a time on top of another — *do not slide one onto another.*

If storage space is limited, use cabinet organizers. Dinnerware may be protected from nicks and accidental breakage by using dinnerware racks. These racks may hold a service for eight in a minimum of space. Also available are cup stackers, revolving or sliding cup racks, plate racks and platter racks that are made from welded steel frames covered with a protective cushion-coating.

CARE OF DINNERWARE

Follow the following suggestions in order to preserve dinnerware:

1. *Fine china* can be washed either in a dishwasher or by hand.

2. China with hand-applied precious metal borders should always be hand-washed.

3. Coffee or tea stains should be removed using borax on a soft cloth.

4. Use paper napkins or rinse with water to remove remains of food off plates. Never scrape or use abrasive cleaning powder.

5. A soft brush is useful when washing fluted china.

6. Always wash china separately from silverware, cutlery, and pans.

7. When washing fine china by hand, place a rubber mat in the bottom of the sink and use a water sprayer with a nozzle.

8. Wash china in warm water using a soft brush or sponge and a mild soap or detergent.

9. Remove diamond rings from your hands; they may scratch any surface.

10. Do not use soap pads or steel wool.

11. Use hot water to rinse china dishes and air-dry them upright in a rubber or plastic-coated dishrack.

12. Polish china with a clean, dry cloth.

13. If an automatic dishwasher is used to wash fine china, certain precautions must be taken. Load the plates so that they do not touch and scratch each other. Select and use a mild soap or detergent.

14. Do not place china directly on a burner or open flame. Always use insulated pot holders to handle warm dishes.

15. Fine china that has a precious metal band is *not* safe for use in microwave ovens.

16. *Earthenware, ironstone, and stoneware dinnerware* are usually washed in the same manner as fine china. Use mild soap and a soft dish cloth and avoid steel wool and gritty cleaners which scratch the glazed surface.

17. Some hand-painted dinnerware that has been inproperly fired will not withstand any kind of vigorous washing. If in doubt about any particular type of dinnerware, follow the manufacturer's directions.

18. Many brands come with washing instructions included. You may have to precool or preheat dishes before placing them in the refrigerator or in water.

19. Ovenglaze coloring on handles may rub off; therefore, place cups so they do not touch.

20. Ironstone and stoneware are usually dishwasher and microwave oven safe. They may have oven-table-freezer use. Do not freeze pitchers, cups, or high wall vessels when filled with liquid or cracking may result.

21. *Plastic dishes* require little care. Although break-resistant, they may chip or crack if they hit a hard surface.

22. Plastic dishes may be washed in a dishwasher.

23. Melamine dishes resist temperature extremes such as boiling water and use in refrigerators. No plastic ware should be put in an oven over 270 degrees Fahrenheit.

24. Coffee and tea stains in cups may be removed by soaking the cups in a little baking soda in water or by using commercial cleaners sold for this purpose. Do not scrub the cups with cleaning pads or any type of gritty cleanser.

25. Sharp knives will scratch the surface of plastic dishes.

SELLING POINTS

Salespersons selling dinnerware should observe the following selling points:

1. Suggest that china should be selected first in the table arrangement. Because of its color, the type of pattern, its size and shape, it is the most important part on the table and should dictate the scheme of the setting and establish the mood of the entire table. All other appointments should be chosen to harmonize with it.

2. Rather than focusing on tableware, talk about a fine dining atmosphere, tasteful home decoration, harmonious design, enduring pride in ownership of distinctive tableware for special entertaining and for regular home use.

3. Select china that reflects the customer's lifestyle.

4. Emphasize the qualities of various types of china, china designs, manufacturers, and imports.

5. Offer your expert help to customers, especially brides, who need help in selecting patterns, in deciding what pieces to buy, and in estimating costs to fit their budgets.

6. Customers are interested in the differences between fine china, bone china, earthenware, and pottery and the qualities offered by each one.

7. Fine china has a bell-like tone when struck lightly with a pencil.

8. Hold a fine china plate against the light and notice the shadow of the fingers showing through it. It is delicate, but also hard and durable.

9. Point out how patterns can be matched and bought later from open stock by the customer or as gifts by friends. Broken pieces may be replaced and extra pieces may be purchased to match present patterns through open stock.

10. Tell customers how to take care of their dinnerware.

KEY TERMS

1.	Biscuit	7.	Open stock
2.	Closed stock	8.	Overall measurement
3.	Coupe dish	9.	Place setting
4.	Decalcomania	10.	Sets
5.	Foil	11.	Stamping
6.	Gravy boat	12.	Transfer printing

STUDY QUESTIONS

1. Explain the differences between vitreous and semivitreous wares. Give an example of each.
2. What is meant by chinaware, bone china, ironstone, and stoneware?
3. What raw materials are used for adding strength, shape retention, and translucency? What is the basic raw material of china?
4. Explain how handles, spouts, etc., are formed and joined to the dishes.
5. Explain the following ways of decorative ceramics: in-the-clay, underglaze, in-the-glaze, and overglaze.
6. Name the three different combinations in which dishes may be purchased.
7. Explain briefly the three ways that clay objects are shaped.
8. What two measurements are used with dinnerware? Explain each briefly.
9. Name two basic shapes for plates and other flat dishes.
10. Why is it important to know how to care for ceramic and plastic dishes?

STUDY ACTIVITIES

1. Clip several advertisements or pictures from catalogs, magazines, or newspapers of the dinnerware listed below and mount them on paper:

Earthenware	Porcelain china
Ironstone	Bone china
Stoneware	Plastic ware

   Under each advertisement or picture give the price and selling points of the dinnerware.

2. Visit the dinnerware department in a store. Study the displays of earthenware, stoneware, chinaware, glassware, and plastic ware. Write a brief report about your visit, including comments on price range and the amount of information conveyed to the customer (quality, durability, care).

3. Diagram the various steps in the manufacture of a dish.

CHAPTER 19

Housewares

After completing this chapter, you should be able to:

1. Explain the advantages and disadvantages of cast iron and copper as major materials used in the manufacture of cooking utensils.

2. Describe two ways to prevent cast iron and steel from rusting. Also describe the effects cast iron and steel utensils have on preparing food.

3. Compare the effect that the gauge of sheet and cast aluminum has on cooking.

4. List the various types of cooking utensils given in the chapter and describe their use and how to care for each utensil.

5. Describe and compare two nonstick coatings currently used to prevent food from sticking on pans.

6. Explain how to care for the small electric appliances discussed in the chapter.

Cooking utensils were once the cook's private concern, but now they are also the decorator's. As objects of art, they hang from pegboards on the kitchen wall or from chef's racks above the stove.

The amount of money spent on pots and pans imported into the United States has more than tripled in the 1980s. Copper pans come from Portugal and France; porcelain-on-iron from Denmark, France, and Japan; cast iron from Korea and Taiwan.

Most pots and pans are available as open stock, but cookware can also be bought in sets, usually at some savings per piece. The typical set has six to nine pieces. The nonstick revolution of the early 1960s has stuck, and more than half the cooking utensils sold today have nonstick coatings.

Important features of cookware include heat distribution and ease in handling and cleaning. Sturdiness of construction, the kind and amount of materials used, the price, the design, the finish, the usage, the size, and the workmanship are also important considerations.

MATERIALS USED TO MAKE COOKING UTENSILS

Each of the materials commonly used for cooking utensils has its good points. Knowing the characteristics of different materials will help you decide which to choose for different uses.

Metals

The following metals are used for cooking utensils.

Cast Iron

The Pilgrims brought cast iron pots with them to this country. Cast iron utensils have been the choice of cooks for years because they last a lifetime and improve with use year after year. Cast iron heats slowly but builds up to a medium-to-high surface temperature that maintains heat for economical food preparation. Cast iron is excellent for slow stewing.

Most manufacturers *preseason* their cast iron ware, then lacquer it to prevent rusting. To season a cast iron ware after it has been stored for a length of time, rub it with cooking oil and place the ware in the oven for several hours. The pores in the cast iron become well-lubricated with the cooking oil, leaving a surface excellent for preparing breaded foods, fish, meats, and potatoes.

Advantages of cast iron are that it is inexpensive, durable, and excellent for browning, frying, and stewing foods. Cast iron also imparts good flavor to foods cooked on it.

Some of its disadvantages are its color, it can rust if not carefully and immediately dried, its heavy weight, and certain foods stick to it. Cast iron will not warp, but it may crack if dropped or placed in cold water while hot.

Steel

Steel is made from pig iron that has had impurities removed and carbon added. It can be rolled into sheets from which thin utensils like cookie sheets or saucepans may be shaped by stamping.

Sheet Steel.   Sheet metal utensils, such as frying pans, are thinner and lighter than cast iron and can be easily produced and varied with finishes. However, they do not cook food as slowly, retain heat as long, or heat as evenly as the iron ware, and they may warp or bend after use. Sheet steel utensils may turn dark or rust if not cared for properly.

Stainless Steel. One of today's most glamourous, versatile, and useful metals, stainless steel is exceptionally durable and takes an excellent polish. Once stainless steel has been stamped, spun, or formed into a utensil, it takes an extremely hard blow to dent it. Its shiny finish won't corrode or tarnish permanently, and its hard, nonporous surface resists wear and scratches.

Like other steels, stainless steel is an alloy. It is a combination of iron and other metals. What makes it different from other steels, however, is that it contains at least 11 percent chromium. It is the chromium that makes the steel "stainless" all the way through.

Stainless steel may also contain other elements, such as nickel, molybdenum, columbium, or titanium. These materials can contribute special hardness, high temperature resistance, and resistance to scratching and corrosion to the finished stainless steel alloy.

Aluminum

Aluminum is one of the most commonly used metals for cooking utensils. It is a naturally soft metal and can be made into pots and pans of all shapes. The addition of small amounts of other metals to make aluminum alloys and various manufacturing processes give the better aluminum wares resistance to bending and warping. Aluminum utensils are either cast or formed from sheet metal.

Sheet aluminum is made in different thicknesses or gauges. Pans made from medium to heavy gauges are very durable. Utensils of very light weights are the least expensive, but they are too thin to stand up under daily use and the food may scorch easily. Thin metal is satisfactory for pans that are used only occasionally. For ovenware, lighter gauge aluminum than that found in good quality top-of-stove pans may be used.

Cast aluminum is heavier than most of the sheet aluminum used in pans. It is rigid, does not warp, is very durable, and in good quality resists pitting. It is not often used for baking pans.

Whether cast or sheet, aluminum distributes heat evenly. Except for large pieces of cast or extra-heavy-gauge sheet metal, aluminum utensils are light enough to be handled easily.

Brightly polished aluminum ovenware reflects heat so that food browns very lightly. Unpolished or dull-finished aluminum absorbs heat and produces a browner crust.

Though easily darkened by alkalies in foods and water, aluminum responds readily to polishing with steel wool. A fine cleansing powder should be used on a highly polished or chrome-plated finish. Rubbing with ordinary household acids such as cream of tartar, lemon juice, or vinegar will brighten darkened areas. You may also cook an acid food such as tomatoes or rhubarb in the pan. There is no evidence that the darkening of aluminum has any harmful effect on food or that aluminum can have any effect on health.

Do not leave salty food or liquids standing in aluminum; they may cause pitting of the metal. Manufacturers advise that baking soda should not be added to foods cooked in aluminum because it will discolor the metal.

Glass

Manufacturers have developed three types of heat-resistant glassware for cooking: (1) borosilicate, (2) glass-ceramic, and (3) laminated glass.

Borosilicate glassware contains boric oxide which helps prevent expansion and contraction when exposed to temperature extremes. Familar trademarks of these baking dishes and cookware are Fire King, Glassbake, and Pyrex. This glassware must be preheated with hot water before placing on a hot surface to prevent breakage. It should never be placed on a cold surface.

Glass-ceramic glassware is made from a substance of part glass and part ceramic. It is used mostly for cook-and-serve ware. Other products may be coffee pots, teapots, and frying pans. This glass can withstand extreme temperature changes, but will break if dropped on a hard surface. Familiar trademarks of this glassware are Pyroceram and Centura.

Laminated glassware resembles chinaware and is made of a dense glass core covered on both sides by a thin coating of clear glass. Corelle and Flameware are examples of laminated glassware trademarks. Advantages of laminated cookware are that it is easily cleaned, holds heat better than metal utensils for baking, may be used as dinnerware or be placed directly in the freezer, and food being cooked may be observed through transparent tempered glass lids.

Plastics

The two basic types of plastics found in kitchenware are *thermoplastic* and *thermosetting*.

Thermoplastics soften, melt, and change shape when heated and harden when cooled. Many kitchenware items, such as spatulas and mixing bowls, are made of thermoplastics. This ware is formed under heat and pressure from a dry state, and permanent patterns are applied during the molding process. Acrylics, cellulose plastics, nylons, polyolefins, styrenes, urethanes, and vinyls are among the thermoplastics used.

Thermosetting plastics are shaped by the use of heat and are rigid. Phenolics, melamines, polyesters, and ureas are found in this classification. These plastics are represented by the knobs and handles on many appliances and utensils, as well as items like melamine dishes. These items may char but will not melt under high heat. Kitchenware that comes in contact with mild heat of less than 400 degrees Fahrenheit is usually made of thermosetting plastics; an example is microwave ovenware which uses thermoset polyester.

Care must be taken to purchase the right plastic article for its intended use. The consumer should be cautioned to read the manufacturer's labels.

CONSTRUCTION FEATURES

Metals may be shaped in their molten state by *casting,* or in their solid form by first rolling into sheets and then *stamping* or *drawing* the metal into shape by means of accurately machined dies. Better quality cutlery is shaped by *forging,* which is a method of shaping metal by heating and pounding it into form. Note the development of cookware in America in Figure 19.1.

Casting

Metal is cast when it is too brittle to be shaped by another method. Cast iron utensils are shaped this way when the impure iron ore is poured into a sand mold while it is still molten.

Casting is used when a utensil of more than usual thickness is wanted, such as cast aluminum. Cast items often have a pebbly outside surface and a smooth inside surface. Their weight and thickness may be a disadvantage.

Stamping

Sheet metal is used in making thin, shallow utensils such as lids, cookie sheets, and trays. These utensils are stamped into shape by a die in a shaping press machine.

Drawing

Seamless, hollow products where considerable depth is needed are made by the drawing process. A sheet of metal is repeatedly compressed into gradually deeper shapes by a series of dies in large presses. Metals and alloys formed by drawing are aluminum, brass, nickel silver, stainless steel, and steel.

Spinning

Spinning may be the method used for shaping ornamental bowls or trays from aluminum or copper. This shaping is done by hand and is used mainly for small jobs. The craftsperson uses a blunt tool to shape the sheet metal against a mold as it revolves on a lathe. After the item is completed, the mold is removed.

Forging

Products such as knife blades and handles of some pots and pans are shaped by forging. Dies are hammered repeatedly against the heated metal to force it into the desired shape. Some aluminum alloys, nickel silver, stainless steel, and steel are shaped by this process.

Stainless Steel Construction

Stainless steel is made of a combination of metals to improve its heating qualities. The resulting combinations are described as two-ply, three-ply, bottom clad, three-ply/bottom clad, and five-ply/bottom clad and five-ply (Figure 19.2).

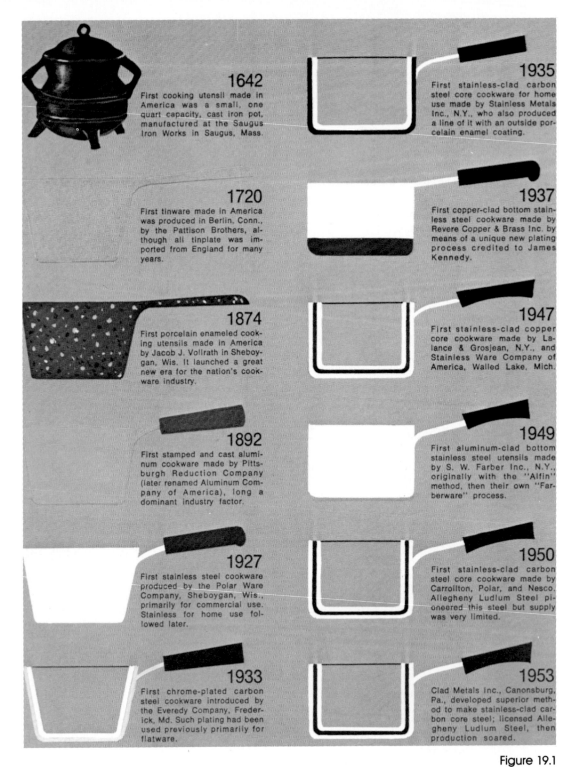

1642
First cooking utensil made in America was a small, one quart capacity, cast iron pot, manufactured at the Saugus Iron Works in Saugus, Mass.

1720
First tinware made in America was produced in Berlin, Conn., by the Pattison Brothers, although all tinplate was imported from England for many years.

1874
First porcelain enameled cooking utensils made in America by Jacob J. Vollrath in Sheboygan, Wis. It launched a great new era for the nation's cookware industry.

1892
First stamped and cast aluminum cookware made by Pittsburgh Reduction Company (later renamed Aluminum Company of America), long a dominant industry factor.

1927
First stainless steel cookware produced by the Polar Ware Company, Sheboygan, Wis., primarily for commercial use. Stainless for home use followed later.

1933
First chrome-plated carbon steel cookware introduced by the Everedy Company, Frederick, Md. Such plating had been used previously primarily for flatware.

1935
First stainless-clad carbon steel core cookware for home use made by Stainless Metals Inc., N.Y., who also produced a line of it with an outside porcelain enamel coating.

1937
First copper-clad bottom stainless steel cookware made by Revere Copper & Brass Inc. by means of a unique new plating process credited to James Kennedy.

1947
First stainless-clad copper core cookware made by Lalance & Grosjean, N.Y., and Stainless Ware Company of America, Walled Lake, Mich.

1949
First aluminum-clad bottom stainless steel utensils made by S. W. Farber Inc., N.Y., originally with the "Alfin" method, then their own "Farberware" process.

1950
First stainless-clad carbon steel core cookware made by Carrollton, Polar, and Nesco. Allegheny Ludlum Steel pioneered this steel but supply was very limited.

1953
Clad Metals Inc., Canonsburg, Pa., developed superior method to make stainless-clad carbon core steel; licensed Allegheny Ludlum Steel, then production soared.

Figure 19.1
The evolution of metal cooking utensils in America.
Courtesy of National Housewares Manufacturers Association, *The Housewares Story.*

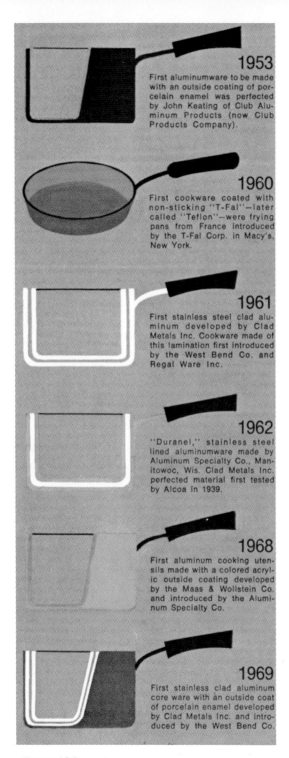

1953
First aluminumware to be made with an outside coating of porcelain enamel was perfected by John Keating of Club Aluminum Products (now Club Products Company).

1960
First cookware coated with non-sticking "T-Fal"—later called "Teflon"—were frying pans from France introduced by the T-Fal Corp. in Macy's, New York.

1961
First stainless steel clad aluminum developed by Clad Metals Inc. Cookware made of this lamination first introduced by the West Bend Co. and Regal Ware Inc.

1962
"Duranel," stainless steel lined aluminumware made by Aluminum Specialty Co., Manitowoc, Wis. Clad Metals Inc. perfected material first tested by Alcoa in 1939.

1968
First aluminum cooking utensils made with a colored acrylic outside coating developed by the Maas & Wollstein Co. and introduced by the Aluminum Specialty Co.

1969
First stainless clad aluminum core ware with an outside coat of porcelain enamel developed by Clad Metals Inc. and introduced by the West Bend Co.

Figure 19.1
continued

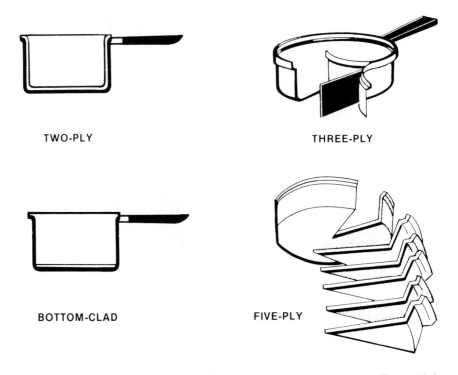

TWO-PLY

THREE-PLY

BOTTOM-CLAD

FIVE-PLY

Figure 19.2
Techniques of combining stainless steel with other metals.
Courtesy of Cookware Manufacturers Association.

Two-ply utensils either have a stainless steel interior with another metal on the exterior or vice versa. Three-ply utensils have stainless steel on the inside and outside surfaces with a layer of copper, aluminum, or carbon steel in the core.

Bottom clad utensils are formed with solid stainless or three-ply constructions, and copper is plated to the bottom or aluminum is applied to the bottom by casting, bonding, or metal spraying. Five-ply/bottom clad utensils are made by the three-ply process, with two clad layers on the bottom. Five-ply utensils are made with stainless steel on the inside and outside surfaces with three layers of aluminum forming the core.

Heat conduction may be improved by plating copper to the bottom of stainless steel pans. Copper will help prevent food from scorching while it is cooking faster. Copper is not used inside pans because it gives food a metallic flavor. Aluminum also conducts heat well and is used to coat stainless steel cookware. Aluminum may be added as a thick coating to the bottom, to serve in distributing heat evenly. A disadvantage of using aluminum and copper is that they both stain easily.

Edge Shaping and Finishing

Cast utensils need to have the edges smoothed and polished. Utensils made of sheet metal may have the edges smoothed and rounded by abrasive polishing. A beading may be applied on the edge of sheet utensils by curving the metal under. This forms a thicker edge and an attractive, smooth surface.

Handles and Knobs

Pots and pans rarely have metal handles. When the utensil is heated, it becomes too hot to touch. Therefore, handles and knobs may be insulated. This is done by forming the handle in sections and placing a nonconductor of heat material between the parts of the handle. Thermosetting types of plastic are used as handles and bases of many products, such as irons, electric griddles, toasters, and waffle irons. They are nonconductors of heat; also, they are smooth and attractive in appearance. Wooden or thermoset handles need no insulation and are attractive, but they may char if the heat gets too high.

Handles and knobs are secured to the products by welding, riveting, screwing, or bolting. Welding compatible metals leaves a permanent joint that will not work loose. Riveting a metal piece through two metal pieces, then compressing the end, is used in lower quality utensils; the rivets may work loose and make cleaning more difficult. Bolts and screws also have a tendency to work loose.

Lids

Lids should fit evenly and snugly. Some lids are held in place on certain liquid-pouring utensils when they are tipped to pour.

METAL FINISHES AND DECORATIONS

Plated Iron and Steel

Cast iron and steel may be plated with chromium or nickel to improve their appearance and to prevent rust. These silver-colored metals are resistant to scratching and rusting. The plated surface will not chip or peel. The plating will last for years before wearing away and the pan will still be useful. Nickel wears easily and is often covered with a chromium finish to protect the nickel. Because abrasives increase the wear of plating, utensils should be scoured as little as possible.

Zinc-Coated Steel

Zinc-coating steel items, called *galvanized* ware, protects steel from rusting. Zinc is attacked by ordinary food acids and by alkalies when hot and forms poisonous compounds. Therefore, it cannot be used to coat products in which food is to be cooked. Steel garbage cans and wash pails are galvanized with zinc. Abrasive powders and steel wool should not be used in cleaning galvanized items.

Tinware

Tinware is made by plating silver-colored tin over steel. The best tin-plated ware is dipped into a bath of molten tin twice. This is called "block" or "retinned" ware. Inexpensive grades of tinware may have pinpoint holes in the coating that cannot be seen until rust appears at these spots. It is a material for ovenware; it is not suitable for top-of-stove use because tin melts at about 450 degrees Fahrenheit. Tin is also used as a plating for such items as cake pans, break boxes, cannister sets, and pie pans.

Since tin is soft, abrasives such as scouring powders and steel wool should not be used to clean it. Tin may stain—acid from certain foods such as apples, tomatoes, and vinegar may attack the tin. Tinware should be washed and dried immediately after using.

OTHER FINISHES AND DECORATIONS

Acrylic Finish

Acrylic enamels applied to the exterior surface of aluminum or stainless steel cookware come in many colors. They are dishwasher safe and stain- and chip-resistant.

Alkyd Finish

Alkyd enamel is an organic resin coating applied to exterior surfaces of metal cookware. Decorative alkyd enamels come in many colors and are chip- and scuff-resistant.

Anodized Finish

The anodizing process gives the oxide film of aluminum a hard finish so that it can be dyed and sealed to give a colored and decorative surface to bakeware, aluminum cookware covers, and specialty items. Products with the anodized finish are heat absorbent, stain- and scratch-resistant, and cannot chip or peel.

Chrome Plate Finish

The chrome plate finishing process involves the electrolytic deposition of nickel, chrome, and copper to cookware with a base metal such as aluminum, brass, carbon steel, or copper. Cookware with this finish is hard, dishwasher safe, and easy to clean.

Decalcomania

Decalcomania is a colorful, decorative printed design which is applied to exterior surfaces of porcelain enameled utensils and uncoated aluminum or stainless steel cookware by using porcelain frit, or many fine glass particles. Cookware with the decalcomania finish is easy to clean, dishwasher safe, and resistant to stains and abrasives.

Epoxy Finish

Epoxy coatings of organic resin may be applied to the exterior of metal cookware. This decorative finish comes in many colors, is dishwasher safe, and is stain- and chip-resistant.

Hardcoat Anodized Finish

A hardcoat anodized finish gives the interior and exterior of aluminum cookware and bakeware a hard finish that cannot chip, peel, scratch, or stain. Its surface is harder than the regular anodized finish, and it is easy to clean and heat absorbent.

Polyimide Finish

Polyimide is a thermosetting organic polymer material applied usually to the exterior of aluminum or stainless steel cookware to make it dishwasher safe and chip- and stain-resistant.

Polyurethane Finish

Polyurethane enamel is an organic resin coating applied to exterior plastic and metal cookware surfaces. It is available in many colors. This finish is decorative, dishwasher safe, and resistant to stains and chipping.

Acrylic Silk Screen

The acrylic silkscreen process forces special ink or paste through a design on a screen which is then applied to uncoated exterior surfaces of stainless steel or aluminum cookware. Such cookware surfaces are decorative, colorful, dishwasher safe, and resistant to stains and chipping.

Porcelain Enamels

Porcelain enamel for exterior surfaces of aluminum or stainless steel consists of a glassy inorganic material that produces a glossy coating when bonded to the metal (Figure 19.3). This porcelain enamel is easily cleaned, resistant to abrasives and stains, dishwasher safe, and available in many colors.

Porcelain enamel for the interior and exterior surfaces of steel or cast iron is made of a glassy inorganic material that requires bonding to the metal by fusion to achieve a glossy coating. Porcelain enamel applied to steel or cast iron is available in many colors, dishwasher safe, resistant to abrasives and stains, and easy to clean.

How Porcelain Enamel Finishes Are Made...

Steel parts or parts to be finished in porcelain enamel

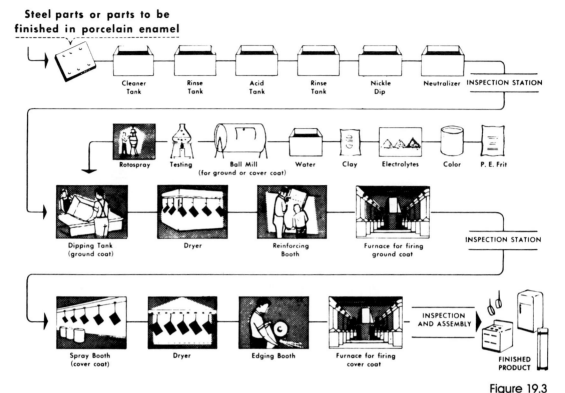

Cleaner Tank   Rinse Tank   Acid Tank   Rinse Tank   Nickle Dip   Neutralizer   INSPECTION STATION

Rotospray   Testing   Ball Mill (for ground or cover coat)   Water   Clay   Electrolytes   Color   P. E. Frit

Dipping Tank (ground coat)   Dryer   Reinforcing Booth   Furnace for firing ground coat   INSPECTION STATION

Spray Booth (cover coat)   Dryer   Edging Booth   Furnace for firing cover coat   INSPECTION AND ASSEMBLY   FINISHED PRODUCT

Figure 19.3

When porcelain enamel is applied to steel, a decorative, easy-to-clean, abrasion-resistant surface is created.
Courtesy of Porcelain Enamel Institute.

Porcelain Silkscreen

Porcelain silkscreening is the process in which a porcelain enamel is forced through a design on a screen, then applied to exterior surfaces of porcelain enameled utensils, or uncoated exterior surfaces of aluminum or stainless steel cookware. Cookware that has a porcelain silkscreen finish is decorative, colorful, chip- and stain-resistant, and dishwasher safe.

Nonstick Fluorocarbon Finish

Fluorocarbon coatings have inherent nonstick properties and are applied by one of the following methods.

1.   Single coat method—a single coat of fluorocarbon resins is applied to metal cookware.

2. Two coat method — a primer coat and a finish coat of fluorocarbon resins are applied to metal cookware to make them nonstick.

3. Two coat method with substrate — a coat of ceramic or hard metallic material is applied to metal substrates, followed by a primer coat and a finish coat of fluorocarbon resins to make cookware nonstick.

4. Three coat method — fluorocarbon resins are applied to a specially prepared metal cookware surface in a prime coat, intermediate coat, and a finish coat.

Some tradenames which identify nonstick fluorocarbon finishes are Teflon, SilverStone, Fluon, and Debron (Figure 19.4). These coatings may be found on sauce pans, frying pans, popcorn poppers, and deep fryers.

Nonstick High Temperature Resin Finish

High temperature resin coatings consist of nontoxic plastic resins that are capable of withstanding cooking and baking temperatures. They may contain fluorocarbon resins for better nonstick properties. These materials are applied to specially prepared interior surfaces of metal cookware and bakeware to guarantee that they are dishwasher safe, nonstick, easy to clean. They come in many colors.

Nonstick Silicone Finish

Silicone finishes are made of nontoxic synthetic resins that are applied to the interior and exterior surfaces of metal bakeware to make them glossy, nonstick, easy to clean. They are available in many colors.

Almost every cookware and bakeware item is available with a nonstick surface. Many kitchen tool accessories also have nonstick finishes, such as spatulas, ice cream scoops, and rolling pins for use with nonstick cookware.

METRIC GUIDELINES FOR BAKEWARE AND COOKWARE

Metric guidelines have been developed for manufacturers, retailers, consumers, and other users of bakeware and cookware products. These guidelines are intended to bring metric bakeware and cookware products to the consumer in an orderly and effective manner.

Figure 19.4
This skillet features a "Silverstone" finish, the tradename for a nonstick fluorocarbon finish.
Courtesy of Regal Ware, Inc., Kewaskum, Wisconsin.

All countries in world trade are converting to the International System of Units, SI (Systeme International d'Unites). The sizes of bakeware and cookware products are expressed using this system. A product's size is defined in linear (length), in capacity (volume), or in mass units. Linear dimensions of bakeware and cookware products are represented in centimeters (cm). Capacity of bakeware or cookware products if smaller than one liter (1000ml) is expressed in milliliters (ml). Products one liter (1000ml) or larger are expressed in liters (l). If the mass of a bakeware or cookware product is smaller than 1000 grams (g), it is expressed in grams. If it is 1000 grams or more, it is expressed in kilograms (kg). Guidelines for measuring bakeware and cookware are shown in Figure 19.5.

COOKING UTENSILS

Cooking utensils occupy the main position in the kitchen. Based on their usage, the three types are (1) top-of-stove cookware (Figure 19.6), (2) bakeware (Figure 19.6), and (3) service ware.

Top-of-Stove Cookware

Saucepans are deep pans that hold from one to four quarts and have long single handles. Saucepans usually come with lids, but their use is optional.

Saucepots are similar to saucepans, but are generally larger and have a handgrip on either side rather than the long single handle. The two handgrips are more convenient than the single handle of the saucepan when both hands are needed to lift a filled pan. Because of their size, saucepots are usually used for cooking stews, pot roasts, soups, and for making jams and jellies.

Double boilers consist of two pans, a smaller top pan with a cover that fits into a larger bottom pan used for boiling water to heat the food in the top pan. The part of the inset pan below the supporting pan should be deep enough so that a large proportion of the pan can be surrounded by steam to provide a good-sized cooking area. Both pans of a double boiler may be used for making all sorts of creamed dishes, puddings, and sauces; for cooking and melting chocolate; for keeping foods warm; and for reheating leftovers. The water in the base of the double boiler regulates the heat which prevents delicate foods from scorching and eliminates the need for constant watching. The pans are designed so that they may serve as two separate utensils.

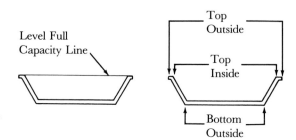

Figure 19.5
Method of measuring bakeware and cookware.

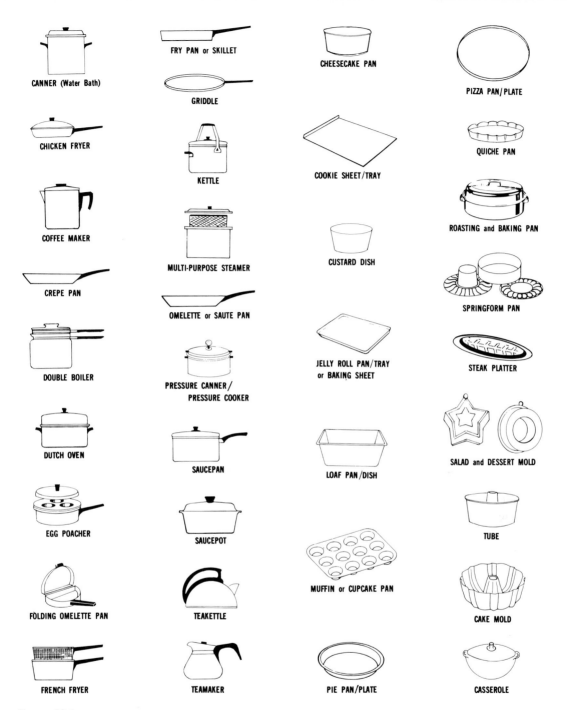

Figure 19.6

Cookware and bakeware.

Courtesy of Cookware Manufacturers Association.

CANNER (Water Bath)

FRY PAN or SKILLET

GRIDDLE

CHEESECAKE PAN

PIZZA PAN/PLATE

CHICKEN FRYER

KETTLE

COOKIE SHEET/TRAY

QUICHE PAN

COFFEE MAKER

MULTI-PURPOSE STEAMER

CUSTARD DISH

ROASTING and BAKING PAN

CREPE PAN

OMELETTE or SAUTE PAN

SPRINGFORM PAN

DOUBLE BOILER

PRESSURE CANNER/
PRESSURE COOKER

JELLY ROLL PAN/TRAY
or BAKING SHEET

STEAK PLATTER

DUTCH OVEN

SAUCEPAN

LOAF PAN/DISH

SALAD and DESSERT MOLD

EGG POACHER

SAUCEPOT

TUBE

FOLDING OMELETTE PAN

TEAKETTLE

MUFFIN or CUPCAKE PAN

CAKE MOLD

FRENCH FRYER

TEAMAKER

PIE PAN/PLATE

CASSEROLE

Dutch ovens are made of heavy aluminum, stainless steel, or cast iron. They have close-fitting covers. The large saucepot usually has either two side-handles or an overhead bail handle with one side handle for balancing. They hold five quarts or more and may be used on top of the stove, over an open flame, or in the oven. Since they are deep, they will hold thicker pieces of meat and are useful for soups and stews.

Deep-fry pans come with a wire-net pan that fits inside and may be removed from the oils and outside pan. These saucepans are used for deep oil frying croquettes, doughnuts, french fried potatoes, and fritters.

Pressure cookers reduce cooking time from hours to minutes. They use small amounts of water. The covers usually interlock and contain gaskets that seal. Different pressure regulators are used to indicate the pressure. There are top-of-stove or electric types of pressure cookers. Both types are equipped with safety devices to relieve excess pressure if the regular controls should fail to operate for some reason. Some types have a cooking guide built into the cover handle. Electric types can be plugged in and used anywhere since they have built-in heating units and are thermostatically controlled. They also double as electric saucepans or electric skillets for braising, boiling, frying, and preparing casserole dishes. Electric units may be set at "warm" to keep foods hot until served. The pressure cooker cooks the foods at the heat of about 250 degrees Fahrenheit. With this temperature under pressure, it is possible to cook foods three to ten times faster. Meats, potatoes, vegetables, a custard, and even onions can be cooked at the same time without intermingling of flavor or color. Natural vitamins, minerals, flavors, and colors are retained since it is air and water that remove, transfer, and boil out these items.

Frying pans or skillets are used for frying foods. They are wide, shallow, open pans with a long side handle. They come in sizes from six to twelve inches in top outside diameter linear measurement of their surface. Cast iron skillets are available in a complete range of sizes from six to twenty inches in diameter. They are called *spiders* in some cookbooks. A frying pan with a domed, close-fitting cover may be used for braising and other cooking methods that require moisture. A deep pan with a domed cover is sometimes known as a *chicken fryer*. Nonstick interiors are popular in some frying pans.

Griddles are frying pans that are flat and have a ridge or a small lip around the edge of a large cooking surface. Some have nonstick coatings. They are used for pancakes, french toast, and such food as grilled sandwiches.

Kettles are large cooking pans with an overhead metal bail handle and lid. They are used for cooking large amounts of food, ranging from six to eighteen quarts or more. Kettles are used for cooking large quantities of soup or stews, a whole ham, or for cooking fruits and vegetables for canning or freezing. Tea kettles are smaller and designed with wide spouts for quick, easy filling and pouring. They are used to boil water for tea and instant cereal, coffee, or soup. Some have whistles to indicate when the water is boiling. These kettles should be washed regularly to prevent formation of lime deposits. A mild solution of vinegar and water should be used.

Coffee makers are available in three common types: percolators, vacuum coffee makers, and drip coffee makers or dripolators (see Figure 19.7). The important difference in them is the way in which the water contacts the ground coffee.

In one type of percolator, boiling water rises through a tube, strikes a glass top, falls back over the ground coffee that is placed in a perforated basket, and then drains into the bottom of the coffeepot. The removable tube and coffee will fit in the center of the pot. Most electric percolators, and some of the more expensive nonelectric percolators, have a valve instead of a domed place at the base of the tube; the valve rests in a cup located in the bottom of the percolator. Percolating starts almost immediately because only the water in the cup has to be heated to start the boiling action. The cup makes the percolator more difficult to clean.

The vacuum coffee maker has two bowls, the lower one for water, the upper one for brewing coffee. When the water boils, it rises through a tube into the coffee at the bottom of the top bowl. The water only rises once and is brewed over a

Figure 19.7
Common types of coffee makers.
Percolator courtesy of The West Bend Company; copyright Dart Industries. Drip coffee maker courtesy of Proctor Silex.

low heat. Once brewed, the heat is turned off, and as the top bowl cools, the coffee filters down to the bottom bowl.

A drip coffee maker, or dripolator, is considered to be the oldest coffee maker. It consists of three parts and a cover. A middle perforated basket holds the ground coffee. Over it is a container for hot water, with a few well-spaced holes in the bottom to allow the water to drip slowly over the coffee. The hot, ready-to-serve coffee collects in the bottom pot.

Bakeware

Bakeware includes many different utensils from casseroles to microwave ovenware. These items are used for foods which cook by indirect heat produced in an oven.

Casseroles are saucepots that are made in a wide variety of sizes, usually with covers. The two-quart size is a useful one for families of four to six. They are usually made from attractive materials that may go from the oven to the table. Ceramics, glass, porcelain enamelware, and Pyroceram are often used in making casseroles. Both casserole and cover need handles that can be grasped firmly with pot holders. Casseroles are used for baking many kinds of main dishes and desserts such as scalloped foods and puddings.

Roasters are built in different sizes and shapes (see Figure 19.8). They are available in oval, round, or square shapes. For open-pan roasting, any kind of pan large enough for meat and deep enough to hold the drippings can be used. A pan about fourteen by ten by two inches is a good size for most roasts, such things as baked apples, or a large quantity of scalloped potatoes. A wire rack or pan that fits into the pan is needed to hold meat up out of the drippings and to let hot air circulate around the meat and prevent scorching. The rack may have handles on it to help in lifting the roast from the pan. In covered roasts, size is usually designated by the weight of roast the pan will hold. A pan large enough

Figure 19.8
Round roaster and Dutch oven.
Courtesy of Regal Ware, Inc., Kewaskum, Wisconsin.

for a big, special-occasion turkey may be too cumbersome for ordinary use and may monopolize the oven space. A quality covered roaster has handles for easy lifting.

Tube, or angel, cake pans are used mostly for angel, sponge, or chiffon cakes. These delicate cakes are usually baked in aluminum or tinware pans with a hollow tube in the center that allows the heat to go to the center of the cake to give a lightly brown crust. The tube should be taller than the pan sides to keep the top of the cake from touching the table when it is inverted for cooling. The bottoms of tube pans may be loose or solid.

Muffin pans are sized in two ways: (1) by the size of each cup, or (2) by the number of cups in each pan. Cups vary in dimensions. For general use a medium-sized cup is good, one about two and one-half inches in diameter by one and one-fourth inch in depth, or three inches wide and one and one-half inch deep. Most muffin pans have six or twelve cups. Sometimes two pans of six cups each rather than one twelve-cup pan are purchased because they are more adaptable to different purposes and different occasions. The average recipe calls for the twelve-cup size. Muffin pans can serve several purposes. They are often used for cupcakes, rolls, and tart shells as well as for muffins. Unless paper linings are used, muffin cups should be greased so cleaning will take less time.

Pie pans are usually shallow and round with flared sides and are available in a wide range of sizes. Most recipes call for a nine-inch pie pan. To be good, a pie must have a well-baked bottom crust. This means that pie pans should be made of materals that absorb heat readily and distribute it evenly to the pie. Aluminum, glass, and darkened tinware will bake undercrusts well.

Layer cake pans are shallow, oblong, square, or round pans with straight sides. Most are round and are eight to nine inches in diameter. Cake recipes generally call for eight-inch pans about one and one-fourth inch deep or nine-inch pans one and one-half inches deep. Layer cake pans are available with solid or loose bottoms.

Square and oblong cake pans are a little deeper than layer cake pans and many cake recipes call for these kinds of pans. Square pans are often either eight inches on a side and two inches deep, or nine by nine by one and three-quarters inches deep. An oblong pan is usually eleven by seven by one and one-half inches. Larger oblong pans are available for extra large cakes that may be iced in the pan. These pans may be used for roasts as well as rolls or cornbread.

Loaf cake pans are deep pans that may be round, square, oval, or oblong in shape. They come in a variety of dimensions. They are used for baking bread, loaf cakes, or meat loaf. People who bake usually use more than one.

Cookie sheets are available in small, medium, and large sizes. There should be at least one inch clearance around the cookie sheet. If it touches the sides or the back of the oven, it will shut off the circulation of heat. The cookie sheet always has at least one turned-up edge so that you can get hold of it easily and at least one open side to allow you to slide the food off. Besides cookies, the cookie sheet pan is good also for baking rolls, biscuits, and cream puffs. Because the cookie sheet has no sides, hot air can circulate directly over the food to brown it evenly.

Microwave ovenware is available for use in microwave ovens. It can also be used in gas and electric ovens up to 400 degrees Fahrenheit. Thermoset polyester is the plastic normally used. The ware is freezer-to-oven safe and dishwasher and detergent safe. A microwave ovenware set may include a roasting rack, baking ring, bacon rack, muffin pan, various quart sizes of casseroles, and a meat and vegetable cooker/steamer.

Other microwave ovenware is available for roasting, baking, thawing, reheating, steaming, and simmering. A separate product available is a "micro-go-round" food rotator that slowly rotates food in a microwave oven. It is spring-wound with about a thirty-minute cycle.

Glassware and paper products may be used for cooking in microwave ovens, but no metal should be used.

Service Ware

Cutlery

The world of cutlery has developed in recent years from the use of one knife for every task to the development of a proper knife for every specific task. A home-maker should have a paring knife, utility knife, steak slicer, cook's or chef's knife, roast slicer, pot fork, and a sharpening steel. Other knives that may be used in the kitchen are the boning knife, scalloped or saw-toothed bread knife, curved blade grapefruit knife, ham slicer, light cleaver, and flexible spatula. High content carbon steel is used to make the best cutting edge of knives. Stainless steel is used to make knives that do not rust or stain.

The better knife blades are made by *forging* rather than stamping. A round bar of steel is used to make individually forged blades. The bar is rolled and shaped under high pressure. Regular blades do not have as sharp a cutting edge as hollow-ground blades.

Less expensive knife blades are *stamped* from a thin gauge of metal and then are ground to a sharp edge. Better knives have a one-piece blade securely placed in the handle. Materials used in the handles include bone, metal, plastic, and wood. When rivets are used to hold the handle and blade, there should be three rivets. The following cutlery is needed in most kitchens (Figure 19.9).

A *paring knife* has a three- to three and one-half-inch blade and is used to peel and section fruits and vegetables. A *utility knife* has a five- to seven-inch blade used for dicing, halving, and slicing fruits and vegetables. A *cook's knife*, also called a *butcher's* or *chef's knife*, has an eight-inch large, wide blade and is used for carving roasts and mincing small quantities of onions and peppers. A *steak slicer* is eight inches long and has a long, flexible, thin blade for slicing bread, cold meats, etc. A *pot fork* is seven to eight inches long, has a long handle, and two or three tines. It is used for taking food from a cooking utensil, for turning foods, and for holding meat and vegetables steady while being cut. A *roast slicer* is nine inches long and is used for slicing large roasts and hams.

A *sharpening steel* is a tubular bar with small ridges to help in straightening the edges of knives. When used often, the steel keeps the edge straight and razor sharp.

Figure 19.9
Basic kitchen cutlery—a utility knife, a paring knife, and a cook's knife.
Courtesy of Russell Harrington Cutlery Inc.

Other cutlery items that are suggested for use in the kitchen are *grapefruit knives* with a curved blade to core the fruit and *spatulas* with dull flexible blades and rounded edges for spreading filling and icings.

Knives will last a long time if they have proper care. A wooden knife rack with special sized slits will protect the knives and edges.

Miscellaneous Service Ware

Many types of service ware are used in the preparation and serving of food (see Figure 19.10). These include mixing bowls, which are available in a variety of shapes and sizes for mixing and stirring foods; bowl-shaped sieves or strainers called *colanders,* made of metal or plastic and used to drain boiled foods or vegetables; and pitchers of many shapes and sizes used to serve hot and cold liquids.

ELECTRIC KITCHEN HOUSEWARES

Electric kitchen appliances add to comfort, save time and effort, and eliminate drudgery. They use the most common type of electric current, called *alternating current* (AC), a pulsating current. The *voltage* is the pressure behind the current. Residential wiring commonly uses 120 volts of electricity. Large electrical appliances, such as a dryer or range, use 240 volts. The *amperage* indicates the size of the current or the number of electrons flowing through the electrical wires. Most homes are wired for 100 amps so that several appliances can be operated at the same time. Electric current is sold by the *watt* (w) by electric companies. One watt is equal to the amount of work done by one volt pushing one ampere through a circuit. One *kilowatt* equals 1,000 watts. One *kilowatt hour* indicates the number of kilowatts used in one hour. *Horsepower* is the amount of energy a motor has at normal speed. A motor using 746 watts has a rating of one horse-

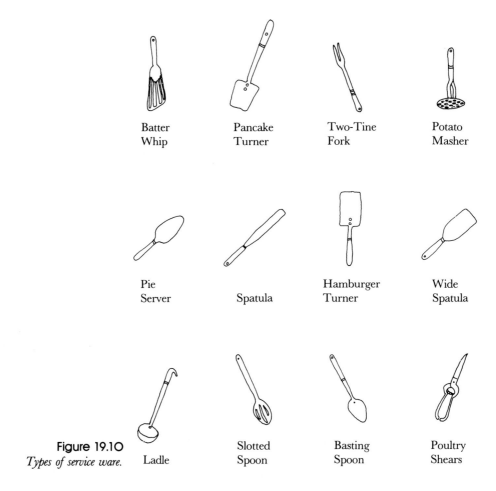

Figure 19.10
Types of service ware.

Batter Whip · Pancake Turner · Two-Tine Fork · Potato Masher

Pie Server · Spatula · Hamburger Turner · Wide Spatula

Ladle · Slotted Spoon · Basting Spoon · Poultry Shears

power. Electric current flowing through a wire creates heat. Heating and lighting products use more current than products powered by electric motors that do not produce heat or light. Most electrical appliances have a plate on them that indicates the number of volts and amperes and the kind of current to be used. Also, the number of watts the appliance uses in an hour is given. Once the cost of electricity per watt is known, the cost of operating the appliance per hour can be determined.

Some of the electric appliances have wires that resist the flow of electric current. These wires are called *heating elements.* These elements can convert electricity into heat as high as 1000 degrees Fahrenheit. Elements found in some toasters are wires that are wound around mica. The elements used in certain waffle irons may be coiled wires secured in cement. Insulation is used in parts of the appliances to prevent shock and burns. Some of the more common appliances are shown in Figure 19.11.

Figure 19.11

Small kitchen appliances—a two-slice toaster, a food processor, a regular style waffle baker, and an electric griddle.
Toaster and food processor courtesy of Sunbeam Appliance Company, a member company of
Allegheny International Company. Waffle baker courtesy of Oster, Division of Sunbeam Corporation,
An Allegheny International Company. Griddle courtesy of Farberware, a subsidiary of Kidde, Inc.

Toasters may be automatic or semiautomatic. Automatic and semiautomatic
toasters toast both sides of the bread at once and eject the toast when it is ready.
A heat control will give light, medium, or dark toast. Some toasters have a
crumb tray. The body is usually made of chrome-plated steel.

Griddles are square or oblong in shape and have a nonstick cooking surface. Most quality griddles have an automatic thermostat with signal light, an all-around grease moat for easy grease drainage, and a dial to control heat settings. They are used for cooking foods like toasted sandwiches, frying bacon and eggs, and frying pancakes.

Grills and waffle bakers are mostly square shapes with nonstick coated, reversible grills. They may be used for grilled sandwiches, eggs, waffles, etc. There is a variable heat control and an automatic thermostat.

Food processors are several appliances in one. They knead dough, mix dressings and batters, slice vegetables, shred cabbage, grate cheese, and chop nuts. They also beat, blend, and make purees. A powerful, quiet, direct-drive motor has no belts to slip or break. A safety interlock system keeps the machine from operating unless the container is properly positioned. Some models adapt to additional attachments, such as ice crushers, can openers, and juicers.

Can openers and knife sharpeners have magnetic lid holders that secure the attached lid while the can is held in place. The steel cutter and lid holder may come off for easy cleaning. A knife sharpener restores the edge to any nonserrated blade. The cord usually is stored in the base.

Mixers are used for beating, mixing, and whipping food. The motors vary in power and in the job that they can perform, ranging from mixing bread doughs to whipping cream. Some mixers have motor heads that tilt, making it easier to remove the beaters. Other mixers are portable and are used for light mixing jobs. Convenient controls are provided for speed and types of jobs. Some models rotate the mixing bowls, assuring even mixing. Various attachments are generally available for blending, juicing, grinding, shredding, and slicing.

Microwave ovens feature an automatic defrost cycle and a slow cooking cycle. Since the walls of the microwave oven remain cool, foods and spills do not bake on. Oven cleanup is as simple as wiping with a damp sponge. These ovens are stingy users of electricity. None of the microwave energy is wasted on heating the air around the food, the utensil, or the oven walls, or preheating an empty oven.

The microwaves are high energy frequency radio waves generated in an electron tube called a *magnetron,* which converts alternating current into electromagnetic radiation. The energy causes the molecules in the food to vibrate, setting up a motion that builds heat. This heat cooks the food. No metal containers should be used in a microwave oven.

Most microwave ovens operate on ordinary household current, 110 to 120 volts. The cost of operating a microwave oven is generally one-fourth to two-thirds less than a conventional range, which needs its own 220-volt line. Standards on radiation emission from microwave ovens began October 6, 1971, and are regulated by the Environmental Health Service's Bureau of Radiological Health of the Department of Health and Welfare.

Glass-ceramic top-of-stove electric ranges have designs etched into the counterlike surface to identify the places where the heating units are located. Six- and eight-inch heating elements are sealed beneath the surface. These range tops provide a space to work when not in use, are attractive, and are easy to clean.

CARE OF HOUSEWARES

Some basic safety precautions and rules for care should be followed to give housewares and appliances longer life.

1. Nonstick surfaces clean easily and quickly and are dishwasher safe. Very little oil or butter is needed to prepare food in nonstick ware.

2. Nonstick cookware and bakeware require plastic, rubber, or wooden spatulas to prevent scratching the coating while removing food. The scratches affect only the appearance, not the nonstick properties.

3. Light-colored nonstick coatings may become discolored or stained in time. Use a special cleaner for nonstick finishes to remove the stains.

4. High heat may warp nonstick utensils; therefore, low to medium heat settings should be used to achieve good cooking results and to make utensils easy to clean.

5. Nonstick utensils should be washed in hot sudsy water using a dishcloth. Scouring pads or powder may scratch the surface of the coating.

6. Read the care-and-use booklet that comes with an electrical appliance to understand its function. Read cleaning instructions to find out what parts of the appliance can be washed or are dishwasher-safe. To protect against electrical hazards, do not immerse an appliance in water.

7. Do not place electrical appliances on or near hot gas or electrical burners or in a heated oven.

8. Unplug an appliance from the outlet when not in use and before cleaning. Do not let the cord hang over the edge of a table or counter, or let it touch hot surfaces. If a cord is frayed, it should be repaired immediately by wrapping with friction tape. Badly worn cords should be replaced to avoid short circuits.

9. Do not overload the electrical capacity of the wiring of your home or the four-way electrical outlets as overloading may result in a fire. If a light dims slightly when an appliance is turned on, that is a warning sign that there is an overload on the wire and some appliance should be disconnected.

10. Do not use electrical appliances outdoors or while standing in a damp area.

11. To clean exterior chrome finishes of appliances, use a damp, sudsy cloth. A glass or nonabrasive cleaner may be used for stubborn stains. Do not use metallic scouring pads as they may scratch the finish. Polish appliances with a dry cloth to remove cleaning agent.

12. Most electrical appliances are coated with a nonstick, easy-to-clean finish. Before using nonstick electrical appliances for the first time,

wash them with hot, sudsy water, using a dishcloth or soft sponge. Rinse thoroughly with hot water and dry. Then condition the interior nonstick surface by applying cooking oil with a paper towel. This is not necessary to prevent foods from sticking, but the oil or butter helps give added flavor and aids in the browning and crispness of foods.

13. Electrical kitchen appliances such as mixers need to be oiled occasionally to lengthen their life and efficiency.

14. Glassware or porcelain enamel pans should not be stacked because this may cause them to break or chip. They should not be subjected to extreme temperature changes; instead, they should be heated and cooled gradually.

15. Pour water into pans after removing food to prevent the remaining food from sticking.

16. Utensils plated with chromium or nickel should not be cleaned with strong cleaning powders, steel wool, or metal scrapers that will scratch the surface plating and expose the base metal. Enamelware may also be scratched this way.

17. Avoid scorching food in utensils. Cover the bottom of the pan with water and cook over low heat once boiling begins.

18. Carefully wash and dry cast iron, sheet steel, and tinware immediately to prevent rust.

19. Handle aluminum pans carefully to prevent denting and warping. Discoloration caused by alkaline food can be removed by boiling a weak solution of water and vinegar in the pans. Foods and hard water left in the pans may cause pitting. Wash and dry aluminum pans immediately.

SELLING POINTS

Some selling points that the salesperson may suggest to the customer about housewares include the following:

1. Aluminum cookware has the highest rate of heat conductivity among the materials currently practical for cooking utensil use.

2. Aluminum utensils are strong, yet lightweight.

3. Aluminum is nontoxic.

4. Aluminum cannot impair the flavor, nutritive value, or color of foods cooked in it.

5. Good aluminum cookware is available at prices within the reach of virtually every family budget.

6. Attractive porcelainized enameled finishes are applied to cast aluminum to match the home decor.

7. An anodized finish is applied to sheet aluminum to make it more attractive.

8. A brilliant polish is used on cookie sheets to keep the cookies from becoming too heavily browned on the bottom.

9. The best pots and pans are not the most inexpensive; the most expensive ones are not necessarily the best. A convenient, durable, and even-heating pan, though it does not guarantee a superb meal, makes any cook's job easier and can be bought for a modest price.

10. Although most people buy their pots and pans piece by piece, they should be encouraged to buy them in sets to save money per piece. Sell the right sizes and type to meet their needs.

11. Most cookware is available as open stock.

12. The most important test of a pan's performance is how well it distributes heat. A pan's performance can be predicted, generally, by knowing of what metal it is made. The type of metal and its gauge affect not only heat distribution, but durability, ease of cleaning, and ease of handling.

13. The design, construction method, and materials used in making handles are important factors in cooking. Plastic handles are usually better than wood for all-around purposes such as handling the pan when hot or placing in the oven, dishwasher, or sink.

14. Lids should fit and seal tightly so that little vaporized water and heat are lost. Rivets inside the pan are difficult to clean around.

15. Spouts should be shaped and placed so that contents will pour easily without dripping.

16. Lips on both sides of the cookware make it usable by either hand. A lid should fit both lips.

17. Electric appliances, like other cookware, should be energy efficient, easy to use, and easy to clean.

18. People take pride in the fashionable appearance of their kitchenware. Explain advantages of the best cookware first; one can always trade down.

KEY TERMS

1. Alloy
2. Casserole
3. Cast iron
4. Colander
5. Dutch oven
6. Element
7. Enamelware
8. Forging
9. Galvanized
10. Gauge
11. Pyroceram
12. Stainless steel
13. Thermoplastic ware
14. Thermosetting ware

STUDY QUESTIONS

1. Name three finishes used to keep cast iron or steel from rusting. How are they applied?
2. Why would a cast iron frying pan need to be seasoned?
3. What are the advantages of using copper in making pots and pans? How is copper used in the construction of cooking utensils?
4. How is stainless steel made? What is the best quality stainless steel for pots and pans? Why do qualities of stainless steel differ?
5. How should a customer care for nonstick coatings on pans?
6. How do aluminum pots and pans differ? What are the advantages and disadvantages of using aluminum ware?
7. What are the advantages and disadvantages of using glassware utensils for cooking?
8. Name the advantages and disadvantges of porcelain enamelware. What is the best quality?
9. What safety features would you look for in buying electrical appliances? What suggestions should be pointed out to customers about the care of electrical appliances?
10. Explain the purpose of Dutch ovens, double boilers, pressure cookers, percolators, and dripolators.

STUDY ACTIVITIES

1. Visit a housewares department. List the different types of pots and pans and electric appliances on display. How many different materials were used in making them?
2. Obtain a catalog featuring cooking utensils. Analyze the utensils as to types, materials, sizes, weights, prices, and country of origin.
3. Select three different coffee pots and write down the advantages and disadvantages of each that may be used in a sales presentation.

CHAPTER 20

Leather and Footwear

OBJECTIVES

After completing this chapter, you should be able to:

1. Understand the different methods used in producing leather.

2. Know the major leather finishes.

3. Be able to explain the difference between the major kinds of leather.

4. Know the basic manufacturing processes used in making footwear.

5. Identify the parts of a shoe.

6. Understand the differences between the basic types of footwear.

7. Explain the difference between materials used in making footwear.

8. Explain how to care for leather and footwear.

Leather is made from the treated hides and skins of certain animals. Most leather comes from domesticated animals like cows and calves, pigs, goats and kids, sheep, and horses. Leather is a by-product from these animals, and therefore it is fairly inexpensive. Leathers made from domesticated animals are used mainly in consumer products such as footwear, handbags, wearing apparel, furniture upholstery, and interiors of cars. The Endangered Species Conservation Act of 1969 makes it a federal offense to purchase or sell any amphibian, crustacean, fish, reptile, or wildlife that is obtained against state or foreign law. Rare animals that provide exotic leathers that are in danger of becoming extinct include alligators, seals, sharks, and lizards.

The different kind of leathers are identified by their natural *grain* markings. When the hair is removed from the skins of hair-growing animals, the hair follicle openings form a pattern known as grain. The size of the hair follicle openings creates the distinctive grain of each leather. Fine hair leaves small holes while coarse hair leaves large holes. Reptiles, such as alligators, lizards, and snakes, have scale patterns also called grain. These natural grain patterns are valued for their distinctive beauty.

Today's footwear articles are comfortable and durable. Shoes are found in an almost unlimited number of sizes, widths, styles, colors, finishes, and materials. Men and women today own several pairs of casual footwear, an assortment of dress footwear coordinated with their suits and dresses, and assorted footwear for play.

QUALITIES OF LEATHER

The best leather comes from the center back section of most animals. The animal develops a thick, tough hide there to protect itself from the natural elements and from its enemies. The most durable, the firmest, and the best quality of sole leather for *footwear* comes from this section of cowhide, called the *bend*. The belly and shank sections are the poorest quality for making leather soles because they will not wear nor resist moisture as well as bend leather. Some animals, such as alligators, lizards, and snakes, crawl instead of walk; therefore, they develop leathers that are of excellent quality in the belly section. Figure 20.1 shows the side view of a cowhide and the location of qualities of cowhide used in making footwear. Number 1 represents the best quality and number 6, the poorest.

There is a name difference in skin sizes. If an animal's skin weighs fifteen pounds or less when it is sent to the tannery, it is called a *skin*. Calfskin, goatskin, kidskin, and sheepskin are examples. Skins that weigh between fifteen and twenty-five pounds are called *kips*. Kipskins usually come from the skins of oversized calves. Large animal skins that weigh more than twenty-five pounds are called *hides*. Examples are cowhide, buffalo hide, and horse hide.

Figure 20.1
Qualities of cowhide.

MAKING LEATHER

Tanning

Tanning is a process by which various chemicals and bark extracts are used on animal hides and skins to produce leather. There are three major steps in the tanning process: (1) preparation, (2) tanning, and (3) finishing. In the *preparation* step the hide is cleaned and scoured. In the *tanning* process the actual chemical change occurs which converts hide into leather. The *finishing* process involves rolling, adding oils, and forming a pattern. Some of the tanning methods are oil, vegetable, mineral, formaldehyde, and combination tanning.

Oil Tanning

An oil solution, usually cod oil, is worked into the skin until a chemical reaction changes the skin to leather. Oil tanning creates a washable, porous, supple leather that is creamy yellow in color. Chamois skins used for cleaning purposes and for gloves are oil-tanned. Doe skin and buckskin may be oil-tanned.

Vegetable Tanning

Vegetable tanning requires from two weeks to six months for completion, depending on the thickness of the hide. Bark extract (tanning acid) is used to produce thick tan-colored leather that is firm, durable, attractive, and porous, yet water-resistant. Items produced with vegetable-tanned hides include shoe soles, upholstery, luggage, and belts.

Mineral Tanning

Alum Tanning. The skins are tumbled in an alum mineral salt solution that turns them into leather in several hours. Then they are seasoned for weeks or months before they are ready to be used for leather goods such as gloves. The leather is soft and flexible, white in color, and must be dry-cleaned—not washed.

Chrome Tanning. A solution of chrome salts is used to change skins into leather in about five to eight hours. The skins are tumbled in a drum, and when the process is completed, the leather has a grayish-blue color. Most of our leather is chrome-tanned because the process costs less and takes less time to complete than other methods. Chrome-tanned leather is more durable and less water-resistant than vegetable-tanned leather. It is somewhat slippery when damp, and may be carefully sponged when soiled. This leather is used extensively for articles such as gloves, handbags, and shoe uppers.

Formaldehyde Tanning

Formaldehyde, a colorless gas, is used along with water to convert skins to leather. Several hours in the solution makes the tanned leathers white in color, soft and pliable, and washable. Leathers tanned by this method are considered superior for use in making gloves and certain shoe uppers.

Combination Tanning

Some leathers are tanned by two processes in order to combine the good qualities of both, such as durability, elasticity, porosity, and attractiveness. For example, formaldehyde and alum tanning make good glove leather. Chrome and oil tanning also make a good glove leather. Chrome and vegetable tanning make leathers that are sought after for farm, military, and heavy-duty work shoes.

Finishing Tanned Skins

Splitting

Skins vary in thickness and may need to be split into as many as five layers (Figure 20.2). Leather articles may be made from all the layers. The top layer or natural grain layer is the strongest, the most beautiful, and the most expensive; it is called the *top grain*. The rest of the layers of the skins are called *splits*. Figure 20.2 shows how the different layers are named. All of the splits may be sueded or may have imitation grains embossed on them. Split leather usually is not as durable and is less expensive than top grain leather. Only top grain leather may be labeled and sold as "genuine leather."

Boarding

Boarding gives a special grain effect to leather. It is accomplished by folding the grain over on itself and rubbing the two surfaces together, under pressure, by hand or machine. Examples of this creased texture may be seen on boarded calf and cow, morocco, and pin seal leather.

Coloring

Some leather is made more appealing by dyeing it. *Brush dyeing* is applying dye to the outside surface only. As wear takes place on the finger tips of gloves, the original tanning color will show. *Dip dyeing* is an expensive process where the articles are immersed in dye; all sides are colored thoroughly. *Spray dyeing* on one side with air sprayers may give articles novel tones and shades.

Embossing

An imitation grain is placed on leather by an *embossing* process. The selected grain or pattern is etched on a steel plate and put on leather permanently under

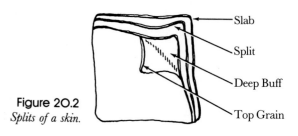

Figure 20.2
Splits of a skin.

Slab

Split

Deep Buff

Top Grain

tremendous pressure. Split leathers and scarred grainside leathers are often embossed. Less expensive leathers look more expensive when embossed with a top grain look. Leathers that are embossed must be correctly labeled; examples are alligator-grain calfskin and lizard-grain sheepskin.

Fat Liquoring

Replacing natural oils removed from skins by the tanning process with animal, mineral, or vegetable oils is called *fat liquoring*. It helps prevent leather from cracking and drying out. Polishing shoes is the same as fat liquoring them.

Metallic Finishes

Leathers are given metallic finishes by placing thin sheets of selected metal on the leather and applying high pressure to bond them. Thin sheets of gold are used for gold finishes. Thin aluminum sheets are used for giving silver-looking finishes.

Patent Finish

A plastic urethane coating is placed on any smooth surfaced leather, giving it a shiny, smooth, *patent finish*. The grain is visible and usually of calfskin, cowhide, coltskin, or kidskin. Lacquer and varnish coatings were used prior to urethane plastic. Patent leather lacks the porosity and elasticity characteristics of other leathers.

Sueded Finish

A buffing wheel raises the fibers on the flesh side of the leather, causing a soft, velvetlike surface called *suede,* or *nap.* Some leathers that have grainside blemishes are napped or sueded. Mocha and doeskin-finished lambskin are sueded on the grain side. Many garments today are made of sueded pigskin and cowhide, sometimes called roughouts, split cowhides, or bushcoats.

TYPES OF LEATHER

Cowhides and Calfskins

Most of the leathers that are used in the United States come from cows and calves. The leathers are considered by-products of the meat-processing companies in North and South America.

Leather from a young calf, several days to several weeks old, is firm, fine-grained, smooth-surfaced, and in short supply today. Calfskin is durable and does not scuff easily. It cleans easily, takes a high polish, and stretches moderately. It will take a patent or a suede finish. Coarse calfskin suede may be called *reversed calf.* As a calf ages, its skin gets heavier and thicker, and the grain becomes more visible. Cowhides are used for durable footwear, leather briefcases, luggage, upholstery leather, and many other leather articles.

Elk side is cowskin that has been finished to look like elkhide. *Genuine leather* is whole grain or top grain leather. Cowhide that has been oil-treated but not tanned is called *rawhide*. *Retanned cowhide* is cowhide that is tanned by the chrome and vegetable process and then saturated with oily grease to make it acid- and moisture-resistant. *Saddle leather* is a vegetable-tanned calfskin or cowskin used in making footwear and handbags.

Scotch grain is a rough, embossed leather used for men's heavy-duty walking and sport footwear. *Side-leather* is a cowhide that has been cut into two sides before tanning. The top grain leather is used in making shoe uppers. *Vellum* is cowhide and calf skin processed to be used like parchment.

Sheepskins and Lambskins

Sheepskin and lambskin leather that is used in this country comes from domestic and imported sources. Sheepskin leather is less expensive and less durable than most other leathers. It also stretches and damages easily. It is grain-finished or sueded for gloves and sueded for jackets. When it is tanned with the wool left on it, it is called *sheepskin* or *shearling leather* and is used as a lining in caps, coats, gloves, and footwear. Lambskins used for glove leather come mostly from Europe. The leather is slightly coarser in grain than kidskin and is less durable and less elastic.

Capeskin is a skin of a South American haired sheep. The leather has a tight, close grain and is sturdy and pliable. It has a very strong grain, which enables it to be split to light weights without serious loss of strength. Its tight grain will take a high luster. It is desirable for formal types of gloves.

Cabretta is made from the skin of a hair sheep found in South America, mainly Brazil. It is similar to capeskin. It is becoming popular as a glove leather.

Chamois skins are made from a split layer of oil-tanned and sueded sheepskin. They are used for cleaning purposes.

Doe skin originally came from the female deer, but now it is commonly made from lambskin. The grain side is removed and a velvet nap finish is applied. It is tanned in formaldehyde and readily takes fashion colors used for warmer dress gloves.

Electrified sheepskin is a fine velvetlike textured wool pile developed by straightening the hair with a chemical.

Flesher is a coarse flesh split of lamb or sheep skin. It is alum-tanned, dip-dyed, and sueded for inexpensive gloves.

Mocha leather is made from African or Asian hair sheep. It has a velvet finish. Mocha skins are alum-tanned, then chrome-tanned so that they are washable. Mocha is used mainly for men's gloves, semiformal and formal wear, and women's tailored gloves.

Parchment is an alum-tanned sheepskin with a smooth finish. It is used for items such as diplomas and documents.

Skiver is a top grained layer of sheepskin that is thin and used in shoe linings, sweat bands in hats, and small leather goods.

Goatskins and Kidskins

Goatskins are obtained from Africa, Asia, Europe, and South America. This naturally tough skin is made pliable, soft, and attractive through a chrome-tanning process. The pebbled grain can be given a gloss and is used for sport gloves. Morocco leather refers to goatskin that has been vegetable-tanned and boarded (creased) to give it a pebble-like surface. It is used for wallets.

Kid leather is made from the skins of young goats that are generally imported from Europe. The term *kid* applies to skins from milk-fed animals. They are no longer considered kids after they are put to pasture. Kid is a very fine leather, with a close tight grain. Kid leather is capable of taking a pleasing finish. It has good elasticity, high strength, durability for its weight, and is used for gloves and shoes. This leather must be handled carefully to prevent scratching or peeling. Kidskin is used for shoe linings and uppers, belts, bookcovers, and handbags.

Bronze kid is made by coating the leather with a metallic powder. It must be used with care. *Crushed kid* is creased in different directions to give a rough texture that does not show scratches or wrinkles. It is used for casual footwear. *Glacé kid* refers to a polished shiny finish on glove leather. It is also called *smooth kid*, whereas a *matte finish* is dull.

Pigskins

Pigskin comes from a wild hog (peccary) or water rodent (carpincho) from Central and South America. Skins of domesticated pigs appear in small quantities. These skins are used in gloves imported from England, usually for heavy work gloves. The peccary makes the best quality leather, and the carpincho makes a leather that is heavier. All three pigskins are similar in appearance, having a coarse pebbled grain, marked with visible bristle holes in groups of three. The holes serve as beauty marks and for ventilation. Scratches, caused by the wild animal brushing against thorns, may appear on the finished leather. These scratches do not affect durability nor do they lessen the style appeal. If there are excessive scars, the leather will be embossed and called *pig-grained pig*. The leather is chrome-tanned and is generally finished in natural cream, cork, or similar colors. Pigskin is used for small leather articles, driving and sport gloves, and occasionally for shoe uppers.

Deer and Elk Skins

The supply of domestic deerskins and elk skins is very limited. Their skins have similar characteristics. Deerskins for grain-finish leathers usually come from China and Central and South America. Exceptionally durable and with a stout-plump, though flexible, feel, deer skin is suitable for men's dress and sport gloves. *Buckskin* usually has the grain skived off, and a velvet or suede finish is given to this side. If deeply scratched, the flesh side may be finished. Clay dyes are brushed on the surface, and oil tanning is generally used. It is porous, soft, warm, and suitable for dress and sports gloves. *Doeskin* originally came from the female deer, but because of the limited supply of these skins, the term is commonly applied to leathers made from lambskins. The grain side is removed and a velvet nap finish is applied. It is tanned in formaldehyde and readily takes fashion colors. It is lightweight, porous, absorbent, and washable. Consequently, it is suitable for women's dress gloves in summer and in winter.

Other Leathers Used

Horsehides

Horsehide, when available, comes from domestic and imported sources. It is usually chrome-tanned. The better hides, when split to lighter weights, have gained acceptance in dress gloves. The less perfect hides are useful for work gloves. *Cordovan* leather comes from the hindquarters. It is nonporous, very strong and durable, and resists scuffing.

Buffalo Hides

Buffalo hides, in limited supply, are imported from Asia and Eastern Europe. These hides, coarser and more durable than cowhides, are usually scarred so much that they are embossed with an imitation grain. They are made into handbags, work gloves, and shoe uppers.

Kangaroo Skins

Kangaroo skins, when available, are imported mainly from Australia. They are similar to but stronger than kidskins and do not scuff as easily. Kangaroo skin may have a glazed finish or be sueded and takes the same tannage as kidskin. It is more expensive than kidskin and is used for the same kinds of footwear, especially where comfort and durability are wanted.

Seal Skins

Seal skin, in limited supply, makes a smooth, soft leather that has a pebblelike grain when boarded. *Pin seal* is the best quality leather from the skin of young seals; when boarded, it is made into small leather goods.

Sharkskins

Sharkskin, when available, has a diamond-shaped grain. It is very scuff-resistant. Tips of children's shoes may be reinforced with this skin.

Walrus Hides

Walrus hide, when available, is heavy and may be several inches thick. The thick durable hide is used on wheels to polish gold and silver jewelry. Split walrus hide is almost always embossed.

Alligator and Crocodile Skins

The Endangered Species Conservation Act of 1969 made alligator and crocodile skins virtually unavailable. These exotic skins were in great demand in expensive handbags, footwear, and small leather goods. Their top grain patterns are popular in embossed designs on other leathers (calfskin and sheepskin) and plastics. The top grain ranges from squarelike markings from the belly section (the most valuable part) to the tiny oval, round, horny markings on the back section.

Lizard Skins

Lizards are on the endangered species list and their skins are scarce. The skins have unusual markings which look like grains of uncooked rice. Certain species have grains that resemble miniature alligator markings. These leathers are very durable. They are used in handbags and small leather accessories.

Snake Skins

Snake skins, domestic and imported, are in limited supply. Cobra, diamondback, and water snake skins are among those used for making handbags and small decorative leather goods. The skins are so thin that they are reinforced with a fabric backing.

Ostrich Skins

Ostrich skins are scarce and expensive. It is the only bird skin frequently used for leather goods. The beauty of this leather comes from the spiral-shaped markings with a hole near the edge of the marking. This is caused when the ostrich plumes are removed from the skin, leaving "rosettes." This leather is used for western boots and small leather goods. Embossed leathers, calfskin and sheepskin, imitate the rosette of ostrich.

Imitation Leather

Man has not been able to reproduce the leather that comes from animals, even though imitations have been produced that feel like leather, look like leather, and have some of the characteristics of leather. *Bonded leather* (reconstituted leather) is made from waste leather fibers mixed with a plastic binder. This mixture is formed into sheets and then cut into patterns designed to resemble leather.

Plastic materials are usually used to imitate leather. The plastic most commonly used is vinyl, the generic name for materials made from polyvinyl chloride. Vinyl is produced under several trade names and comes in a variety of well-known types. *Expanded vinyl* has cells of air that make the material crushable and soft. *Nonexpandable vinyl* may look like calf, kid, or patent leather, or may have designs embossed on it. Stretch vinyl expands and contracts with movement.

Polyurethane plastic materials are used widely as imitation leather for footwear uppers, wearing apparel, and small accessory items. Porosity has presented a problem in shoe uppers. Imitation leather has to be broken in every time it is worn.

A variety of man-made materials have been developed that have taken over the majority of the shoe-sole market. The low cost, availability, durability, and special use needs, such as molded treads, have been some of the reasons.

FOOTWEAR

The primary purpose of footwear is to protect the wearer's feet from contact with the ground. Once the basic need was met, early civilizations gradually refined footwear with frills and extras. The art of making footwear developed to such a degree that in recent centuries people of all economic levels stopped making their own footwear and started relying on footwear specialists. The emerging boot-maker did custom work for a small number of people. It took several weeks to complete an expensive pair of footwear. Emphasis was on style and functional use, not on comfort. Breaking in footwear was not easy until left and right foot-wear developed around 1860. The American Civil War and industrial revolution brought about mechanical development, which greatly changed shoe construction and distribution.

Parts of the Foot

Today's shoes are constructed to provide comfort, fashion, and protection for the feet. They are built to fit the various parts of the foot: toes, ball joint, waist, in-step, heel, arch, and ball (see Figure 20.3). The foot includes twenty-six bones which serve as a framework to support other parts of the foot. The bones are held in place by ligaments and move by means of muscles and tendons. Movement is produced by expansion and contraction of the muscles. The action of the muscles, tendons, and ligaments is controlled by the nerves of the feet. These nerves carry messages and sensations to and from the brain, making you conscious of pain, wet feet, cold feet, or any other good or bad sensation. When shoes do not fit properly, these nerves are irritated and tell you something is wrong. Continued irritation will spread to the entire nervous system and thus affect other parts of the body. That is the reason properly fitted shoes are important.

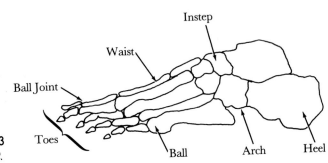

Figure 20.3
Parts of a foot.

Determining Shoe Size

The most common method used to indicate shoe sizes is the American system, which is based on a three- or four-digit number. The width is indicated by the first figure, the length by the remaining figures. For example, 595 is size 9½ E. The first figure stands for the letter of the alphabet designating the width (E is the fifth letter of the alphabet), and the next two figures show the length (5 indicates ½). For sizes that are not half sizes, a zero takes the place of the 5; for example, 470 is 7 D. Applying the preceding rules, note the following sizes:

065	= 6½ AA		495	= 9½ D
285	= 8½ B		575	= 7½ E
1120	= 12 A		6105	= 10½ EE
3105	= 10½ C		780	= 8 EEE

Several size ranges may be used to measure shoe sizes by lengths. The following chart indicates how children's and adult shoe sizes overlap:

Children's: 8 9 10 11 12 13 1 2 3 4
Boys': 23456
Women's: 56789 10
Men's and prep's: 6789 10 11 12 13 14 15

Half sizes run about one-sixth of an inch larger than whole sizes.

The width of shoes runs from quadruple A (AAAA) to quintuple E (EEEEE). Widths are measured by the circumference of the foot at the ball. About one-fourth inch separates the widths. For example, a triple A (AAA) shoe is approximately one-fourth inch narrower than a double A (AA) shoe. This indicates that there is a difference of approximately one-twelfth to one-sixteenth inch across the flat sole. A shoe width of AA in a larger size is actually wider than an AA shoe in a smaller size.

Measuring the Foot

Three common measuring devices are used to measure a customer's foot. They are the (1) *Ritz size stick*, (2) *Brannock measuring device*, and (3) graphs for tracing the feet called *Fedo Graphs*. The Ritz stick measures the foot in three different operations. The Brannock device can measure the foot in three ways at once: heel-to-toe, heel-to-ball, and width. All three measurements are needed to determine the proper size shoe. The Brannock device is extremely accurate on length, but it can be off on width because of the varieties of manufacturers' lasts. This device will measure the feet of men, women, and children. Both of the customer's feet should be measured because one foot is sometimes larger than the other. In that case, fit the larger foot. Measure the length and width of the feet in a standing position and in a sitting position; some feet become longer and others become wider when one stands. Properly fitted shoes allow for this.

In checking the fit, watch the shoe when the customer walks. Check to see if the shoe slips on the heel. In fitting slip-ons, for example, some slippage is normal, but the shoe should not open too much if the foot is bent. Blisters will develop if the shoe is too tight. The top line should normally fit snugly but not rub against the ankle bone. There should be at least one-half inch of space beyond the big toe. Children are normally fitted with shoes three-quarters to one inch longer than the foot measures. Little or no breaking in is needed for shoes that are properly fitted.

Shoes with pointed toes should be fitted longer than those with oblique or square toes. Open-toe shoes are fitted shorter than regular shoes because they do not restrict movement of the toes.

Parts of the Shoe

The three major parts of a shoe are the sole, heel, and uppers (see Figure 20.4).

The Sole

The sole of the shoe is made of one or more layers of leather, plastic, rubber, or wood, according to the construction, type, and quality of the shoe. The five parts of the sole are outsole, insole, filler, shank, and welt.

Outsole. The outsole is the bottom of the shoe exposed to wear. Top-grain leather is used for outsoles in quality shoes. Other materials used for outsoles include plastics, neolite and vinyl, crepe and plain rubber, and wood. Irons are used to measure the thickness of leather outsoles. An iron is $\frac{1}{48}$ inch thick. Outsoles on men's shoes are generally nine to twelve irons thick. Women's outsoles are generally two to six irons thick.

Insole. The insole is the sole underneath the sock lining. The insole serves as a foundation for the shoe and adds comfort and durability. Leather is used in good quality insoles. Plastic materials are used to make less expensive insoles. Specially made fiberboard (cardboard) is used in making inexpensive insoles.

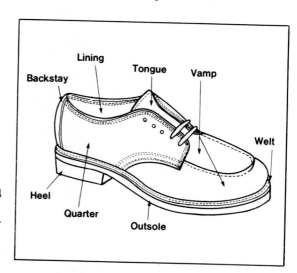

Figure 20.4
Parts of a shoe.
Courtesy of Footwear
Industries of America, Inc.,
Philadelphia

Filler.   The filler is the space between the insole and the outsole. In good quality shoes, the filler is often made of leather, cork, felt, rubber, or polyurethane. This filler stops squeaks, adds comfort, and provides a water-resistant sole. Polyurethane foam and foam rubber also add comfort.

Shank.   The shank is a wooden, leather, or tempered steel bridge between the ball of the foot and the heel of the shoe. The shank adds support to the arch of the foot and helps keep the shape of the shoe.

Shoe Welt.   The shoe welt is a narrow strip of leather about one-eighth to one-half inch wide used on oxford type or heavy-duty shoes to hold the upper of the shoe to the sole. It may be used as decoration. It may be shaped and stitched to make the shoe more water-resistant.

The Heel

Heels support the heel portion of the foot. They come in various sizes and shapes. *Breasted heels* are common on women's dress shoes. They have an extended graceful curve toward the arch of the shoe. Fashion determines whether they will be slender, medium, or bulky. Materials used in heels include wood, leather, reconstructed leather (waste leather ground up and bonded with a special glue), plastic, or wood with a metal reinforcement. Wooden or plastic heels are often covered with material or spray-paintd to match the uppers. This is done on inexpensive shoes. Heels done this way may not maintain their beauty because of damage. *Heel lifts* are attached to the base of the heel and are made of leather, metal, nylon, or rubber; they are generally replaceable if it becomes necessary.

A greater variety of style selections in clothing has increased the style selections in men's footwear. The heels of men's footwear are affected by fashion trends, working demands, health considerations, and other reasons. Casual shoes may have wedge heels; oxfords may have walking-style or stacked-look heels; cowboy boots may have cowboy or walking-style heels; and linesman's boots may have pole-hiker heels. Footwear is also manufactured with the sole and heel in one piece, called a *unit bottom.*

Toe and heel shapes for women's shoes vary according to the accepted fashion of the time. Nevertheless, there are nine toe shapes and eleven heel shapes that are basic (see Figure 20.5).

The Uppers

All the inside and outside sections of the shoe above the sole and heel are called *uppers.* Uppers are usually made from leather, plastic, or fabric (Figure 20.6).

The Upper-Inside Sections.   Inside sections of the shoe that are not visible or that form the lining of the shoe are the toe box, the counter, linings, and the doubler.

The *toe box* is the stiff reinforcment used under the tip of some shoes. It protects the toe and helps the shoe retain its shape. Toe boxes are constructed from leather, plastic, or stiffened paper (used in some inexpensive shoes). Safety shoes have steel toe boxes to protect industrial workers from falling objects.

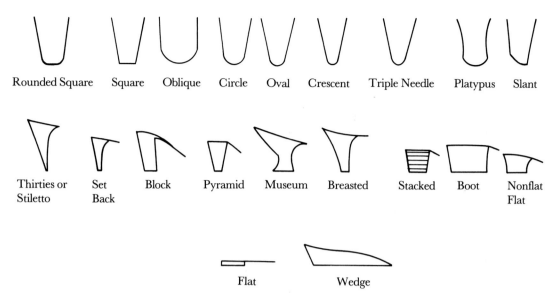

Rounded Square   Square   Oblique   Circle   Oval   Crescent   Triple Needle   Platypus   Slant

Thirties or   Set   Block   Pyramid   Museum   Breasted   Stacked   Boot   Nonflat
Stiletto   Back   Flat

                    Flat   Wedge

Figure 20.5
Toe and heel shapes used for women's shoes.

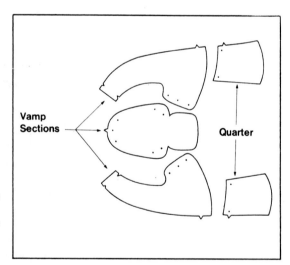

Figure 20.6
An upper for a moccasin style shoe.
Courtesy of Footwear
Industries of America, Inc.,
Philadelphia.

The *counter* is the stiff reinforcement in the heel under the quarter (the part of the shoe extending from the instep to the center back of the heel). It preserves the shape of the shoe and gives a snug fit at the heel. In better shoes the counter is made of leather. In medium quality shoes, plastic or stiffened fabric is used. Stiffened paper is often used in inexpensive shoes.

There are several *linings* within a shoe; they are quarter linings, vamp linings, sock linings, and tongue linings. The linings are made of cloth, plastic, or leather inside layers that help absorb perspiration. These linings cover the joining and seams and make the insides of the shoes more comfortable and attractive. Better linings are made of sheepskin, kidskin, or good quality cotton drill. Split leather, imitation leather (plastic), or heavily sized cotton fabric are used as inexpensive linings.

The *doubler* is a cotton-felt pad between the outer material and inside lining. It improves the appearance and adds comfort by providing insulation for the shoe.

The Upper-Outside Sections. Outside sections of the upper are the vamp, tip, quarter, saddle, and tongue.

The *vamp* is the front part of the shoe from the toe to the instep.

The *tip* is a separate piece of material covering the toe section of the vamp. It is often used on oxford-type shoes.

The *quarter* covers the heel from the instep to the center back of the heel.

The *saddle* is a separate piece of material covering the instep section of certain sport oxfords.

The *tongue* is the reinforcement section under the lacings that protect the foot. It may be a separate stitched-on piece or may be part of the vamp.

Shoe Construction

Once a shoe has been designed and priced, marketing researchers will conduct studies to see if the shoe will sell profitably. If so, mass production will begin using one of several methods. Computer programs may be used to grade patterns for desired sizes and widths, to determine the number of pieces to be cut, and to activate the laser beam mechanism which cuts the pattern material. Other methods may begin by using cardboard patterns for different parts of the shoe. Steel cutting dies are made from the patterns for each style and size of shoe. Shoe parts are cut from large pieces of leather, man-made materials, or fabric. The various pieces are tied and bundled by size and type.

The quarter, lining, and upper are sewn together in a stitching room. The upper, when completed, then moves to the lasting room. The innersole is tacked to the last, a form resembling a human foot, and then the upper is attached to the inside. The upper is made to conform to the shape of the last with a machine called a heat setter.

The outsole is then attached to the innersole by cementing, sewing, or nailing. One widely used method of attaching the upper to the sole is the Goodyear Welt Construction.

Heeling machines are used in many shoe factories to attach the heel to the outersole. Heel pads and sock lining are then added to the shoe. Finally, heels are dyed and uppers are polished.

Each of the many types of construction depend on the means whereby the outsole is attached to the innersole or upper part. Common construction methods of attaching the upper to the sole are shown in Figure 20.7.

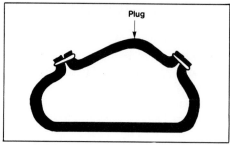

Moccasin construction

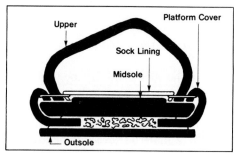

Slip lasted construction

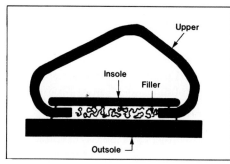

Cemented construction

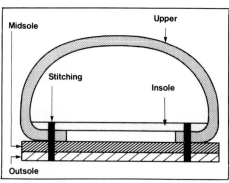

Littleway construction

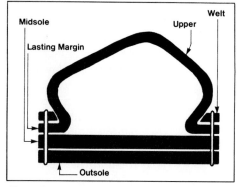

Two sole stitchdown construction

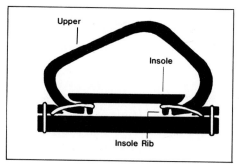

Goodyear welt construction

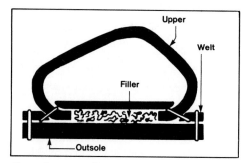

Pre-welt construction

Figure 20.7
Methods of constructing shoes.
Courtesy of Footwear Industries of America, Inc., Philadelphia.

Goodyear Welt Construction

This construction method is commonly used in men's and boys' shoes that take rugged wear. Some expensive men's quality dress shoes are made by the Goodyear Welt method. First, the insole, upper, and lining are stitched to the welt. Then the outsole is stitched to the welt to complete the shoe. The shoe may be cork-filled between the insole and outsole. None of these seams come in contact with the foot at any point. The shoe is easily repaired.

Injection Molded Sole Construction

The injection-molding process to attach vinyl soles to uppers came about in the 1960s. Polyvinyl chloride is heated to a flow state and injected into a mold; the process forms the one-piece outsole and heel and, at the same time, bonds it to the insole. These shoes cannot be resoled, but the sole withstands unusually rugged wear very well. The 1970s brought about a polyurethane injection-molding compound that was used to produce a sole that was cushioned.

Vulcanized Sole Construction

This vulcanization process joins rubber soles to canvas uppers, such as seen in athletic shoes and sneakers. A completed upper, rubber mudguards, and the rubber sole are fitted over a metal last and then placed in an oven and baked under pressure. This cures and hardens the rubber and permanently joins the parts.

Cement Construction

The cementing process has become practical with the development of waterproof rubber and plastic cements. In this process the sole is affixed to the upper by means of a strong adhesive. This process holds expenses down; offers a neater, cleaner, and lighter look, and increased flexibility; and is adaptable to newer stylings. Most shoes made in the United States today are cemented. Shoes without linings, such as slippers, are made by cementing various fabric or plastic uppers to sole materials.

Stitchdown Construction

Using this process, the shoe can have one, two, or three soles. In the three-sole construction, used for work shoes, the lining is pulled over the bottom of the insole, after which the midsole and the upper are attached by a chainstitch. Lastly, the welt and the outsole are attached to the upper and midsole by a lockstitch.

Slip Lasted Construction

In the slip lasted shoe, the sock lining is stitched to the upper prior to inserting the last, giving the upper a partial shaping. During lasting, the last has to be forced into the partially formed upper. This process is sometimes called *force lasting*.

The main feature of this construction is the comfortable "cushioned" effect caused by a thick midsole, or platform, which is used.

Slip lasting is particularly suitable for cloth-type shoes and is usually employed in casual designs with open toes and open heels.

Littleway Lockstitch Construction

This process is of the flat lasted type, with the upper joined to the insole by staples that curve and do not exit on the inside of the insole. While partially constructed, the shoe is removed from the last, and the sole is attached with a lockstitch. Then the last is replaced and the rest of the construction is finished.

Moccasin Construction

A shoe formed by moccasin construction consists of one piece of leather to which a sole has been added to permit longer wear. This single-piece leather unit is affixed to the bottom of the moccasin by two rows of lockstitches. The heel is attached later.

McKay Construction

Few shoes are made using pegs, nails, or screws to attach outsoles to insoles. Examples are ski boots and heavy-duty shoes.

Molding

Since the 1950s the upper parts of the shoe have been cemented together; then the shoe is placed over a metal mold. Then the rubber is attached by hydraulic pressure and heat to vulcanize the rubber and attach the sole permanently.

Finishing Procedures

A heel is affixed to the back part of shoes with cement, nails, pegs, or screws. Then toplifts of leather, rubber, or certain man-made materials are nailed or cemented to the heels. The shoes are then removed from the last. Sock linings may be put in, and the edges are trimmed. After this the shoes are cleaned or polished, inspected, placed in wrapping paper, and placed in appropriate boxes. They are now ready for delivery.

The Last

Figure 20.8 shows how important a last is in making shoes. A last, over which a shoe is produced, is usually made of maple wood or of plastic. Fit, comfort, and walking ease all depend on the last. There are three distinct types of lasts: (1) standard, (2) combination, and (3) orthopedic. One of these types should meet the size and shape requirements of most feet.

Standard Last. A standard last is designed for the average foot. It has the standard length, width, instep, heel, and ankle.

Combination Last. The combination last is designed to provide a proper fit for the person who has a long, slim foot, and a thin instep or thin heel. The total fit is usually narrower, although the other measurements are standard. Usually the use of the combination last is indicated by the way in which the width is indicated. This is done by a combination of markings, such as D/B, B/AA, AA/AAAA. These markings mean, in the first instance, that the shoe is of B

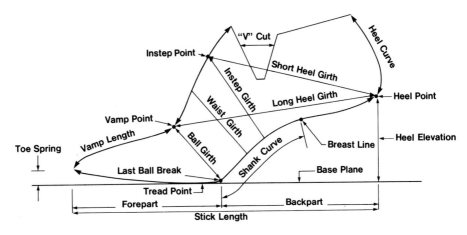

Figure 20.8
A last.
Courtesy of Footwear Industries of America, Inc., Philadelphia.

width through the instep and heel, with a D width across the ball. In the third instance, the shoe is of AAAA width through the instep and heel, with AA width across the ball.

Orthopedic Last.   An orthopedic shoe has corrective or preventive features and has almost no resemblance to the conventional last, because it is actually constructed for a specific type of foot ailment. Expert knowledge of shoe construction and human anatomy is required to construct an orthopedic last and shoe.

Buying Footwear

There is a direct relationship between quality and price in buying footwear. Knowledge about last and fit are important. Being fashion conscious about colors and styles is important. Knowledge about the footwear market and fashion may be obtained through publications such as *Footwear News* and *Women's Wear Daily.* In order to help aspiring buyers compare materials, features and benefits, or advantages and disadvantages of selected materials used in making footwear, Tables 20.1 and 20.2 are presented.

GOVERNMENT REGULATIONS

The following Federal Trade Commission rules on the labeling and advertising of shoe content became effective January 1963:

1.   The term *leather* may be used to describe shoes and slippers that are made of top grain leather in all parts, excluding heels, stiffenings, and ornamentation.

TABLE 20.1 SHOE UPPER MATERIALS

FEATURES (FACTS)	BENEFITS
Vinyl	
Can be made in a spectrum of colors.	Provides the wearer with colors to coordinate with apparel, relate to seasons, follow a fashion trend or special occasions.
Poromerics breathe.	Provides the wearer with a dry, cool, comfortable foot.
Textures can be made to look like any leather—from shiny patent to suede.	Provides the wearer with a wide choice of textures and styles that resemble leather.
Materials can be produced in a wide range of qualities usually costing less than leather.	Offers fashion-conscious customers shoes at reduced prices.
Stretches when worn and after wearing returns to its original shape.	Provides the wearer with a good fit, comfort, and shape.
May be cleaned with a wet cloth.	Uppers are easy to clean and do not require polishes, creams, or suede protectors.
Leather	
Is porous and breathes.	Keeps the foot dry, cool, and comfortable
Stretches to fit the shape of the foot and returns to the foot-conforming shape whereas vinyl returns to the original shape.	Provides the wearer a very comfortable fit.
Top grain leather is usually used in best quality shoes.	Provides the wearer with the most fashionable, finest quality shoes.
Can be dyed a spectrum of colors.	Provides the wearer with colors to coordinate with apparel, relate to seasons, follow a fashion trend or special occasions.
Costs more than other materials used in uppers.	If cared for has a more lasting beauty than vinyl materials. Customers who want the best are willing to pay for it.
Can be renewed with creams and polishes.	Properly cared for, can provide years of attractive wear.

2. The term *leather* must be used to describe shoes and slippers that are made of split leather or ground, pulverized, or shredded leather in all parts.

    Examples: "Split leather"
                   "Imitation leather"

3. Shoes made partly or wholly of split leather which simulates top grain leather must be clearly labeled.

    Example: "Upper made of split cowhide"

TABLE 20.2 MATERIALS USED IN SHOE LININGS AND SOLES

Linings		
LEATHER	SYNTHETIC LEATHER	FABRIC
Sheepskin: inhibits conditions like athlete's foot and irritation. Used in fine footwear. Durable, porous, and absorbent. Split leather: used to cut costs—less expensive than top grain leather.	Vinyls: May have the leather-look. Durable as leather. Less expensive than leather. Not as porous and absorbent as leather.	Cotton drill and cotton duck: closely woven for strength and durability. Very absorbent. May be heavily sized to lower costs. Soils easily. Cotton prints: used in girls' and women's shoes for fashion effect; very absorbent; soil easily. Nylon tricot: sheer fabric backed with polyurethane foam to provide soft, cushioned comfort. Acrylic pile: soft and fluffy to provide warmth and softness.

	Soles			
QUALITY	LEATHER	PLASTIC (Neolite)	CREPE RUBBER	WOOD
Comfort	Comfortable, resilient, flexible, porous—it breathes	Not resilient; foot gets hot; not very flexible	Very comfortable, flexible; does not breathe; hot; very resilient	Not as comfortable as leather; not very resilient
Durability	Less durable than crepe; will wear out; shoe may be resoled	Most durable; polyvinyl chloride (PVC) withstands very hard wear. Additives make synthetics resistant to deterioration, oils, acids, etc.	Very durable; color darkens with wear	Less durable than leather, Neolite, or crepe rubber
Fashion	Top grain leather is very fashionable	Less fashionable than leather	Very fashionable for certain shoe styles	Fashionable for certain shoe styles
Price	More expensive than Neolite	Least expensive material	Costs about 10 percent more than leather	About as expensive as leather

4. Shoes made of split leather which has been embossed, dyed, or otherwise processed to simulate the appearance of a different kind of leather must disclose the actual type of leather used.

Example: "Simulated alligator made of split cowhide"

5. Shoes whose parts are composed wholly or partly of nonleather material, having the appearance of leather or split leather, must be clearly labeled indicating the material is simulated or imitation leather.

    Examples: (a) "Outsole, innersole and linings composed of imitation leather"
    (b) "Midsoles composed of cellulose fibers," or "Cellulose fiber shoeboard"
    (c) "Sock lining, quarter lining, and heel pad are imitation leather made from ground leather fibers"
    (d) "Vinyl linings"

    Nonacceptable example: "Shoeboard innersole"

6. In labeling shoes and slippers no trade name, trademark, depiction, coined name, symbol, or other words may be used to convey the idea that the shoes are made of leather when in fact they are not.

    Examples: "Duraleather"
    "Barkhyde"

7. All labeling must be clearly affixed to the shoe and remain affixed until the completion of the sale to the retail customer. These labels must be easily observed and understood upon casual inspection of the shoe or slipper. Shoes containing inner parts made of nonleather material and outer parts made of leather must be clearly labeled to disclose the nonleather parts.

    Examples: "Innersole of nonleather shoeboard"
    "Innersole of cellulose fiber"
    "Cellulose fiber shoeboard"
    "Innersole of rubberized felt"

    Nonacceptable example: "Shoeboard innersole"

8. In advertising as in labeling, the purpose is to provide an accurate, nondeceptive description of the shoe material content.

TYPES OF FOOTWEAR

Footwear may be divided into four main types: (1) shoes, (2) slippers, (3) boots, and (4) waterproofs. There are many shapes and styles within each type being worn. Fashion merchandising helps determine how popular the styles become. Footwear varies from plain to ornate.

Types of Shoe Footwear

Shoes usually are categorized into one of five different groups: (1) oxfords, (2) pumps, (3) sandals, (4) slip-ons, and (5) high-top shoes. Popular shoe styles for men and women are described in the following material. Shoe buyers and salespeople must be able to identify types and styles of shoes.

Popular Shoe Styles for Men

Oxfords.   There are many variations of oxford shoes. The oxford is a low-cut shoe that is held on the foot by laces tied in the center of the instep. Laces may also be tied on the side of the shoe. The height of the heel may vary or may be a wedge. Sneakers and tennis oxford shoes have fabric uppers and rubber soles. Other athletic oxford shoes may have spiked soles and cleats; for example, golf and baseball shoes. Described below are some of the various styles of oxford shoes.

1. *Bal*—Bal is a front-laced shoe of medium height in which the quarters meet and the vamp is stitched over the quarters at the front of the throat.

2. *Blucher*—The blucher is distinguished from the bal shoe by the extension forward of the quarters over the throat of the vamp; quarters are left loose at the inner edge and made to lace across the tongue. It may have a plain toe, wing tip, or long wing tip.

3. *Brogue*—The brogue is a heavy-soled shoe sometimes having a plain toe, wing tip, or long wing tip. This shoe is sometimes trimmed with pinking, perforations, and stitching.

4. *Saddle*—The saddle oxford has a piece of leather extending from the shank over the throat of the vamp and upward to the top of the quarter on both sides; it forms a part of both vamp and quarter. This construction is generally used in sport shoes; the piece of leather often is of some material or color which contrasts with that of vamp and quarter. This piece of leather may be stitched over a whole vamp and quarter, or these parts may split, the part under the saddle being cut away.

Pumps.   The pump is a casual low-cut shoe that is not held to the foot by any adjustable fastener.

Sandals.   Sandals use straps to hold the shoe on the foot. Thongs are one style of sandal.

Slip-Ons.   Slip-ons are casual or step-in low-cut shoes worn indoors or outdoors. There are several variations of these shoes that are cut below the ankle but have no laces. They may be held to the foot by the shape of the upper part of the shoe. They may have an elastic goring in front or side. The heel may vary in height. Described below are two styles of slip-ons.

1. *Monk*—The monk is a closed shoe held to the foot by means of a strap across the instep; the monk strap is generally, but not necessarily, buckled or otherwise fastened at the side of the shoe. The terms *monk* and *monk strap* are used interchangeably.

2. *Moccasin*—Moccasin shoe construction makes use of a single piece of leather for the vamp extending all the way under the foot; slippers may

be made from a single piece of leather or with a soft leather and, unlike the original moccasin, frequently have heels; the genuine moccasin has no innersole or bottom shoe filler. The vamp of a moccasin shoe has a U-shaped plug or insert extending to the toe cap, attached to the vamp with a butt seam.

High-Tops.   This type of shoe laces above the ankle to give extra ankle support. Work shoes, hiking shoes, and some athletic shoes are common styles worn by men.

Popular Shoe Styles for Women

Oxfords.   The oxford is a low-cut shoe laced or tied over the instep or side of the shoe. It is a casual shoe.

Pumps.   The pump is a low-cut shoe that is not held to the foot by any adjustable fastener. It is a popular dress shoe (sometimes referred to as "heels").

Sandals.   All sandals use straps to hold the shoe on the foot. They usually vary in shape and coverage of the foot. There are many variations of design and ornamental techniques, including braiding, cut-outs, stripping, perforating, cross-strapping, and banding. Some sandals may be worn for dress, and others are worn as informal shoes. Various types of sandals are described below.

1. *Ankle strap*—A sandal having a strap which *encircles* and fastens at the ankle. Its anchor point is at the top or at the sides of the quarter.
2. *Open shank*—Any sandal in which the upper is cut away at the shank, leaving the insole exposed. Usually refers to women's dress shoes.
3. *T-strap*—A shoe having a strap rising from the center of the vamp throat to the instep line, where it is finished with a loop through which another strap is run around the ankle to form a T.

Slip-Ons.   The slip-on (step-in) is a low-cut shoe worn indoors or outdoors that does not use laces. It may have elastic gores or elasticized uppers. This shoe is used for women's dress or casual wear.

High-Tops.   The high-top shoe is one that laces above the ankle. It gives support to the ankle while hiking and playing sports like basketball.

Styles of Slipper Footwear

Slipper footwear is designed for indoor wear. A slipper can be slipped on the foot and held there by pressure of its upper without fasteners. Some slippers are made for wearing indoors and outdoors. Materials used vary considerably.

Styles of Boots and Waterproof Footwear

Boots for dress and outdoor wear may be made with elasticized uppers or with elastic gores, zippers, and toggle closers. There are styles of waterproof footwear for many activities with various heights, weights, treads, upper materials, and fasteners.

CARE OF LEATHER AND FOOTWEAR

In order to maintain leather and footwear, follow the suggestions listed below.

1. Apply a coat of transparent paste wax to new leather shoes before wearing.
2. Leather must be polished often to keep it supple and in good condition.
3. Suede can be cleaned with a suede brush or art-gum eraser. Do not overrub.
4. Clean leather with a cream. Protect and polish it with a wax.
5. Leather athletic shoes should be hand-washed periodically.
6. Increase the waterproofing of boots and shoes by keeping them well-polished and by spraying silicone on the sole line and seams of dark-colored leather. Seek advice from a shoemaker on a variety of products made for light, delicate leathers and suedes regarding water-resistance. *Do not use* heavy oils to waterproof fine leather boots; they dull the finish and make them impossible to polish.
7. Wet leather boots or shoes must be cared for immediately. Place paper in the toes and dry away from heat for at least twelve hours.
8. Salt can corrode and stain leather if it is not washed off quickly. Use a soft sponge, warm sudsy water with a small amount of vinegar, and wash *all* outside parts of the footwear.
9. Fabric shoes with cemented soles should be washed by hand. Do not soak the soles.
10. Fabric sneakers may be cleaned in the delicate cycle of a washing machine.
11. Fabric shoes may be spray-protected to resist soil and moisture. They may be cleaned with soap and water.
12. Synthetic shoes are easy to clean with a damp cloth and do not need polishing. They are scuff-resistant. If they get scuffed, use a liquid scuff coat.
13. Use shoe trees in shoes between wearings. They prevent shoes from curling up or wrinkling. Boot trees will help keep soft leather boots upright and prevent cracking. Boot trees may be made from stiff cardboard rolled into tubes and placed inside boots.

14. Keep heels and soles in good repair on boots and shoes. Worn heels cause boots and shoes to lose their shape and create uneven walking patterns which can lead to body pain.

15. Wear hosiery and socks inside shoes. Upper linings are difficult to replace.

16. Rotate wearing at least three pairs of boots or shoes. This will prolong the life of the boots and shoes, and keep them looking attractive.

17. Place blocks of camphor inside boots and shoes to help remove foot odor after wearing.

18. Ask the manufacturer for care instructions on new materials and for information on care products recommended by manufacturers.

19. Instruct customers on the care of their newly purchased footwear. A satisfied customer comes back in the future to buy more.

SELLING POINTS

Salespeople should observe the following selling points for leather and footwear.

1. Find out the customer's needs and then point out the features of the footwear that you present.

2. Show at least three pairs of footwear so that the customer has a choice of styles, colors, finishes, and materials.

3. Remember that most men and women own several pairs of casual footwear, dress shoes coordinated with their suits and dresses, and assorted footwear for play. This means that footwear may be sold in multiple pairs.

4. Utilize the nomenclature of parts of a shoe or the manufacturing process used in making specific footwear when making the sales presentation.

5. Always measure the customer's foot for size. Then, while the customer is trying on the shoes, discuss styles, colors, finishes, or materials. The customer's comfort in footwear should be considered foremost.

6. Explain to customers how to care for the footwear purchased and how related items such as polish and shoe forms will help preserve the shoes.

KEY TERMS

1.	Blucher	21.	Oxfords
2.	Boarding	22.	Patent finish
3.	Bond	23.	Peccary
4.	Bonded leather	24.	Pin seal
5.	Brogue	25.	Pumps
6.	Cabretta	26.	Quarter
7.	Capeskin	27.	Saddle
8.	Cordovan	28.	Scotch grain
9.	Counter	29.	Shank
10.	Crushed kid	30.	Skin
11.	Embossing	31.	Slip-ons
12.	Fat liquoring	32.	Split
13.	Filler	33.	Suede
14.	Glacé kid	34.	Throat
15.	Hide	35.	Tongue
16.	Lace stay	36.	Top grain
17.	Last	37.	T-Strap
18.	Linings	38.	Uppers
19.	Monk	39.	Vamp
20.	Morocco	40.	Welt

STUDY QUESTIONS

1. How does top grain leather differ from split leather?
2. Explain why there are small scars on finished pigskin.
3. Explain what the word *bend* means when referring to cowhide leather.
4. What finishes are used to keep wrinkles from showing in kidskin?
5. Which method of dyeing leather gives it the most dye and the longest-lasting finish?
6. Why is it important to buy footwear that fits?
7. What is a last? How is it used in making shoes?
8. What are three measuring devices that are used for shoe fitting?
9. How are shoe sizes determined?
10. What materials may be used in making the three major parts of the shoe?
11. Name five basic shoe styles for women. When can each style be worn?
12. Name six oxford shoe styles for men. When can each style be worn?

STUDY ACTIVITIES

1. Go to a shoe department or shoe store that sells men's, women's, or chil-den's shoes. Select three shoes from shoe displays. If unable to go to a store, use a catalog. Analyze each shoe and fill out the form shown below.

ITEM ANALYZED	SHOE 1	SHOE 2	SHOE 3
1. Sole Material			
2. Upper Material			
3. Heel Material			
4. Style			
5. Finish			
6. Texture of Surface			
7. Toe Shape			
8. Heel Shape			
9. Shoe Size			
10. Color			
11. Where Shoe Will Be Worn			
12. Price			
13. Decoration(s)			

2. Leather items and shoes need care. Visit a dry-cleaning business and ask the employees how they care for leather apparel. Visit a shoe department or shoe store and examine the shoe-care items. Complete the following columns.

SHOE-CARE ITEMS AND/OR PROCESSES	SHOES OR LEATHER THAT CAN USE THE PRODUCT	BENEFITS OF USING THE ITEM AND/OR PROCESS
1.		
2.		
3.		
4.		
5.		
6.		
7.		
8.		
9.		
10.		

3. Obtain a Brannock measuring device. Assume you are a shoe salesperson. Measure the feet of two males and two females. Record the feet measurements of each person, and compare them with the shoe sizes each is wearing. You may want to obtain assistance at a shoe store in finding a Brannock measuring device.

CHAPTER **21**

Fashion Accessories

OBJECTIVES

After completing this chapter, you should be able to:

1. Identify six styles of gloves, name six parts of a fine leather glove, and explain how this information is important to the consumer and retailer.

2. Recognize fine workmanship of the articles discussed and explain how this information affects consumer expectations.

3. Discriminate and recognize the advantages of articles made from one material over another. Discuss how this information affects its usage.

4. Give examples of eight different handbags. Classify each into the appropriate group of handbags and explain consumer expectations of handbags.

5. Identify six different pieces of hand luggage, and give six construction features. Explain why this information is important to the retailer.

6. Give three different styles of umbrellas. Name each style and state the proper term used for eight of the ten parts of the umbrella. List reasons why these details are important to know.

Gloves, handbags, belts, luggage, and umbrellas are known as accessories. They serve both a functional and a decorative need. Accessories center attention and may emphasize or detract from a pleasing or undesirable feature of a clothing ensemble. They may express individuality or create certain moods for the person wearing them. Together, accessories and apparel carry out a fashion trend.

Buyers and salespeople of accessories need to know how they are constructed, the materials used in making them, the basic styles, and how to take care of them in order to be successful. This chapter covers five accessories in detail: gloves, handbags, belts, luggage, and umbrellas.

GLOVES

Gloves serve two functions: (1) they keep the hands dry and warm, and (2) they compliment the clothing ensemble in color, style, or texture. They are made for various occasions: as formal wear for gowns and tuxedos, or as informal wear for driving or sports. Many materials are used, from fine leather to crocheted lace. Gloves may be worn to detract from hands or arms. Minimum attention is given hands that are covered with gloves that have the same color as clothing. A person with long arms may want to wear gloves longer than wrist-length to make the arms look shorter.

Materials Used in Gloves

Leathers, fabrics, plastics, furs, and various combinations of these materials are used in making gloves. The leathers that are used must be thin enough for comfort, strong enough for durability, and soft and flexible. Commonly used glove leathers are calfskin, capeskin, cabretta, chamois, goatskin, kidskin, doeskin, finished lambskin, mocha, pigskin, and suede. Cowhide, horsehide, and deerskin are heavier leathers that may be used for men's gloves and sports gloves.

Leathers may be used in all-leather gloves, as the palms of gloves with fabric backs, or as the backs of gloves with fabric palms. Leather gloves may have fur linings and trim made of rabbit, squirrel, mink, muskrat, and sheepskin with wool attached. Wool, silk, and acrylic pile linings are also used in the leather gloves.

The most popular synthetics used are vinyl and polyurethane. These are often finished to resemble leather. Glove fabrics include canvas, cotton flannel, cotton fleece, cotton jersey, cotton poplin, nylon, stretch nylon, acrylic, rayon, cashmere, and wool, along with lace, meshes, and tricot. Certain cold-weather mittens use goose down and feathers as filler insulation inside the linings.

Construction of Gloves

There are twenty to thirty separate operations in making leather gloves. Fewer operations are needed in making fabric gloves. The main operations in making leather or woven fabric gloves are taxing; cutting the trank; slitting the gloves; pointing, seaming, and binding; and laying-off.

Experts determine by marking how many pairs of gloves can be cut from a skin or a woven fabric. This operation is called *taxing*.

When the trank is cut, the marked skin or fabric is cut in the oblong form of the glove. The *trank* of the glove is the general outline that forms the palm, the back, and the fingers. See Figure 21.1 for more information. The three methods of glove cutting are table cutting, pull-down cutting (pattern cutting), and block

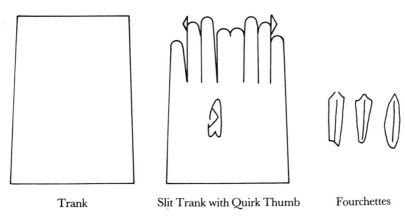

Trank   Slit Trank with Quirk Thumb   Fourchettes

Figure 21.1
Construction of a glove.

cutting (die cutting). In the *table cutting method* the leather is moistened and then stretched over the edge of the table until it is the correct size for cutting. Each trank is then cut by hand using shears. Gloves that are table-cut fit well and give with the hand to permit maximum flexibility of movement. This is also the most expensive method of cutting tranks for leather gloves. The trade stamp "table cut" is usually found inside these gloves.

The *pull-down cutting method* is an adaptation of table cutting. After being cut, the trank is pulled down to fit the pattern. This is not as exact as the first method, but it is less expensive. These gloves are less expensive than table-cut gloves. Although they do not assure perfect fit and comfort, they will give good service.

The *die-cutting method* is generally used for the heavier leathers that are difficult to cut by hand. The gloves are die-cut directly from the skins without the middle step of cutting a trank. The whole pieces of leather are placed under a sharp metal die which stamps out the pattern. Thumbs, fourchettes, and quirks are also cut by this process. It is an easier manufacturing process than the other two methods and is less expensive in making leather, work, and fabric gloves. A fourchette is the side piece of a glove finger (see Figure 21.1). A quirk is a small, triangular section at the base of some fourchettes. Steel dies are used for *finger slitting*. A slitter presses a steel die down. The die cuts fingers, holes for thumbs, and the quirks in one operation.

Pointing, or silking, is the use of seams for decoration. This forms the three rows of stitching or embroidery seen on the back of most gloves. It usually requires at least two operations on different machines, or it may be done by hand. Pointing is also used to place braids or beads on the back of gloves.

In sewing or stitching the seams of the glove, the thumbs are inserted, the fourchettes and quirks sewn in place, and the fingers and sides closed. There are different types of closing stitches (see Figure 21.2). Each type affects the appearance, durability, and price of the glove. The various types of stitches are discussed below.

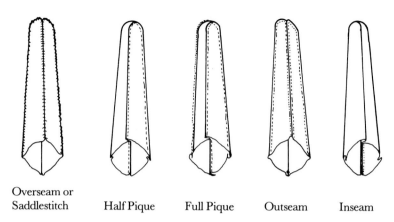

| Overseam or Saddlestitch | Half Pique | Full Pique | Outseam | Inseam |

Figure 21.2
Stitching seams used in closing fingers and sides of gloves.

1. The *inseam stitch* is the easiest closing and the least expensive stitch. The edges are turned in and stitched on the inside. No raw edges are visible when the glove is turned wrong side out. Although easy to do, it is not as durable as other stitches.

2. The *outseam stitch* (Pixseam) allows both raw edges and the seam holding the edges to be visible. This stitch gives the fingers a bulky look. It is used mostly on men's gloves, women's sports gloves, and lightweight dress gloves. It is more expensive and durable than the inseam stitch.

3. The *overseam stitch* is made by placing both raw edges of the leather together on the outside of the glove and sewing them over and over. This stitch is more attractive and durable than the other two stitches.

4. With the *full pique seam stitch,* one edge is lapped over the other edge so that only one raw edge shows on the outside. This is the most difficult stitch to make. It is a finger-slimming and durable stitch used for fine quality, expensive, dress gloves.

5. The *half-pique seam stitch* is made by using a sewing machine. Only the seams on the back of the glove are overlapped; on the palm side, the fingers are closed either by an outseam or an inseam. It imitates the full pique sewed gloves but does not give the same slim fit and is less expensive.

Laying off (pressing) is the final operation in the construction of gloves. The pressing is done on heated brass forms shaped like hands.

Knitted gloves are knitted by hand or by knitting machines. The tips of the fingers are closed after the gloves are knitted. Knitted gloves are warm and comfortable to wear because air is trapped between the fibers and they stretch to fit the hand. Usually, they are machine-washable.

Parts of a Glove

Salespeople and buyers of gloves need to know the different parts of a glove. It is important to know the purpose of the small sections of gloves, in order to be able to explain how to make the glove fit properly.

The *trank* of the glove is the general outline that forms the palm, the back, and the finger. The *thumb* is made from a separate piece of material that is stitched around a hole cut in the trank. There are two types of thumbs: (1) the *Bolton thumb,* and (2) the *quirk thumb* (Figure 21.3). The Bolton thumb has a bulkier appearance but gives freedom of movement. The quirk thumb makes the thumb appear thinner but restricts movement of the hand. Men's and women's driving gloves generally have a Bolton thumb. The quirk thumb is found in women's dress gloves.

The side pieces of the glove fingers are called *fourchettes.* When the fingers of gloves are made in four sections, the front and back sections are part of the trank. The fourchettes provide space for the finger width and for extending the length of the fingers. The small, triangular sections at the base of some fourchettes are called *quirks.* They allow for more flexibility between the fingers. Gloves in which quirks are used indicate quality workmanship. Some gloves have a *lining,* which is a material used inside gloves to make them warmer, comfortable, and perhaps more colorful. Skeletal linings are used to cover only the trank. Full linings cover the fingers and wrists; they are more costly than trank linings. Linings are made of cotton, nylon, acrylics, silks, furs, or blends of two or more of these materials.

Styles of Gloves

There is an appropriate glove style for almost all occasions, formal and informal. Various styles of gloves are listed below.

1. *Mittens* — gloves having one part for the thumb and a larger part covering the fingers and the wrist. They are used mainly for warmth for children's wear and for men's and women's sportswear.

2. *Shorty glove* — a dress or sports glove that comes to the wrist. It usually has a side or center opening for inserting the hand or a center for placing fasteners.

Bolton Thumb

Quirk Thumb

Figure 21.3 *Construction variations for thumb of glove.*

3. *Slip-on glove*—a popular style glove for women. It is loose at the wrist and has a slight flare above the wrist. Some slip-ons are available in longer lengths. It has no fasteners at the wrist.

4. *Gauntlet glove*—this glove has a wide flare above the wrist made by a triangular-shaped piece (gore) set into the side section. The gore may be of the same or a contrasting material.

5. *Formal glove*—a formal glove is a longer length glove with an opening at the wrist which is fastened by buttons or snaps. It may have a six-, eight-, twelve-, sixteen-, or twenty-four-button length. A sixteen-button length glove, between elbow and shoulder, is worn only for very formal occasions (with completely bare arms). A wrist opening called "mousquetaire" allows the hand to be free with the glove still on (for example, when eating at a formal function). As a general rule, if sleeves are elbow length or below, the glove should meet the sleeve. Very short gloves are appropriate with sleeveless or short-sleeved dresses, even for evening, except for the very formal occasions when the long, sixteen-button glove would be worn. Men wear wrist-length white gloves for very formal occasions.

6. *Driving or sport glove*—a glove that has a leather palm and other leather/knit combinations. It is usually a shorty style and may have an opening with a fastener on the back. Specially designed gloves are found for almost every sport and kind of work. Any gloves with unusual combinations of materials, decorations, trimmings, and cuffs are called *novelty gloves*.

7. *Fur-lined glove*—a sporty, casual glove lined with fur, mostly rabbit. It is used for leather gloves worn in the winter.

8. *Sting glove*—a sporty, casual glove knitted of wool and synthetic fibers; it has automatic stretch because of knitting method. The knit is comfortable, retains body heat, and is often combined with leather palms.

Sizes in Gloves

Sizes in men's and women's leather gloves run in quarter inches. Sizes in fabric gloves run in half inches. Women's glove sizes range from 6 to 8½. Some women's gloves and mittens are sized small (6–6½), medium (7–7½), and large (8–8½). Men's sizes range from 8 to 11½. Some men's gloves are sized small (8–8½), medium (9–9½), large (10–10½), and extra large (11–11½). Children's sizes are usually one-half the age of the child. A one-year-old would wear size 0, a ten-year-old would wear size 5, and so on. Stretch gloves usually fit all sizes.

Women's gloves are measured by lengths called *buttons*. Each button equals one inch of length from the base of the thumb to the edge of the arm part of the glove. A one-button glove is wrist-length and is used for daytime and evening wear. The two-button glove is the most popular length glove. A four-button glove is above wrist length and is worn with three-quarter-length sleeves. An eight-button glove comes to the middle of the forearm. Sixteen-button gloves come between the elbows and shoulders and are worn during very formal occasions.

Gloves that are fitted improperly can be uncomfortable and wear out quickly at the seams and fingertips. To determine proper glove size, use a tape measure around the largest part of the hand over knuckles while making a fist, excluding the thumb. The number of inches is the size. For example, a women buying a pair of leather gloves whose hand measures $6\frac{1}{4}$ inches should buy a size smaller, or a 6. A lined glove should be bought a size larger. Gloves should be tried on because glove sizes vary with different materials and manufacturers.

HANDBAGS

Handbags are an important fashion accessory in a well-dressed person's wardrobe. A woman rarely goes out without carrying a handbag. Today, women often carry their personal items like glasses, keys, wallets, and memorandum books in their handbags. A woman may also need a handbag for a special occasion. The handbags will vary in color, material, size, and style because the buyer wants them to be both functional and fashionable.

Materials Used for Handbags

Many manufacturers are operating in new classifications of materials. The majority of the materials are discussed in this section.

The quality of a handbag depends largely on the quality of the materials used in making it. The basic exterior materials used are leathers, synthetics, fabrics, and straw.

Leathers used in making fine quality handbags are calfskin, kipskin (oversized calf), cowhide, sheep and lambskin, and reptile. Reptile skins may come from certain types of snakes, turtles, lizards, alligators, and crocodiles when they are removed from the endangered species list. Various leather treatments and finishes that are used include top grain, split cowhide, sueded, antiqued, crushed, glazed, embossed, and patented. Bonded leather (reconstituted leather) is used for medium priced handbags.

Man-made synthetics were originally developed as less expensive substitutes for leather; now they are accepted on their own merits and are used in a large percentage of the popular- or volume-priced handbags manufactured in the United States. Vinyl is the most widely used plastic in making handbags. Its textures may be crinkled, smooth, napped, or expanded. Smooth, napped, and crinkled polyurethane plastics are also widely used. Their popularity has been due to their light weight, the wipe-clean factor, and a great color variety. Flow molding is a major innovation in handbag technology. The liquid matter flows into a mold and comes out as a finished handbag, complete with all the details of stitching and texture.

Fabric materials used to make handbags include the following. *Burlap* (jute) is used in casual handbags. *Canvas* is the most popular material. *Duck*, a heavy canvas, is also used. *Cotton* is used in novel summer handbags. *Faille* is used in dressy styles. *Linen crash* is used as a spring favorite. *Needlepoint* and *tapestry* are used in knitting bag styles. *Nylon circ* or *Parachute nylon* is used in casual and sportbags; these handbags are often trimmed with leather or vinyl. *Oil cloth* or *rubberized cotton* is a rubberized fabric adapted to handbags with leather, vinyl, or canvas trims. *Peau de soie* is used in evening handbags. *Silk brocade, crepe, bengaline, moiré,* and *satin* fabrics are used for elegant evening handbags. *Ultrasuede*, a brushed polyester fabric, takes a suede look. *Velvet*, in solids, prints, and cuts, has a lustrous and rich look in dressier handbags. *Pique, gingham, boucle, broadcloth, felt, taffeta,* and *metallic cloth* are all used in making handbags. Some of the fabric bags are embroidered, and others are quilted for various decorative effects. Evening bags are often decorated with beads, embroidery, rhinestones, sequins, or marcasites.

Straw handbags have been basic summer fashion accessories for years. Most of the straw handbags that are imported are soft and clothlike, with some having a glazed finish. Rigid shapes are made of willow or rattan.

Parts of a Handbag

Besides the exterior material of a handbag, there may be a frame, handles, or straps; fasteners or zippers; linings; inside coinpurse, compartments, or pockets; along with the filler paddings and reinforcements that give a full, rich appearance on the outside and help the bag retain its shape.

Handbag frames give a distinct shape to the bag. They are usually made of steel or brass. Expensive bags may be gold, silver, or chromium-plated, or covered with leather or fabric. Inexpensive bags may have frames that have been gold- or silver-colored, or sprayed with an enamel that harmonizes with the exterior material. These frames will chip easily.

Handles or straps are used on many handbags. They may be small to hold in the hand, medium length to cover the arm, or shoulder length. All three types are known as top handles and extend across the top of the bag. A handle that is located on the side of a handbag, used for carrying it, is known as a side handle. Handles may be made from the same material as the handbag, or they may be made from wood, chains, bone, or hard plastics.

Fasteners may include buckles, drawstrings, latches, turn locks, Velcro, toggles and loops, snap closures, or zippers.

The *linings* found inside the handbags may be made from leather, plastic, or fabric. *Interlinings* are not visible and are usually glued to the inside of the bag to help hold its shape. They may be made from cardboard, muslin, paper, stiff plastic, cotton felt, or duck fabric.

Manufacturing Handbags

A designer's drawing of a handbag is worked out in an inexpensive material to show how the handbag would look when finished. Upon approval, the material is used for the basic pattern from which the many patterns that are needed for the different parts of the bag are cut.

The leather or other material to be used is cut by hand or with metal dies, just as parts of shoes are cut. Then the job of assembling and sewing the parts of the handbag continues. Certain workers stitch parts together with sewing machines; others glue the linings, filler, and other materials into the bags. Once the lining and outside materials are completed, the bag goes to a frame worker, who puts all the parts into the necessary frame or attaches the necessary fasteners to the bag. The most costly and difficult construction process is the framing.

The last step in making a handbag is the inspection of a finished handbag. The bag is then filled with tissue paper to hold its shape and packed for the marketplace.

Styles of Handbags

Many handbag manufacturers are operating in new classifications of style and price. The new price range is as follows: L—Low, M—Medium, H—High, and C—Couturier. There are many classifications of style including attaché, beach, blazer, casual, classic, clutches, contemporary, daytime, dressy, evening, late day, nylon, shoe coordinates, soft classics, sports, tailored, totes, and travel. Whether you are buying in the marketplace or selling handbags in a department, get to know and use the right names. In general, handbags may be classified into four major areas: (1) box, (2) envelope, (3) pouch, and (4) novelty. Figure 21.4 shows the first three types.

The *box* bag is one that is small, rigid, and not expandable. It usually has a mirror and a space for small items of makeup and coins. It may be cylindrical in shape and is often jeweled and designed in gold, silver, or metal. Minaudier (men-o-dee-ay) is a name for a box bag.

The *envelope* handbag has a flap over the top. It may have a handle attached flat on the back side. This small bag may be carried in the hand or under the

Pouch Style

Envelope Style

Box Style

Figure 21.4
Styles of handbags.

arm. The *clutch* bag may be an envelope bag that is popular for daytime and evening wear. The *belt* bag that attaches to the belt is an envelope bag. A *shoulder-strap* bag may have an envelope flap and may be an envelope or a pouch-style handbag.

The most popular bag used for every kind of occasion is the *pouch* handbag. Handbags that may close on top, have a frame, a top handle, and a shoulder strap are known as pouch bags. Some styles of pouches are as follows.

1. *Attaché bag*—square-shaped, it has handles that may disappear into the body of the bag. Sometimes it has outside pockets, a shoulder strap, and a top zipper closing.

2. *Body bag*—a body-conforming bag that is long, fairly thin and may be carried in the hand or on the shoulder.

3. *Duffle*—barrel-shaped, it has soft sides, a top handle, a shoulder strap, and usually a zippered closing.

4. *Hobo*—a very soft bag with a top zipper. It usually has a shoulder strap.

5. *Sport*—a carryall for athletic gear, it is multipocketed to hold essential items. It may have handles and an adjustable shoulder strap. It may be closed with zippers or snaps.

6. *Swagger*—this bag has two handles for security when in use. It may have a zipper top closing.

7. *Tote*—large carryalls that have room for books, clothing, knitting, or packages.

Labeling Guidelines for Handbags and Small Leather Goods

The Federal Trade Commission provided guidelines for the handbag industry in 1969. Handbags and small leather goods must be labeled correctly. All materials that look like leather must be labeled so that customers will know what they are buying. The terms *scratchproof* and *scuffproof* may not be used unless the finish will not scratch or scuff.

Selecting the Right Handbag

Selecting the right color, the right look, and the right fabrication of handbag will help achieve a fashion-wise look. Handbags should blend with the clothing being worn or provide a pleasing contrast. Some people select handbags to coordinate and harmonize with their shoes and clothing.

Using good style sense means using proportion properly. A tiny bag should not be sold to a heavy person, a round bag to a round customer, or an oversized bag to a small person. A shoulder bag calls attention to the wearer's hips. A wide, thick shoulder bag can make the wearer's hips look broader. Clients who buy few handbags should select beige or light brown neutral tones.

BELTS

As accessory items, belts are either decorative or functional. They are used to add color or interest at the waist or to hold up pants. Fashion trends often determine the types of belts worn and whether or not they will be worn. They can make a waistline look smaller, lower, or higher. Tall people often wear belts to give the appearance of a shorter waistline by placing the belt above the waist. Customers of average height and with slender waists can wear almost any color and style of belt. Customers who do not want to emphasize their waists should wear plain-looking belts.

Belt Materials

Materials that are used in making belts include leather, plastic, cotton, straw, macrame, and metallic fabrics. Top grain cowhide, split cowhide, sueded split cowhide, bonded leather fibers, and oil tanned leather are commonly used in making belts. Common plastics used in making belts are nylon, polyester, polyurethane, and vinyl.

Belts are made by cutting the material to designated lengths and widths, stitching edges and designs on the material; tapering and staining the edges; crocheting, knitting, braiding, embossing, handpainting, decorating with various objects; adding tabs; and perforating or adding holes. Belts are often reversible and various materials, including cardboard, are used for backing. Different devices and methods are used to fasten belts, but buckles are the most commonly used. The most common buckle is the harness-style metal buckle. Others include fabric-covered, center bar, military-style, two prong, and center-hook. Metals used include solid brass and steel with finishes like brass-plated, gold-colored, copper-colored, silver-colored, nickel-plated, or chrome-plated.

Belt Styles

Belts are selected that go with the rest of the wardrobe. Below some styles of belts are explained.

1. *Cinch or cinch tie belt* — wide belt or tight, elastic belt that laces and ties up the front to show off the waist. It may be a self-fabric belt.

2. *Cummerbund belt* — wide sashlike fabric belt. Usually worn by men or women with formal clothes. It may be a self-fabric belt.

3. *Metallic belt* — any metal belt. It may be a stretch-type, or it may be composed of interlocking links, such as a chain link.

4. *Rope or string tie belt* — cord-type belt that can be wrapped and tied. It may be a self-fabric belt. It is also called a spaghetti tie belt.

5. *Sash belt* — soft ribbon or fabric worn around the waist. Sometimes referred to as an Obi-sash. It may be a self-fabric belt.

6. *Self-fabric belt*—made of the same fabric as the garment with which it is being worn. Narrow self-fabric belts are especially becoming to a person with broad hips and a large waist.

Belt Sizes

Belts are usually sized according to waist measurements. Men's sizes range from 28 to 60 inches. Women's sizes range from 22 to 34 inches. Belts are also sized small (24–26), medium (27–30), large (31–33). Velcro and stretch elastic make some belts adjustable.

In measuring a customer for a belt to wear with pants, measure around the waist over well-fitting pants on which the belt will be worn. Number of "even" inches measured is the size to select. If the measurement is between even sizes, select the next higher even size. If the customer is wearing slacks, place the tape measure through the belt loops. For a blouse or dress, wrap the tape measure around the waist.

LUGGAGE

Nearly everone travels somewhere at some time or other. People are going away to school, commuting to work, representing businesses, going on vacations, visiting friends and relatives, or traveling for other reasons. They may be going by car, bus, airplane, train, or ship. The mode of travel has influenced the size, shape, and style of luggage to a great extent.

The luggage manufacturers design different luggage with the appropriate amount of space to match each traveler's needs for these many types of trips. Each new piece of luggage is generally given a trade name by each manufacturer. There are general or basic classifications used for certain sizes and styles, such as garment pack, boarding pack, shoulder tote, square and duffle bag, beauty case, twenty-two-inch carry-on, twenty-four-inch pullman, and twenty-eight-inch overseas with wheels. *Hand luggage* and *trunks* are the two basic types of luggage.

Construction and Materials

Hand Luggage

There are three methods by which hand luggage is made—(1) hard-side, (2) soft-side, and (3) soft-construction.

Hard-side luggage is rigid, with boxes or molded shapes (see Figure 21.5). The materials used for boxes include fiberboard (quality ranges from treated cardboard with rag content to plain cardboard) and basswood (three-ply and lightweight), which is used in quality luggage. Outside covering materials include leather, vinyl, vinyl-coated fabrics (canvas), and paper-covered cardboard for inexpensive luggage. Some luggage is made of aluminum, and others of thin steel. Molded luggage is usually made of polypropylene, and styrene is used in less expensive luggage. Glass fibers bonded with vinyl plastic may also be molded.

Figure 21.5
Hard-side luggage.
Courtesy of *Travelware* Magazine.

Soft-side luggage has a material stretched over a frame (Figure 21.6). Several materials may be used including various thicknesses of vinyl, vinyl-coated fabrics, nylon fabric, and leather. Leather has lost its place as the most used material in making luggage; however, top grain leather is used in expensive luggage, and split leather is used in less expensive luggage. The center frame usually is made of steel. A steel wire spring may be inside the welting to help retain the shape. Corner stays also help retain the shape.

Soft-construction luggage uses neither frames nor boxes in its construction (Figure 21.7). Examples include some tote bags and travel bags. They are made from nylon fabric, vinyl, a vinyl and nylon fabric combination, or an inexpensive fabric like cotton canvas.

Figure 21.6
Soft-side luggage.
Courtesy of *Travelware* Magazine.

Hand luggage may be lined with rayon, nylon, sheepskin, cotton, or paper. Expensive hardware (hinges, clasps, rings, and locks) is made of brass or stainless steel. Less expensive hardware is brass-, chrome-, or nickel-plated. Handles are usually made of polypropylene or other rigid plastics. Large pieces of hand luggage may be easily converted to luggage with easy-rolling wheels for pulling instead of carrying. Most pieces of hand luggage have zippers.

Figure 21.7
Soft-construction luggage.
Courtesy of *Travelware* Magazine.

Trunks

Most trunks and foot lockers are made of plywood and covered with a heavy gauge vinyl or sheet steel. The interior materials may include vinyl, a rose-colored plywood impregnated with oil of cedar, plywood with a red cedar veneer, fabric, printed paper, and paint. The hardware (hinges, wraparound, riveted steel bindings, hasp lock, tension draw bolts, metal bumper corners, and steel tongue and groove closure) is an important feature of trunk luggage. The best hardware is made of brass or stainless steel. Luggage having nickel-, chrome-, or brass-plated steel hardware will rust if scarred. The center or end handles are made of leather.

Types of Luggage

Hand Luggage

The names and descriptions of popular hand luggage are below.

1. *Pullman*—this luggage holds the business person's wardrobe. Popular sizes are approximately twenty-four, twenty-six, twenty-eight, and thirty inches in width. This luggage usually has dividers and straps to hold clothes. It may be used for storage (the smaller size goes inside the larger size).

2. *Weekender, boarding, or underseat*—these cases are sized to fit under airplane seats or overhead on racks. They have space for a change of clothes. They are approximately twenty to twenty-two inches in width.

3. *Garment bag*—garments may be packed in this bag at full length. The bag may be folded in half for carrying by a handle. It may also be called a suit pack or a suitbag.

4. *Travel bag*—garments may be packed in this bag at full length and the bag carried by an end loop handle or by the hangers. Dress length is approximately fifty inches and suit length is approximately forty-two inches. It is lighter in weight and less expensive than the garment bag.

5. *Cosmetic case*—this small case is used for cosmetics. It has a handle on the lid, has a lid mirror, and may have a lift-out tray. It usually is deep enough to carry bottles upright and has a plastic lining.

6. *Tote bag*—this small pouch-type bag usually has a zipper top, zipper pockets, and an adjustable shoulder strap. Other tote bag styles may be called *open, barrel,* or *roll totes* which may have handles, adjustable shoulder straps, and top zippers.

7. *Back-pack tote*—this is a sport bag to wear on the back or to hand-carry as a tote bag. It has adjustable shoulder straps and may have three compartments for carrying books. It can be used when going to the beach, gym, or on short hikes.

8. *Attaché case*—a small, hard-sided case with handle and lock for carrying legal and letter size papers, personal documents, and order forms. It also has a small space for clothing and toiletries. It often has dividers, an organizer with pockets for eyeglasses, calculator, and snap-in key ring. It may be used as a lap desk.

9. *Portfolio*—a small, flat, versatile case resembling a briefcase, but having a single divider for legal size papers, rather than two or three dividers as usually found in a briefcase. The portfolio may have retractable handles, detachable shoulder straps, zipper pockets, an interior organizer for calculator, and other business-related items.

Trunks

Trunks may be divided into the following two categories:

1. *Trunks*—these are large, rigid cases that are too large for the traveler to carry. The box or packing trunk is used for packing bedding, woolens, clothing, and linens for storage. A trunk may also be used for long trips.

2. *Footlockers*—these smaller, rigid cases are too large for the traveler to carry. They may have a tray and may be used for home storage. They may be used in a school dormitory room for securing personal items. Footlockers are also used by military personnel.

UMBRELLAS

Umbrellas are both a functional and a fashionable accessory. They can be found in a wide variety of colors and styles for men and women. They are functional because they protect the user from the sun and the rain. Umbrellas have also become an important accessory because they may add to the appearance of a wardrobe. For example, a neutral-colored umbrella may blend with a raincoat, a specific item of clothing, or different colors of clothing. Children's umbrellas and raincoats may be brightly colored for safety reasons so that motorists can see them easily.

Parts of an Umbrella

Using the right name is important when you are buying or selling an accessory such as an umbrella; this lets other people feel confident that you know your merchandise. An umbrella has the following parts (see Figure 21.8).

1. *Canopy*—water-repellent fabric or plastic that stretches over the ribs and protects the user from the rain or sun. Nylon or cotton fabrics and vinyl plastic are some of the materials that may be used.

2. *Ribs*—narrow, thin metal pieces that arch radially and give the desired shape to the canopy. Grooved steel is generally used for these pieces. The strength of the ribs, not the number, determines the quality of the umbrella.

3. *Tips*—rounded metal or plastic pieces placed at the end of the ribs. Tips serve as a safety feature and hold the canopy in place when the umbrella is open.

4. *Tape*—a material used to fasten the umbrella that is attached to the canopy. A snap fastener is commonly used at the end of the tape.

5. *Sheath*—a protective cover that may be slipped over the canopy when the umbrella is not being used. Covering materials used include fabric, plastic, and simulated leather.

6. *Spreaders*—narrow, thin metal pieces attached to the center of the ribs that open and close the canopy. They are usually made of grooved steel.

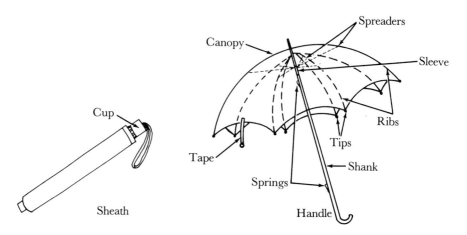

Figure 21.8
Parts of an umbrella.

7. *Shank*—a shaft located between the canopy and the handle. A shank is usually made from wood. A shank made from metal is called a rod.

8. *Sleeve*—a metal piece which slides up and down the shank and enables the spreaders to which it is attached to be opened for use or collapsed for carrying.

9. *Springs*—two small metal parts that can hold the metal sleeve in position when the canopy is opened or closed by slight finger pressure. Some umbrellas have push-button, self-opener spreaders that open and close with a hidden spring.

10. *Handle*—a part at the end of the shank used to hold the umbrella when it is opened or closed. A metal or plastic *cup* may be used to fit over the tips of a closed umbrella and also be affixed to the shank. Materials used in making handles range from inexpensive to very expensive. The materials used include woods, plastics, bone, horn, leather, and metal. The handles may be carved, engraved, or hand-painted. The most commonly used shapes for handles are the *straight,* the *crook* (a question-mark shape), and *golf* or *opera* (modified crook) shapes. Additional *straps, cords,* or *chains* are usually attached to women's umbrellas to permit easy carrying.

Styles of Umbrellas

Umbrellas are available in the following styles.

1. *Ballerina*—the ruffled edge resembles a ballerina skirt. It has a delicate look.

2. *Beach*—the covering materials are waterproof and usually have stripes or patterns and bright colors. The center pole is made of aluminum or wood and may have a point at one end to sink in the sand or soil. Sizes vary from five to eight feet in diameter.

3. *Bubble-shape*—the dome is designed to cover the head and shoulders; the materials are transparent so that the user can see. Clear vinyl is generally used.

4. *Folding*—the ribs fold to reduce the size for easy carrying or packing. Umbrellas may be carried in a briefcase or other carryall bag.

5. *Parasol*—a lightweight umbrella used to shade from the sun.

6. *Regular*—umbrellas approximately twenty-four inches in length. They may have eight, ten, or sixteen ribs.

7. *Stadium*—dome-shaped; large enough to cover two people.

8. *Self-opening*—umbrellas with a push button that works a hidden spring that releases the sleeve, pushing the ribs into position. When closed, the tip ends of the ribs are held in place in a metal or plastic cup.

9. *Windproof*—these umbrellas can be snapped back into shape if blown inside out. They may have a spring between the spreaders and ribs just under the canopy, which helps to keep the umbrella in shape, or they may have hinges at the point where the spreaders and the ribs join. These hinges allow the ribs to be turned back without bending them out of shape.

CARE OF ACCESSORIES

In order to maintain the quality and lifetime of accessories, observe the following procedures.

1. The durability and appearance of leather depend mostly on the care which is given to it. The first time a leather glove is put on, the wrist should be turned back, and the fingers of the glove should be worked on simultaneously with a sliding motion. Afterward, the thumb is slipped on and the wrist drawn into place. Gloves should be tried on slowly the first time to make sure of a good fit.

2. Leather dress gloves should always be removed by drawing them off backwards or wrong side out by the wrist. Then they should be turned and drawn back into shape, folded carefully, and lain flat with palms together in a box or dust-free drawer. White and light-colored leather gloves should be further protected by wrapping them in tissue paper. If the gloves are damp from perspiration or rain, allow them to dry in the air to prevent mildew and spotting before putting them away.

3. Check the labels to make sure leather gloves are washable. Never wash gloves that have been previously dry-cleaned. Lined gloves should be dry-cleaned. Gloves should be washed in lukewarm-to-cool

mild soap suds. Chamois and doeskin gloves should be washed while on the hands and rinsed in clean water. All other leathers are washed off the hands and rinsed in clear lukewarm water.

4. Leather gloves should not be wrung out or dried near intense heat. Use a terry cloth towel to remove excess moisture. Blow into the gloves, shape them, and place on a towel or wooden board to dry at normal room temperature. When dried, the gloves can be softened by rubbing them between moistened fingers; then they can be fitted to the hands.

5. Washable gloves should not become too soiled before washing because extra rubbing to remove the dirt causes extra wear. Fabric gloves that are washable should be pulled into shape while they are damp. Gloves that are tagged nonwashable should be dry-cleaned by a leather method.

6. Clean fabric handbags by brushing, spot cleaning, or dry cleaning.

7. Clean the handbag lining by wiping, brushing, or vacuuming.

8. Clean washable leathers and plastic compositions by wiping lightly with a damp cloth. *Do not place the handbag in water.*

9. Store vinyl and patent leather handbags in tissue paper to hold their shape. Do not store these handbags in plastic bags. They often adhere when they touch. Do not store in extremes of cold, dryness, heat, or humidity. Repair damages immediately.

10. Brush suede with a dry rubber sponge to remove dust and dirt without matting the surface. If in doubt, take sueded items to a dry cleaner. Wet or water-spotted suede handbags should be emptied, stuffed with tissue paper to hold their shape, and dried at room temperature. Then they should be brushed with a terry cloth or dry sponge to restore their looks.

11. Clean dark-colored leathers with vinegar to remove surface scratches. Restore polish with use of a good leather cream.

12. Use neutral leather creams that are prepared especially for different types of leather.

13. Read the label for cleaning instructions—especially for light leathers or grained leathers.

14. Avoid overloading a handbag because doing so distorts the handbag's shape, weakens the fastening, pulls fabric from the frames, and breaks seams.

15. When belts are not being worn, they should hang or be rolled.

16. Leather belts, except oil-tanned ones, should be polished with wax shoe polish. Wipe patent leather belts with a damp cloth.

17. Follow the same care instructions for fabric belts as for the whole garment unless the belt has a cardboard, leather, or vinyl backing. Dry clean all fabric belts with these backings so that they will maintain their appearance and shape.

18. Refer to the manufacturer's instructions when caring for luggage.

19. Vinyl luggage may be wiped clean with a damp cloth.

20. Molded hard-side luggage wipes clean easily with a damp cloth.

21. Umbrellas require very little care. If they get damp or wet, open them until they dry. Then close them, slip the sheath on, or carefully roll them, and use the tape. This helps prevent mildewing, spotting, and unnecessary wrinkling.

22. Store umbrellas in a safe place away from the sun, which may fade fabrics, and away from excessive heat, which melts vinyl.

23. On a windy day direct the top of the umbrella into the wind to avoid its being blown inside out. This procedure should be followed even with a windproof umbrella.

SELLING POINTS

Salespeople should observe the following guidelines when selling accessory items.

1. Mention parts of the glove, when appropriate, during the sales presentation. For example: A Bolton thumb gives better freedom of movement than a quirk thumb. Linings are used for warmth, comfort, and color.

2. Explain that appropriate glove styles and sizes are available for most occasions. Determine the customer's needs.

3. Point out the features of handbags such as construction methods, colors, materials, sizes, and styles that meet the function and fashion needs of the buyer.

4. Determine whether the customer wants belts that are decorative or functional. Help the customer select belts that will go with the rest of the wardrobe. Plain-looking belts should be selected for the customer who does not want to emphasize the waist. Customers of average height and with slender waists can wear almost any color and style of belt. A tall person may wear a belt to give the appearance of a shorter waistline by placing the belt above the waist.

5. Find out the traveler's needs; then match the types of luggage to meet those needs.

6. Use the correct names of the parts of an umbrella when demonstrating a specific style to meet the customer's needs.

KEY TERMS

1.	Attaché	14.	Portfolio
2.	Box	15.	Pouch
3.	Bubble-shape	16.	Pullman
4.	Canopy	17.	Rib
5.	Cinch	18.	Sash
6.	Clutch	19.	Self-belt or self-fabric
7.	Cummerbund	20.	Shorty
8.	Envelope	21.	Slip-on
9.	Fourchette	22.	Soft-sided
10.	Gusset	23.	Tote
11.	Interlining	24.	Trank
12.	Mitten	25.	Weekender
13.	Pique seam		

STUDY QUESTIONS

1. Describe the following types of glove closing stitches: inseam stitch, overseam stitch, outseam stitch, pique seam, and half-pique seam.
2. Explain how you would measure a customer's hand to fit a pair of leather gloves.
3. What care is given leather gloves that are washable compared with non-washable leather gloves?
4. Identify six styles and name and describe five important parts of a handbag.
5. What materials are used in making handbags?
6. What special care should be given handbags made of leather, fabric, and plastic?
7. Identify five styles of belts and explain how to determine the appropriate size.
8. Explain why brass and stainless steel is desired more than plated steel for hardware in handbags and luggage.
9. Give an example and describe each of the following: soft-side luggage, hard-side luggage, and soft-construction luggage.
10. What are the advantages of the following types of umbrellas: folding, bubble-shape, regular, self-opening, and windproof?

STUDY ACTIVITIES

1. Obtain a tape measure and measure the hands of two men and two women. Determine the size of unlined and lined leather gloves that would fit each.
2. Visit an accessories department in a store or obtain a catalog in which handbags are sold. List the terms that describe the handbag styles, materials, construction, finishes, and size.
3. Visit a store or obtain a catalog that sells a variety of luggage. Make a list of the luggage styles, construction, materials, finishes, sizes, and hardware.

Suggested Readings

Alexander, Patsy R. *Textile Products.* Boston: Houghton Mifflin Co., 1977.

Aronson, Joseph. *The Encyclopedia of Furniture.* 3d ed. New York: Crown Publishers, 1965.

Beveridge, Elizabeth. *Choosing and Using Home Equipment.* 6th ed. Ames: The Iowa State University Press, 1971.

Bigelow, Marybelle S. *Fashion in History.* Minneapolis: Burgess Publishing Co., 1979.

Bogle, M. *Textile Dyes, Finishes, and Auxiliaries.* New York: Garland Publishing, 1977.

Brett, Vanessa. *Phaidon Guide to Pewter.* New York: Prentice-Hall, 1983.

Context. Vol. 12, No. 1. Wilmington, Del.: E.I. duPont de Nemours and Co., 1983.

Contini, Mila. *Fashion: From Ancient Egypt to the Present Day.* New York: Odyssey Press, 1965.

Corbman, B.P. *Textiles: Fiber to Fabric.* 6th ed. New York: McGraw-Hill, 1983.

Crawford, Joan. *Introducing Jewelry Making.* New York: Watson-Guptill Publications, 1974.

Cudlipp, Edythe. *Furs.* New York: Hawthorn Books, 1978.

Davenport, Millia. *The Book of Costume.* New York: Crown, 1966.

Encyclopedia of Textiles. 3rd ed. Englewood Cliffs, N.J.: Prentice-Hall, 1980.

Feirer, John L. *The Woodworker's Reference Guide and Sourcebook.* New York: Charles Scribner's Sons, 1983.

Grace, Evelyn. *Introduction to Fashion Merchandising.* Englewood Cliffs, N.J.: Prentice-Hall, 1978.

Hollen, Norma; Saddler, Jane; and Langford, Anna L. *Textiles.* 5th ed. New York: Macmillan Publishing Co., 1979.

Hood, Graham. *American Silver.* New York: Praeger Publishers, 1971.

Joseph, Marjory. *Introductory Textile Science.* 2d ed. New York: Holt, Rinehart & Winston, 1972.

_____. *Essentials of Textiles.* 2d ed. New York: Holt, Rinehart & Winston, 1980.

Kaplan, David G. *World of Furs.* New York: Fairchild Publications, 1974.

Kaufman, Morris. *Giant Molecules.* New York: Doubleday and Co., 1968.

Kleeberg, I.C., ed. *The Butterick Fabric Handbook.* New York: Butterick Publishing, 1975.

Laver, James. *The Concise History of Costume and Fashion.* New York: Charles Scribner's Sons, 1969.

Lyle, D.S. *Performance of Textiles.* New York: John Wiley & Sons, 1977.

Man-Made Fiber Producers Association. *Man-Made Fibers: A New Guide.* Washington, D.C.: Man-Made Fiber Producers Assoc., 1982.

Mark, Herman, *Giant Molecules.* New York: Time Inc., 1966.

Mason, Anita. *An Illustrated Dictionary of Jewelry.* New York: Harper & Row, Publishers, 1973.

Mason, Joseph Barry, & Mayer, Morris Lehman. *Modern Retailing: Theory and Practice.* Dallas, Tex.: Business Publications, 1978.

Meilach, Dona Z. *Ethnic Jewelry.* New York: Crown Publishers, 1981.

Needles, H.L. *Handbook of Textile Fibers, Dyes, and Finishes.* New York: Garland STPM Press, 1981.

Pizzuto, J.J. *Fabric Science.* New York: Fairchild Publications, 1978.

Smith, Betty F., and Block, Ira. *Textiles in Perspective.* Englewood Cliffs, N.J.: Prentice-Hall, 1982.

Stepat-DeVan, D. *Introduction to Home Furnishings.* New York: Macmillan Publishing Co., 1971.

Textiles Handbook. 4th ed. Washington, D.C.: American Home Economics Association, 1970.

Tolman, R. *Guide to Fashion Merchandising.* Vol. 1. New York: Milady Publishing Corp., 1978.

Tortora, Phyllis G. *Understanding Textiles.* New York: Macmillan Publishing Co., 1978.

Wingate, Isabel B., and Mohler, June F. *Textile Fabrics and Their Selection.* Englewood Cliffs, N.J.: Prentice-Hall, 1984.

Wingate, I.B.; Gillespie, K.R.; and Milgrom, B.G. *Know Your Merchandise.* New York: McGraw-Hill Book Co., 1975.

Index